Higher Education Leadership

Higher Education Leadership

Challenging Tradition and Forging Possibilities

Rozana Carducci, Jordan Harper,
and Adrianna Kezar

Johns Hopkins University Press
Baltimore

© 2024 Johns Hopkins University Press
All rights reserved. Published 2024
Printed in the United States of America on acid-free paper

9 8 7 6 5 4 3 2 1

Johns Hopkins University Press
2715 North Charles Street
Baltimore, Maryland 21218
www.press.jhu.edu

Library of Congress Cataloging-in-Publication Data

Names: Carducci, Rozana, author. | Harper, Jordan, 1997– author. |
    Kezar, Adrianna J., author.
Title: Higher education leadership : challenging tradition and forging
    possibilities / Rozana Carducci, Jordan Harper, and Adrianna Kezar.
Description: Baltimore : Johns Hopkins University Press, 2024. |
    Includes bibliographical references and index.
Identifiers: LCCN 2023029967 | ISBN 9781421448787 (paperback) |
    ISBN 9781421448794 (ebook)
Subjects: LCSH: Educational leadership—Philosophy. |
    Education, Higher—Research. | Education, Higher—Administration. |
    Educational change.
Classification: LCC LB2805 .C2668 2024 | DDC 371.2/011—
    dc23/eng/20230708
LC record available at https://lccn.loc.gov/2023029967

A catalog record for this book is available from the British Library.

*Special discounts are available for bulk purchases of this book. For more
information, please contact Special Sales at specialsales@jh.edu.*

Contents

Acknowledgments   vii

PART I: THE CONTEMPORARY CONTEXT OF LEADERSHIP IN HIGHER EDUCATION

CHAPTER 1   The Evolution of Leadership Research and the Work Left Undone   3

CHAPTER 2   Leadership Paradigms   22

CHAPTER 3   Neoliberalism and Higher Education Leadership   46

CHAPTER 4   Whiteness and White Supremacy in Higher Education Leadership   77

PART II: PERSPECTIVES ON LEADERSHIP RESEARCH AND PRACTICE

CHAPTER 5   Transformational Leadership Perspectives   117

CHAPTER 6   Cognitive Leadership Perspectives   147

CHAPTER 7   Chaos and Complexity Leadership Perspectives   181

CHAPTER 8   Cultural Leadership Perspectives   202

CHAPTER 9   Processual Leadership Perspectives   242

PART III: LEADERSHIP FOR LIBERATION

CHAPTER 10   Looking to the Future of Leadership Practice and Research   271 vi *Contents*

Appendix: Case Studies   *303*

1. Merger at Cañada College   303
2. Rethinking Technology at Chumash State   310
3. New Program and Leadership Process at Webster University   315
4. Addressing Student Success at Westgate Community College   320

References   *327*

Index   *385*

Acknowledgments

The order of authorship is alphabetical. All authors equally contributed to the development of this book.

Rozana Carducci would like to express deep gratitude to her dad, Professor Bernardo J. Carducci, for cultivating her love of learning and intellectual curiosity. She would also like to acknowledge the gifts of wisdom and mentorship shared by Cynthia Wolf Johnson, Peter Magolda, Denny Roberts, and Judy Rogers, all of whom fostered Rozana's passion for the study and practice of critical leadership. Thanks to Jordan and Adrianna for their good company on this journey of deep reflection and writing. Melissa, you are dearly missed; thank you for embodying liberatory leadership. Finally, Rozana would like to thank her daughter, Caiden, for serving as a constant source of motivation, inspiration, and hope for a better tomorrow.

Jordan Harper wishes to thank grassroots leaders across the world for their work to dismantle oppressive systems and imagine a liberatory world. Their insights have been deeply influential in the shaping of this book.

Adrianna Kezar would like to acknowledge the late Melissa Contreras-McGavin for her contributions to fighting for racial justice. She would also like to thank other scholars who have contributed to her thinking about leadership, such as Estela Bensimon, Cynthia Cherrey, Susan Elrod, Lorelle Espinosa, Sharon Fries-Britt, Tricia Gallant, Lynne Gangone, Elizabeth Holcombe, Jaime Lester, Julie Posselt, Judith Ramaley, Rob Rhoades, Darsella Vigil, Marissiko Wheaton, and her two coauthors. Adrianna is inspired to see what the next generation of more diverse leaders will bring to a transformed campus life.

We would all like to thank Diane Flores—a staff member at the Pullias Center for Higher Education—for her support of the book. We would also like to collectively thank the generous anonymous reviewers for their incisive and useful comments on the entire manuscript.

PART I / The Contemporary Context of Leadership in Higher Education

Chapter 1

The Evolution of Leadership Research and the Work Left Undone

In the fall of 2015, the University of Missouri-Columbia made national headlines as students, faculty, and administrators engaged in a series of public protests and confrontations concerning the institution's response to campus racial tensions. Influenced by the Black Lives Matter movement and protests for justice in the police shooting of Michael Brown in nearby Ferguson, Mizzou students established Concerned Student 1950 (a reference to the year Black students were first admitted to the university) and demanded the institution take meaningful action to improve the campus racial climate. Frustrated by the lack of substantive proposals for change advanced by senior administrators—including the University of Missouri System president, Tim Wolfe, and the Columbia campus chancellor, R. Bowen Loftin—members of Concerned Student 1950 decided to take more direct action, blocking President Wolfe's vehicle during the homecoming parade and using a megaphone to share examples of racism experienced by Mizzou students from 1839 to 2015. Wolfe did not engage with the protesting students; instead, he silently sat atop his convertible as several members of the parade crowd attempted to move the protesters out of the way. Police officers eventually arrived on the scene and asked the protesting students to move.

More than two weeks after the parade, Wolfe met with representatives from Concerned Student 1950. After the conversation, the students said Wolfe seemed unaware of how systemic oppression influenced campus life

4   *The Contemporary Context of Leadership in Higher Education*

and was unwilling to meet their demands for concrete actions the university could take to improve resources and support for students of color (e.g., additional mental health funding, greater diversity in faculty and staff hiring, and mandatory racial awareness programming). Wolfe argued that many of the student demands were already folded into a draft system-wide strategic plan that focused on improving diversity and inclusion. Tensions continued to escalate when Mizzou graduate student Jonathan Butler announced he would engage in a hunger strike and members of the Mizzou football team communicated an intention to boycott all football activities until Wolfe resigned or was removed from office. Elected Missouri officials from both political parties joined the chorus calling for Wolfe's resignation, and on November 9, he stepped down, followed six and a half hours later by Chancellor Loftin (Izadi, 2015; Kingkade, 2015).

This brief vignette certainly does not capture the depth and complexity of the systemic oppression and racial hostility that gave rise to and framed the Concerned Student 1950 protest, nor does it fully depict the sequence of events that took place leading up to the resignations of President Wolfe and Chancellor Loftin. For a detailed analysis of the fall 2015 Mizzou protests that captured national attention and sparked similar campus movements around the country (Hartocollis & Bidgood, 2015), we encourage you to consult the numerous scholarly and multimedia works that shed light on this historical moment (Gill et al., 2020; Kezar & Fries-Britt, 2018; S. Lee, 2016; McElderry & Rivera, 2017). We open this book on the nature, limitations, and possibilities of higher education leadership theory and research with a reminder of the Mizzou Concerned Student 1950 protests because this campus movement and series of events effectively illustrate the ways in which the twin pillars of white supremacy and neoliberalism prop up oppressive leadership systems and structures in American higher education. A neoliberal focus on using market principles to improve operational efficiency and increase revenue streams likely led the University of Missouri to hire Tim Wolfe, a former software company executive with no professional higher education experience, as the system president. Although Wolfe may have possessed the business acumen the University Board of Curators was seeking in an organizational leader, it became evident during the fall of 2015 that he lacked the knowledge and skills (e.g., active listening, empathy, willingness to speak from the heart, and understanding of oppression and collective racial trauma; Kezar & Fries-Britt, 2018) needed to effectively lead Mizzou through the unfolding racial crisis. Ironically, Mizzou's deep entrenchment in neoliberal ideology likely ended Wolfe's tenure as president. While legislators and administrators had been willing to tolerate the repeated harassment of students of color on campus and the disruption of the beloved homecoming parade, the specter of lost revenue associated with the football team's boycott (Mizzou would have had to pay Brigham Young University $1 million for canceling an upcoming game) almost certainly motivated campus stakeholders to increase their pressure on Wolfe to step aside.

Inextricably intertwined with the neoliberal forces shaping the Mizzou racial crisis were the insidious norms and values of white supremacy, which fostered and perpetuated a racially hostile campus climate and leadership structures that were unable to recognize and address the systemic oppression deeply embedded in campus culture, policies, and practices. Inadequate leaders and leadership presented substantial barriers to action, change, and healing at the University of Missouri (Kezar & Fries-Britt, 2018). The Mizzou racial crisis also illustrates how equity-centered, collective leadership perspectives, such as those displayed by Concerned Student 1950, can disrupt discrimination and facilitate material change. It is this dual understanding of leadership—as a barrier to social justice and as a pathway to equity—that frames the analysis of higher education leadership theory and research presented in this book. In this opening chapter, we expand on the barrier-pathway framework and map out the book's key aims and arguments.

The Contemporary Landscape of Higher Education Leadership

American colleges and universities are facing unprecedented political, economic, human rights, public health, and environmental challenges. In many cases, these compounded pressures threaten institutional survival. At a minimum, the challenges undermine the ability of schools to fulfill their multifaceted missions of preserving American democracy, fostering economic prosperity, advancing scientific discovery, and promoting peaceful and productive global interdependence. Now more than ever, higher education institutions require leadership processes and (in)formal leaders capable of identifying and eliminating behavior that implicitly and explicitly thwarts justice within and beyond campus borders (G. Anderson, 2020; Santamaría & Santamaría, 2016b). This demand for more nimble and just higher education leadership raises the question, Do college and university educators possess the leadership knowledge needed to tackle complex challenges centered on issues of racial injustice, economic inequality, environmental degradation, and political incivility? Put another way, Are contemporary leadership theory and research capable of guiding higher education organizations and individual actors toward the development of policy and practices that foster anti-racist learning environments, make college more affordable, and treat the postsecondary labor force with dignity and respect? These are a few of the pressing and interdependent issues demanding leadership attention and action. In this book, we survey the contemporary landscape of leadership theory and research, including general leadership scholarship and research specific to higher education contexts, in the interest of both synthesizing knowledge that can be used to inform action and highlighting knowledge gaps to guide future inquiry.

In this chapter, we review the evolution of leadership theory and research over the last three decades, noting the expansion of scholarly attention paid to collective, nonhierarchical, process-centered, and context-bound frameworks rooted in social constructivist and critical paradigms (Dugan, 2017; Kezar et al., 2006). These collectivist perspectives and their emphasis on mutual power and influence processes stand in contrast to the postpositivist hierarchical views of leadership that have dominated leadership scholarship for centuries (Dinh et al., 2014; Dugan, 2017; Kezar et al., 2006; Northouse, 2019) and continue to inform policy and practice in the contemporary neoliberal academy (Kezar et al., 2019; Kezar & Posselt, 2020). Classic leadership theories rooted in the traits and behaviors of great white, upper-class men focus on those in positions of power, study leadership as the actions and responsibility of individuals, and search for universal characteristics that can be used to predict outcomes and guarantee leadership effectiveness (Dugan, 2017; Northouse, 2019). Our review of contemporary leadership scholarship reveals that both of these competing perspectives (hierarchical and collectivist) continue to frame leadership research and practice. Despite evidence of the positive outcomes associated with adopting shared-power approaches to leadership, including enhanced team satisfaction, innovation, learning, and performance (D'Innocenzo et al., 2016; G. Drescher & Garbers, 2016; S. Liu et al., 2014; Serban & Roberts, 2016), the assumptions and norms of top-down, individual-centered leadership remain deeply entrenched in society broadly and higher education specifically (Dugan, 2017; Young & López, 2011).

A central argument of this book is that higher education researchers and practitioners seeking to understand and advance leadership knowledge and practice in the interest of fostering more just organizations need to examine the contemporary landscape of leadership scholarship as well as question the ways the hierarchical and collectivist leadership frameworks simultaneously serve as pathways to transformative change and mechanisms for maintaining an oppressive status quo. This dual project of synthesis and critique serves as the framework for this book, which is intended as a valuable resource for higher education scholars, particularly emerging scholars, seeking to develop research agendas that center questions of leadership. Higher education professionals committed to engaging in leadership for social change will also find this book to be a useful guide for action. We detail how classic, hierarchical views of leadership have metastasized and gained power under a neoliberal and white supremacist regime despite the existence of more inclusive leadership theories and practices that have existed for decades (in some cases centuries) yet remain marginalized within the leadership discourse. These sidelined forms of leadership (women's, racial and ethnic, Indigenous, spiritual, etc.) continue to assert themselves and work to gain recognition in the lexicon of leadership, with mixed results. This book outlines the continued struggle to make leadership more inclusive while also naming traditional forces that work against such recognition.

One such force thwarting the progress and influence of collective leadership perspectives may be these inclusive frameworks themselves. Specifically, we question whether and how collectivist conceptualizations of leadership are working to name and disrupt leadership's long-standing association with domination, oppression, authority, and white supremacy in the neoliberal academy. Given the continued dominance of neoliberal and racist hierarchical leadership perspectives, we argue that collectivist leadership theorists and practitioners need to couple their articulation of culturally inclusive, shared leadership values and assumptions with the explicit identification of the oppressive norms embedded within historical structures of leadership and the way their vestiges prevent leadership from providing a pathway to change. Left unattended, normative leadership structures reinforce authority- and domination-based views of leadership that instantiate themselves and co-opt inclusive perspectives. In this book, we make the case that in order for leadership to serve as a pathway to change and achievement of institutional objectives for equity and the public good, higher education leadership research and practice must critically examine and seek to overturn the interdependent ideologies of neoliberalism and white supremacy that continue to shape leadership and campus contexts. Although inclusive leadership perspectives have helped us imagine what it looks like to engage in shared leadership and prioritize the justice and public-good aims of higher education, they have not necessarily shed light on how to go about dismantling existing racist, sexist, classist, and other systems and structures of oppression. Indeed, McNair et al. (2020) observe that many higher education leaders are comfortable engaging in "equity talk," expressing their commitment to cultivating inclusive and equitable learning environments, but struggle to translate this talk to an "equity walk," the tangible actions (assessment practices, decision-making processes, policy development, etc.) necessary for overturning oppressive structures and achieving equitable outcomes. A contribution of this book is to spotlight the work of critical leadership scholars (e.g., Santamaría & Santamaría, 2016b) who are developing theory and studying higher education professionals focused on naming and overturning oppressive systems of power and privilege while simultaneously promoting inclusive leadership beliefs, norms, and behaviors.

A key assumption framing this book is that there is a relationship of mutual influence between leadership research and practice. As scholarly conceptualizations of leadership change, so do leadership practices (Young & López, 2011). Scholarly shifts stem from both theoretical and methodological developments. New and evolving leadership theories (e.g., applied critical leadership theory; Santamaría & Santamaría, 2015) as well as novel approaches to collecting and analyzing leadership data (e.g., Arnold & Crawford, 2014; Rodela & Rodriguez-Mojica, 2020) contribute to the development of new leadership perspectives that inform action. Simultaneously, shifts in daily leadership commitments and practices necessitate that researchers revisit, update, or abandon altogether older theories and models of leadership. By centering the relationship between leadership research and practice, we aim to demonstrate the ways new approaches to thinking about and studying leadership may facilitate the systemic, structural change needed to realize the public-good aims and ideals of American higher education.

Having articulated the key arguments and assumptions framing this book, we now turn to a discussion of the historical origins of our work on this project and the evolution of thinking about leadership. We close the chapter with an overview of the book's organizational framework and suggestions for using the end-of-chapter discussion questions and case studies for further reflection and inquiry.

Revisiting the "L" Word in Higher Education

We trace the intellectual roots of the present book to Bensimon et al.'s (1989), *Making Sense of Administrative Leadership: The "L" Word in Higher Education*, which offered an interdisciplinary review of six major leadership theories (trait, power and influence, behavioral, contingency, cultural and symbolic, and cognitive) as well as the organizational frames in Bolman and Deal (1984). It considered the implications and applications of this scholarship within higher education administrative contexts. Bensimon et al. noted that, at the time, studies of higher education leadership centered the formal role of the president and were guided by a "traditional and directive view when they define[d] the leadership role; few appear to [have] emphasize[d] the importance of two-way communication or social exchange processes of influence or to identify leadership as facilitating rather than directing the work of higher education professionals" (p. iv). Additionally, Bensimon et al. observed the beginnings of a paradigmatic shift from traditionally dominant rational leadership perspectives toward cultural and symbolic perspectives within higher education leadership research, noting, however, that these cultural and symbolic leadership views were not yet widely adopted in practice despite their usefulness for navigating many of the academy's defining features (e.g., ambiguous goals, diverse constituencies, and bifurcated authority).

Curious as to whether Bensimon et al.'s early observations of a shift toward cultural and symbolic views of leadership had gained momentum in the seventeen years since their scholarly review, Kezar, Carducci, and Contreras-McGavin (2006) revisited the project and offered an updated analysis of leadership theory and research in *Rethinking the "L" Word in Higher Education: The Revolution of Research on Leadership*. The authors situated their examination of leadership scholarship within a contemporary context characterized by growing demand for leaders capable of tackling the multitude of challenges confronting higher education at the dawn of the twenty-first century, including diminished state funding, increased revenue generation expectations, globalization, the rise of the accountability and assessment movements, an increasingly diverse student demographic, expanded community engagement ambitions, and calls for more attention to improving college access and affordability. Kezar et al. suggested that new theories and concepts of leadership were needed to understand and cultivate higher education leadership processes capable of bringing about the bold changes demanded by higher education's diverse constituencies. Based on their review of the literature, the authors asserted that the paradigmatic shift toward cultural and symbolic perspectives observed by Bensimon et al. in 1989 had expanded in the ensuing years and a revolution in leadership research and practice was underway at the turn of the twenty-first century. Although the traditionally dominant models of hierarchical, individual-centered, control-based leadership frameworks had not lost total favor within the leadership research community, an increasing number of leadership scholars were examining and advocating for leadership perspectives founded on collective and contextual notions of leadership. Kezar et al. argued the leadership revolution underway was the product of both dramatic shifts in leadership scholarship and the return of long-forgotten topics that were becoming influential again. For example, concepts such as spirituality

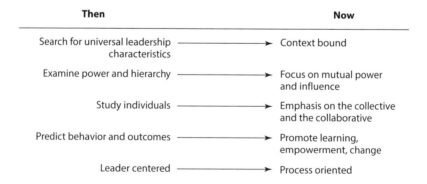

Figure 1.1   The Revolution in Leadership Research. *Source:* From *Rethinking the "L" Word in Higher Education*, by Kezar et al. (2006), p. 34. Copyright 2006 by Jossey-Bass.

were revolving back into prominence within the leadership scholarship. Kezar et al. developed an image to depict their understanding of the revolution in leadership research, offering an explicit mapping of the conceptual shifts in leadership theory and research that characterized scholarship published after Bensimon et al.'s 1989 literature review (fig. 1.1). Specifically, they noted the increasing prominence of research that examined the contextual nature of leadership; emphasized mutual power and influence as opposed to top-down unilateral power; studied the collective and collaborative dimensions of leadership processes; moved away from individual, position-centered studies toward an understanding of leadership processes; and generated insights regarding the leadership dynamics of learning, change, and empowerment as opposed to searching for universal and predictable leadership "truths."

Kezar et al. (2006) attributed the late twentieth-century leadership revolution to the interdependent influences of a changing social context and the emergence of new scholarly perspectives associated with the radical social movements of the 1960s and 1970s (e.g., those for civil rights, women's rights, gay liberation, and Movimiento Estudiantil Chicano de Aztlán) that challenged authority, emphasized empowerment, and conceptualized collective action as a pathway to social change (Rhoads, 1998). The late twentieth century was also characterized by the rise of a global economy predicated on coordination and collaboration across national borders made possible through rapid technological advancement (Burbules & Torres, 2000). Emerging global leadership perspectives and practices shed light on the unique cultural and social dimensions of leadership, underscored the importance of teams as well as local leadership, and paved the way for a more complex and process-oriented understanding of leadership. Kezar et al.'s examination of the leadership research revolution encompassed both developments in leadership theory (i.e., contingency, cultural, cognitive, complexity, organizational learning, processual, and teams) and new thinking pertaining to leadership concepts (e.g., ethics, empowerment, collaboration, and networks). In the interest of producing a comprehensive landscape analysis of leadership research published from 1990 to 2005, they reviewed scholarship both within and beyond higher education. As we do in the current book, they included vignettes and case studies throughout in the interest of providing opportunities to apply revolutionary theories and concepts.

Rethinking the "L" Word (Kezar et al., 2006) highlighted major shifts in late twentieth-century leadership research, specifically the following: (1) an expanded focus from senior positional leaders (presidents) to broader academic leadership roles (deans, department chairs, students, and nonpositional leaders); (2) movement past command-and-control leadership frameworks in favor of inclusive and empowering models (e.g., servant leadership and team); and (3) challenges to leadership myths that valorize domineering, all-knowing actors and universal leadership traits. Kezar et al. identified academic capitalism and managerialism as two countermovements to the leadership revolution. These conceptually distinct but related neoliberal approaches to higher education administration continued to reaffirm hierarchical and individualistic leadership perspectives that prioritized the accumulation of power, prestige, and wealth over the common good. At the time, the authors were optimistic that the paradigm shift toward social constructivist, critical, and postmodern leadership perspectives would take root and begin to overshadow the historically dominant postpositivist discourses within higher education leadership research and practice communities. Sixteen years later, we revisit the project of surveying the landscape of leadership inquiry with a particular interest in examining the extent to which the "revolutionary" leadership theories and concepts featured in *Rethinking the "L" Word* have continued to expand leadership discourse and practice.

Now that we have traced the historical origins of the book, it is time to reflect on whether Kezar et al.'s optimism regarding the expansion of inclusive leadership perspectives was justified. The answer is a tepid yes. Informed by our analysis of published leadership research and scholarly observations of postsecondary responses to global, national, and local crises (Kezar et al., 2019; Kezar & Posselt, 2020), we have revisited and refined some of Kezar et al.'s (2016) arguments regarding the status and future of inclusive leadership inquiry and practice. First, we now recognize that Kezar et al. were perhaps a bit too hopeful regarding the fading influence of hierarchical views of leadership. Upheld by principles of neoliberalism and white supremacy that have gained prominence and fueled global movements, traditional and dominant leadership perspectives continue to frame higher education leadership research and practice (Santamaría & Santamaría, 2016b; Young & López, 2011). This argument is a major focus of chapters 3 and 4.

The Evolution of Leadership Research and the Work Left Undone 13

Second, we find it necessary to temper Kezar et al.'s characterization of collective, nonhierarchical leadership perspectives as "revolutionary." Although many collectivist and shared leadership theories and concepts featured in *Rethinking the "L" Word* represented "major or fundamental change" (Merriam-Webster, n.d.) to Western leadership views, they would not be considered revolutionary by those who adopt a broader lens and recognize them as extensions of Indigenous or non-Western perspectives with rich histories. For example, complexity and chaos leadership theories have connections to Eastern philosophies (Wheatley, 1999), and some collective leadership theories that have gained prominence in the twenty-first century are rooted in centuries-old Indigenous principles (Spiller et al., 2020). In this book, we again highlight and laud the continued evolution of inclusive and collective leadership perspectives; however, we soften the description of them as "revolutionary" in the interest of honoring their historical legacies.

A third argument that marks a departure from the thinking in *Rethinking the "L" Word* was introduced earlier in this chapter—the assertion that leadership (in both research and practice) serves simultaneously as a barrier and a potential pathway to the systemic change needed to transform the academy and realize espoused equity commitments. Institutional agents committed to enacting the public-good missions of higher education must recognize the role that historically dominant leadership perspectives rooted in the tenets of neoliberalism and norms of white supremacy play in maintaining inequitable policy and practice structures (leadership as a barrier) and the promise of critical leadership perspectives to name and overturn systemic oppression (leadership as a pathway). We have developed figures 1.2 and 1.3 to visually depict the key arguments and assumptions framing this book.

The status quo in leadership inquiry, encompassing both traditional (postpositivist, hierarchical) perspectives and some of the inclusive leadership theories and concepts highlighted in *Rethinking the "L" Word*, are represented in figure 1.2. This body of scholarship is supported by and often maintains the twin forces of neoliberalism and white supremacy, advancing our understanding of effective leadership within and beyond higher education but rarely explicitly naming, contesting, or changing the norms, policies, and structures that reify racial, economic, and gender inequity. To be sure, contemporary leadership scholars and practitioners have expanded knowledge

14   The Contemporary Context of Leadership in Higher Education

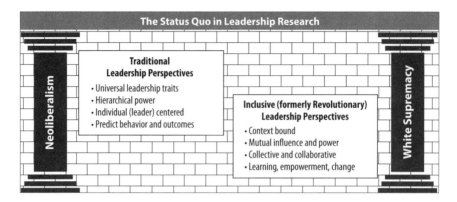

Figure 1.2   Leadership Research as a Barrier to Social Justice

of contextual, collective, and empowerment-oriented approaches to shaping individual actions and organizational outcomes (Dinh et al., 2014; Kezar & Lester, 2011; Pak & Ravitch, 2021a; Santamaría & Santamaría, 2016b), knowledge that has the potential to bring about meaningful change on campus (e.g., curricular reform, community partnerships, or increased demographic diversity). But some of the scholarship characterized as revolutionary in 2006 and inclusive in our most recent literature review remains rooted, albeit implicitly, in assumptions and experiences of white supremacy (e.g., whiteness as property, interest convergence) and neoliberalism. For example, cultural and symbolic theories of leadership and organizational dynamics highlight the importance of attending to the socially constructed and contextual nature of norms, values, and symbols, but these theories often explicitly fail to examine the ways in which symbols and leadership discourses can serve as instruments of hegemonic power and oppression, determining criteria of organizational fit, value, and belonging (Gonzales et al., 2018). Additionally, some newer theories have been usurped by traditional forces, rendering them inert. For example, we describe how chaos and complexity theories have been neutralized by traditional forces that limit the revolutionary potential of these leadership perspectives. Despite espoused commitments to engage in leadership theory building and research with the aim of advancing social justice objectives inside and beyond the academy, the absence of direct engagement by many inclusive or revolutionary leadership perspectives with the concepts of power, hegemony, cultural imperialism, white supremacy, and neoliberalism leaves the roots of systemic inequity undisturbed and free to become more deeply entrenched in higher education institutions. In this way, we see contemporary leadership theory and research as a barrier to achieving espoused social justice goals.

Although we argue that traditional and *some* inclusive leadership perspectives are complicit in maintaining oppressive systems and structures in the academy, we also view leadership theory and research as a pathway to equity. To bolster this view, we turn to the work of critical leadership scholars (e.g., Pak & Ravitch, 2021a; Santamaría & Santamaría, 2016b). Guided by the aims and principles of critical social theory, which emphasize the systemic nature of discrimination, the intersection of social identities, and the role of mainstream research practices in the reproduction of oppression (Young & López, 2011), critical leadership scholars advocate for alternative theoretical and methodological approaches unequivocally focused on examining and disrupting leadership dynamics that foster oppression and discrimination (Collinson, 2011). Specifically, critical leadership scholars study and critique normative leadership ideologies and practices (e.g., power dynamics, language, authority, identity constructions, values, beliefs, rituals, and myths) that foster inequality. Within the context of higher education leadership research and practice, critical leadership scholar-practitioners examine and critique normative leadership discourses and institutional practices

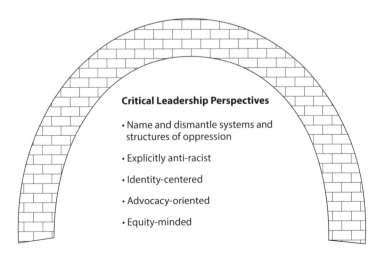

Figure 1.3   Leadership Research as a Pathway to Social Justice

that contribute to a relatively homogeneous (white, male, heterosexual) cadre of senior institutional leaders. We identify in figure 1.3 the characteristics of critical leadership perspectives that facilitate the development of knowledge and practices essential for excavating the systemic roots of white supremacy and neoliberalism with the aim of bringing about substantive and sustained racial, economic, and gender equity.

In the following chapters, we revisit our conceptualization of leadership as both a barrier and a pathway to social justice, drawing on contemporary leadership theory and research to illustrate how decisions concerning what is studied (e.g., focal concepts, behaviors, and individuals) and approaches to inquiry (e.g., paradigms, methodology, and methods) serve to constrain or expand leadership knowledge and practice. In the interest of cultivating leaders and leadership processes capable of addressing the complex challenges confronting higher education, including deep-seated racism, higher education leadership scholars and practitioners must continue to develop, examine, and adopt inclusive, collective, and equity-oriented leadership perspectives that explicitly seek to dismantle oppressive systems and structures (Kezar et al., 2021). For example, in their case study of the 2015 Mizzou racial crisis, Kezar and Fries-Britt (2018) called for higher education organizations to proactively build leadership capacity for addressing campus racial crises rather than waiting for crises to erupt before identifying response strategies. Specifically, Kezar and Fries-Britt called for leadership characterized by a deep appreciation for the roles that social, cultural, and political contexts play in shaping human interactions and perceptions; a commitment to active listening; a willingness to speak from the heart and engage in honest communication rooted in emotion rather than political spin; an understanding of collective trauma; and a belief in the power of "acting with" community members to address immediate and underlying racial tensions. The leadership knowledge and skills highlighted in the Mizzou case study transcend the focal context of addressing campus racial crisis; they reflect inclusive and equity-oriented leadership perspectives essential for creating socially just learning and work environments and fulfilling the public-good mission of higher education. In addition, the leadership processes and characteristics described by Kezar and Fries-Britt challenge hierarchical, individual-centered, command-and-control models of leadership that dominated foundational leadership theory and research (Kezar et al., 2006; Northouse, 2019) and continue to thrive in organizational contexts steeped in neoliberal and white supremacy ideology. Higher education leadership scholars and practitioners committed to advancing inclusive, equity-oriented leadership perspectives must continue to conceptualize, study, and practice leadership phenomena in new ways that both build on the collective-, process-, and context-oriented theories that have gained prominence in the twenty-first century and advance our thinking with respect to what it looks like and means to engage in leadership work that is explicitly committed to resisting and dismantling the twin influences of neoliberalism and white supremacy. In this book, we map the contemporary landscape of leadership theory and research as well as point to possible futures in the interest of contributing to a leadership research agenda that informs the development of individual and organizational leadership capacity for deep, sustained structural change focused on creating a more equitable society in and beyond higher education. Now that we have introduced the premise and central arguments shaping this book, it is time to provide a general overview of the book's structure and content.

Organization of the Book and Intended Applications

This book is designed to provide readers with a comprehensive overview of contemporary higher education leadership theory and research. Although some may choose to read the book from cover to cover as organized, others may opt to turn directly to chapters of particular professional relevance. The chapters in part I introduce key ideas that are threaded throughout the book, so we recommend spending some time familiarizing yourself with this part before moving on to material presented in part II. Whatever your approach, we invite you to actively engage with the ideas and reflective activities presented throughout the book in the interest of expanding your understanding of contemporary leadership theory and developing the capacity to engage in leadership research and practice with a focus on dismantling the twin forces of white supremacy and neoliberalism.

The book is divided into three parts. The four chapters in part I (including this introduction) detail the key assumptions and arguments framing our analysis of contemporary leadership theory and research. In chapter 2, we review five paradigms—postpositivist, social constructivist, critical, postmodern, and participatory—that shape leadership inquiry, succinctly describing each paradigm's approach to conceptualizing and studying leadership as well as explaining how paradigmatic assumptions serve to constrain and advance leadership knowledge and practices focused on dismantling systemic oppression and bringing about positive social change. Chapters 3 and 4 provide deep dives into neoliberal and white supremacist ideologies and the role these knowledge regimes (which are rooted in the postpositivist paradigmatic assumptions and values of universal truth, objectivity, control, prediction, and efficiency) play in cementing oppressive hierarchical power and leader-centered constructions of leadership within and beyond higher education.

Each of the five chapters in part II provides a detailed overview of a theoretical domain applied to the study and practice of leadership. Specifically, we examine transformational, cognitive, chaos and complexity, cultural, and processual leadership theories, reviewing the historical roots, major assumptions, significant contributions, and key findings of these frameworks. We also synthesize the critiques leveled against these well-worn leadership approaches and describe new evolutions in each approach that hold promise for fostering more inclusive and transformative leadership perspectives and processes. In each chapter, we revisit the concepts of neoliberalism and white supremacy and reflect on how these ideologies manifest in contemporary leadership scholarship and practice within the focal frameworks. Although all of the chapters in part II are organized similarly, the chapters vary in length, reflecting differences in the depth and breadth of research undertaken on each approach.

In part III, chapter 10 synthesizes major insights from our analysis of contemporary leadership research and imagines what the future may hold for the study and practice of leadership in and beyond higher education. Consistent with our argument that neoliberal and white supremacist ideologies serve to maintain individual-centered and hierarchical power–oriented notions of leadership, we identify research topics and questions that may prove useful in identifying and dismantling oppressive leadership norms and practices. Additionally, our proposed research agenda builds on the critiques and new evolutions in each of the five leadership approaches featured in part II, highlighting promising new directions for expanding knowledge and practice within these well-established leadership frameworks. Acknowledging that the way we study leadership profoundly shapes what we know (Young & López, 2011), chapter 10 also includes a call for emerging and seasoned re-

The Evolution of Leadership Research and the Work Left Undone 19

searchers to expand their methodological toolkit and adopt critical, participatory, decolonizing, and Indigenous methodologies that promote engagement in data collection, analysis, and representation activities and relationships that dismantle oppressive power dynamics in the research process and produce new, transformative ways of knowing and practicing leadership.

We begin each chapter in parts I and II with a brief vignette that presents a contemporary higher education issue and highlights the potential value of adopting more inclusive and liberatory leadership perspectives to address these challenges. To help readers translate theory and research into practice, each chapter concludes with a summary of key points as well as a set of questions that can be used to frame individual reflection or group dialogue. The appendix includes four integrative case studies designed to illustrate how higher education scholar-practitioners might draw on several of the leadership approaches and concepts featured in the book to make sense of and tackle complex challenges. These are excellent resources to support teaching these perspectives and understanding the contemporary challenges of leadership.

We have written this book with several audiences and applications in mind. It provides a foundational overview of contemporary leadership theory and research within and beyond higher education. Accordingly, faculty teaching graduate-level higher education leadership seminars may find the book of value as a primary text, drawing on chapter discussion questions and integrative case studies to frame in-class activities and written reflections. Scholars seeking to engage in higher education leadership research will find the book's comprehensive literature review and extensive reference list helpful as they frame their proposed studies and synthesize current knowledge. The new directions for inquiry mapped out in the concluding chapter are intended to inform the development of research projects that will advance understanding of contemporary leadership dynamics with a particular focus on naming and dismantling the pernicious influences of neoliberalism and white supremacy within (higher education) leadership theory, research, and practice. Higher education professionals who seek to better understand and expand their capacity to engage in leadership for positive change may also benefit from reading this book individually or as part of a reading group. Chapter reflection questions and the integrative case studies can help these professionals identify their current, potentially oppressive, leadership frameworks and guide them in exploring and developing more

20   *The Contemporary Context of Leadership in Higher Education*

inclusive leadership processes. Finally, those responsible for designing and facilitating leadership development opportunities for higher education faculty and staff may find this book helpful for conceptualizing new approaches to both the content and structure of leadership development programs. Regardless of where you are situated within higher education (graduate student, faculty, researcher, staff, supervisor, leadership educator), we invite you to actively engage with the book's ideas and tools for guided reflection and dialogue in the interest of thinking about, studying, and practicing leadership in potentially new and complex ways that dismantle deeply entrenched oppressive systems and structures.

Conclusion

In 2006, Kezar et al. used the notion of a revolution to frame the disruption of traditional leadership views, articulating a hope that these perspectives would grow in influence. We see more than fifteen years later the continued dominance of traditional and neoliberal perspectives coupled with the continued evolution and expansion of non-Western, collectivist leadership. In *Higher Education Leadership: Challenging Tradition and Forging Possibilities*, we move away from the term *revolutionary* for reasons explained earlier in this chapter but continue to examine the extensions of collectivist leadership frameworks featured in *Rethinking the "L" Word*, offering a more realistic assessment of the neoliberal and white supremacist constraints actively resisting culturally inclusive leadership. In this book, we discuss various new leadership theories and concepts influenced by inclusive perspectives that can create pathways for leadership to achieve organizational aims that represent the full span of humanity rather than just the elite. We also note how various inclusive and critical ideas and movements tend to be disconnected, taking away from their power to disrupt the overarching neoliberal, white supremacist narrative. We describe ways leadership theorists and practitioners can work together to create a uniform front focused on disrupting leadership as part of the problem and moving it toward a pathway for solutions.

Key Points

- Contemporary leadership theory and research serve as both barriers and pathways to the systemic change needed to transform higher education and realize espoused equity commitments.

- Neoliberalism and white supremacy ideologies serve to maintain and advance individual-centered, hierarchical power–oriented leadership frameworks and practices.
- Equity-centered, collective leadership perspectives can facilitate the dismantling of oppressive systems and structures.
- Despite the continued evolution and expansion of shared-power and process-oriented leadership frameworks, the assumptions and norms of top-down, individual-centered leadership remain deeply entrenched in society.
- Collective leadership theorists and practitioners need to couple their articulation of culturally inclusive, shared leadership values with the explicit identification of the oppressive norms embedded in contemporary leadership structures.
- New approaches to thinking about and studying leadership (e.g., new methodologies) will likely facilitate the systemic, structural change needed to realize the public-good aims of higher education.

Discussion Questions

1. What do you see as the most pressing leadership issues confronting American higher education? What about at your particular institution or organization?

2. Write your personal definition of leadership. What has informed the development of this definition? Now review figures 1.2 and 1.3. In what ways does your personal definition of leadership align with the traditional, inclusive, and critical leadership perspectives depicted in these figures? How might your personal definition shape or constrain your approach to studying and practicing leadership?

3. When have you observed leadership serving as a barrier to the achievement of equity and social justice aims? When have you observed leadership serving as a pathway to equity and social justice? For your examples, describe how context, social identities, relationships, and systems and structures of power shaped the experience.

Chapter 2

Leadership Paradigms

Michelle, a second-year doctoral student in higher education administration, has set aside time to prepare for an afternoon meeting with her faculty adviser. The purpose of the meeting is to discuss Michelle's preliminary dissertation ideas and develop a consensus on a general direction for the project so that Michelle can begin to explore relevant literature and conceptualize the study in the research practicum she will complete next term. Students in Michelle's program typically use the practicum as the launching pad for their dissertations, and Michelle is eager to work with her adviser to map out a research plan that aligns with her interests in higher education leadership, particularly the experiences of Black women in academic leadership roles.

Before going back to school as a full-time doctoral student, Michelle was the associate director of an undergraduate honors program, a role that placed her in frequent contact with academic leaders (e.g., department chairs, deans, and provost staff) and allowed her to observe a variety of leadership styles in action, some empowering, others quite toxic. As a queer Black woman, Michelle frequently reflects on the ways her intersectional identities have influenced her experiences in the academy. Specifically, she contemplates how her leadership style and approach to organizational change have been informed by her social identities, her life history (her parents met at a civil rights organizing event), the professional socialization she received as a chemistry major, the microaggressions and overt discrimination she frequently experienced as the only Black staff member in her office, and the community and commitment to collective action she derived from her active involvement in the campus Black professionals network. Recognizing that her approach to leadership is deeply rooted in her life story, Michelle is now eager to explore how other Black women experience and enact leadership in academic environments characterized by implicit bias and overt racism.

Having settled on a general topic of inquiry that she is confident her adviser will approve of (they have frequently discussed Michelle's experience and emerging scholarly interest in Black women's leadership during advising conversations), Michelle knows her next task is to generate a set of preliminary research questions that might guide her review of the literature and initial research design decisions. For guidance, Michelle turns to the readings and notes from the introductory research methods course she completed during her first semester in the doctoral program. Chapter 1 of the required methods text introduces the notion of research paradigms and explains how a researcher's paradigms (also commonly referred to as worldviews) shape the research process, including the aims of inquiry, framing of research questions, approaches to data collection and analysis, and representation of findings. Although she is familiar with the broad themes of the paradigms featured in her textbook, she is not sure in which paradigm she wants to situate her dissertation research. It seems that the next logical step in preparing for her afternoon meeting is to review the major research paradigms and consider how their principles, assumptions, and associated research methods might inform the study of leadership in general and her exploration of Black women academic leaders in particular. In this chapter, we provide Michelle and other leadership scholars with a concise introduction to five paradigms (postpositivism, social constructivism, critical, postmodern, and participatory), illustrating how paradigmatic tenets inform contemporary leadership inquiry and play a role in supporting (or constraining) the development of leadership knowledge and practices that contribute to the creation of socially just and equitable organizational environments.

An Introduction to Paradigms

In chapter 1, we traced the evolution of leadership theory and research, calling attention to the continued preoccupation with hierarchical, individual-centered notions of leadership and the simultaneous advancement of process- and context-based leadership perspectives that emphasize shared power and collective action. Underlying these diverse approaches to understanding and practicing leadership are paradigms. Mertens (2020) described a paradigm as "a way of looking at the world . . . composed of certain philosophical assumptions that guide and direct thinking and action" (p. 8). Within the context of leadership research and theory development, paradigms influence beliefs and assumptions regarding the essential nature of leadership (i.e., "leadership is . . ."), the purpose of research (e.g., to predict, interpret, critique, or transform), the most appropriate approaches for studying the phenomenon of leadership (e.g., surveys, interviews, ethnographies, or action research), and the role of values in leadership. In *Rethinking the "L" Word in Higher Education*, Kezar et al. (2006) closely examined the ways the assumptions, beliefs, and values of the social constructivist, postmodern, and critical paradigms influenced the evolution in leadership research and practice in the late twentieth century, contesting the historical dominance of the postpositivist paradigm and its corresponding assumptions regarding the existence and value of universal leadership truths. In this chapter, we revisit and update Kezar et al.'s review of the paradigms shaping leadership scholarship, noting the persistence of the postpositivist worldview (rooted in neoliberal principles that place a premium on quantifying and measuring productivity, effectiveness, etc.) as well as the continued influence and expansion of the social constructivist, postmodern, and critical paradigms. We have added a fifth leadership paradigm to this discussion—the participatory paradigm—to recognize the role participatory inquiry plays in developing research practices and leadership knowledge that advance positive, material change. Table 2.1 summarizes the leadership paradigms featured in this book.

At the outset of this discussion, it is important to distinguish between paradigms and theories. Paradigms are concerned with overarching assumptions regarding the philosophical issues of ontology (the nature of reality), epistemology (beliefs about knowledge), axiology (examination of values), and methodology (approaches to inquiry). Paradigmatic assumptions are not typically grounded in empirical evidence, but they do play an important role in the research process, informing decisions regarding the nature of research questions, approaches to data collection and analysis, and

Table 2.1 Leadership paradigms

	Postpositivism	Social constructivism	Critical	Postmodern	Participatory
Major assumptions	Leadership is a social reality that can be described, has an essence, and has generalizable qualities and predictable outcomes.	Leadership is a social construction; subjective experience is important to how leadership emerges. Culture and context have a significant effect on leadership, an ever-evolving concept that has changed over time.	Leadership has a history of oppression and is therefore viewed with suspicion. Leadership is typically used by those in power as a means of maintaining authority and control. It is possible for leadership to serve a broader goal of social change if power dynamics are watched carefully and new language is used that empowers historically marginalized individuals and groups.	Leadership has been an expression of the will to power but is more complicated than that generalization; it is a contingent, human construction affected by local conditions, history, and the ambiguity and complexity of the human experience; it is a reflection of human identity shaped by history.	Leadership knowledge and practices are highly experiential (leadership as experience and action) and situated in particular contexts; accordingly, it is necessary to study and theorize leadership at the local level.
Purpose of research	To predict leader outcomes based on behavior; to develop generalizable principles to help direct the actions and behavior of leaders	To interpret and understand what people perceive or attribute as leadership; to help leaders understand their frameworks and how their perspectives as leaders affect a leadership process	To develop representations and strategies of leadership that are empowering and create social change	To question the concept of leadership itself; to examine whether it is merely the will to power; to explore whether certain complex conditions can result in leadership	To improve local conditions through transformational actions rooted in the lived experience of coresearchers

(continued)

Table 2.1 (continued)

	Postpositivism	Social constructivism	Critical	Postmodern	Participatory
Approach to research	Survey of leader traits, behaviors, and influence strategies	Interviews of leaders in a particular setting; surveys of perceptions of followers; study of interaction of leaders and followers	Case study and ethnography of leadership contexts focused on power dynamics and interactions	Case study and ethnography of local contexts with a focus on examining contradictory perspectives and ambiguity; explore alternative approaches to representing research (e.g., playwriting, a/r/tography)	Collaborative inquiry processes in which researchers and local stakeholders work together to design and conduct research; an iterative process characterized by identification of a focal challenge, reflection on lived experience, and transformational actions; may employ both qualitative and quantitative data collection methods
Role of values	Functionalist theories take a neutral stance on values	Values seen as shifting based on perspectives and situations	Values believed central for creating leadership that empowers and creates social change	Values questioned as inherently serving some power interest	Varies based on particular participatory approach—for example, values are believed central to creating leadership that empowers and creates social change in critical participatory perspectives; other forms of participatory inquiry (e.g., action science) espouse a neutral stance on the role values play in evaluating leadership
Criticisms or limitations	Fails to acknowledge the influence of context, culture, and individual differences on leadership; limited ability to create universal or general principles of leadership	Provides few specific directives for action; does not examine the role of power	Does not emphasize effectiveness or outcomes important for societal and organizational survival	Provides few specific directives for action; some people question whether the global economy and postmodern condition truly exist	Focus on local, experiential knowledge limits transferability of leadership research to other settings; difficult to authentically and consistently enact collaborative inquiry principles and practices

Source: Adapted from *Rethinking the "L" Word in Higher Education*, by Kezar et al. (2006), pp. 16–17. Copyright 2006 by Jossey-Bass.

strategies for representing, sharing, and applying findings. In contrast, theories advance organized, multifaceted, and often empirically grounded explanations for why and how a phenomenon (e.g., leadership or cultural capital) works. Leadership theorists draw on paradigmatic assumptions to frame their research processes as well as articulate the nature and aim of their theory (e.g., to explicate universal leadership traits or name and dismantle gender biases embedded in leadership discourses). Paradigms and theories are inextricably linked, and the development and implementation of leadership perspectives that contribute to the advancement of socially just postsecondary educational institutions necessitate the continued expansion of inquiry and theories anchored in critical, postmodern, and participatory paradigms.

Now that we have reviewed the foundational role paradigms play in shaping knowledge production, it is time to examine the major paradigms shaping contemporary leadership scholarship. As you read about each paradigm, consider how the paradigm's guiding assumptions concerning the nature and aim of leadership research might inform Michelle's study of Black women academic leaders.

The Postpositivist Paradigm

Early leadership research was firmly grounded in the assumptions and tenets of the (post)positivist paradigm, which emphasizes ontological realism—that is, the existence of a singular, objective reality that transcends culture and context—and a commitment to utilizing the scientific method to discover universal and generalizable knowledge that can serve as a guide for action and a tool for predicting outcomes. As Mertens (2020) explained, positivism, the precursor to postpositivism, was predicated on a belief that social phenomena such as leadership could and should be studied using value-free methods of scientific experimentation, observation, and measurement in the interest of uncovering objective facts and causal explanations. Recognizing that many facets of human behavior cannot be observed (e.g., cognition and emotions), postpositivists moved away from limiting inquiry to that which could be observed and instead pursued "understandings of truth based on probability rather than certainty" (Mertens, 2020, p. 12), all the while holding on to the principles of objectivity and generalizability. In the context of leadership research, the postpositivist paradigm guides empirical efforts to generate objective, universal, and generalizable leadership knowledge that, when applied by individuals in formal leadership roles, results in predictable outcomes. Classic and modern leadership trait and behavior theories illustrate the prominence of the positivist paradigm in leadership research (Northouse, 2019). Leadership scholars are in a never-ending empirical quest to identify universal leadership traits associated with individual or organizational effectiveness. Additional strands of leadership inquiry and theory historically guided by postpositivist assumptions include power and influence theories and contingency theories predicated on universal interpretations of a singular reality (the organizational context).

In addition to influencing the aims of leadership research (i.e., the discovery of universal leadership truth), postpositivist assumptions also influence the process of inquiry, resulting in research designs (typically quantitative) that seek to strip the influence of values, identity, context, and so on from data collection and analysis. The result is the discovery of objective facts that can be used to control and predict leadership behavior, resulting in expected outcomes. We conceptualize traditional postpositivist leadership perspectives as barriers to realizing the social justice and equity aims of higher education institutions given that they are typically silent on or seek to erase multiple interpretations of context, intersectional identities, and critical analysis of hegemonic, top-down power structures (see fig. 1.2). Although contemporary leadership scholars continue the quest for objective, universal, generalizable leadership knowledge (Northouse, 2019; Zaccaro, 2012), the recognition that leadership is a product of human interaction, culture, and context paved the way for the rising influence of social constructivist, critical, postmodern, and participatory paradigms.

The Social Constructivist Paradigm

Social constructivists reject the postpositivist assumption of an objective reality that can be observed, measured, and replicated, embracing instead a view of reality as socially constructed and characterized by numerous possible interpretations and meanings (Mertens, 2020). Thus, the aim of inquiry anchored in the social constructivist paradigm is not to discover universal facts that can be used to predict or create future outcomes but rather to examine multiple interpretations of a focal phenomenon (e.g., leadership or sense of belonging) from the perspective of those with lived experience, resulting in the development of a shared, albeit partial and imperfect, understanding. When applied to the study of leadership, social constructivism shifts attention away from the search for universal leadership traits and skills that can be generalized to all settings and instead explores how perception, interpretation, context, culture, experience, and social identities influence the understanding and practice of leadership.

Operating from the premise that leadership is a socially constructed phenomenon continuously produced through interaction, social constructivist leadership scholars seek to identify and understand the factors that influence individual and collective leadership beliefs and actions. One strand of social constructivist leadership inquiry examines how identities and experiences shape leadership views (e.g., Chávez & Sanlo, 2013; Eagly & Chin, 2010; Fassinger et al., 2010; Kezar & Lester, 2010). A prime example of this scholarship within the field of higher education is Kezar's (2002) ethnographic study of thirty-six community college faculty and staff, which drew on positionality theory to shed light on how overlapping aspects of identity (e.g., race, gender, professional role, academic discipline, and experiences with power) influence personal leadership beliefs.

In the absence of a uniform, universally adopted definition of leadership, notions of leadership quality and effectiveness are in the eye of the beholder; thus, social constructivist leadership researchers seek to understand how individuals throughout the leadership setting (i.e., formal and informal leaders, collaborators, and followers) interpret leadership (Birnbaum, 1992; Grint 1997). Two significant influences on interpretations of leadership are culture and context (Bryman et al., 1996; Osborn et al., 2014; Schein, 2010). Specifically, cultural and contextual norms concerning leadership qualities and behaviors shape individual and group expectations and interpretations of leadership, including who can fill leadership roles and how they are to act. The importance of context in constructions and interpretations of higher education leadership can be seen in the concern expressed by campus constituencies in response to news that an institution has hired a president or chancellor with military, political, or corporate leadership experience rather than a leader who has risen through the ranks of academic leadership (Krupnick, 2015; L. McKenna, 2015). Operating from the assumption that there are significant differences between the leadership norms and behaviors deemed appropriate in hierarchical organizations like the military and for-profit businesses (e.g., top-down decision-making and consolidated power)

30   *The Contemporary Context of Leadership in Higher Education*

and those appropriate in higher education, faculty and staff often bristle at the prospect of an "outsider" leading their campus.

Attribution theory and research also shed light on meaning-making in leadership. Specifically, this line of inquiry examines how and why individuals attribute outcomes and processes to leaders. Attribution researchers have found that individuals are biased when assessing the importance of leader behavior for organizational outcomes (both positive and negative), attributing more influence to leaders than they likely exhibit (Yukl, 1998). In an organizational context characterized by organized anarchy and loose coupling (Hendrickson et al., 2013), individuals seek to bring clarity and order to their meaning-making by attributing outcomes to formal leaders.

In addition to examining how organizational members make sense of the social construct of leaders and leadership, researchers have also explored the ways positional leaders may utilize the socially constructed nature of leadership to advance their preferred agenda or version of reality. For example, in what ways do individuals vested with positional or other forms of power leverage their influence to shape constituent perceptions of meaning and reality? In these situations, leadership can become a form of social control (Chemers, 1997). This line of thinking is evident in Bolman and Deal's (2017) discussion of how leaders manage symbols (stories, myths, artifacts, rituals, ceremonies, etc.) to convey a shared sense of organizational beliefs and values as well as influence action. For example, institutional leaders seeking to diminish support for a unionization movement among contingent faculty may draft messaging (e.g., press releases, speeches, or emails to the campus) that lauds the university's commitment to the principles of shared governance and frames union efforts as a threat to the prized value of collegiality. These symbolic communications seek to construct a common understanding of what shared governance means and looks like for all faculty, regardless of rank, labor conditions, or job security. Through the manipulation of symbolic communications, leaders who oppose the union effort aim to control individual and collective constructions of a collegial work environment, framing collective bargaining as antithetical to their shared best interests.

In addition to shaping how leadership is conceptualized (as a fluid and ever-evolving phenomenon produced through interaction), the social constructivist paradigm also influences the nature of leadership inquiry. Rather than adopting research designs that adhere to the principles of the scientific method (e.g., data collection methods such as surveys that minimize the influence of values and context), social constructivist researchers recognize that they themselves play an active role in the construction and interpretation of meaning and engage in highly interactive data collection methods (e.g., interviews and participant observation) that allow them to mutually construct insights with those participating in the study. Furthermore, the recognition that context and culture shape leadership beliefs and processes necessitates that researchers must situate their studies in a particular context and adopt research methodologies like case study and ethnography that allow for careful examination of cultural norms, artifacts, values, assumptions, and so on (Bryman, 2004; Bryman et al., 1996). The influence of context on postsecondary leadership can be seen in studies situated in particular institutional types or sectors. For example, a prominent strand of higher education leadership research focuses on the particular leadership dynamics, needs, and norms embedded within American community colleges (Boggs & McPhail, 2019; Eddy, 2012, 2018; Eddy & Khwaja, 2019; Tarker, 2019). Leadership scholars recognize that community colleges' unique culture and context (e.g., connections to local industry, posttraditional student demographics, heavy reliance on contingent labor, and bureaucratic governance structures; Cohen et al., 2014) shape human interactions and thus leadership perceptions and performances. Similarly, examinations of higher education leaders and leadership have also been situated in the specific institutional contexts of Historically Black Colleges and Universities (Freeman & Gasman, 2014; Freeman et al., 2016; Gasman, 2011; Palmer & Freeman, 2020), Hispanic-Serving Institutions (Cortez, 2015; Garcia & Ramirez, 2018; Palmer et al., 2018), Tribal Colleges and Universities (Bowman, 2009; Crazy Bull, 2018; Krumm & Johnson, 2011; Sorensen, 2015), and faith-based institutions (Frawley, 2014; Longman & Anderson, 2016; Webb, 2008).

As elaborated on earlier in this chapter, social constructivist approaches to conceptualizing and studying leadership challenge historically dominant assumptions regarding the existence of universal leadership traits and behaviors that can be discovered through rigorous and objective (scientific) methods. Framing leadership as a socially produced phenomenon that reflects evolving and contextualized individual and collective beliefs, norms, and principles shifts the higher education leadership research agenda from questions of prediction and a preoccupation with formal (often senior)

32   The Contemporary Context of Leadership in Higher Education

positional leaders toward inquiry framed by the aim of understanding multiple realities, interpretive processes, and human interactions across identities, power, and cultures. Accordingly, social constructivist leadership researchers center concepts of meaning-making, language and discourse, perception, interpretation, and culture, among others. Although social constructivist approaches to leadership theory and research significantly challenge postpositivist notions of hierarchical, individual-centered, and universal leadership truths, this body of scholarship does not typically engage explicitly with questions of power and oppression or seek to develop leadership theory and practice overtly focused on advancing positive social change. Critical leadership scholars have taken up these projects.

The Critical Paradigm

Critical leadership research is rooted in critical social theory's philosophical tenets and aims, an expansive body of scholarship characterized by shared foundational principles and distinct schools of thought. Often traced back to scholars affiliated with the Institute for Social Research founded in 1923 at the University of Frankfurt (commonly referred to as the Frankfurt School), critical theory extends Karl Marx's critique of the subjugation embedded in industrial capitalism and typically encompasses "all work taking a basically critical or radical stance on contemporary society with an orientation toward investigating exploitation, repression, and unfairness, asymmetrical power relations (generated from class, gender, race or position), distorted communication and false consciousness" (Alvesson & Deetz, 2006, p. 256). Critical theory rejects social constructivism's neutral aim of interpreting human and organizational dynamics; rather, critical scholars engage in the explicitly political and revolutionary project of examining oppression and injustice with the aim of empowering those who have been historically oppressed to create a more just and equitable society (Brookfield, 2005; Kincheloe et al., 2012; Tierney, 1991). The critical paradigm also seeks to engage individuals with power and privilege, demanding they reflect on their positionality and leverage their influence to advance positive social change (Shields, 2012). While the breadth and depth of critical social theory and scholarship cannot be condensed into a single uniform definition or framework, scholars have identified foundational assumptions of critical social theory:

Leadership Paradigms 33

> That all thought is fundamentally mediated by power relations that are so-
> cial and historically constituted; that facts can never be isolated from the
> domain of values or removed from some form of ideological inscription; . . .
> that language is central to the formation of subjectivity (conscious and un-
> conscious awareness); that certain groups in any society and particular socie-
> ties are privileged over others and, although the reasons for this privileging
> may vary wildly, the oppression that characterizes contemporary societies
> is most forcefully reproduced when subordinates accept their social status
> is natural, necessary, or inevitable; that oppression has many faces, and fo-
> cusing on only one at the expense of others (e.g., class oppression versus
> racism) often elides the interconnections among them; and finally, that
> mainstream research practices are generally, although most often unwit-
> tingly, implicated in the reproduction of systems of class, race, and gender
> oppression. (Kincheloe & McLaren, 2005, p. 304)

Although critical social theory may share a common set of underlying assumptions and principles, this body of scholarship is broad, encompassing
numerous disciplines (e.g., arts, humanities, and social sciences) as well as
diverse theoretical perspectives (e.g., critical and Black feminisms, critical
race theory, LatCrit [Latino and Latina critical race theory], queer theory,
critical Indigenous theory, critical disability theory, and postcolonial theory)
(Martínez-Alemán, 2015; Shields, 2012). The common thread connecting
these diverse schools of thought is a commitment to critiquing, interrogating, and transforming systems of power and oppression (Gonzalez et al.,
2018).

When applied in the study and practice of leadership, the critical paradigm rejects value-free notions of leadership advanced by postpositivism and
moves beyond the social constructivist aim of understanding diverse interpretations of leadership, focusing instead on the role power and identity constructions play in leadership, with a particular eye toward how individuals
and organizations leverage power to perpetuate oppression and maintain
control (Collinson, 2011; Dugan, 2017; Santamaría & Santamaría, 2016b).
Beyond examining leadership as a tool of domination, critical leadership
scholars also seek to develop theories and promote practices that honor the
empowering potential of leadership characterized by collaboration (e.g.,
shared leadership and teams), an ethic of care, and reflection focused on

equity and social change rather than profit maximization and the accumulation of power. Finally, critical perspectives also call on researchers to reconsider processes of leadership inquiry to alter the power dynamics that traditionally define the roles of researcher and subject (Shields, 2012).

Disrupting traditional notions of leadership as centered in formal roles of power and authority, critical leadership perspectives often examine leadership processes embedded throughout organizations. As Collinson (2011) noted, "Critical studies emphasize that leadership dynamics can emerge informally in more subordinate and dispersed relationships, positions, and locations as well as in oppositional forms of organization such as unions (Knowles, 2007) and revolutionary movements (Rejai, 1979)" (p. 181). This line of critical leadership inquiry is evident in Kezar and Lester's (2011) examination of grassroots leadership in higher education. Building on insights generated from a multi-institution case study, Kezar and Lester developed a grassroots leadership model that details the individual, group, and organizational dynamics that support bottom-up change efforts to challenge the status quo. Kezar and Lester's study aligns with "postheroic" notions of leadership that disrupt tendencies to attribute organizational outcomes to formal positional leaders, instead recognizing the collective and relational nature of leadership and underscoring the need for more attention directed toward understanding shared leadership and followership (Crevani et al., 2007). Within the critical leadership perspective, scholars of followership seek to examine and transform asymmetrical power dynamics between positional leaders and their followers (Collinson, 2011).

Critical leadership scholars also place social identities at the center of inquiry, exploring the ways leadership processes perpetuate inequality along the intersecting dimensions of race, class, gender, faith, sexual orientation, nationality, ability, and so on. Seeking to address the omission of social identity considerations within traditional (postpositivist) educational leadership theory, Young and López (2011) called on scholars to examine educational leadership through the theoretical lenses of critical race theory (focusing analysis on issues of race and racism), queer theory (examining gendered, heteronormative, and homophobic assumptions embedded in leadership), and feminist poststructuralism (exploring manifestations of patriarchy and the possibility of resistance in educational leadership). Critical leadership scholars assert that the adoption of critical theoretical perspectives and accompanying methodologies (e.g., counterstorytelling, testimonio, and auto-ethnography) is an essential step toward disrupting oppressive master leadership narratives. Leadership scholars cannot come to know leadership differently until they change the lenses and tools of inquiry (Ospina & Foldy, 2009; Young & López, 2011).

Within the field of educational leadership, Santamaría and Santamaría's (2016b) model of applied critical leadership exemplifies the aims and theoretical orientations of critical leadership scholarship. Moving beyond an examination of how asymmetrical power relations embedded in educational systems create and sustain oppression, applied critical leadership offers a strengths-based leadership framework that draws on critical theory (e.g., critical race theory, queer theory, LatCrit, TribalCrit, and feminist theory) and culturally responsive pedagogy to explain the transformative, equity-oriented leadership practices of historically marginalized individuals. As Santamaría and Santamaría (2016b) explained, the premise of applied critical leadership is that

> when leaders of color, otherwise marginalized individuals, or those who may choose to practice leadership through a CRT [critical race theory] lens, make leadership decisions, they reflect and draw upon positive attributes of their identities and life experiences within their societal locality, asking themselves questions such as: In what ways does my identity (i.e., subjectivity, biases, assumptions, race, class, gender, and traditions) enhance my ability to see other perspectives and therefore provide effective leadership? Hence, what are the affirmative attributes that render me different and unique that might be explored and developed in order to build and improve my leadership practice? (p. 5)

Explicitly eschewing a deficit perspective toward the intersecting social identities and lived experiences of historically oppressed individuals, applied critical leadership examines the ways leaders draw on their embodied knowledge of inequity, bias, and discrimination to engage in transformative leadership practices that advance social justice. Santamaría and Santamaría (2016b) made a point of noting that applied critical leaders are not only changing the way they think about leadership (theory) but also, and perhaps most importantly, reimagining what it looks like to do leadership (practice), including regularly engaging in deep self-reflection and consciousness-raising. Applied critical leadership embodies the perspective of leadership as a pathway to social justice that we visually depict in figure 1.3. We will return to the applied critical leadership model in chapter 8, which explores cultural models of leadership in detail.

Leadership theory and research rooted in the critical paradigm has gained prominence in recent years (Collinson, 2011; Santamaría & Santamaría, 2016b) as researchers and practitioners seek both to critique functionalist (postpositivist) leadership perspectives that perpetuate discriminatory (e.g., racist, heteronormative, gendered, or nationalist) leadership assumptions and to advance transformative leadership theories and practices that actively contribute to the establishment of a more equitable and just society. Although critical leadership scholarship draws on a diverse array of theoretical frameworks, this body of work shares a focus on systems of power (and domination), intersectional identities, resistance, and positive social change (Collinson, 2011; Santamaría & Santamaría, 2016b; Young & López, 2011).

In addition to framing leadership inquiry topics, critical paradigm tenets may also guide data collection, analysis, and representation strategies. Critical methodologies seek to disrupt hierarchical, "objective," and oppressive constructions of data, research relationships, and knowledge dissemination to transform not only what we know about leadership but how we know it (Shields, 2012). Eschewing the facade of neutrality, critical scholars engage those with lived experience in the gathering, interpretation, and sharing of knowledge, dismantling repressive notions of evidence, rigor, and grand narratives in the process (Pasque et al., 2012). Despite a well-developed and growing body of scholarship on the principles and practices of critical research (L. Brown & Strega, 2005; R. N. Brown et al., 2014; Cannella et al., 2015; Shields, 2012), critical methodologies such as counterstorytelling, photovoice, arts-based inquiry, and critical performance ethnography remain muted and marginalized within (higher) educational leadership scholarship (Klenke et al., 2016; Young & López, 2011). The perpetuation of methodological conservatism (Lincoln & Cannella, 2004) within higher education leadership literature contributes to a narrow understanding and practice of leadership, as well as the cultivation of educational leaders who are ill-equipped to confront and dismantle the twin forces of white supremacy and neoliberalism. We return to this argument in chapter 10, issuing a call for the adoption of more critical methodologies in future higher education leadership research.

The Postmodern Paradigm

A fourth paradigm shaping contemporary leadership research is postmodernism. Developed in the 1980s, postmodernism has been conceptualized and applied in a diverse array of disciplines, including the arts, architecture, cultural studies, history, literature, economics, political science, and philosophy. A foundational premise of postmodernism is a rejection of totalizing narratives, making it difficult to develop a coherent and consistent definition of postmodernism that captures its complexity and multiple permutations (S. R. Jones et al., 2022). In *Rethinking the "L" Word in Higher Education*, Kezar et al. (2006) described the postmodern paradigm as "a rejection of modernist views of the world—including a belief in an objective, continuous, linear view of reality with an autonomous individual who controls his or her destiny" (p. 23). In opposition to postpositivist assumptions of grand narratives and objective, universal truths, postmodernists view reality and knowledge as socially constructed and produced through interactions that are local, particular, fleeting, and laden with power (Alvesson & Deetz, 2006). Although not a definitive list (indeed, the postmodern perspective rejects the premise of definitive lists), concepts such as reflexivity, subjectivity, local history and context, chaos, fluidity, change, textuality, fragmentation, complexity, and simultaneity frame postmodern examinations of the social world (Alvesson & Deetz, 2006; Kezar et al., 2006; Tierney, 1996).

When applied to the study of leadership, postmodernism (like social constructivism) challenges postpositivist assumptions of universal leadership traits and qualities. Postmodern leadership theorists recognize that leadership is a socially constructed phenomenon produced in particular moments and spaces and thus focus on examining how cultural norms and assumptions influence perceptions and expectations of leadership. Postmodernists reject the notion of stable, shared cultural constructions of leadership that can be coherently conveyed and uniformly understood by organizational members. Rather, postmodern organizations are made up of humans who possess agency to construct their own realities, contributing to an organizational life and perceptions of leadership characterized by difference, opposition, ambiguity, and complexity. As Tierney (1996) explained,

> The implication for studies of leadership is that the idea of leadership becomes contested, and the assumption about what constitutes good leadership

is open for interpretation and redefinition. Thus, when a researcher enters a research site his or her struggle is to search for inconsistencies and contradictions. Postmodernists eschew the search for clarity or persuasion through rational logic because absolutes no longer exist, and one assumes that multiple representations exist within one organization. The struggle becomes first how to develop those multiple interpretations, and then how to portray them. (p. 374)

This quote highlights a foundational premise of postmodern leadership research: postmodern scholars are not seeking to identify and develop stable, coherent, uniform definitions of leadership; rather their aim is to explore the multiple perspectives on leadership operating within a particular context and call attention to the factors (e.g., power and identity) that shape leadership beliefs and behaviors.

One strategy for surfacing different constructions of leadership within the postmodern paradigm is to examine language (including speech, text, and images). Specifically, postmodern scholars explore the ways language and (in)formal communication (conversation, speeches, email, memos, etc.) are used to construct and convey leadership ideology (Alvesson & Deetz, 2006). Similar to critical theorists, postmodern leadership scholars seek to understand how language and discourse can be used as tools of oppression, establishing hegemonic power structures that center the leadership values, beliefs, and expectations of those who possess dominant identities (i.e., wealthy, white, heterosexual, cisgender men). Through the textual analysis process of deconstruction, postmodernist scholars seek to "displace or unsettle taken-for-granted concepts, such as the unity of the text, the meaning or message of the text, and the authorship of the text" (Schwandt, 2001, p. 53). Within the context of higher education leadership inquiry, postmodern analysis of leadership discourse might examine the multiple and contested interpretations of leadership conveyed in formal speeches (e.g., presidential remarks or student protests), routine interactions (e.g., department meetings or hallway conversations), institutional documents (e.g., press releases, publications, or websites), and campus symbols (e.g., building names, monuments, and art or artifacts).

Underscoring the contingent and indeterminate nature of language, Tierney (1996) highlighted the importance of attending to context when analyzing leadership discourse with a postmodern lens, including developing an understanding of the local context's historical roots, present conditions, and ties to broader global trends. Returning to the Mizzou vignette from chapter 1, postmodern scholars seeking to understand the multiple constructions of leadership framing this particular moment and movement for racial justice would need to analyze historical narratives of leadership and racism at Mizzou, the rhetoric and actions of the individuals at the center of the 2015 protest (i.e., President Tim Wolf, the members of Concerned Student 1950, Chancellor R. Bowen Loftin, the Board of Curators, and members of the football team) as well as the broader international Black Lives Matter movement.

The notion of fragmented identities is another foundational postmodern concept of particular interest to leadership scholars. Specifically, postmodern scholars reject the modernist notion of the autonomous individual with a well-developed, coherent, and unified sense of self (Alvesson & Deetz, 2006; Tierney, 1996). Alvesson and Deetz (2006) noted the modernist "fiction" of the unified self can serve as a tool of oppression, masking the complexity of fragmented, intersectional identities and privileging those who seek to emulate the normative behaviors of white masculine rationality and control. Within the context of leadership research, this refutation of autonomous, unified identities calls into question the possibility of establishing distinct categories for leadership, leaders, and followers, recognizing that these are fluid and highly contextualized concepts and roles.

Finally, as in the critical paradigm, scholars situated in the postmodern paradigm are also interested in the analysis of power, and specifically how power manifests in language, norms, and material practices and how power serves to establish and reinforce ideology and organizing categories that can perpetuate oppression (e.g., gender and race). Within the context of leadership inquiry, this focus on power shifts attention away from the study of leadership traits or the leader-follower dichotomy and toward questions centered on how organizational discourse and practices (e.g., hiring protocols, reward structures, and office layouts) privilege some constructions of leadership and marginalize others (Alvesson & Deetz, 2006; Tierney, 1996).

As with the other paradigms highlighted in this chapter, adopting a postmodern perspective in leadership inquiry not only informs the focus of inquiry but also holds implications for research methodology. Research designs that emphasize the examination of local contexts, contradictory perspectives, fragmentation, ambiguity, and multivocality align with the postmodern paradigm. Of particular interest to postmodern researchers are issues of representation, how to present research findings in ways that honor the fragmented realities and multiple voices that compose postmodern narratives (Guba & Lincoln, 2005; Tierney 1996). As Guba and Lincoln (2005) noted, postmodern efforts to explore alternative approaches to representation typically result in messy texts, "texts which seek to break the binary between science and literature, to portray the contradiction and truth of the human experience" (p. 211). Poetry, playwriting, storytelling, auto- and duoethnography, a/r/tography, photovoice, and other representational approaches drawn from the disciplines of art and literature may prove useful to postmodern leadership scholars seeking to disrupt the highly structured narrative norms of the scholarly journal article (Guba & Lincoln, 2005).

THE PARTICIPATORY PARADIGM

The fifth and final leadership paradigm highlighted in this chapter is the participatory paradigm, an approach to knowing and inquiry that is "fundamentally experiential" (Heron & Reason, 1997, p. 276). The participatory paradigm was not featured in *Rethinking the "L" Word* (Kezar et al., 2006), which limited the discussion of prominent leadership paradigms to postpositivism, social constructivism, critical, and postmodern. We have added participatory inquiry to our discussion of paradigmatic approaches that advance the study and understanding of contemporary leadership because this worldview holds promise for engaging in leadership theorizing, research, and practice that actively construct pathways to more equitable educational organizations.

Although the participatory paradigm encompasses a number of distinct research approaches, including action research, action science, pragmatic action research, participatory action research, collaborative inquiry, and cooperative inquiry (Schwandt, 2001), participatory approaches to inquiry share a belief that knowing is a product of experience and that knowledge production processes should be situated in local contexts and result in transformational action that brings about positive change first and foremost in the immediate setting, with broader implications a secondary consideration (Heron & Reason, 1997).

Heron and Reason (1997) articulated the foundational tenets of the participatory paradigm, which include a subjective-objective ontology that defines reality as cocreated through interaction between one's subjective perception and "tangible entities" (p. 278), as well as an epistemology rooted in critical subjectivity that is characterized by four ways of knowing: experiential knowledge (direct engagement), presentational knowledge (expression of experience through language, music, visual, and material forms), propositional knowledge (conceptual knowledge expressed in theories and statements), and practical knowledge (knowing as doing). With respect to axiology, participatory inquiry's value system, Heron and Reason (1997) asserted, "Within the participative worldview, the primary purpose of human inquiry is practical: our inquiry is in the service of human flourishing. Our knowledge of the world is consummated as our action in the world, and participatory research is thus essentially transformative. Although some inquiry projects may be primarily informational and result in propositional knowing, transformational projects are primary (Heron, 1996)" (p. 288). Seeking to establish connections with existing paradigms while simultaneously articulating the unique aims of participatory inquiry, Heron and Reason (1997) noted that both the participatory and critical paradigms share an axiological commitment to social transformation that is not foundational to constructivist research; however, the emphasis placed on practical knowing and local action in participatory inquiry distinguishes this paradigm from both constructivist and critical worldviews.

Another distinctive feature of the participatory paradigm is a methodological commitment to collaborative inquiry—developing research designs that disrupt the traditional and separate roles of researchers (experts who carry out the research) and subjects (those who are studied). In many forms of participatory inquiry, distinctions between researcher and subject are blurred as researchers and local stakeholders work together to develop research questions, design the research process, collect and analyze data, and formulate action plans to bring about material change in the immediate context. Although distinct methodologies encompassed within the broad participatory paradigm differ in the extent and nature of local stakeholder engagement in the research process (Bensimon et al., 2004), Heron and Reason (1997) advocated for a participatory methodology guided by the principles of epistemic participation (i.e., "research is grounded by the researchers in their own experiential knowledge") and political participation defined as a belief that "research subjects have a basic human right to participate fully in designing research that intends to gather knowledge about them" (p. 284). Although constructivist, critical, and postmodern paradigms view knowledge as contextual and thus engage in inquiry practices that examine the lived experience of their research "subjects," the participatory commitment to epistemic and political participation calls for inquiry processes that engage local stakeholders in both the design and implementation of research projects in which they examine and make meaning of their own experiences—it is research *with*, not on or about, community members (Heron & Reason, 1997).

Moving from an abstract overview of the participatory paradigm to its application in practice, leadership research and theory guided by the principles of participatory inquiry are characterized by an iterative, localized process of observation, reflection, and action with an explicit aim of bringing about material change in the immediate context (Malcom-Piqueux, 2016). Within the participatory perspective, leadership knowledge and practices are highly experiential (leadership as experience and action) and situated in particular contexts; thus, it is necessary to study and theorize leadership at the local level (in a particular organizational setting). Gonzales and Rincones's (2013) examination of the emotional labor embedded in the work of department chairs is an excellent example of participatory leadership research. In this study, Gonzales and Rincones drew on participatory action research and photo-elicitation methods to explore how Rincones (a department chair) experienced and made meaning of emotions in his administrative role. Consistent with the participatory principles of collaborative inquiry, the situation of research in local contexts, and the generation of knowledge that contributes to material positive change, Rincones actively participated in each phase of the study and described the research process and findings as energizing and fostering heightened understanding and new insights that will inform his leadership practice. Another robust line of participatory leadership inquiry examines participatory action research as a space to engage in shared leadership for social justice and a vehicle for leadership development (G. L. Anderson & Middleton, 2014; Bertrand, 2018; Fox & Fine, 2015; James et al., 2008; Zuber-Skerritt, 2011; Zuber-Skerritt et al., 2015).

While participatory inquiry approaches share a commitment to fostering local change, not all participatory researchers are focused on bringing about

Leadership Paradigms   43

positive social change—what Heron and Reason (1997) described as transformational change or inquiry "in service of human flourishing" (p. 288). The neoliberal aims of increased efficiency, productivity, and profit may also be advanced through participatory inquiry. For example, Chris Argyris and Donald Schön's action science framework does not explicitly call on researchers to examine issues of power and oppression as they work with collaborators in particular contexts to address problems of practice (Schwandt, 2001). In contrast, participatory action researchers do center issues of politics and power in the inquiry process with the aim of collaboratively generating applied knowledge rooted in lived experience that can empower local stakeholders and contribute to more equitable and just practices (Malcom-Piqueux, 2016).

The participatory paradigm was not featured in Kezar et al.'s (2006) discussion of paradigmatic influences on leadership theory and research at the start of the twenty-first century, reflecting the limited role participatory inquiry principles played within "mainstream" leadership scholarship published before 2006. We include the participatory paradigm in this chapter to recognize its growing prominence within contemporary leadership research and practice and honor its potential for framing transformative leadership scholarship. Operating from the participatory paradigm principles of epistemic and political participation, leadership scholar-practitioners can draw on the four ways of participatory knowing and the axiological commitment to inquiry as a vehicle for local social change to examine and cultivate leadership perspectives that serve to dismantle the twin forces of neoliberalism and white supremacy and advance leadership commitments and practices rooted in equity, anti-racism, and the public good.

Conclusion

In this chapter, we have reviewed the five major paradigms that guide leadership research within and beyond higher education: postpositivism, social constructivism, critical, postmodern, and participatory. Paradigms significantly influence both the nature and process of inquiry, guiding the development of research questions, the selection of sensitizing concepts, and decisions regarding data collection, analysis, and representation. Emerging higher education scholars like Michelle, the doctoral student introduced in the chapter's opening vignette, who are embarking on the development of a leadership research agenda should spend considerable time reflecting on their paradigmatic orientations and alignment of particular paradigms with topics of interest. Researchers need not settle on one particular paradigm; Kezar and Dee (2011) highlighted the potential value of multiparadigmatic inquiry. It is important, however, for scholars to understand the epistemological (knowledge), ontological (reality), axiological (values), and methodological (research design) implications embedded in particular paradigms as they conceptualize and carry out their leadership research.

As documented in the subsequent chapters of this book, contemporary leadership scholarship is framed by all five inquiry paradigms. Although research anchored in the tenets of postpositivism and social constructivism certainly serves to advance understanding of higher education leadership processes, we contend that scholarship rooted in the critical, postmodern, and participatory paradigms—inquiry that explicitly names, critiques, and disrupts oppressive power structures—is most likely to develop knowledge and inform actions essential for dismantling systems and structures of oppression associated with neoliberalism and white supremacy. If leadership is to serve as a pathway, rather than a barrier, to realizing positive social change and the public-good mission of higher education, postsecondary leadership scholars must continue to advance critical, postmodern, and participatory perspectives that center questions of intersectional identities, context, power, and resistance. We develop this argument more fully in subsequent chapters.

Key Points

- Paradigms are framed by distinct epistemological (knowledge), ontological (reality), axiological (values), and methodological (research design) beliefs and assumptions that play an important role in framing theory development and research design.
- Within the field of leadership, paradigms influence beliefs and assumptions regarding the essential nature of leadership, the purpose of research, the most appropriate approaches for studying the phenomenon of leadership, and the role of values in leadership.
- Contemporary leadership theory and research are framed by five paradigms: postpositivism, social constructivism, critical, postmodern, and participatory.

- It is imperative for higher education leadership scholars and practitioners to identify and reflect on their preferred paradigms with respect to framing, studying, and practicing leadership.
- Theory and research rooted in the critical, postmodern, and participatory paradigms—inquiry that explicitly names, critiques, and disrupts oppressive power structures—are most likely to develop knowledge and inform actions essential for dismantling systems and structures of oppression associated with neoliberalism and white supremacy.

Discussion Questions

1. Take ten minutes and engage in a free-writing exercise in response to the following prompt: "Leadership is . . ." Don't edit yourself, just write. At the end of the time period, reflect on the assumptions, beliefs, and values embedded in your personal leadership framework. Compare your leadership framework with the paradigm overview presented in table 2.1. Which paradigms best align with your current leadership perspective?

2. The chapter's opening vignette introduces Michelle, a second-year doctoral student interested in examining the experiences of Black women in academic leadership roles. Michelle is in the process of considering which leadership paradigms will inform her dissertation research. All five of the paradigms reviewed in this chapter hold potential relevance for Michelle's study; however, each of the paradigms would approach the study of Black women in academic leadership roles differently given their distinct leadership assumptions and ontological, epistemological, axiological, and methodological principles. Help Michelle think through the implications of paradigms in her dissertation research by considering how each of the paradigms featured in this chapter would inform key aspects of the study, including (a) the study's foundational assumptions about leadership, (b) the purpose of the research, and (c) research methodology. What do you see as the benefits and limitations of each paradigm for a study of Black women's academic leadership experiences?

3. Identify three empirical research articles on higher education leadership published within the last ten years. Review each article and attempt to identify the paradigms framing the study. How do the author's paradigms inform the research questions, theoretical or conceptual framework, methodology, and findings?

Chapter 3

Neoliberalism and Higher Education Leadership

Juanita is new to her campus as the director of the Office of Institutional Research. Her doctoral training program emphasized the possibilities for institutional research to support student success and equity, which is what attracted her to pursuing the position when she finished her degree. As she starts to meet with campus stakeholders to talk about her perspective and to learn about their expectations of the office, she is quite confused about her role. As she meets with the provost, he emphasizes his need for reports on enrollment patterns across different majors. He is considering conducting a major restructuring and laying off faculty and staff. He also talks to her about a system of metrics that he is interested in putting in place and hopes that she will monitor over time. The metrics relate to the economic efficiency of different departments and units. This way, he says, he can start winnowing away staff earlier and not have to do this kind of major restructuring in the future.

Juanita next meets with the deans, who are also asking for data for program reviews; they seem anxious about the current types of data requested and are trying to recommend some different metrics. She asks the provost if she can meet with the head of the academic senate and the vice president of student affairs. He says that is probably not a good idea and that decisions are largely made among the cabinet members and senior administrators like the deans. He suggests meeting with the vice president of human resources and the chief financial officer instead. This was not how Juanita imagined her role. She is trying to reconcile her incoming student success and equity goals with the provost's performance metrics demands and narrow conceptualization of her institutional role, expectations echoed by the academic deans.

This scenario illuminates the ideas that will be discussed in this chapter concerning the neoliberal philosophy driving campus decision-making. This philosophy reflects the deeply embedded corporate style of management, which is oppositional to the more progressive forms of leadership highlighted in this book. Revisiting our conceptualization of leadership as both a barrier and a pathway to realizing the equity aims and public-good mission of higher education, this chapter highlights the structural and systemic barriers to justice-oriented leadership constructed and reinforced by neoliberal ideology.

Traditional Views of Leadership

As discussed in chapter 1, until the 1980s, leadership research and practice were embedded in what were called positivist or functionalist theories (Kezar et al., 2006). These theories emphasized that leadership was an individual practice by those in positions of authority. In addition, leadership was largely seen as social control that was executed by those in elite positions. In fact, the emphasis on management that undergirded early views of leadership was based on the association of leadership with those in functional roles of organizational management. Additionally, leadership was often assumed to be vested in those who have power in hierarchical systems. As a result, the study of leadership largely focused on identifying the traits, behaviors, and power and influence strategies of individuals in positions of authority. The paradigm of positivism that undergirded these traditional studies of leadership asserted a realist ontology that emphasizes a singular, objective, and shared reality. This helped to reinforce this dominant view of leadership that was developed from the perspectives of white, male, and privileged leaders or individuals in positions of authority. If there is only one view of leadership and it is an objective statement of truth, then other views or perspectives on leadership are not explored or seen as legitimate—for example, the views of people of color, Indigenous people, and women as well as others typically not in positions of authority. Those conducting the research as well as the individuals who were studied were mostly white, male, and privileged, which continued to reinforce the norm of a transcending set of leadership qualities and characteristics that reflected the views of white, male, and elite people. Positivist studies encourage the study of phenomena separate from their context, which also mitigates challenges to the elite's perspectives from women, racialized minorities, and other groups within the organization, reinforcing the universal white male elite norms.

In the 1980s, however, significant critiques of traditional views of leadership scholarship emerged, advancing the perspective that leadership can be executed by anyone, not just individuals in positions of authority. Drawing from studies of social movements, these new leadership theories viewed leadership as collective and a process, and because it involved individuals throughout organizations and society, mutual forms of power and influence were emphasized (Kezar et al., 2006). Informed and inspired by the social and political movements in the 1960s and 1970s that pushed for racial, gender, and environmental equity and justice, the inclusive leadership frameworks that gained prominence at the dawn of the twenty-first century applied feminist, Marxist, and critical race theory to the study of leadership, resulting in democratic, collaborative, and nonhierarchical perspectives that explicitly named social change as the desired outcome. The changes of the 1960s and 1970s gave way to new theories of leadership that critiqued traditional views but also provided a vision for leadership that looks quite different from past conceptions. Kezar et al. (2006) labeled this new vision the revolution in leadership—in which chaos and complexity theories, cultural and symbolic theories, and the concepts of transformational leadership, professional leadership, and leadership teams were articulated in the 1980s and 1990s and began to be fairly mainstream thinking by 2006.

The 1980s were also seeding another revolution, a reaction to the social and political efforts aimed at racial and gender equity (R. Brown, 2011; Smythe, 2017). This conservative movement, called neoliberalism, began to spread simultaneously with the revolutionary principles that we described in Kezar et al. (2006). At its core, neoliberalism aims to bring back traditional perspectives of leadership that emphasize authority, control, hierarchy, managerialism, and leaders in formal positions of power as the epitome of leadership (R. Brown, 2011). These views of leadership comport with the politically conservative perspective of neoliberalism and work to assault the emerging progressive views within social, political, and other institutions. Neoliberalism has often been described as the invisible hand that reshaped global political, economic, and social philosophies, as it took decades for social commentators to realize the way it had taken over institutions and reshaped social and organizational structures. In this chapter, we look at the way this hidden hand moved into higher education and its leadership and has hindered the efforts of scholars to establish the newer progressive, inclusive, equity-oriented, and democratic leadership concepts (R. Brown, 2011). Neoliberalism has made the goals of social change leadership for the public good extremely difficult to achieve, and it is this tension that we explore in this book (Marginson, 2007; Smythe, 2017). Before diving more deeply into the ways neoliberalism is shaping leadership, it is important to get some background on what neoliberalism is and how it has manifested in higher education through academic capitalism and the Gig Academy. Throughout this chapter, we also note how neoliberalism supports whiteness and white supremacy, and identify how racism itself emerged out of capitalism. These connections will be drawn out further in the next chapter, which is dedicated to exploring the other pillar blocking progressive forms of leadership: whiteness.

Defining Neoliberalism

While the term *neoliberalism* was coined at the beginning of the last century and its philosophical elements were debated from 1930 to the 1970s, it was not until the ideas were adopted by US president Ronald Reagan and UK prime minister Margaret Thatcher in the 1980s and embedded in major political systems that they gained significant power in daily affairs (Giroux, 2014; D. Harvey, 2007). By the 1970s, economic stagnation and increasing public debt prompted some economists to advocate a return to classical liberalism, which in its revived form came to be known as neoliberalism (D. Harvey, 2007).

Neoliberalism is a reassertion of liberalism and sees individualism, the free market, and competition as the best way to orient society and defining characteristics of human relations (R. Brown, 2011). It applies a market and economic perspective to political matters and redefines citizens as consumers whose democratic choices are best exercised by buying and selling, a process that rewards merit and punishes inefficiency (R. Brown, 2011). This belief in the power of markets indicates that government should be minimized and

50   *The Contemporary Context of Leadership in Higher Education*

market solutions to social and political issues championed. Attempts to limit competition are treated as an assault on liberty. Market principles and competitive philosophy argue for minimizing taxes and regulations and privatizing public services (R. Brown, 2011; D. Harvey, 2007). Over the years, we have seen all sorts of public services, from prisons to the military to schooling, be privatized based on neoliberal perspectives. Unions and collective bargaining are undermined as forces working against market principles. As Monbiot (2016) noted, "Inequality is recast as virtuous: a reward for utility and a generator of wealth, which trickles down to enrich everyone. Efforts to create a more equal society are both counterproductive and morally corrosive. The market ensures that everyone gets what they deserve" (para. 5).

Neoliberalism has its roots in colonialism and its associated racism, which is taken up in chapter 3. Neoliberalism continues the same forms of hierarchy and elitism that led to Europeans colonizing other countries as well as the slave trade (Quijano, 2000). Kendi (2019) reminded us that racism is tied directly to capitalism and its most recent incarnation as neoliberalism. Today's disparities along racial lines were brought on by capitalism and started with the colonization of the Americas, Africa, Asia, and Oceania by Europeans who brutally reconfigured labor, race, space, and peoples for their economic advantage. These same capitalist inequalities have been revived under neoliberalism, perpetuating the same patterns of earlier colonization under a slightly different logic (Stein, 2017). Instead of colonization and slavery, neoliberalism uses modern institutions and political systems to reinforce the same racial hierarchies (as well as long-standing gender and class hierarchies that capitalism seized on). Over the last four decades, neoliberal capitalism has created the greatest wealth gaps in centuries, reversing trends toward equality started during the Progressive Era at the turn of the last century (Stein, 2017). Therefore, as we speak about the impacts of neoliberalism on leadership, it is not surprising that we report how it is negatively affecting people of color and women moving into leadership, for example.

The 2007 worldwide recession is often attributed to the thirty-year implementation of neoliberalism, which created perverse economic incentives and pitted individual and national interests against the collective public good. Immediately after the recession, there were an increasing number of critiques of neoliberalism, yet it continues to dominate many political, economic, and social policies (R. Brown, 2011; Smythe, 2017). It is particularly troubling that it remains such a dominant force when several examples of its failure have been described.

In education, the move toward neoliberalism can be dramatically illustrated with the charter school movement to privatize K–12 education, which has weakened public education across the country (Giroux, 2014). It can also be seen in various other forms of the marketization and privatization of school activities ranging from after-school programs, to technology and curricular programs offered within public and private schools, and to the emphasis on testing by private-sector companies. All of these trends have in common the intrusion of private companies into K–12 education and their profiting from public functions traditionally administered by the government. The testing regimes that have proliferated in K–12 are another aspect of neoliberalism that favors productivity and efficiency over effectiveness and management strategies as ways to understand the operations of education (Giroux, 2014). While the battles over and critiques of K–12 education have been quite visible, the changes in higher education have been much more subtle and went undocumented for decades (Kezar et al., 2019). The critiques that have been made of neoliberalism in higher education have been much more prevalent in countries such as Australia and New Zealand (Croucher & Lacy, 2020; Marginson & Considine, 2000); countries such as the United States with a strong alignment to capitalism have been less likely to document this trend (exceptions include Cantwell, 2015; Dougherty & Natow, 2020; Slaughter & Rhoades, 2004).

In higher education, neoliberalism is illustrated through the trends documented in academic capitalism as organizing principles for higher education (Kezar et al., 2019). Academic capitalism was first identified by Slaughter and Rhoades (2004) as they tried to make sense of operating logics (e.g., marketization/corporatization, individualism, and privatization) that were reshaping the behaviors and routines of administrators, faculty, and staff. For example, they saw administrators increasingly focused on generating revenues through patents, licensing, and monetizing research that had formally been a public good. Slaughter and Rhoades also described marketing and branding of campuses as a way to raise money through merchandising and sports. Likewise, they described marketing becoming prominent in admissions and necessary to justify rising tuition costs. We now describe, in detail, how these logics began to reshape campus operations.

According to market or corporate logic, universities are best operated as businesses and through corporate approaches to management (Jameson, 2019; Kezar et al., 2019). We have seen this manifested in the concentration of power among board members and senior-level administrators for decision- and policymaking. Traditional approaches to decision-making through shared governance have been dismantled on most campuses and authority generally taken away from faculty for most major decisions. We can also see these business approaches affecting staff who are asked to meet performance metrics, engage in activities designed to move the institution and academic programs up in the rankings, and more closely monitor staff (Letizia, 2016). Student affairs staff find themselves increasingly conducting the work of assessment to demonstrate their value institutionally, particularly around student retention, which improves the bottom line for the institution (Torres & Renn, 2021). And we see this influence on staff in terms of the use of predictive analytics that try to maximize our understanding of students and their success so that tuition dollars are not lost to attrition. Discussions of student engagement and success rarely focus on the way students thrive or the quality of their experience and are driven by the need to retain students for their tuition dollars. Corporate/market logics can be observed in the opening vignette, notably the provost's request for metrics around efficiency that he can use to shutter departments and fire staff.

Individualism is fostered by promulgating values of entrepreneurialism so that workers and leaders see themselves as solely responsible for revenue generation and competition with others (Kezar et al., 2019; Levin & Aliyeva, 2015; Slaughter & Rhoades, 2004). This entrepreneurialism has resulted in the rise of contingent research faculty who compete to get grants as well as tenure-track faculty who fund their own jobs through grants. We can also see entrepreneurialism foisted on administrators and staff as they are pressed to bring in more students in order to increase the revenue of the institution, particularly individuals in enrollment management but also those in traditional academic roles such as department chairs who are being asked to increase the enrollments of their programs (Slaughter & Rhoades, 2004). Returning to the vignette once more, the provost focuses on individual and departmental performance. The provost also creates competition to perform according to neoliberal metrics, fostering greater entrepreneurialism and revenue to units. We also observe how Juanita struggles to balance equity and student success goals in her work because of demands around revenue generation.

In terms of privatization, higher education has experienced privatization with the development of a substantial for-profit higher education market that grew to 15% of the overall sector until regulations put in place under the Barack Obama administration reined in growth and abuses (Kezar et al., 2019). This increased pressure on profit-driven higher education was short-lived, however, as the transition to the Donald Trump presidency saw a return of good favor with Secretary of Education Betsy DeVos repealing many Obama-era rules (Green, 2019). Despite the intensive criticism leveled against the for-profit education industry for luring in poor and racialized minority students and leaving them in debt, as well as for its low retention and graduation rates (Body, 2019), support for this sector is likely to ebb and flow in alignment with shifting federal power structures.

Another sign of neoliberalism's influence in higher education is the increasing vocationalism of higher education curriculum and narrowing of options for students, particularly in community colleges (Giroux, 2014). In addition, this sector has seen a decline in public funding for higher education that resulted from less funding for public institutions more generally (R. Brown, 2011; Giroux, 2014). Higher education has also seen greater competition among public institutions for scarce resources, pitting higher education against the K–12 system as well as other public institutions like health care (D. Harvey, 2007). We can also see privatization on campuses with the drive to brand campus athletics and identity so that it can be sold and marketized (Slaughter & Rhoades, 2004).

In the next section, we detail how changes in decision-making and authority structures are linked to broader changes in leadership. Higher education has been rapidly transformed by forces that favor managers, market-based interests, hierarchy, and elite interests, shifting the sector away from efforts to maintain its status as a public or collective good, fulfill the equity imperative, and foster worker empowerment and participation in decision-making, as well as community formation and organizing among workers (R. Brown, 2011). Values of individualism, entrepreneurialism, marketization, and the privatization of higher education shape campus operations and leadership, working against equity goals that higher education has recently fought hard to implement, goals seen in leadership models focused on teams, social change, and empowerment (Slaughter & Rhoades, 2004).

Academic Capitalism and the Gig Academy

In the previous decade, Kezar et al. (2019) identified how academic capitalism continues to morph and neoliberalism becomes further embedded within colleges and universities through Gig Academy logic. Colleges and universities have adopted a model in which almost all of their employees (faculty, staff, postdoctoral employees, and graduate students) are contingent, with virtually no job security. This labor shift further advances the goals of corporatization, where a few administrative leaders have all the decision-making power and staff and faculty live in fear for their survival because they have little job security, making resistance and collective action extremely difficult. Although contingency started with faculty through adjunct professorships, it is now the contractual arrangement for all employees. The Gig Academy is characterized by several trends underlying all contingent positions—unbundled, deprofessionalized, and atomized roles; forced micro-entrepreneurialism; managerial influence over labor supply and demand; the offloading of costs onto workers; the use of technological means of reducing labor costs; and increased structural discrimination. While several of these characteristics exist within academic capitalism—unbundling and contingency, for example—they are further deployed or transformed within the Gig Academy. We briefly describe each of these trends and then describe their impact on leadership.

Contingency is the most prominent feature of the Gig Academy, as it allows many of the other conditions to exist. The most prominent scholarship in this area focuses on faculty, particularly the dwindling number of tenured and tenure-track faculty and concomitant growth in contingent hires (Kezar et al., 2019). Contingent faculty—a minority in the workforce just a few decades ago—now represent nearly three-quarters of all instructors. The number of contingent faculty averages 50% across all institutional types; in community colleges the number is higher, averaging 80% (Kezar et al., 2019). Contingent faculty's working conditions are extremely poor—these positions lack a living wage, benefits, pension, long-term contracts, career advancement, involvement in governance, protection of academic freedom, and autonomy to define one's role and work, all features of professional roles.

Unbundling refers to the decoupling of work activities that are often synergistic for the purposes of efficiency over effectiveness (Kezar et al., 2019).

This process allows for cost reductions often at the expense of quality. Unbundling has occurred with faculty roles—for example, in the move to have teaching-only and research-only faculty and to break out teaching tasks, such as having separate individuals do advising and assessment. The same process is occurring with staff positions, as student affairs staff are becoming increasingly specialized—for example, as academic coaches—with the goal of eventually automating their various roles. A related trend is deprofessionalization. Because of the complexity of occupations such as those in medicine, law, and education, professional associations emerged to protect the integrity and quality of this work by ensuring that decisions about working conditions remained in the hands of qualified and committed experts who do the work. But autonomous, collective decision-making by faculty and staff inhibits the ability of administrators to optimize resource flows and production processes. In response, administrators have dismantled shared governance and minimized professional authority and autonomy. Deprofessionalization is tied up with unbundling because as work is made less complex, administrators can standardize a process and take over control of it (Kezar et al., 2019). The nature of the work is no longer the same, however, and is typically not as high in quality or as effective.

While entrepreneurialism was already noted under academic capitalism, this principle is accelerated in the Gig Academy. It is fostered by administrators creating a greater number of research faculty positions, individuals who are only employed if they get grants to fund their own salaries. And tenure-track faculty are incentivized to get grants, as this is the only way to meaningfully be involved in research and creative work and have any autonomy. Staff are also encouraged to generate revenues for activities, and administrators are rewarded for being in full-time development mode. In general, the goal is to foster competition between employees, units, and institutions for scarce funds. This fixation with revenue generation deters education institutions from serving the public-good mission, causing higher education to become unmoored from the egalitarian values of collectivism and citizenship and to be increasingly bound up in neoliberal approaches that prize individual advantage (Marginson, 2007).

The Gig Academy employs the tools of scientific management—contingency, forced revenue generation and entrepreneurialism, and unbundled and deprofessionalized work—in order to provide an advantage to elites' interests and disempower and atomize workers, making resistance and collective leadership extremely difficult. When workers are forced to compete against each other, with limited time for any collective interaction, faculty and staff on campus are at the whim of administrators' interests. And once every role has been unbundled into the simplest units of work, each one can be administered in the manner of a "gig"—that is, as a self-contained production process. Similar to the managers of gig economy platforms like Uber, academic managers can now simultaneously maximize institutional returns and flexibility over workers while minimizing risks and waste. One result of this is employers foisting all costs back onto the worker. The typical adjunct must provide their own office space, computer supplies, copies, telephone, internet, and so forth, not to mention health care and insurance. If they sign a contract to teach forty people three credits' worth of instruction in English and composition over four months for a fee of $3,000, that rate is fixed regardless of whether the professor commutes five miles or fifty, whether it takes twenty minutes or two hours to grade an exam, or whether they must manage a chronic health condition, provide for children, or care for elderly family. The employer's concern can be confined to the wage and nothing else.

And as in the broader gig economy, technologies are applied with the goal of cutting costs (with little evidence this is happening) and controlling worker processes, exacerbating the process of taking away autonomy. An example of where gig technologies are gaining a foothold in higher education is in the use of workforce management software. As more postsecondary work is unbundled and outsourced to many different staff providers, the use of human capital management tools such as Oracle and Workday, which have the capacity to manage large organizational ecosystems of contingent labor, has started to proliferate in higher education. Workday, for instance, is an increasingly popular software system that is advertised as uniquely designed for higher education. Targeting colleges and universities specifically, Workday's website describes uniting financial and workforce planning within one flexible, modern platform that can adapt to your changing needs.

To oversee the large disempowered, contingent workforce and deploy and manage the required technologies, administrators are outsourcing work to other companies, privatizing their workforce, and hiring droves of middle managers to oversee processes. We have seen an incredible growth of outsourcing, with 30% to 40% of campus staff being outsourced. For example, bookstore workers are being outsourced 50% of the time, food services 75% of the time, vending 63% of the time, and groundskeeping 20% of the time (Bushman & Dean, 2005). Core functions long considered off limits are now being targeted for outsourcing, including admissions, financial aid, housing, budget management, human resources management, and information technology (Bushman & Dean, 2005). In terms of hiring more midlevel managers, the College and University Professional Association for Human Resources (CUPA-HR) identified almost six hundred thousand workers in 353 distinct positions within this growing area of employment on campus, a group that largely did not exist a few decades ago (Higher Ed Workforce Trends, n.d.). Their function in the Gig Academy is to oversee and manage the growing contingent workforce and create a layer between the executive or senior administration and the "rank-and-file" instructors and staff members, which provides administrators additional control because employees do not have access to those who make decisions about their working conditions.

The Gig Academy, like the gig economy, is rife with workplace discrimination, some of which is due to quality-control issues that manifest when large, fluid populations of contingent workers are employed. Many issues are left unaddressed and the perpetrators unaccountable in the current scenario. For example, adjunct workers typically do not take the sexual harassment training that is mandated by employees. University managers may try to partly address the problem through outsourcing. By subcontracting with a labor provider that has its own review and quality-control procedures, the institution can be absolved of liability for most accusations of discrimination, exploitation, or harassment, so long as workers answer to the external firm. Each of these problematic features—contingency, forced revenue generation and entrepreneurialism, unbundled and deprofessionalized work, foisting costs for production onto workers, workplace discrimination—can be seen in trends within neoliberal leadership in postsecondary institutions today.

It is important to understand how neoliberalism and the Gig Academy become manifest and how leadership is implicated in this process. Today,

58   The Contemporary Context of Leadership in Higher Education

leadership is becoming synonymous with a new concept called new managerialism, which is embedded with the logics of neoliberalism and the Gig Academy (J. Clarke & Newman, 2004). New managerialism is how the principles of neoliberalism and the Gig Academy become ingrained within managers and eventually organizational structures and cultures (R. Brown, 2011). New managerialism's legitimization and implementation of new organizational forms originated from a view that professional modes of organization were inefficient and could not cope with the challenges arising from increasing globalization (Pollitt, 1990). To restructure organizations so they could achieve neoliberal goals, businesslike practices based on a neo-Taylorist (corporate) view of work were appropriated. In such a view, organizations are thought to operate most efficiently by standardizing, automating, and breaking down tasks and allocating responsibilities to find the most efficient way of performing each task (Handy, 1999). Work tasks are monitored and controlled to improve productivity (through performance indicators), motivating individuals through financial reward (Letizia, 2016; S. M. Mullins et al., 2002). Efficiency is thought to be driven by having to meet customer needs within a competitive marketplace. Public services are reconfigured with business approaches so students are consumers, marketing strategies are used to attract students, and competitive approaches are used to increase enrollments.

New managerialism's reach is extended in the Gig Academy, bringing in new tools such as outsourcing, contingent labor, entrepreneurialism, and automation. While higher education has always operated as a corporate form and utilized some business approaches, what is different is that new managerialism now dominates all processes and professional norms have been largely eradicated (Jameson, 2019; Letizia, 2016). This new environment has been described as the toxic university, where administrators are identified as zombie leaders utilizing these managerial practices in ways that amount to bullying and harassment (Smythe, 2017). While not all critiques are this heavy-handed, many concerns have been raised about neoliberalism in the academy generally; however, we are suggesting that not enough direction attention has been paid to the role it has played in reconfiguring leadership. As we argue in this book, neoliberalism has rendered leadership both a problem to be described and a potential solution to ameliorate neoliberalism's worst iterations.

Neoliberalism's Reshaping of Leadership

Neoliberalism has taken traditional, functionalist views of leadership and amplified them in such a way as to allow a corporate takeover of higher education and the ascendance of perspectives about administration and leadership that advance the principles of new managerialism. This neoliberal shift shapes every aspect of leadership, such as who is seen as a leader, including the criteria for hiring; the goals and roles of leaders; and the possibilities for leadership among faculty, staff, and students, which have been reduced due to the imbalance of power, lack of autonomy, and limited time for thoughtful reflection and wise action. Smythe (2017) characterized the many changes to leadership vis-à-vis neoliberalism as creating zombie leadership approaches that have thoroughly transformed leadership into a set of managerial routines—measuring, calibrating, ranking, rating, comparing, and auditing. F. Wood (2014) explained, "Universities have been duped into making a pact—the adoption of business and commercial ideas and practices, in return for the promise of continued survival in a context of precariousness around 'uncertain . . . student numbers, status, [and] funding'" (p. 152). Next we outline how leadership has been fundamentally altered in terms of who leaders are, what their roles and responsibilities are, how they lead, and the outcomes of leadership.

WHO IS SEEN AS A LEADER AND THE CRITERIA FOR HIRING/ APPOINTING LEADERS

As a result of neoliberal corporate, individualistic, and market logics (embedded in both academic capitalism and the Gig Academy), leadership power has been increasingly concentrated among administrators and academic managers who are largely male and white (Kezar et al., 2019). Very little progress has been made in recent decades to diversify leadership positions, particularly among leaders of color. In terms of college presidents, for example, in the 1970s, 9% of women held presidencies, compared with 32.8% in the latest survey in 2023 (American Council on Education, 2023). Women of color are highly underrepresented within leadership roles in higher education (H. L. Johnson, 2017). They have been less than 5% of college presidents from the 1980s through the 2000s and only just recently met the 5% threshold. Women of color are less likely to emerge into and hold other senior academic

60   *The Contemporary Context of Leadership in Higher Education*

positions and hold only 7% of all senior administrative positions. For example, they represent only 3% of chief academic officers, compared with 6% for men of color and 33% for white women (J. E. King & Gomez, 2008).

Gig Academy logic is premised on a leadership philosophy where a managerial class maintains decision-making power to continue to maximize profits and institutional benefits (new managerialism). Accordingly, hiring for administrative and leadership roles has been based on criteria related to fundraising and managerial experience, with hires often coming from other fields such as law or military (R. Brown, 2011). Furthermore, leader selection is conducted through searches for candidates with managerial qualities rather than academic merits. Administrators are thus increasingly separate—both in terms of function and in terms of experience and knowledge base—from the actual processes involved in teaching and learning and from campus life.

Leadership Concentrating Power

In a dramatic departure from the leadership evolution described in *Rethinking the "L" Word in Higher Education* (Kezar et al., 2006), leadership is no longer seen as a broad and collective process but is instead viewed primarily as a function executed by those in positions of authority. Various studies have identified how the role of leaders is being repositioned again as synonymous with that of administrators (Marginson, 1997; Rubins, 2007). So a central tenet of neoliberal leadership is that power must be centralized so that leadership is both conceptually (shifting the understanding of who is considered a leader) and practically (removing the decision-making power of faculty, staff, and students) vested in positional authority (Marginson, 1997). Activities described earlier such as greater activism among governing boards and more top-down decision-making among presidents and their leadership teams represent this shift toward the centralization of power, which is critical to defining leadership in a narrow and exclusive fashion (Marginson, 1997). This new view of leadership, captured within the literature on new managerialism, makes the direct connection between neoliberalism and universities serving the goals of this philosophy, including the rise of potent administrative power structures in higher education globally and declines in faculty and staff power (Bleiklie, 2005; Rubins, 2007). Administrative leaders need to centralize power and diminish governance to ensure a standardized and controllable handling of the growing number of faculty conducting the activities of teaching and research. Contingency has led to a greater number of sheer faculty since most faculty are no longer full-time (Bleiklie, 2005). A timely and striking example of the material consequences embedded in neoliberal efforts to centralize power can be seen in institutional responses to the COVID-19 global pandemic. Eager to minimize financial losses associated with declining enrollments, housing and dining refunds necessitated by campus closures, and increased expenditures for personal protective equipment, senior campus administrators on many campuses made centralized decisions regarding campus operations and instructional modes, often with minimal or no input from shared governance (Burke, 2020; Flaherty, 2020). And a recent study by the American Association of University Professors (2021) based on investigations of campuses across the country documented empirically how severe the loss of shared governance was: "Some institutional leaders seem to have taken the COVID-19 crisis as an opportunity to turbocharge the corporate model that has been spreading in higher education over the past few decades, allowing them to close programs and lay off faculty members as expeditiously as if colleges and universities were businesses whose CEOs suddenly decided to stop making widgets or shut down the steelworks" (pp. 2–3). Put more succinctly: *"The COVID-19 pandemic has presented the most serious challenges to academic governance in the last fifty years"* (American Association of University Professors, 2021, p. 34, original emphasis). Marjorie Hass (2020), president of Rhodes College, argued that shared governance and broad constituent engagement in decision-making actually improved her college's COVID-19 response, challenging neoliberal assumptions that centralized power increases efficiency and outcomes.

Reorienting the Overall Aim of Leadership

Bleiklie (2005) summarized the reorientation of leadership into the notion of the business executive role, which reflects the perspective of new managerialism. This new view directly ties neoliberalism and new managerialism together in a process in which the university is refashioned in market terms as a producer of educational and research services for the broader neoliberal government and economic goals. The university is seen as a business enterprise in service to neoliberal goals, and leaders thus emphasize the importance of

62   *The Contemporary Context of Leadership in Higher Education*

education for national economic growth (Bleiklie, 1998; Kauppinen, 2015). Therefore, a major aim is to increase the capacity to produce larger numbers of students more efficiently and cheaply. The role of administrators is to create incentive policies and performance indicators to drive these goals. The broader public purposes of higher education, described in more detail later, are abandoned for a much narrower view of the role of higher education, which then shapes the more corporate and marketized role and goal of leaders. One contemporary instructional reform movement that aligns with the neoliberal aims of increasing the efficiency and market responsiveness of higher education is the growing popularity of microcredentialing, digital badges, and the like, which break down education into bite-size commodities that can be bought and stacked by consumers in the hope of increasing their vocational and economic mobility (Ralston, 2020). In addition to generating revenue, microcredentialing efforts also provide colleges and universities with opportunities to create and strengthen for-profit enterprises. As Ralston noted, "Support for microcredentialing is particularly strong among higher education executives, administrators, and financial/tech-oriented staff who appreciate its value as an innovative profit center" (p. 84).

Goals and Role of the Leader

Leadership has undergone a significant redesign under an enterprise now characterized by marketization and corporatization—captured within new managerialism. The administrator's role has dramatically changed in recent decades to focus on market goals like revenue generation, efficiency, production, productivity, monitoring, and entrepreneurialism. Research has identified revenue generation as the key goal for leadership, pushing other historical priorities to the side and reshaping who is seen as a leader as someone who is good at revenue generation (Marginson & Considine, 2000; Rubins, 2007; Slaughter & Rhoades, 2004). For example, Slaughter and Rhoades (2004) documented how the revenue-generating goals of academic capitalism are replacing the traditional public-good orientation of higher education. In order to achieve revenue-generation goals, leaders are tasked with fundraising and development activities as the most prominent goal of campus administrators. The public-good orientation is characterized by valuing knowledge as a public good to which the general citizenry has claims. Public goods are no longer supported as one of the ideals of the administrative leader, which formerly included increasing access among underrepresented students, aiding the moral development of students, creating civic engagement, preserving integrity in science, providing technical assistance abroad, serving the economic and social needs of local communities, taking political positions on important issues, being careful in accepting gifts, avoiding undesirable relationships with commercial interests that are unethical, and becoming involved in boycotts (Bok, 2003). Cantwell (2016) also found that endowment management has taken on a much more prominent place within leadership activities than in previous years, reinforcing that the main activity of administrators is financial management and growth.

Additionally, leaders work to foster an entrepreneurial ethic among faculty and staff so that they are also bringing in money and seeing revenue generation as a primary goal of the work and activities of all individuals on campus. The press for revenue generation can be seen in leadership literature that emphasizes the need for administrators to be entrepreneurial (Fisher & Koch, 2004). McClure (2016) illustrated how administrative leadership is championed and idealized if it is focused on entrepreneurial activities that raise both the profile and the revenues of the campus. McClure's study of administrators identified five main roles that executive and managerial administrators tend to focus on and that reflect the principles of academic capitalism and the Gig Academy: building infrastructure, creating new programs, cultivating donors and raising funds, setting a vision around entrepreneurship, and changing policies. The findings show that an institutional orientation to knowledge privatization and profit taking is largely an administrator-driven project (McClure, 2016).

The earlier description of the Gig Academy illustrates another pivot in the role of leaders (now identified as only individuals in positions of authority) to efficiency and productivity strategies such as outsourcing and fashioning contingent and deprofessionalized labor. So, in addition to all of the revenue-generating roles and goals, higher education leaders are also focused on cost cutting and increasingly using corporate gig strategies for executing this role (Kezar et al., 2019). The main goal of leaders is setting expectations of increased efficiency by formulating production goals and incentive systems to drive worker behavior (Bleiklie, 2005). This focuses administrators' activities on also creating productivity goals and the monitoring and assessment regimes that have been put in place over the last few decades (Torres &

Renn, 2021). The efficiency strategies around outsourcing are justified by the overarching goals of increased efficiency and productivity, which cannot be met by current revenue streams and require constant cost-cutting measures. Administrators find themselves in an endless cycle of growth for growth's purposes and cost cutting to achieve the growth goals of revenue generation (Gaffikin & Perry, 2009).

Another strategy for increased efficiency is competition. Competition is reinforced through managerial practices such as performance-based funding for both campuses and individuals that pit them against others rather than encouraging them to work toward a collective good (P. Blackmore & Kandiko, 2011; Torres & Renn, 2021). Ranking and benchmarking systems have also become prominent as a vehicle to push institutions to perform more efficiently and productively. Studies have documented the rise in ranking systems worldwide as a symptom of neoliberal competitiveness, which seeks to drive more market behaviors among institutions and their leaders globally (Marginson & Considine, 2000). In general, various metric systems, benchmarking, and rankings are used as tools to drive systems toward market-desirable outcomes.

We could see this orientation to altering roles in the opening vignette. The provost saw his primary role as creating efficiencies, reducing costs, developing performance metrics, cutting staff, and generating new revenues through entrepreneurial mechanisms.

Removing Ethics from Leadership

Smythe (2017) argued that neoliberalism ultimately removes any moral imperative from leadership. Leadership loses its conscience and is fully consumed with profit seeking. He likened this thinking to a disease or pathology that has taken over the consciousness of leaders within colleges and universities. It is this diseased type of thinking among leaders that has moved higher education away from its public purposes and created the exclusive focus on areas such as marketing and public relations that are helpful for the profit-seeking motives but take away all attention to traditional public responsibilities. And the push for profit seeking creates anxiety and fear for college and university stakeholders in a never-ending search for additional funding that eventually becomes a zero-sum game, as there are only so many funding sources and funds to go around. There is a Darwinian fight for survival and the creation of an environment in which, if you do not play by the rules of the game, you as a leader or the institution will cease to be. So the fear is existential. The leader's role is to instill that competition and a set of audit, accountability, and benchmarking systems that perpetuate fear and promote competition (Gaffikin & Perry, 2009). Smythe's view is that leadership has become completely dysfunctional and counterproductive to the goals of higher education.

In prior decades, faculty and administrators made decisions jointly through a system of shared governance. Faculty members' professional expertise was considered important to making decisions about curriculum and the teaching and learning environment. Shared governance helped to facilitate positive relationships and communication between administrators and faculty as they made decisions together about important areas related to academic programs. Yet in the Gig Academy, shared governance has declined. For example, Schuster and Finkelstein (2006) and more recently Finkelstein et al. (2016), in national studies of faculty, found a significant decline in tenure-track faculty participation in governance and consistently reported that faculty perceived themselves as having less influence over important campus matters. When faculty have significantly less influence on issues like campus priorities and budgets, while being saddled with more local service responsibilities that underutilize their expertise, such as course scheduling, decisions of consequence come to rest with the exclusive and largely unchallenged authority of a few senior administrators. Leadership, under managerialism, renders governance obsolete except as performance.

The contingent nature of faculty and staff appointments makes involvement in leadership extremely difficult (Gonzales et al., 2014; Kezar et al., 2019). Additionally, these workers are no longer empowered, as noted in the last few sections, with the decision-making authority that they once had or allowed input into important decisions that are part of the work of leaders. Campuses are increasingly trying to identify superficial ways to obtain input quickly from overworked groups that do not have time to participate in real decision-making processes anymore (Kezar et al., 2019). Tenure-track faculty, particularly in striving institutions, report that faculty members feel under constant surveillance and experience pressures induced by academic capitalism to pursue revenue, limiting time for service and leadership (Gonzalez et al., 2014). Staff are increasingly outsourced and not part of the

66   *The Contemporary Context of Leadership in Higher Education*

campus community, so they are also not a part of decision-making or leadership. And students now designated as consumers are not looked to for leadership, nor are their skills cultivated (Furedi, 2011).

Smythe (2017) emphasized that leadership is also extremely difficult among groups outside of administrators because of the fear and anxiety that administrators have created by making workers contingent and outsourced. It is hard to play a leadership role when you are unsure day to day whether you have a job and will make enough money to survive. All of the employment practices that are currently utilized under the new managerialism regime create the fear that makes leadership an exceptional and challenging activity. Juanita from our opening vignette really struggled with the ethical implications of the leadership environment she was in. She felt she was unable to pursue her goals of equity and student success given the market/corporate priorities of the provost. Neoliberalism brings about tensions that are difficult for leaders like Juanita to make sense of and navigate.

Dehumanization of Leadership

Clearly undergirding the new managerialism is a dehumanization of leadership as well as the environment (Smythe, 2017). Neoliberalism defines human relationships in transactional terms, as the means to an end, the end being high performance and productivity (R. Brown, 2011). Leaders are encouraged to depersonalize their interactions to focus solely on the institutional goals and broader political interests, which are prioritized by boards of trustees. This activity has become much easier because administrators have hired over half a million midlevel managers across higher education who buffer them from interacting with faculty and staff who would communicate the challenges of current leadership aims and goals and the impact of the changes on them as people (Kezar et al., 2019). Additionally, since administrators have adopted centralized power and shifted away from shared governance modalities for making decisions, they also have much less interaction with faculty and staff in decision-making processes (Marginson & Considine, 2000). The centralization of authority and power amplifies the dehumanizing element of leadership, as the interests of campus stakeholders are taken out of the pool of ideas and needs. This kind of dehumanization is present in the opening vignette where the provost exhibited little to no concern about openly gathering data with the intent to fire staff who were seen as less efficient without any information to contextualize these data.

The Neoliberal Context and Its Impact on Leadership

Not only do we see neoliberalism asserting a new set of parameters for leadership under the guise of managerialism, but neoliberalism also affects the possibilities for leadership on campuses, including who is becoming a leader and the outcomes of leadership. A general impact of neoliberalism on leadership is the move to frame managerialism as a form of governance and to downplay references to leadership, which has been associated in recent years with social change (Kezar & Lester, 2011). By portraying managerialism as a new way that groups interact through systems of accountability and control, and making less reference to leadership itself, neoliberal ideologies have caused leadership to be paralyzed by silence about its very existence. The ways that neoliberalism is affecting leadership have only been studied in a limited fashion, but the studies that exist suggest negative impacts for groups who have traditionally been marginalized or disempowered in society (J. Blackmore et al., 2015; Smythe, 2017). This certainly illustrates a problematic trend and the need to combat neoliberalism.

Extricating Faculty, Staff, and Students from Leadership

Every group on campus has been refashioned in a manner that directly influences the possibilities for the progressive types of leadership we describe within this book. Luke (2001), in his study, identified how the rise of contingent faculty at a time when women and people of color are finally being hired into these positions affects the ability of these groups to move into leadership roles. Very few contingent faculty move into leadership roles on campus, and contingent faculty have difficulty leading in the first place because their time is so constrained and their authority limited. Collective forms of leadership are hard to come by among outsourced and contingent workers. Students have been encouraged to see themselves as consumers, so their energies are directed toward evaluating cost, considering job possibilities, and making educational choices that best position them for work. And of course, the global recession and challenging economic times put pressure on students

68   *The Contemporary Context of Leadership in Higher Education*

to focus on economic concerns over social concerns that have long been a part of student leadership and advocacy.

Neoliberalism aims to take away individual agency and create workers who live in fear and anxiety for their jobs. So not only does neoliberalism shape the possibilities for leadership, but it also works to render people passive so that the possibility of resistance is reduced, and collective action is much more challenging. The casualization of labor through outsourcing and part-time employment is one of the best strategies for making collective leadership and action extremely difficult.

One of the significant ways neoliberal approaches to leadership have reduced the possibility for collective action, resistance, and leadership is through the thwarting of unions. Over the past thirty years, academic unions have been discouraged and administrators have engaged in lawsuits to block the rights of adjunct faculty and staff to unionize. For example, the legal doctrines from the *NLRB v. Yeshiva University* (1980) and *NLRB v. Catholic Bishop of Chicago* (1979) cases have long stymied growth in private-sector unionization. *Yeshiva* had a chilling effect on private-sector unionization; for years, only the most militant faculty or staff at private four-year institutions attempted to form unions, with rates of unionization at 3% and 8% for full-time and part-time faculty, respectively (Kezar et al., 2019). Then, in 2015, a new ruling (against Pacific Lutheran) revised many of those restrictions, clearing the way for a new wave of faculty organizing that was swiftly overturned by later rulings under Trump's National Labor Relations Board (Kezar et al., 2019). Campus administrators continue to relentlessly block and discourage unionization, which is seen as incompatible with the new managerialism goals of efficiency, cost cutting, and hyperproductivity.

Reestablishing Whiteness and Male Dominance in Leadership

In addition to employing tactics that make it extremely difficult for faculty, staff, and students to play leadership roles, neoliberalism also seeks to centralize power under governing boards that are mostly made up of white, male leaders from industry, business, and the military (Marginson & Considine, 2000). Since governing boards set the priorities for campus and generally hire the president, neoliberal views are instantiated in the most powerful entities on campus, ensuring the entrenchment of neoliberal ideologies

(Rubins, 2007). As noted earlier, shared governance in which faculty and sometimes staff had input into decision-making has been in decline on most campuses or made advisory so that neoliberal values and beliefs prevail under the centralized power.

Scholars have also documented how neoliberalism has further disadvantaged women and people of color (Lafferty & Fleming, 2000). While there remain tremendous barriers to these populations being selected into leadership roles, the way these roles are now constructed are not desirable to women and people of color impacting their interest in assuming them. Studies identify that women are refusing, resisting or dismissing senior leadership and making strategic decisions not to apply for positions which they evaluate as unattractive, onerous and undesirable (J. Blackmore, 2014). Specifically, the corporatization of the academy has produced academic disenchantment due to managerial dominance, commercialization and privatization and disengagement with the dominant values, practices and images of university leadership. J. Blackmore (2014) asks a key question at this juncture—What is it about contemporary university leadership that 'turns off' many academics, and who will take up these positions if that continues?

Studies by Kreissl et al. (2015) in Austria, O'Connor (2014) in Ireland, and J. Blackmore et al. (2015) in Australia showed that the competitive and entrepreneurial orientation to leadership results in universities aggressively positioning themselves to be more favorable in global rankings and to be seen in the academic and student markets as "world class." The result of these aspirations for campuses is the hiring of white men who are more likely to assert these values and goals. Luke (2001) uncovered the need for greater attention to be paid to how institutional micropractices differ in culturally specific sites in ways that marginalize women. Neoliberalism works against such a focus on culturally specific practices since market values are universal and move attention away from local needs that are attentive to contextual and culturally appropriate leadership responses. Ignoring culturally specific needs and practices results in the continued lack of hiring of leaders of color across postsecondary institutions worldwide.

Diminishing Academic Values in Leadership

The impact of neoliberalism has also been seen in the break with the long-time tradition of hiring higher education leaders from among the professoriate and among candidates who possess an academic identity and values (Smythe, 2017). The role and identity of leaders are significantly altered within the new neoliberal view of leadership, in which leaders from outside academic institutions are seen as not only legitimate but better choices to lead institutions. Academic values such as autonomy, professional expertise, intellectualism, critique, community, colleagueship, inspiration, mentoring, and moral argumentation are no longer considered normative. The values that undergird the leadership practices in new managerialism have thoroughly replaced these traditional values as well as the identity of who is a leader on campus. Smythe (2017) captured this issue in the following way: "The decoupling of the skills of academic leadership from the substantive understanding of and commitment to the serious work of scholarship and research, is to all intent and purposes, complete in the modern university context" (p. 78). Not only are leaders not grounded in the important values that traditionally were part of the university and college cultures, but the new structures and environments on campuses characterized by layers of managers who remain insulated in market logics result in a lack of any understanding of the day-to-day work of faculty and staff that might illuminate their thinking with some of these academic values.

INCREASE IN DISCRIMINATION, BULLYING, AND LOW MORALE

Many have hypothesized that the move to a more dehumanized and corporate form of leadership might result in more discriminatory practices and negative relationships and interactions between people on campus. Studies are indeed finding these types of relationships. Erdemir et al. (2020) identified a statistically significant relationship between leadership approach and mobbing (e.g., bullying) in the academic context. According to the findings, when academics observe positive (humanistic and prosocial) leadership behaviors in their departments rather than corporate and bureaucratic approaches, they are less likely to be exposed to mobbing behaviors. Kezar et al. (2019) demonstrated how neoliberalism has eroded a sense of community and fostered experiences of anxiety and fear about job insecurity, subjecting staff to abuse by their supervisors. This feeling was recently captured in a survey by Gallup of employee engagement across many industries, which revealed that universities and colleges are among the least engaged workplaces in the world. The survey found that 52% of higher education faculty are not engaged in their work, and 14% are actively disengaged. Only 34% of faculty and staff were found to be engaged in their work (Kezar et al., 2019).

Careless Institutions

The intensified focus on technical management processes and procedures in leadership has significantly downplayed the more human and affective elements of leadership. While there has long been an indifference to and undervaluing of the affective domain in leadership, some theories, such as transformational and team leadership, had oriented leadership to the importance of emotions within the leadership process. Current studies identify how higher education leaders anchored in neoliberalism and subject to performance measurement and rankings focus even less on human interactions and colleagueship. Grummell et al. (2009) documented that, as a result, senior managerial posts are careless positions, with emotional work being nonexistent. Additionally, women, who take up more responsibility for caring for children and elders, are at a disadvantage as leaders, according to worldwide surveys (McKinsey & LeanIn, 2020). The researchers have also documented the advantages to those who are carefree, who are disproportionately men in societies where the moral imperative to do primary care work applies mainly to women. The data suggest that understanding how the care ceiling (similar to the concept of the glass ceiling, but with emphasis on the care role and not just gender) operates is also crucial for understanding why women do not occupy senior leadership roles.

Destroying Collegiality and Community

Other studies have focused on how neoliberal leadership practices are destroying collegiality and community. The managerial tactics of employing contingent labor, unbundling roles, and atomizing work are the main culprits for destroying working relationships on campus. Administrators are better able to oversee activities if they are atomized, rather than leaving the entire process to be overseen by experienced faculty or staff. Breaking down the activities into component parts also means deprofessionalizing the workers who play a role in each part. As a result, staff across units, faculty in different departments, and faculty and staff find it more challenging to collaborate and interact. Additionally, the growth of middle management means

72   *The Contemporary Context of Leadership in Higher Education*

that many staff members have very little interaction with their senior supervisors. And most of the interactions are around auditing or surveilling their work. Rosser (2009) documented how the quality of interpersonal relationships between educational support staff and their supervisors has become increasingly negative over the past few decades. In surveys, staff list interpersonal experiences in general and with supervisors as a central matter of concern and describe feeling that they are treated like second-class citizens, that supervisors and administration do not respect them, and that communication is poor. While there are few studies on the issue to date, the emerging picture is that new managerialism is creating a negative work environment. And as community and collegiality break down, this prevents interactions that might have led to resistance and collective action. Therefore, neoliberal leadership helps to constrain the rise of any other forms of collective and progressive leadership.

Destroying Innovation

Smythe (2017) argued that neoliberalism has negatively shaped innovation, as zombie leadership creates fear and anxiety that make faculty and staff feel vulnerable and less likely to be innovative and creative. Also, the hierarchy that is entrenched even further with neoliberalism discourages thinking outside the norms of the hierarchy. Routines around control also work against creativity and innovation. Other studies identify how neoliberalism focuses on control and conformity to standardize goals and processes, which has stifled innovation and experimentation (A. Davis et al., 2016). While market logic extols creativity and innovation as important to economic returns, the leadership that is in place actually is detrimental to the very innovation and creativity that it holds up as an ideal. But as has been emphasized throughout this chapter, the very goal is social control and maintenance of the status quo, so innovation is only valued if it supports elite and white interests.

Neoliberalism in Contestation with the Public Good

Slaughter and Rhoades (2004) documented how academic capitalism is in contestation with public-good views of higher education. More recent studies have revealed that the two visions continue to exist simultaneously but that neoliberal values are reshaping public-good (and progressive leadership) views and goals (Marginson, 2007). So while the two ideologies continue to exist simultaneously, neoliberalism's colonization of traditional public-good goals and views of leadership threatens their very existence. As Lynch and Grummell (2018) argued, the difficulty with neoliberalism and managerialism is that they do not just prioritize efficiency; they suppress other organizational values so that they become incidental to the running of the organization (Ball, 2012). The net effect of the devaluation of public-good purposes, in and of themselves, is that public institutions, such as higher education, are increasingly defined as commodities to be delivered to customers in the marketplace, and increasingly only those who can afford to buy them (Jessop, 2017; Lynch & Grummell, 2018).

This suggests that leaders and leadership are being colonized by neoliberal values that will make it difficult for the two ideals—that of the public good and that of neoliberalism—to exist, and the neoliberal values will likely smother public-good values and the visions of higher education and approaches to leadership that were embedded in those values. Without active resistance and attention, colonization is common because neoliberalism is becoming so deeply entrenched in structures and culture. One study helps highlight this challenge. Schulze-Cleven and Olson (2017) studied higher education leaders' views of thirty-two key issues for the future of Australian higher education in the next ten to twenty years. The traditional academic goals of knowledge generation, dissemination, and application were seen as high priorities. Rated among the top ten issues were student learning outcomes and student access to higher education, as well as efforts to address the needs of society through research on grand challenges facing humanity, such as climate change and food security. At the same time, higher education leaders viewed most of the issues related to both marketization and academic capitalism as important, including issues of internationalization, the balance between tenured and contract academics, and the role of university-industry joint research. But research also indicates that leaders are seeing public-good goals through the lens of neoliberalism—student access and success, for example, in relation to serving economic goals.

A second study of administrators found neoliberalism has produced tensions with democratic commitments (Croucher & Lacy, 2020). Government policies creating incentives for organizational (and individual) entrepreneurship have weakened checks on neoliberal and capitalist leanings by undermining the power and collective identities of both academic professionals and student populations. Most notably, the rise of contingent faculty and the commercialization of students as consumers have weakened critiques of market values. Increased competition has reduced faculty self-governance, as faculty are chasing revenues or bogged down with service. Thus, all the traditional counterforces to neoliberal goals have been squelched (Gildersleeve, 2016; Joseph, 2015).

One of the more progressive theories of leadership promotes distributed and shared forms of leadership. Yet studies of shared leadership within a neoliberal regime have shown that sharing is often performative rather than real (S. Jones, 2014). S. Jones's (2014) critical analysis of the experience of a distributed leadership approach used to build leadership capacity in learning and teaching in an Australian university identified this growing tension. The study showed that even when more individuals were included in the leadership process, the competition and forced entrepreneurialism of neoliberalism hindered the development of the forms of collaboration needed for shared leadership. Surprisingly, distributed leadership, while it may increase the participation of academics in decision-making, may not lead to more democratic decision-making because voices are not authentically considered. Studies are reinforcing that even efforts that may look progressive in terms of leadership are being colonized by academic capitalism. It is challenging to reach public-good goals when institutions' operating structures and cultures are aligned with neoliberal processes. Until we decolonize the campuses and eradicate the new managerialism—rankings, auditing, benchmarking, efficiency regimes, revenue generation, student consumerism, faculty and staff contingency, and outsourcing, among many other practices—progressive forms of leadership will likely be co-opted and diluted.

Conclusion

Understanding leadership in today's colleges and universities requires comprehending and interrogating the neoliberal context and the way this ideology has shifted the conceptualization of leadership, which has moved from a collective and public-good vision to a narrow corporate and marketized one. In addition, it is important to see how neoliberalism has limited and continues to limit a broader and more diverse set of leadership voices and the ascent of women and people of color to leadership roles. This chapter also outlines how neoliberalism, as a universal set of operating procedures and philosophy, denies the plurality of leadership voices and possibilities. Neoliberalism actively disempowers other perspectives by placing power among elites who are largely white and male. It is also important to understand how neoliberalism works against democratic, collective, equitable, and progressive views of leadership through its infiltration into the very fabric of higher education organizations and operating principles. Studies have documented the ways that traditional authoritative views of leadership have become reinvigorated through larger political and economic systems that reinforce capitalist and corporate views of organizations and leadership but that also are in contestation with more progressive views. It is this context of competing ideologies that we ask scholars and leaders reading this book to consider as they study or lead institutions of higher education. Without an understanding of the complexities of the current context, efforts to combat this long-hidden and invisible force will not succeed. As was the case in our opening vignette, leaders become confused, demoralized, and ineffective when they are unaware of or disregard the impact of neoliberalism on campus operations. We hope our articulation of neoliberalism is empowering and helps leaders better understand the challenges they face.

Key Points

- Neoliberalism and the Gig Academy have become dominant ideologies that have oriented higher education to corporate and market values and moved it away from historical public-good values.
- Neoliberalism has become embedded in leadership through the concept of new managerialism, in which leadership is moved away from its transformative potential and instead focuses on the status quo and elites' interests.
- New managerialism has removed progressive goals and aspirations from higher education leadership.
- Neoliberalism and public-good ideologies remain in contestation, but public-good views are being colonized by neoliberalism and seemingly progressive leadership practices are increasingly performative.
- Without acknowledging and resisting neoliberalism, the Gig Academy, and new managerialism, leaders in higher education are likely to replicate neoliberalism in its many manifestations.

Discussion Questions

1. How do you see neoliberalism and the Gig Academy present on your own campus?
2. How do you see the concepts of new managerialism operating through leadership on your campus?
3. Have you seen tensions between progressive forms of leadership and new managerialism on your campus? What has been the result? Have you seen instances in which progressive forms of leadership were colonized by neoliberalism?
4. Which impacts of neoliberalism on leadership have you seen in your career?
5. How might you address some of these trends? Can you think of ways to work with others to make these practices more visible so they do not have the power they currently derive from being invisible or taken for granted?
6. Among your colleagues, do you see a trend of shying away from leadership because it no longer represents the values and goals they share?

Chapter 4

Whiteness and White Supremacy in Higher Education Leadership

Nikole Hannah-Jones, a Black woman and a University of North Carolina at Chapel Hill (UNC–Chapel Hill) alumna most known for developing the 1619 Project, a long-form journalism project that sought to tell the unvarnished truth about slavery and the overall history of the United States, was being considered for the coveted Knight Chair in Race and Investigative Reporting position at UNC–Chapel Hill. She was actively recruited by the dean of the UNC Hussman School of Journalism and Media, Susan King. When Hannah-Jones agreed to join the faculty, she began the rigorous tenure process, which included writing separate teaching, creative, and service statements and teaching a class while being observed by faculty, as well as the dean's solicitation of letters from others in the field whom Hannah-Jones did not know personally, all normal steps in the tenure process. Her tenure dossier was reviewed by all the full professors in the School of Journalism and Media, who overwhelmingly supported granting her tenure. The dossier was then submitted to the university tenure and promotion committee, which also supported her tenure overwhelmingly. Hannah-Jones herself explained what happened next:

> My tenure package was then to be presented for a vote by the Board of Trustees in November so that I could start teaching at the university in January 2021. The day of the Trustees meeting, we waited for word, but heard

78   *The Contemporary Context of Leadership in Higher Education*

nothing. The next day, we learned that my tenure application had been pulled but received no explanation as to why. The same thing happened again in January. Both the university's Chancellor and its Provost refused to fully explain why my tenure package had failed twice to come to a vote or exactly what transpired. (NAACP Legal Defense and Educational Fund Media, 2021, para. 8)

Hannah-Jones signed a five-year contract and was set to be the first Knight Chair to not have tenure. Days after she signed the contract, news began to circulate regarding the board of trustees' refusal to consider her for tenure. A reporter from NC Policy Watch, Joe Killian, broke the story that the board refused to consider Hannah-Jones for tenure because of pressure from conservatives. The board of trustees was also allegedly worried about a nontraditional academic like Hannah-Jones being granted tenure. The chair position, however, was designed to bring professional journalists into academia, and no past chairs were ever denied tenure. The past chairs also all happened to be white. The board spent an overwhelming amount of time and energy debating the validity of Hannah-Jones's work and her ability to meaningfully contribute to the school and the university more broadly.

As time went on, more details began to emerge. Walter Hussman, the megadonor whom the School of Journalism and Media is named after, actively lobbied against Hannah-Jones and exerted pressure over her hiring. He pledged $25 million to the school in 2019. Killian (2021) noted, "Most of that money hasn't yet been delivered, leading some to speculate Hussman felt he had leverage with which to pressure the school to abandon its plan to hire Hannah-Jones" (para. 3). Hussman dismissed any speculation that he pressured the school or members of university leadership, but he did share that he expressed his concerns regarding Hannah-Jones's hiring to many university stakeholders, including at least one board of trustees member. Hussman's emails were eventually leaked and exclusively obtained by *The Assembly* (J. Drescher, 2020). In an email to Dean Susan King (with the chancellor and the vice chancellor for university development copied), he wrote,

I worry about the controversy of tying the UNC journalism school to the 1619 project. . . . I find myself more in agreement with Pulitzer prize winning historians like James McPherson and Gordon Wood than I do Nikole Hannah-Jones.

Whiteness and White Supremacy in Higher Education Leadership 79

He continued,

> These historians appear to me to be pushing to find the true historical facts. Based on her own words, many will conclude she is trying to push an agenda, and they will assume she is manipulating historical facts to support it. If asked about it, I will have to be honest in saying I agree with the historians. (J. Drescher, 2020, paras. 9, 10)

Hussman's hands were far from clean and his opinions were a long way from objective in this debacle. As a donor, he felt he had the power and authority to name his concerns, most of which had a racist undertone.

As more information became public and available to Hannah-Jones and organizations like the NAACP, she threatened to file a lawsuit against the university for discrimination. Students began to protest, faculty started coming out with letters of support, and some even threatened to leave the university. Feeling the weight of their inaction and discrimination against an acclaimed Black woman journalist, the board of trustees finally decided to consider her tenure package. Hannah-Jones was granted tenure with a nine-to-four vote. Mere days after her approval for tenure, she released a statement asserting that she would not be joining the faculty at UNC–Chapel Hill. We share her words at length:

> I cannot imagine working at and advancing a school named for a man who lobbied against me, who used his wealth to influence the hires and ideology of the journalism school, who ignored my 20 years of journalism experience, all of my credentials, all of my work, because he believed that a project that centered Black Americans equaled the denigration of white Americans. Nor can I work at an institution whose leadership permitted this conduct and has done nothing to disavow it. How could I believe I'd be able to exert academic freedom with the school's largest donor so willing to disparage me publicly and attempt to pull the strings behind the scenes? Why would I want to teach at a university whose top leadership chose to remain silent, to refuse transparency, to fail to publicly advocate that I be treated like every other Knight Chair before me? Or for a university overseen by a board that would so callously put politics over what is best for the university that we all love? These times demand courage, and those who have held the most power in this situation have exhibited the

least of it. (NAACP Legal Defense and Educational Fund Media, 2021, para. 16)

One of the last paragraphs of her statement said,

> For too long, powerful people have expected the people they have mistreated and marginalized to sacrifice themselves to make things whole. The burden of working for racial justice is laid on the very people bearing the brunt of the injustice, and not the powerful people who maintain it. I say to you: I refuse. (NAACP Legal Defense and Educational Fund Media, 2021, para. 32)

Instead, Nikole Hannah-Jones would go on to join the faculty of Howard University as their inaugural Knight Chair.

Many leadership challenges facing higher education are inextricably linked to notions of whiteness and white supremacy (e.g., student debt, tuition hikes, and campus climate) (Mustaffa, 2017; Patel, 2021). When leaders subscribe to whiteness, even implicitly, they are lured into maintaining the status quo, for which they are materially rewarded and experience numerous advantages. The status quo subsequently supports the historically inequitable and racist investments evident in higher education today. The advantage of these investments is enjoyed by a select few and threatens equity and public-good missions and visions for the postsecondary enterprise. This is particularly evident in the Hannah-Jones case, which we return to throughout the chapter. In recent years, scholars across race, gender, and class identities have begun calling out and grappling with issues related to diversity, equity, and inclusion in higher education, but fewer have taken up the charge to explicitly interrogate whiteness. Even fewer have discussed whiteness in higher education leadership processes.

Charles H. F. Davis III (2021) noted, "Beyond the many calls for investments in social justice, commitments to diversification, and rhetorical (but not structural) value of 'inclusive excellence,' a meaningful deconstruction of both *where* and *how* Whiteness paradoxically undermines the presumed public mission of higher education is desperately needed" (p. 6, original emphasis). This chapter attempts to address this need. In so doing, we disentangle the idea that whiteness merely means white people. Whiteness is a complex idea; it is a system made up of distinct structures and ideologies.* Seeing whiteness in this way means that people of color can also be complicit with whiteness. Additionally, whiteness is a shaping, mediating, and interpreting force that defines how we understand higher education leadership and the various outcomes of leadership processes. We demonstrate whiteness as a social construct in this chapter by introducing the idea of plantation leadership, which describes the ways in which the afterlife of slavery and contemporary matters related to whiteness and white supremacy are evident in and throughout leadership processes in higher education.

In this chapter, we first anchor our argument in a review of key concepts around whiteness and white supremacy to construct a shared understanding. Then we introduce readers to plantation leadership and discuss (1) the roles and responsibilities embedded in plantation leadership, (2) the tools used to enact and maintain notions of domination and exploitation necessary for plantation leadership, and (3) the strategies employed to cement plantation leadership in our contemporary fashionings of higher education. Where necessary, we connect these concepts to the previous chapter on neoliberalism and further explore the links among neoliberalism, whiteness, and white supremacy.

Toward a Shared Understanding of Whiteness and White Supremacy

Whiteness has evolved beyond a racial group or identity and into a structuring and gratifying ideology and habit (Ahmed, 2007; Anzaldúa, 1987; Crenshaw, 1989; Garner, 2007; C. I. Harris, 1993). Over the years, whiteness has "gone from something one was to something one did" (Olson, 2004, p. 126).

---

* In some cases, we use the terms *whiteness* and *white supremacy* interchangeably. We do so because white supremacy is an extension of whiteness that offers an explanation for how and why white people and others who conform to whiteness uphold racial hierarchies, hoard power, and sustain a status quo that centers and rewards whiteness exclusively (Bonilla-Silva, 2001; Omi & Winant, 1994). In some instances we also refer to higher education as a neoliberal, white supremacist space. This reference is rooted in the exclusionary history of higher education (i.e., the white male elite only), the enterprise's shift away from the public good and toward market values (see chapter 3 of this book), and the fact that higher education operates under plantation logics where people of color are readily used for economic gain and white patriarchal power continues to have an overwhelming presence in the practice and position of leadership (see Squire et al., 2018).

In this section, we identify the constitutive elements and habits that make up and uphold the ideology of whiteness. In doing so, we begin to make whiteness visible and locate it in higher education leadership discourse and practice.

A number of scholars have offered various definitions of whiteness. Flagg (2005) conceptualized whiteness as a "metaprivilege" at the intersection of power, privilege, and prestige. C. I. Harris (1993) argued that whiteness is a form of property protected by social institutions such as law. Frankenberg (1993) defined whiteness as a social location of structural advantage and privilege and a set of cultural practices that are largely invisible and thus unnamed. Table 4.1 goes into more depth regarding these many definitions. We offer several perspectives on whiteness, as each provides additional insights, offering readers a broader understanding of whiteness as a system and ideology that has its roots in power and oppression.

Inherent to whiteness is the idea that with whiteness come real, material benefits and more power and advantages than other racially and ethnically minoritized individuals (DuBois, 1935; Leonardo, 2009). Table 4.2 outlines the concepts that are essential to understanding whiteness. These concepts help us comprehend how whiteness becomes real and material.

White Settler Colonialism

Discussions of whiteness and white supremacy and how they came to shape our social order begin with the concept of white settler colonialism. Crawley (2016) contended that the ideology of whiteness is predicated on the "acceptance of violence and violation as a way of life" (p. 6). When European settlers took over native lands, they did so by displacing native people through physical violence. Tuck and Yang (2012) argued that settler colonialism is an ongoing process composed of three interdependent elements: land grabs and the extraction of cultural practices and resources, state-sanctioned genocide, and chattel slavery, where people of color are primarily property and workers but not owners. Settler colonialism was meant to be sustainable and advantageous for white people. It sought to preserve a distinct way of life that would only thrive and remain powerful through the use of violence, both physical and nonphysical (e.g., emotional and psychological), against Black and Indigenous peoples. Colleges and universities benefited from and continue to benefit from settler colonialism (Wilder, 2014). Settler colonialism

Whiteness and White Supremacy in Higher Education Leadership   83

Table 4.1   Conceptualizing whiteness

Scholarly contribution to the definition of whiteness	Basic premise	More advanced conceptualization
"Foreword: Whiteness as Metaprivilege," Barbara Flagg (2005)	Whiteness exists as a "metaprivilege" at the intersection of power, privilege, and prestige.	"By 'metaprivilege' I mean the ability of Whiteness to define the conceptual terrain on which race is constructed, deployed, and interrogated. Whiteness sets the terms on which racial identity is constructed. Whiteness generates a distinct cultural narrative, controls the racial distribution of opportunities and resources, and frames the ways in which that distribution is interpreted. Finally, Whiteness holds sway over the very terms in which its own ascendancy is understood and might be challenged" (p. 2).
"Whiteness as Property," Cheryl I. Harris (1993)	Whiteness is a form of property (anything to which people attach value) protected by social institutions such as law.	"As it emerged, the concept of whiteness was premised on white supremacy rather than mere difference. 'White' was defined and constructed in ways that increased its value by reinforcing its exclusivity. Indeed, just as whiteness as property embraced the right to exclude, whiteness as a theoretical construct evolved for the very purpose of racial exclusion. Thus, the concept of whiteness is built on both exclusion and racial subjugation. This fact was particularly evident during the period of the most rigid racial exclusion, as whiteness signified racial privilege and took the form of status property" (p. 1737).
The Social Construction of Whiteness: White Women, Race Matters, Ruth Frankenberg (1993)	Whiteness is a social location of structural advantage and privilege and a set of cultural practices that are invisible and often go unnamed.	"The historicizing of whiteness [is] simply [a] retelling of the same tale. Analysis of the place of whiteness in the racial order can and should be, rather than an end in itself, only one part of a much broader process of social change leveled both at the material relations of race and at discursive repertoires. It is not, in any case, realistic or meaningful to reconceptualize whiteness outside of racial domination when, in practical terms, whiteness still confers race privilege. It would be similarly naive to imagine that political will alone might bring about the kinds of shifts necessary to challenge those discourses that most effectively stabilize the racial order" (p. 243).

84   The Contemporary Context of Leadership in Higher Education

Table 4.2   Essential building block concepts toward understanding whiteness

Concept	Definition	Recommended reading
White settler colonialism	An ongoing process and practice composed of rules, dreams, and desires that are inherently political, violent, and interested in maintaining notions of white supremacy and anti-Blackness. It is also predicated on the theft of land, air, and, more broadly, life from Black and Native people.	• T. L. King et al., 2020 • Patel, 2021 • Rowe and Tuck, 2017 • Tuck and Yang, 2012
Anti-Blackness	An antagonistic relationship between Blackness and the possibility of humanity. Anti-Blackness renders Black people property of the settler state. Anti-Blackness deeply confines the struggle for freedom and liberation and only exists because of white supremacy.	• Dumas, 2016 • Ewing, 2018 • A. F. Gordon, 1997 • Hartman, 2008 • Tichavakunda, 2021a • Wilder, 2014 • B. C. Williams et al., 2021
Racial hierarchies	A distinct and deliberate order that situates whiteness as a norm to which others ought to aspire and where nonwhite people are seen as inferior. Racial hierarchies are used to organize social, political, and economic orders.	• Robinson, 1980, 2000 • Smith, 2016
Whiteness as property	A form of property (anything to which people attach value) protected by social institutions like law. Whiteness as property asserts that white people have the absolute right to exclude.	• Aggarwal, 2016 • Buras, 2011 • C. I. Harris, 1993, 2020
Complicity	The act of employing a conscious ignorance about issues of race and racism, therefore detaching responsibility from dismantling systemic racism and other forms of oppression.	• Applebaum, 2010 • Mills, 2007 • S. Sullivan and Tuana, 2007
The white gaze	The imagination and conceptualization of the world and our (im)possibilities through the lens of what is acceptable and palatable to white people and whiteness.	• Morrison, 1992 • K. D. Stewart and Gachago, 2020

allowed them to acquire the land necessary to erect academic buildings, football stadiums, and residence halls, from which they derive profit. Whiteness and white supremacy attempt to protect what was stolen, not given, and agents of whiteness work actively and tirelessly to maintain their supremacy and racial dominance, at the cost of marginalized and minoritized populations (Bonilla-Silva, 2006).

An example of settler colonialism at play in higher education is dispro-portionate labor expectations. Often, these expectations are placed on Black faculty and staff, especially when it comes to taking on temporary leader-ship roles (e.g., serving in interim positions and chairing committees) (Dancy et al., 2018). This distinct type of colonial labor uses the presence and ge-nius of Black people to perform inclusion without giving Black people a sense of real, permanent power within the institution. Temporary power mini-mizes people of color as workers and not owners (Tuck & Yang, 2012) and fails to create any structural changes that redistribute power to victims of settler colonialism, nor does it disrupt or eradicate whiteness and white su-premacy. It instead maintains the status quo.

Anti-Blackness

Whiteness only knows itself through anti-Blackness. Without the pres-ence of Black people and the power to both dehumanize them and use them for white interests (e.g., diversity committees and anti-racism initia-tives), the ideology of whiteness and white supremacy would be rendered paralyzed. *Anti-Blackness* refers to "an antagonistic relationship between blackness and (the possibility of) humanity" (Dumas & ross, 2016, p. 429). Hartman (2008) continued to explore this idea of anti-Blackness by high-lighting that Black people live in the afterlife of slavery, where the way they live and are able to be fully human is primarily guided by institu-tionalized white supremacist policies, practices, and principles that date back to the era of enslavement. Anti-Blackness creates and cements the conditions for proper personhood by which white people and those who align with whiteness define and give power through quotidian behaviors, actions, and interactions (Gilroy, 2000; Okello et al., 2021; Sharpe, 2016; Sexton, 2008).

Anti-Blackness holds great operative power in higher education and has made systemic inequities normal and legitimate. It manifests in myriad ways. Anti-Blackness is enslaved Black people building colleges and universities nationwide yet being unable to attend for decades (Wilder, 2014). Anti-Blackness is racialized student loan debt and the myth of meritocracy (Mustaffa, 2017; Mustaffa & Dawson, 2021). Anti-Blackness is the failure to fund, thus eventually closing, Black cultural centers in higher education (Patton, 2010). Anti-Blackness is the forced desegregation of Historically Black

86   The Contemporary Context of Leadership in Higher Education

Colleges and Universities as a direct result of anti-Black state and federal policies (S. R. Harper et al., 2009). In all of these pursuits, institutions attempt to otherize Blackness, strip life and access from Black people if they fail to assume an aesthetic associated with whiteness, and enact a type of sanctioned and legitimate violence.*

Racial Hierarchies

While contempt for Blackness is the bedrock of white supremacy, racial hierarchies are also relevant for its legitimacy. Racial hierarchies reflect and perpetuate a belief that white people are superior to nonwhite people and that human differences necessitate hierarchical ordering. This belief—a fallacy, might we add—has existed since the settler-colonial beginnings of the United States, is often seen as natural and inevitable, and continues to hold significance in our contemporary times (Robinson, 1980). Tropes and stereotypes about racial categories have helped create and legitimize racial hierarchies. But because racial hierarchies are socially constructed, they change according to region, new immigrations, and the overarching sociopolitical moment (Gans, 2012; Wilkerson, 2020; Yancey, 2003).

Class, capitalism, and notions of property also play important roles in the maintenance of racial hierarchies (Cox, 1959). In fact, to ignore those connections would be irresponsible. A. Smith (2016) writes that the "racial hierarchy tells people that as long as you are not Black, you have the opportunity to escape the commodification of capitalism. This helps people who are not Black to accept their lot in life, because they can feel that at least they are not at the very bottom of the racial hierarchy—at least they are not property; at least they are not slaveable" (p. 67). This allows white people to feel solid about their standing in the social order and allows organizations to order labor in a way that stratifies nonwhite people while they consolidate power and wealth.

In higher education, we continue to see more people of color occupying traditional blue-collar occupations (e.g., custodians and groundskeepers) (Magolda, 2016). Organizations seldom find the need to diversify these

---

* As a result, higher education scholars have begun to examine practices of Black life-making in higher education when institutions fail to adequately support their Black students (Mustaffa, 2021; Tichavakunda, 2021a).

workers because of their beliefs and assumptions about racial hierarchies and inferiority (Berrey, 2015; Ray, 2019). The numbers of blue-collar workers and other support workers on campus are dwindling while their workloads increase and the number of middle managers continues to rise (Kezar et al., 2019). The racial makeup of these workers cannot be overlooked and, in part, illustrates how the belief about racial hierarchies orders labor in higher education.

Whiteness as Property

C. I. Harris (1993) argued that whiteness as a form of racial identity has been interwoven with moral entitlements to property and power. With property rights, agents of whiteness have the right to exclude and the right to set the parameters of whiteness by making rules, policies, and laws that structurally disadvantage the most marginalized and minoritized. The structural disadvantage also strategically advantages white people and the ideology of whiteness. Whiteness as property situates whiteness as something for people to aspire to because of the real, material benefits and access to power and privilege. In this sense, agents of whiteness can be white, but they can also be people of color.

Black feminists like Patricia Hill Collins, Kimberlé Crenshaw, and Angela Davis highlight the many ways whiteness as property manifests itself in society and promotes a type of death-dealing among and dehumanization of racially and ethnically minoritized individuals. Angela Y. Davis (2010) has written extensively about how whiteness as a form of property supports and legitimizes racialized punishment practices. She contended that prisons are put in place to exclude Black and Brown people from society, and once they are released (if they are released), they experience insurmountable barriers to participation in society. The use of prisons as punishment, she argued, is death-dealing and dehumanizing, and a way to ensure whiteness and anti-Blackness hold a powerful grip on organizing and controlling the social world. Whiteness as property has also been a useful frame to understand the disintegration of affirmative action and the ongoing assault on voting rights across the country (K. Clarke & Rosenberg, 2018; C. I. Harris, 1993; Roth & Ritter, 2021). In these examples, the logic of whiteness as property is animated by an equal distribution of rights but unequal protection of said rights (Aggarwal, 2016).

88 The Contemporary Context of Leadership in Higher Education

Scholars have explored how whiteness as property has manifested in higher education as well. In her study on whiteness and student leadership education, Irwin (2021) found that leadership educators in higher education actively privileged white knowledge about leadership and missed key opportunities to teach students about critical and diverse perspectives of leadership. Irwin used whiteness as property as a frame to understand the benefits of exclusion and leadership legitimacy as a property of whiteness. Scholars such as Bondi (2012) and J. C. Harris (2019) have linked notions of comfort and the use and enjoyment of the benefits of whiteness to experiences in higher education. Bondi (2012) found that white people in student affairs graduate programs privileged their own needs and comfort in contentious conversations about race and racism. They deployed their rights to the use and enjoyment of whiteness and exercised defensiveness when their peers of color would talk candidly about their experiences. Similarly, J. C. Harris (2019) interviewed multiracial women in higher education and found that they believed that their white peers could more easily interact with professors and easily form relationships and a sense of belonging within the higher education landscape. From their vantage point as multiracial women, they clearly observed the advantages experienced through whiteness. Harris argued that whiteness as property actively disadvantages multiracial women if they fail to fit in with monoracial white aesthetic sensibilities.

Whiteness as property affects how leadership is defined and practiced in higher education (Wolfe & Dilworth, 2015). Whiteness as property shapes guidelines and outcomes for higher education leadership processes, whom leadership processes should benefit, and what voices and perspectives the leadership process should privilege. Through the frame of whiteness as property, leadership processes are centered on white, male, heroic norms and constructions of leadership.

COMPLICITY

Complicity, as Applebaum (2010) contended, means employing a conscious ignorance about issues of race and racism, therefore avoiding responsibility for dismantling systemic racism and other forms of oppression. Complicity also comes in the form of saying or knowing and not doing, or witnessing and not acting (Mills, 1997). Dei (1999) argued this point further by noting,

"Dominant group members are usually aware that any acknowledgment of complicity in racial subordination seriously compromises their positions of power and privilege" (p. 401). With this in mind, beneficiaries of whiteness and white supremacy are motivated to act in symbolic ways and in ways that dilute the severity of issues around race and racism.

Patton et al. (2015) noted that "higher education as an entity has been complicit in submitting to ideals of colorblindness and race neutrality" (p. 196). Historically speaking, higher education leaders have played significant roles in the decision to expand the physical space of higher education institutions while displacing vulnerable and marginalized communities (Cole, 2020; P. R. Mullins & Jones, 2005). A lack of awareness and acknowledgment of past wrongdoings and an unwillingness to engage in conversations about reparations work to maintain a status quo that reasserts the fallacy of white supremacy and other notions of racial dominance. Further, Bledsoe et al. (2020) contended that complicity in higher education leadership works to protect hate speech and creates a "right to be racist" (Moore & Bell, 2017, p. 111). A growing body of scholarship about anti-racist educational leadership seeks to disrupt the notion of complicity and advance the study of leadership in education toward equity and justice (e.g., Blaisdell, 2021; Brooks et al., 2013; Welton et al., 2018). Law (2017) presented some key considerations worth noting for higher education specifically. He argued that in order to move away from complicity and toward equity and justice, leaders must develop alliances with accountability mechanisms, prioritize cross-sectional learning, and identify anti-racism as a foundational pillar for moving the campus forward.

The White Gaze

The white gaze also significantly limits the imagination regarding what higher education and society could be. American literary author Toni Morrison (1992) popularized this idea of the white gaze, which she understands as the imagination and conceptualization of the world and our im/possibilities through the lens of what is acceptable and palatable to white people and whiteness. Under the white gaze, people of all races, creeds, and identities may fall into the trap of internalizing whiteness and white supremacy, thus limiting and affecting their imagination and leadership. In higher education, we often see faculty, students, and staff alike hypnotized by the white gaze and what whiteness will allow, which subsequently narrows the scope of higher education's futurity (Shahjahan & Edwards, 2021).

The influence of the white gaze in higher education leadership is evident in conversations regarding strategies for fostering systemic change toward equity and the eradication of racism on campuses. Studies have shown that senior leaders are often interested in pursuing strategies that focus change efforts on racial symbols (e.g., changing names on buildings or creating chief diversity officer positions) rather than initiating larger structural reforms, necessary policy changes, and power and resource shifts (Tichavakunda, 2021a, 2022; Wilson, 2013). These symbol-oriented leadership actions—which can be conceptualized as policy distractions (Farley et al., 2021)—are constructed according to the white gaze, which narrows the scope of palatable change efforts to those that do not materially threaten the status quo of white supremacy. The management of racial symbols through efforts to rename buildings or remove campus statues does not contribute to the deep structural changes (e.g., curricular reform or the establishment of new accountability metrics) needed to dismantle oppressive systems. The cosmetic nature of these reform efforts is exactly what makes them permissible (although not entirely uncontested) actions within the white gaze of higher education leadership. Similarly, institutional leaders operating within the white gaze often tout the establishment of chief diversity officer positions as evidence of a meaningful commitment to equity-oriented change; however, these roles often "lack the power to transform institutions *by design*" (K. A. Griffin et al., 2019, p. 692, emphasis added). Within higher education organizations, the white gaze shapes leadership priorities and actions, undermining the possibility of systemic change by limiting what leadership efforts are perceived as legitimate, feasible, and politically tolerable.

We have seen whiteness shape our past and present—from settler colonialism, to slavery, to our contemporary times, when conversations about race and racism are being demonized and banned at state and local levels (A. Harris, 2021). Whiteness has no regard for people under the weight of systems of oppression. Instead, it is interested in defending itself first and always and working strategically to maintain its systemic advantages and hoarding its power and benefits (Bonilla-Silva, 2001; C. I. Harris, 1993; Cottom, 2019). Concepts like complicity, the white gaze, and anti-Blackness work in concert to ensure that an oppressive and dehumanizing status quo remains unscathed. Here, it becomes evident that whiteness is a vicious, invisible structuring force that must be interrupted, obliterated, and made hypervisible if there is to be equity and justice for marginalized and minoritized groups and the institutions they inhabit.

While we can only provide a brief overview of whiteness in this book, we recommend reading full-length books such as *Displacing Whiteness: Essays in Social and Cultural Criticism* (Frankenberg, 1997), *White Guys on Campus: Racism, White Immunity, and the Myth of "Post-racial" Higher Education* (Cabrera, 2019), *Nice White Ladies: The Truth about White Supremacy, Our Role in It, and How We Can Help Dismantle It* (Daniels, 2021), and *Look, a White! Philosophical Essays on Whiteness* (Yancy, 2012). We also recommend reading *Black Marxism: The Making of the Black Radical Tradition* (Robinson, 1983) for a better understanding of racial capitalism.* Having provided a concise overview of the foundational constructs that frame and illustrate whiteness and white supremacy, we now turn our attention to a particular manifestation of white supremacy in higher education leadership—plantation leadership.

Introducing Plantation Leadership in Higher Education

Though the ratification of the Thirteenth Amendment abolished slavery in the United States, the ideology of whiteness and the fallacy of white supremacy continue in their pursuit to order society to the detriment of people of color. Escaping the logic of slavery is nearly impossible because our society was designed, and continues to benefit from, racial violence and the political economy of white supremacy and anti-Blackness (e.g., prison labor or police acting as modern-day slave patrols) (Alexander, 2010; A. Y. Davis, 2010; Hartman & Wilderson, 2003). As previously stated, scholars like Hartman (2008) have come to understand our contemporary times as the afterlife of

---

* Racial capitalism is a system and ideology that decides differential value to the life and labor of racially minoritized individuals (N. Leong, 2013; Robinson, 2000). Racial capitalism continues where some of the ideas we presented in this chapter leave off by exploring how racial hierarchies, whiteness (as ideology, system, and property), and capitalism work together to place value on racially minoritized individuals, especially in contexts like higher education where diversity is necessary and used for legitimation purposes (Irwin & Foste, 2021; A. Mir & Toor, 2021; Mustaffa & Dawson, 2021).

slavery, which she described as "skewed life chances, limited access to health and education, premature death, incarceration, and impoverishment" (p. 17). In the afterlife of slavery, our institutions, governed by plantationesque arrangements, are helping to keep the logic of slavery alive. Within institutions of higher education, the logic of slavery is institutionalized through the processes and constitutive elements of plantation leadership, an extension of B. C. Williams et al.'s (2021) conceptualization of plantation politics in higher education. Anchored in foundational whiteness concepts such as settler colonialism and whiteness as property, plantation leadership leverages power, order, and control to create and regulate the infrastructure (e.g., policies, practices, and work conditions) necessary to maintain whiteness and white supremacy at the center of the organizational order (Ray, 2019). In a system where whiteness is seen as a valuable form of capital (Tadiar, 2003), leaders are strongly encouraged or even expected to align their identities, actions, and outcomes with whiteness. Accordingly, whiteness and white supremacy can be identified in every element of higher education leadership (i.e., who is a leader, what characteristics define effective leadership, how leadership processes are organized and ordered, and the end goals of leadership). Thus, in order to dismantle plantation leadership, higher education scholar-practitioners must first see and understand whiteness. Here we outline a three-part framework for identifying and analyzing plantation leadership in higher education. It is our hope that the framework not only advances understanding of plantation leadership but also highlights opportunities for resistance and transformational change.

FRAMING PLANTATION LEADERSHIP

We begin our explication of the plantation leadership framework with a reminder from Black feminist theorist Audre Lorde (1984) that "the master's tools will never dismantle the master's house" (p. 179). Lorde contended that those seeking to tear down racist institutions must refrain from relying on the same tools and strategies used to amass the social control necessary for building and maintaining structures of white patriarchal supremacy. The constant use and reuse of the master's tools will only end up strengthening oppressive institutions. Both building on and countering Lorde's dictum, abolitionist geographer Ruth Wilson Gilmore (1993) argued that the tools of oppression are not always the problem; rather it is, without fail,

Whiteness and White Supremacy in Higher Education Leadership   93

who handles the tools and to what end the tools are being used that is worth the worry. Gilmore noted, "If the master loses control of the means of production [tools], he is no longer the master" (p. 79). At the heart of both Lorde's and Gilmore's assertions is a recognition that those seeking to dismantle systemic racism must first develop a deep understanding of the individuals, tools, and strategies that perpetuate oppression. Thus, those seeking to abolish the plantation logic framing contemporary higher education organizations must identify the *individuals* wielding power within plantation leadership (e.g., boards of trustees), examine their *tools of oppression* (e.g., hidden agendas and intellectual property ownership), and scrutinize the *protective strategies* leveraged to preserve a status quo rooted in white supremacy (e.g., boundary control and impression management). All three dimensions of plantation leadership are elaborated on next.

Roles and Responsibilities

Plantation leadership thrives because of strict roles and responsibilities that bind and define individuals in higher education. In their book *Plantation Politics and Campus Rebellions*, B. C. Williams et al. (2021) outlined a number of roles on the plantation that have accompanying responsibilities: enslavers, managers or overseers, and drivers. These roles and responsibilities are racialized, gendered, and classed. We detail these roles and responsibilities in this section to highlight how roles within higher education (plantation) leadership work to uphold whiteness, white supremacy, and neoliberalism. We also describe how Williams et al. make sense of the house slave and the field slave in the context of higher education.

Enslavers

Plantation enslavers are individuals who create the norms and rules—slave codes—that govern the plantation and by which everyone, including managers, must abide (B. C. Williams et al., 2021). Williams et al. categorized members of governing boards as enslavers in contemporary higher education. Similar to enslavers on plantations, these trustee members remain overwhelmingly white and male (McBain, 2021). Enslavers in higher education are in a position of both real and symbolic power and authority where they can advance their white supremacist agendas and ensure that the interests of white people take priority over equity- and justice-related goals and outcomes.

Rall (2021) asserted that while governing boards take great pleasure in using their power to create rules and govern, they often take a "hands-off" approach when crises on campus occur or issues surrounding race, racism, and equity bubble to the surface. Likewise, B. C. Williams et al. (2021) contended that enslavers are often worried about insurrection and rebellion and thus create and uphold slave codes that prevent such an event from happening or, at the very least, present deep consequences for attempts to rebel.

Enslavers in contemporary higher education take the position of barrier, inhibitor, or bystander. Rall et al. (2020) defined barriers as boards that intentionally create policies that prevent the actualization of equity, inhibitors as boards that question or problematize the need for equitable policies, and bystanders as boards that continue business as usual and ignore social justice–related issues. It is important to note that enslavers assume these positions willingly and consciously, as there is nothing unconscious about white supremacy (D. A. Bell, 1992; Mills, 2003).

The concept of racial hierarchies is clearly seen in the role of the enslaver. The enslaver determines who is seen as "slaveable" (A. Smith, 2016, p. 67) and the rules by which those slotted into each level of the hierarchy must abide. Enslavers situate white people and those willing to align themselves with whiteness into the higher levels of the hierarchy (e.g., managers or overseers and drivers).

The denial of tenure for Nikole Hannah-Jones shines a light on the role of the enslaver in contemporary higher education. The UNC–Chapel Hill Board of Trustees, in their role as enslavers and creators of norms and rules, overstepped the shared governance structure of UNC and ignored the faculty's recommendation to grant Hannah-Jones tenure primarily because of their discomfort with the politics of her scholarship, which seeks to tell the truth about America's relationship with slavery. Hannah-Jones's tenure denial illustrates that the elite and privileged few who create the governance structures of higher education also have the power to protect white supremacy by overriding the structures they help put in place. Enslavers, overall, are very particular about whom they bring on as managers and overseers (president, executive administrators, etc.) and even whom they appoint as house slaves (faculty), and white supremacist ideologies and revisionist histories drive them to dismiss anyone who attempts to challenge the status quo brazenly.

Managers and Overseers

Managers and overseers on the plantation ensure everyone is fulfilling their duties and responsibilities, conforming to the needs and desires of the enslavers (B. C. Williams et al., 2021). They also report to enslavers, and enslavers put trust in them to ensure the plantation runs in a smooth and orderly manner. In contemporary higher education, B. C. Williams et al. view presidents, provosts, and executive administrators as people in the administrative chain who assume this role. Managers and overseers are notably responsible for the maintenance of the day-to-day, neoliberal operations of the college or university. They operate under an "any means necessary" approach to ensure that the plantation (college or university) is maximizing the three Ps associated with neoliberalism and capitalism: profit, performance, and productivity (Rhoades & Slaughter, 1997). Their presence, along with their responsibilities, without resistance, situate them as agents of white supremacy and neoliberalism.

Over the last decade, there have been persistent calls to increase racial and gender representation in senior-level administrative positions (managers and overseers) in higher education (D. G. Smith, 2020). Yet individuals in these positions, regardless of race or gender, can perpetuate the violence that emerges from neoliberal and whiteness ideologies. On the plantation, managers and overseers are directly tied to an oppressive and dehumanizing system, carrying out orders given to them by the enslaver. Managers and overseers can be women, they can even be people of color, but they are inherently responsible for the maintenance of a white supremacist system. Thus, the concept of "complicity" is clearly represented in the role of the manager or overseer.

Carr et al. (2021) noted that white women in higher education are becoming the new managers and overseers, roles in which they "self-select through their investments in whiteness to surveil and direct the work of people of color generally, and specifically women of color. They do this all while claiming they lack 'real' power to enact change" (p. 160). H. Liu (2020) extended this understanding by explaining that white women in manager and overseer roles align with notions of white supremacy and patriarchy in an effort to maintain their white privilege and white group membership. In other words, whiteness, along with patriarchy, sustains itself by becoming flexible and malleable to the point where patriarchy has no gender (hooks, 2009) and whiteness has no race. Instead, they become dominant ideologies and organizing forces. Managers and overseers in higher education, regardless of their race or gender identity, do the work of upholding white supremacy and operating within whiteness unless they actively disrupt and resist. Whiteness gains legitimacy, power, and strength through the people who protect, surveil, and (over)police it (Irwin, 2021). And those managers and overseers who fail to work against whiteness and white supremacy in all of its forms run the risk of engaging in harmful and violent leadership that keeps the plantation operating as intended.

Drivers

The role of plantation driver is held by once-enslaved Black people on the plantation. Assuming the position of a driver was like receiving a promotion on the plantation. Enslavers, managers, and overseers sometimes rely on plantation drivers to assign chores for the house and field slaves, monitor their performance, and ensure their "safety" (code for ensuring they do not run away or rebel against plantation leaders) (L. J. Stewart, 2010). Drivers assume the role and responsibility of the overseer in their absence, and some even have direct lines to the enslavers and other plantation owners (Clifton, 1981). Drivers have an extensive amount of privilege and access to power and authority, which ultimately means that their Black peers perceive them to be agents of whiteness. Yet drivers are still viewed as enslaved people, just ones who are now being groomed to become active participants in the project of white supremacy.

B. C. Williams et al. (2021) contended that chief diversity officers are some of the most notable drivers in contemporary higher education. We might add that diversity task force members and other diversity-oriented hires in specific departments (e.g., admissions and global education) are becoming drivers as well. Colleges and universities are creating driver roles at increasing rates in the interest of decentralizing diversity work, minimizing power, and reaping the benefits of racial capitalism (Okuwobi et al., 2021). Drivers have more symbolic, representational power than real, material power. They are often meant to be looked on as symbols of progress and of equality and opportunity. They are often recruited to be actual agents of white supremacy, sometimes in an attempt to pledge loyalty to the institution, not the structural or systemic issue at hand (Tichavakunda, 2021a).

In a comparison between chief diversity officers and plantation drivers, Tuitt (2021) reminded us that chief diversity officers are "chosen by plantation owners and trustees, and not by other enslaved [people]; although some in these positions desire to protect individual slaves, you will owe your power to the trust of your masters, not to your fellow enslaved people" (p. 185). Chief diversity officers, or drivers on the plantation, are put in symbolic positions by design—a forceful and intentional effort to seem progressive while also maintaining white supremacy and operating within oppressive ideologies like whiteness (K. A. Griffin et al., 2019; Wilson, 2013). Ahmed (2007) argued against the notion that diversity—and, by extension, the practice of hiring sole individuals to be responsible for advancing diversity goals—is a positive sign that racism is being eradicated and whiteness is being addressed. Further, D. A. Williams and Wade-Golden (2007) contended that chief diversity officers must be willing to find win-win solutions, which is code for finding solutions that satisfy the ideology of whiteness and the neoliberal, white supremacist institution writ large. When drivers, such as chief diversity officers and other diversity personnel in higher education, must find win-win solutions that miraculously address issues of diversity, equity, and inclusion without poking and prodding the structure and ideology of whiteness, the result is often the increase of racially and ethnically minoritized individuals but the absence of real or substantial cultural and institutional change. Diversity then becomes a mechanism for predatory inclusion (Taylor, 2019).

In sum, the role of the driver on the plantation is largely symbolic and representational. It is created and maintained by concepts like the white gaze in that symbolic and representational power is achieved, but the white gaze is cognizant of who is given material power and resources. Very seldom are drivers afforded that level of power. As a result, they experience copious barriers and challenges that prevent them from meaningfully transforming oppressive and dehumanizing environments. Drivers find themselves again marginalized and powerless, now as agents of white supremacy.

House and Field Slaves

B. C. Williams et al. (2021) identified faculty as house slaves and positioned campus staff and students as field slaves. In the enslavement era, house slaves were subject to slightly better working conditions and clothing and were given a higher-status position (Weiner, 1997). Field slaves took on more manual

98   The Contemporary Context of Leadership in Higher Education

labor and fell at the bottom of the status hierarchy, and their clothing was rationed (Ellis & Ginsburg, 2010). B. C. Williams et al. (2021) did not specify where contingent faculty fell, but given all that we know about their working conditions and experiences (e.g., Kezar et al., 2019), we would argue that they fall into the field slave position. Staff are identified as field slaves because they are more likely to take on the labor to maintain the infrastructure of the plantation (e.g., budget management and administrative processes). Faculty and staff are held accountable to the expectations of the enslavers, managers, and overseers (i.e., neoliberal, quantifiable metrics of success), and often, these expectations limit their freedom to advance critical scholarship, engage in meaningful service work, or support those in the field or other outside community members (Giroux, 2002; Wright-Mair & Museus, 2021). In some cases, faculty members are able to sit on committees or even take on positional leadership roles, but they are still expected to align with the values and priorities of enslavers, managers, and overseers.

Field slaves—specifically students, and especially students of color—are the most poorly treated on the plantation. Much like their antebellum plantation counterparts, contemporary higher education student activists (rebels on the plantation) are chastised and heavily sanctioned for their activist pursuits (Morgan & Davis, 2019). Students, both undergraduate and graduate, are used for their cheap labor (Ross, 2022a) and leveraged as pawns in campus marketing materials that celebrate "diverse student bodies" (Osei-Kofi et al., 2013). Additionally, students of color are dehumanized when they are rendered "at-risk," "remedial," or "unprepared" (Rios, 2011) by a plantation logic that does not value diverse forms of cultural capital. Most importantly, plantation leadership excludes students from actively participating in conversations and decisions regarding the future direction of the institution. Instead, neoliberal and white supremacist leadership approaches champion the individualistic, positional nature of leadership and construct boundaries that avert students' meaningful participation.

It is important to note that the hierarchical, bureaucratic nature of higher education organizations bestows significant power and prestige to those in formal leadership positions and renders students, and other members of marginalized groups on campus, powerless commodities that are easy to use and control. On the plantation known as higher education, people who operate in the roles of enslaver, manager, and overseer are in privileged leadership positions to center and advance white supremacy and neoliberal principles (e.g., color blindness, profit-mindedness, and knowledge as a commodity) and ensure the plantation is functioning as designed. Enslavers, managers, and overseers who fall in line, run higher education like a corporation, and do not question the detrimental effects of inequality, white supremacy, and neoliberalism are rewarded for staying true to the intended goals and outcomes of higher education, some of which date back to the 1600s (Wilder, 2014). Drivers, house slaves, and field slaves are intentionally disregarded in leadership in the interest of preserving the oppressive status quo. Drivers are given symbolic power because symbolism is all that whiteness will allow. House slaves are tasked with balancing a number of neoliberal demands that draw them away from the work of dismantling oppressive systems and ideologies and organizing with field slaves for freedom and liberation. Field slaves are cornered by boundaries and sanctions that render them useful for labor and nothing else.

As stated earlier, enslavers, as well as managers and overseers, are afraid of an insurrection or a campus rebellion (B. C. Williams et al., 2021). Thus, the roles they created and continue to maintain are strategic and intentional, and they serve as a way to protect the power and authority that come with whiteness and hierarchical leadership. This is most commonly demonstrated through higher education leaders' aversion to student activist movements and labor organizing (Kezar et al., 2019; Morgan & Davis, 2019). What is perhaps even more insidious is that plantation leadership and the roles that compose it cause enslaved people and people with less material power and authority to come to terms with the reality that negotiating their freedom and liberation with their oppressors may ultimately compromise their well-being, survival, and overall humanity. Enslavers, managers, overseers, and sometimes drivers make conscious decisions to disregard equity and liberation. They dismiss the chance to activate a liberatory imagination because they find benefit in the control and order they have over the plantation and the enslaved. The most powerful and influential individuals on the plantation make a deliberate choice to uphold and operate within neoliberal and white supremacist ideologies because it is lucrative and personally rewarding to do so. The mere existence of the plantation reproduces neoliberal and white supremacist thought, politics, and desires (Squire et al., 2018).

Tools

Plantation leaders regularly wield tools in an effort to maintain power and create the necessary conditions for domination and exploitation that whiteness requires. These tools are responsible for the maintenance of the master's house and are partly responsible for the continued oppression of marginalized and vulnerable communities in higher education. The tools we explore in this section include individual and intellectual property ownership, hidden agendas, and the politics of representation. This is not meant to be an exhaustive list of plantation leadership tools. Instead, we provide just a glimpse into some of the most prevalent and highly powered tools being utilized in higher education today.

Individual and Intellectual Property Ownership

Plantation leaders are primarily concerned with ensuring ownership of people and property, which feeds into neoliberal capitalist notions of domination and exploitation (Slaughter & Rhoades, 2004). The most common way they ensure ownership is through contracts. Contracts are ways for leaders to guarantee that the most vulnerable and least protected students and faculty fall in line with ideologies of whiteness: civility, ownership, and a sense of order. Such contracts lay out rules and expectations, and failure to follow these may result in a number of sanctions, or even termination. Above all else, the presence of a contract renders marginalized workers such as contingent faculty and graduate students vulnerable and more susceptible to termination, unless they have union protections (Kezar et al., 2019). Because few campuses are unionized and institutions allocate copious resources to thwart union attempts, marginalized and vulnerable workers (e.g., support staff workers and non-tenure-track faculty) are subject to and exist at the whim of the institution and whatever it needs and desires.

Research faculty are one group of faculty that is susceptible to the perils of university ownership. Kezar et al. (2019) noted that research faculty do not belong to the institution but the university "grants them access to its infrastructure while retaining ownership of the products of their research" (pp. 82–83). In some cases, research faculty are given the opportunity to advance through a promotion and reward track like tenure-line faculty. In this case, research faculty are sometimes given access to benefits, but as Kezar et al.

noted, "once the grants run out, the benefits do too" (p. 51). The reality that research faculty face demonstrates how higher education leadership purposely creates an insecure environment for vulnerable workers while also ensuring leaders own the labor produced by those vulnerable workers. To feel financially secure, workers often take on additional responsibilities at the university such as teaching classes. Research faculty are likely to fall into the trap of university ownership since sometimes their benefits and livelihood depend on it.

Some graduate students are also lured into contracts that leave them unable to secure employment outside the university (Kezar et al., 2019). Too often, they find themselves struggling to make ends meet and taking on unpaid work to be successful in the academic job market. The presence of these strict contracts enables colleges and universities to view graduate students as property owned by the institution with very limited freedom or agency. Kezar et al. (2019) noted that higher education leaders are focused on "preventing graduate students from developing the power to demand better working conditions or otherwise influence the academic environment as a cohesive constituency with power and voice" (p. 88). Here, we bear witness once again to the conscious efforts of plantation leadership to ensure the most vulnerable and marginalized stay in their positions as commodities in the neoliberal, white supremacist university. Leaders use the logic of ownership and property to advance ideologies of whiteness and white supremacy and to hoard power at the top and among a few elites. There are numerous examples of institutions that have threatened graduate students for striking and attempting to unionize (e.g., Columbia University). There was even a situation at Indiana University Bloomington in which university administrators called for faculty (house slaves) to keep graduate students (field slaves) in line and quash a strike (Ross, 2022b).

Contracts, when used in the ways that institutions tend to use them, are a manifestation of white settler colonialism. By using the tool of property ownership to the institution's own benefit, plantation leaders align themselves with the settler-colonial idea of resource extraction and "violence and violation" (Crawley, 2016, p. 6), which strips individuals of their power, agency, and autonomy.

Returning to the opening case, conservative criticism of Nikole Hannah-Jones ultimately led the university to offer her a five-year contract with the opportunity to go up for tenure after the initial contract ran out. This contract did not grant Hannah-Jones the protection or academic freedom that comes with tenure, which would have made her an easy casualty if conservative criticism increased during her contract. Presenting Hannah-Jones with a contract instead of tenure was a power move to ensure the board of trustees and other members of university leadership had the opportunity to hold dominion over her teaching, service, and scholarship. The contract rendered Hannah-Jones expendable property of UNC–Chapel Hill. This situation illustrates how contracts, especially as a replacement for tenure, are used to dominate groups and individuals whom plantation leaders may deem threats to the neoliberal and white supremacist regime.

Hidden Agendas

Another plantation leadership tool is the hidden agenda. Hierarchical leadership, which is embedded into plantation leadership, privileges a leader-follower dichotomy rife with notions of powerfulness (leader) and powerlessness (follower) (Hollander, 1995). As it pertains to change, Kezar (2012a) reminded us that "top-down leaders define the change agenda, direction, and others are only brought into the leadership process for 'advice' or in order to implement" (p. 732). From historical evidence derived from slavery and caste subordination and empirical evidence from a study of a small Malay village, J. C. Scott (1990) contended that "the powerful . . . develop a hidden transcript representing the practices and claims of their rule that cannot be openly avowed" (p. xii). He described the hidden transcript, which we fold into the idea of a hidden agenda, as "derivative in the sense that it consists of those offstage speeches, gestures, and practices that confirm, contradict, or inflect what appears in the public transcript" (pp. 4–5). These hidden agendas are meant to advance personal and institutional interests that are not outwardly apparent to other members of the community such as faculty or students. By having a hidden agenda, plantation leaders evade institutional accountability and responsibility by failing to be transparent and open regarding their plans and true intentions.

A particularly compelling analysis of the role that hidden agendas have played in maintaining white supremacy within higher education organizations is offered in Cole's (2020) book, *The Campus Color Line: College Presidents and the Struggle for Black Freedom*. Diving into the archives of a diverse range of institutions (public, private, Historically Black Colleges

Whiteness and White Supremacy in Higher Education Leadership   103

and Universities, and historically white universities), Cole explored how the hidden agendas of senior higher education leaders between the 1940s and the 1960s were purposely formed as a way to expand their personal and political power. Senior higher education leaders did so by getting involved in the shaping of state and federal policies related to segregation and Black freedom during the civil rights era. For example, some presidents and chancellors willingly advocated for university expansion at the expense of Black people through their desire for "slum clearance." Lawrence Kimpton, chancellor at the University of Chicago, was one of them. He actively shaped federal housing policies and further perpetuated housing discrimination and the displacement of Black people for the university's own power, prestige, and profit. When Kimpton stepped down from his leadership role, he was able to use the political influence he garnered in his time as chancellor for personal gain, transitioning into the oil and railroad industries and eventually earning seats on the board of directors of the Chesapeake and Ohio Railway and the Chessie System before his death.

Today, the presidential hidden agenda looks a little different and is concerned with expanding positional power, authority, and influence over decision-making. In 2020, the University of Missouri (Mizzou) system president, Mun Y. Choi, sought and eventually gained the approval of the board to consolidate leadership (Whitford, 2020). This leadership consolidation allowed Choi to serve as both the Mizzou system president and chancellor—increasing his power and influence across the entirety of the system, which includes several satellite campuses. Citing budget restrictions due to COVID-19, Choi began to chip away at administrative costs, cutting the system staff (which included other senior leaders like vice presidents) from ten to two (S. Brown, 2022). Choi argued that his decision to cut administrative positions was related to increasing productivity and performance. Similarly, he argued that because he was now both system president and chancellor, the system would no longer face challenges regarding where and how to make investments, which had apparently been an issue in the relationship between the two senior leaders for years (S. Brown, 2022). Faculty were concerned that Choi had a hidden agenda. They figured that the consolidation was a way to increase his power and significantly change governance structures, much to the detriment of faculty, students, and Mizzou's other, smaller campuses (Bacharier, 2020; S. Brown, 2022). Choi denied and continues to deny that there is a hidden agenda in place, but faculty remain skeptical.

Plantation leaders use hidden agendas to evade accountability and transparency and increase their individual power and influence. Accordingly, concepts such as whiteness as property become evergreen through this plantation leadership tool. Whiteness as property contends that those who align themselves with whiteness and exist in positions of power have rights such as the right to exclude and the right to use and enjoy power and all of its affordances. Thus, plantation leaders are likely interested in keeping these rights. To do so, they may look to expand their power and authority by holding multiple positions of power (as Choi did) or find ways to secure different positions of power and authority that enable them to keep these rights (as Kimpton did).

The hidden agenda tool was of particular significance in the Nikole Hannah-Jones case. The board of trustees had an obvious hidden agenda to remain compliant and answerable to the interests and desires of conservative, white supremacist people and ideologies. That agenda, however, did not remain hidden, as the fragmented elements of the overall situation were pieced together publicly by journalists at NC Policy Watch. There was also a hidden agenda to erode notions of shared governance by dismissing the recommendations of the School of Journalism and Media faculty and the tenure and promotion committee to grant Hannah-Jones tenure. Instead, conservative members of the board of trustees drove a plan into action to reassert the power and authority that come with hierarchical leadership in order to curtail the recommendations of the other, less powerful groups. Hannah-Jones noted that she was never informed why the tenure vote did not happen. Instead, a center founded and supported by one trustee member blew the whistle and demanded that she be denied a tenure vote. This is the only information she received about why the vote did not happen. Decisions were made, and chatter ensued behind closed doors.

The Politics of Representation

A third tool leveraged by plantation leadership to preserve white supremacy is the politics of representation. Plantation leadership posits that increasing racial and gender composition on campus is a sufficient sign of meaningful systemic change (Mayorga-Gallo, 2019). Accordingly, plantation leaders focus a lot of attention on hiring more faculty, staff, and administrators who identify as people of color and women without carefully vetting the politics and stances of new hires with regard to anti-Blackness, white supremacy, and so on (J. Harper, 2020). The result is a more diverse staff who uphold the ideology of whiteness and advance the fallacy that identity equates to critical consciousness.

Higher education plantation leadership's focus on compositional diversity as a proxy for equity aligns with the neoliberal turn that has transformed contemporary conceptualizations of identity politics and notions of representation. Analyzing this transformation from the Combahee River Collective Statement in 1977 to the present day, C. Rodríguez (2019) wrote that "Identity Politics, then, was a declaration of Black women's worth and liberative potential" (p. 109) and an explicit vision for the "destruction of all political-economic systems of capitalism and imperialism as well as patriarchy" (Combahee River Collective, 1977/1983, pp. 267–268). Now, identity politics has been co-opted and "wielded in contemporary discourse to enter systems of power . . . [and] to ensure 'equal representation' in places of privilege" (Rodríguez, 2019, p. 111). The color of faces changes, but structures of power do not. These oppressive systems go untouched. Clemons (2022) suggested that this is largely the result of what he called *the privatization of racial responsibility*, which explains why people with investments in whiteness are more likely to get behind symbolic and expressive forms of antiracism (e.g., representation) rather than support and create systemic policies and initiatives that address structural racial injustices. Concepts of whiteness such as complicity, the white gaze, and settler colonialism are clearly operationalized in this tool. The politics of representation is cyclical and falls flat without contemporaneous systemic change. Thus, a focus on symbolic representation is an ideal tool of plantation leadership.

Protective Strategies

In addition to the tools of oppression just detailed, there are a few strategies that are commonly used by higher education leaders to maintain norms rooted in whiteness and protect the infrastructure of the plantation and the master's house. The strategies we detail in this section are boundary control and impression management. There is a litany of other strategies that leaders use to protect themselves, their institutions, and the investments of the institution (see Patel, 2021, for strategies related directly to settler colonialism and Kezar et al., 2019, for strategies related to neoliberalism and academic capitalism). But we focus on boundary control and impression management specifically because they create illusions of progress, are often used discreetly, and produce and maintain positive images of the institution. These plantation leadership strategies forestall structural change and even reproduce barriers to equity and the collective public good.

Boundary Control: Predatory Inclusion and Interest Convergence

Plantation leadership is predicated on the power and control leaders have to draw, maintain, and police boundaries. Boundaries are meant to define and shape internal organizational structures and behaviors. Boundaries organize action and interaction and define distinct interests, objectives, and responsibilities tied to the various responsibilities of and investments related to the higher education enterprise (Prysor & Henley, 2018; Tilly, 2004). Boundaries must always be (re)negotiated and are even sometimes violated for purposes related to organizational change (Posselt et al., 2017). The power that a select few leaders have to draw, maintain, and police boundaries stems from normalized notions of whiteness and the hierarchical nature of plantation leadership. In this section, we explore what we deem two central concepts connected to boundary control in plantation leadership: predatory inclusion and interest convergence.

In *Race for Profit: How Banks and the Real Estate Industry Undermined Black Homeownership* (2019), Taylor introduced the concept of predatory inclusion. As Taylor conceptualized it, predatory inclusion best describes "how African American home buyers were granted access to conventional real estate practices and mortgage financing, but on more expensive and comparatively unequal terms" (p. 25). Taylor observed, "The concept of predatory inclusion also captures the failures of racial liberalism and its premise that inclusion into American democracy through the vehicles of citizenship, law, and free-market capitalism could finally produce fairness and equality for its Black citizens" (p. 32).

Central to predatory inclusion is the notion that institutions need people to operate and function as intended, and these institutions are hyperconscious of how society and its attendant systems work. As Taylor (2019) noted, the economy needed people to buy homes for the economy to continue functioning. Therefore, Black people were granted access to mortgage loans, but at higher rates, primarily because banks know that homeownership and the notion of owning goods are key elements of the American dream (Rohe & Watson, 2007). In the case of higher education, predatory inclusion manifests in many ways, including the expansion of the contingent academic labor force. In pursuit of profit and productivity, campus leaders situated in all types of higher education institutions actively engage in efforts to grow the ranks of non-tenure-track faculty, a group that now makes up an overwhelming majority of the teaching force in higher education (Kezar, 2012b). Although contingent faculty are granted the privilege of working in higher education institutions, the boundaries of their professional roles are more narrowly defined than their tenure-track and tenured counterparts with regard to participation in shared governance, access to institutional resources and benefits, and opportunities for employment security (Kezar & Maxey, 2014). It is clear that higher education is only fully operational because of non-tenure-track faculty, but traditional and ineffective notions of leadership shut them out of decision-making spaces, while neoliberalism and white supremacy alike have created what is now known as the Gig Academy (Kezar et al., 2019). Higher education leaders and other campus elites have the power to restructure boundaries and invite systematically disadvantaged community members to fully participate in the direction of the institution, but they refrain from adopting more inclusive labor practices in the interest of maintaining their investments in power inequities and other notions of the status quo.

In some cases, boundaries are renegotiated or even violated through the act of interest convergence. Critical race theorists often call attention to the tenet of interest convergence—the idea that institutions and people in power only yield to demands when such demands unite with their own interests (D. A. Bell, 1980; Milner, 2008). Interest convergence suggests that any advancement or opportunity that marginalized groups desire must also benefit white people in some way. Or, better yet, issues such as racism and discrimination have to affect an institution's or organization's political or economic interests or legitimacy for change to occur and demands to be met.

There are many contemporary examples of interest convergence in higher education (Baber, 2015; Ferguson & Davis, 2019; S. R. Harper, 2009). One such example that explicitly engages with the notion of boundary control is

Castagno and Lee's (2007) analysis of interest convergence as a frame for explaining institutional policy (in)action regarding the adoption of an ethnic fraud policy that would protect Indigenous communities' sovereign right to determine tribal affiliation. Drawing on data collected at Midwestern University, a predominantly white research institution, Castagno and Lee found that "the interests of Native people and the institution converge in the sense of wanting to recruit more Indigenous people to the university: both want improved recruitment and retention of American Indian and Alaska Native students. But the cost to the university of implementing a policy guarding against ethnic fraud is simply too high" (p. 8). They further argued that "by not requiring prospective faculty to demonstrate proof of tribal enrollment, the university benefits by getting to 'count' more of its faculty as Native, and the new hires who would otherwise not be considered 'targeted minorities' benefit by being eligible for particular funds, positions, and recognitions" (p. 9). In this sense, administrators responsible for birthing and implementing new policies end up controlling their boundaries to ensure maximum profitability at the expense of systematically disadvantaged individuals and their sacred Indigeneity. Failure to create a meaningful and detailed policy around ethnic fraud only serves the institution and whiteness and no one else. In fact, it actively does harm to Native and Indigenous communities. Higher education leadership, then, is responsible for using Native and Indigenous communities as commodities, cornering them in bounds to keep peace and order, and policing such borders to ensure maximum profitability. These actions elucidate conscious consumption and production of oppressive and dehumanizing ideologies and systems (e.g., neoliberalism, white supremacy).

Higher education plantation leadership uses interest convergence and predatory inclusion as a way to conveniently and strategically answer to powerful corporate interests and notions of whiteness and white supremacy. The protective strategy of boundary control can easily tie back to all of the aforementioned concepts connected to whiteness and white supremacy, since boundary control is deliberately interested in preserving the status quo and keeping a sense of normative order. Predatory inclusion benefits the interests of institutions and what is needed for the institution to remain legitimate in society (i.e., more students and faculty for financial and commodification purposes). Interest convergence as an action allows higher education leaders to police boundaries and open them up in a limited manner when it is advantageous to do so, likely for reactionary purposes such as to respond to student demands or changing market-based demands (Giroux, 2004; Tichavakunda, 2021a).

Impression Management

A second strategy of plantation leadership is impression management. Leaders often idealize their institutions and publicly present a flawless, or close to flawless, public image (Palacio et al., 2002; Sung & Yang, 2008; Weissman, 1990). Leaders do this in a number of ways. They handle issues behind closed doors, silence scandals, minimize the severity of issues related to race and racism, and focus institutional activities on metrics that are measured and valued in rankings and other marks of prestige. They may also construct public images of "inclusive excellence" through communication mediums (e.g., publications or social media). Leaders in positions of power and authority tend to espouse messages of unity and harmony when challenged with issues of race and racism specifically. To take it a step further, leaders in the broader field of education tend to dismiss the centrality of racism and its endemic nature (Bridgeforth, 2021). Hypolite and Stewart (2019) wrote, "By using ambiguous language to bring communities together, university leaders are often absolved from the pressures of having to produce concrete solutions to issues around equity, which is the difference between discourse that preserves rather than transforms campus environments" (p. 8). Thus, impression management is a highly effective plantation leadership strategy that works to maintain a positive public image while exonerating institutions from making structural changes that subvert neoliberalism and white supremacy and challenge the status quo.

Impression management is also a strategy meant to maintain the status quo because it is guided by profit-seeking motives and public relations in the sense that any negative press or participation in institutional activities out of alignment with neoliberal metrics (e.g., rankings) comes with the likelihood of unhappy faculty, students, and staff; questions about legitimacy; or even a decrease in enrollment numbers (Smythe, 2017). Cole and Harper (2017), in their analysis of college presidential statements issued in response to campus racial incidents, supported the argument that impression management is a carefully thought-out strategy by sharing that "academic leaders . . . are crafting statements that respond more favorably to positive public relations than they do to publicly addressing racism on campus. . . . Thus, the historical record of this incident will show that the statement, one of the first artifacts of the institutions' immediate response, had no recollection of the racial incident itself" (p. 327). Publicly addressing racism comes at a cost for the leader operating within the frame of plantation leadership. It also threatens the illusion of a post-racial, race-neutral institution. Notions of order and civility are of the utmost importance. Thus, some leaders act in neutral ways and use impression-management strategies to keep the institution a place of peace and order. But failure to take a stance, along with an inability to attach responsibility to such incidents, outwardly illustrates a disregard for human lives and complicity in racism and white supremacy. Then, impression management becomes not only a priority but also an essential vehicle to preserve whiteness, save plantation leadership, and protect the neoliberal, white supremacist institution.

Impression management as a strategy has distinct ties to concepts like complicity. Plantation leaders' decisions to avoid accountability and systemic change make them complicit in the growing and ongoing violence happening on campuses nationwide under the pretense of whiteness, white supremacy, and even anti-Blackness. Leaders are far more interested in protecting the institution (and its power, profit, and legitimacy) because it in turn protects them. Remaining complicit thus has its benefits.

Impression management was particularly evident in the Nikole Hannah-Jones case. In fact, it was one of the major driving forces in the board of trustees' decision to eventually give Hannah-Jones a tenure vote. Ultimately, they succumbed to public pressures in a last-ditch effort to save UNC–Chapel Hill's reputation and rectify its public image. As stated earlier, however, this action was not taken because the board of trustees believed Hannah-Jones was a victim of injustice. Instead, their public image was becoming tainted as various news outlets picked up on the story, and faculty, students, and staff at UNC–Chapel Hill began to speak up and speak out. Thus, granting Hannah-Jones a vote (not to be confused with granting her tenure) was an impression-management tactic and an effort to save the university's legitimacy, as well as that of the board of trustees. UNC–Chapel Hill was willing

Whiteness and White Supremacy in Higher Education Leadership   111

to do whatever it took to divert attention from the situation, the university, and the board. With the news of Hannah-Jones turning down UNC–Chapel Hill and instead becoming Knight Chair at Howard University, UNC–Chapel Hill and the board could go about their regular operation, gatekeeping white supremacy and advancing the interests of white people and important donors like Walter Hussman.

Conclusion: Oppositional Work and New Possibilities

The plantation leadership framework is meant to provide leaders and scholars of higher education with comprehension and awareness of contemporary higher education leadership roles, tools, and strategies that perpetuate white supremacy. The framework is meant to expose the tensions and contradictions apparent when there is a desire to maintain a status quo order predicated on whiteness and white supremacy while concurrently espousing progressive, often anti-racist, values and commitments (e.g., diversity, equity, inclusion, and the public good). By using plantation leadership as a frame to understand higher education leaders and contemporary leadership processes, leaders and scholars alike should more clearly see neoliberalism, whiteness, and the afterlife of slavery in its fullness. This should create a desire to move into imagination and action. These are inherent to the work of Ruth Wilson Gilmore, Audre Lorde, and countless other (feminist) theorists who have worked to imagine and create otherwise worlds that do not yet exist. The comprehension and awareness of plantation leadership should move us to act and engage in oppositional work—work that pushes beyond the status quo and that seeks to restructure relations and practices in ways that are meaningfully centered on equity and liberation. It is critical that we engage with the comprehension and awareness stage, so that when we imagine something different, "the outcome is not another litany of horror but a re-grounding of the terrain of . . . struggle" (R. W. Gilmore, 2022, p. 37). By challenging plantation leadership and imagining a new system and a new structure, leaders and scholars of higher education alike can dismantle the house and "recycle the material to institutions of our own design, usable by all to produce new and liberating work. Thus, the luxurious [institution] is transformed into the productive. Without both parts of the strategy at work [dismantling and rebuilding], nothing much is different at the end of the day" (R. W. Gilmore, 1993, p. 70).

Mapping the Remainder of the Book

The remainder of the book explores a number of leadership theories and perspectives, such as transformational leadership, processual leadership, and cognitive perspectives on leadership, just to name a few. In each chapter, we explore theories and perspectives in their historical and traditional sense and note how they may support and maintain notions of neoliberalism and whiteness or white supremacy, perhaps unknowingly. We then map new and exciting evolutions of each theory that attempt to engage in the oppositional work that Gilmore (2022) and countless other feminist theorists identify as necessary. These new evolutions are tools, instruments, strategies, and perspectives that scholars have fashioned to help leaders dismantle the master's house, eradicate the plantation, and forge new possibilities rooted in equity and liberation.

Key Points

- Whiteness has transformed beyond a racial group and into a system, structure, and ideology with material benefits, thus shaping higher education and leadership.
- Contemporary higher education leadership operates based on plantation logics and principles that are primarily concerned with institutional legitimacy and power.
- Plantation leadership stifles the actualization of equity and public-good missions and goals in higher education.
- Plantation leadership perpetuates dominant leadership discourse that privileges whiteness, hierarchies, power, control, and order.
- If plantation leadership is not thwarted and equity is not at the center of process and outcome, higher education runs the risk of reproducing harm, institutional power, violence, and inequality.

Discussion Questions

1. How do you see whiteness, white supremacy, and plantation leadership on your own campus?
2. As this chapter has shown, whiteness and white supremacy are at the bedrock of society and institutions of higher education. In recent years, many institutions have espoused commitments to anti-racism, which

could potentially create tensions and contradictions. What can higher education leaders do to ensure that calls for and commitments toward anti-racism are nonperformative and lead to liberatory systemic change?

3. Higher education institutions across the globe are just now beginning to introduce whiteness into their organizational lexicon. In a paragraph or two, create an organizational definition of whiteness and white supremacy for your institution to adapt and reference in their movements toward liberatory systemic change. Be sure to use proper references, some of which can be found in this chapter.

4. What risks does higher education take by introducing and sustaining diversity initiatives without conversations about whiteness and direct action that seeks to disrupt and disassemble structures predicated on whiteness?

5. Refer back to the "Toward a Shared Understanding of Whiteness and White Supremacy" section of the chapter. Continuing applying these concepts to the Nikole Hannah-Jones case.

   a. In what ways was the board of trustees complicit in whiteness?
   b. What anti-Black sentiments were espoused by the board of trustees both in words and in actions?

PART II / Perspectives on Leadership Research and Practice

Chapter 5

Transformational Leadership Perspectives

L eShaun works within the division of student affairs, leading the service-learning program. After a few years, he has noticed that the program really benefits the students but that the community agencies and partners are not getting much out of the partnership. He has also noticed that several of their longtime partners are beginning to drop out and no longer participate in the program. After some community members have a discussion with LeShaun about the lack of reciprocity in the partnerships, they note that they would like to be paid for the training sessions they do for the students and that they desire greater input into the curriculum. LeShaun cannot help but notice that most of the community members are people of color and most of the students from campus are white, which makes these inequalities even worse. LeShaun shares his concerns with other staff members and faculty teaching in the program. Several faculty members state that they appreciate LeShaun's providing such a compelling case for a change, and for inspiring them to act. They work together to create a new vision for the program that better supports community members based on a model of reciprocity. He sets up an appointment with the vice president for student affairs about his concerns. The vice president says they do not really have the money to support these kinds of changes and questions whether there is such a lack of reciprocity in the existing model. She points to all the hours that students put in at these community agencies and notes that the agencies have not complained

118   *Perspectives on Leadership Research and Practice*

in the past, so what is happening now? The vice president seems to be indicating that LeShaun has instigated the complaints. LeShaun is truly surprised and begins to experience leadership as a barrier.

Resisting neoliberal and white supremacist leadership will require embracing and building on transformational theories of leadership through new theories that evolved from this tradition—namely, shared-equity leadership and leadership for liberation. Transformational theories of leadership have the potential to create new, more progressive futures that address the challenges of racial inequity and other forms of inequity. Transformational leadership theories emerged out of social constructivist and critical paradigms of leadership that diverge from traditional, functionalist leadership theories. Such traditional trait and behavior theories reinscribe control, top-down power hierarchies, and purport to have identified effective universal leadership strategies based on studies of white, male leaders. Instead, transformational leadership breaks from these aforementioned approaches to leadership.

In this chapter we review transformational leadership theories that emerged in the late 1970s but deliberately focus on newer extensions of these original theories and concepts that push toward progressive and just ends. Our review of transformational leadership theories includes defining them and tracing their emergence as a response to a long tradition of power and influence theories, exploring key assumptions and contributions, reviewing a select number of major studies, describing studies of transformational leadership in higher education, identifying key concepts, providing critiques, and outlining new theories that address these critiques. We underscore how transformational leadership can be a problem in that it may reinforce white supremacy and neoliberalism through its emphasis on a heroic single leader, often in a position of authority, who has typically been a white male. But transformational leadership is also a pathway in that it emphasizes moral ends, care for others as part of a leadership process, inspiration, and leadership with purpose.

Definition and Emergence

Transformational leadership is an approach in which leaders act in reciprocal and mutual ways with followers (we prefer the term *organizational members*, but *followers* is used in the literature on transformational leadership; throughout the chapter, we will use both terms), appeal to their higher needs, and inspire and motivate followers to move toward a particular purpose—many argue, one tied to moral ends (J. M. Burns, 1978). In Burns's (1978) influential book, *Leadership*, he introduces the concept of transforming leadership, which drew upon his historical research on political leaders. According to Burns, transforming leadership is a process in which leaders and followers help each other to advance to a higher level of moral purpose and motivations. Although transformational leadership is still a fairly new theory, having emerged in the late 1970s, Burns's work is part of a larger tradition of power and influence theories that include charismatic and transactional theories of leadership that have been around for hundreds of years and are among some of the earliest thinking about leadership.

Weber (1924) is credited for labeling both charismatic and transactional theories; both became scholarly topics of study after Weber's articulation of them. Charismatic theories of leadership, popular at the dawn of the twentieth century, explored how successful leaders were able to persuade and inspire followers (Weber, 1924). Communication and vision-setting are two of the foremost concepts related to charismatic theory. Transactional theories emerged in the 1920s, exploring how leaders were able to induce behaviors in followers, typically through reward and punishment. Since Weber's articulation, charismatic and transactional theories have been written about under different labels over time.

J. M. Burns's transformational leadership theory interrogated leaders' motivation for leading and critiqued how many leaders assume a position or role merely to gain power and influence without any moral underpinnings, a typical approach within charismatic and transactional theories of leadership. Burns argued that leaders need to be grounded in an ethical system and morals to pursue socially desirable ends. A focus on *moral* motivation and socially desirable ends of leadership were new concepts to leadership thinking. Earlier leadership theories focused on outcomes, but almost exclusively on the outcomes of organizational effectiveness and performance. Although effectiveness may be socially desirable, in transformational leadership theory, moral ends that lead to human flourishing take prominence over purely functionalist or pragmatic objectives. Burns noted that this new leadership approach was transformational because it caused progressive changes in both individuals and systems. Additionally, transformational leadership enhances the

120   *Perspectives on Leadership Research and Practice*

motivation, morale, and performance of followers by offering a role model for followers, inspiring them with a vision and moral purpose, challenging followers to take greater ownership for their work, and helping them evolve and grow. Burns is also credited with bringing a focus on empowerment and inspiration rather than force or reward, which underlie earlier transactional leadership approaches to influence.

While Burns (1978) has been credited with developing the theory of transformational leadership, it has been elaborated on over the subsequent decades by researchers such as Avolio and Yammarino (2013), Bass (1985), Kark and Shamir (2013), Kouzes and Posner (2002), and Rost (1991), among others. Those who built from Burns's work also focus on moving away from earlier transactional and charismatic theories of leadership, arguing that leadership should focus on moral or ethical ends and that the interaction with followers should demonstrate care and mutuality.

One scholar who has notably extended Burns's work is Bass (1985). Bass's scholarship extended Burns's work from political science into business and other organizational settings, exploring how to fit the concepts of transformational leadership into more institutional spaces while maintaining the same characteristics. Bass also helped to operationalize and test the notion of transformational leadership by developing a survey instrument called the Multifactor Leadership Questionnaire (MLQ). The MLQ was based on his research that asked individuals to describe leaders they considered to be transformational. Bass (1985) conceptualized transformational leadership into four key areas: individualized consideration, intellectual stimulation, inspirational motivation, and idealized influence. Individualized consideration is the degree to which the leader attends to each follower's needs, acts as a mentor or coach to the follower, and listens to the follower's concerns and needs. Intellectual stimulation captures how the leader challenges assumptions, takes risks, and solicits followers' ideas. Leaders in this area stimulate and encourage creativity in their followers. Inspirational motivation is the degree to which the leader articulates a vision that is appealing and inspiring to followers. Leaders with inspirational motivation challenge followers with high standards, communicate optimism about future goals, and provide meaning for the task at hand. Idealized influence is how a leader serves a role model for high ethical behavior, instills pride, and gains respect and trust. Bass and Burns are considered the foundational scholars on transformational leadership.

In the following section, we detail additional elaborations of transformational leadership through a review of major assumptions and findings from key studies.

Major Assumptions and Contributions

Transformational leadership perspectives were a corrective to many earlier leadership theories in which leaders did not act with the best interests of followers in mind. Particularly, scholars advocating for this theory have positioned it against related charismatic theories of leadership, in which leaders strongly influenced followers and motivated them toward ends that sometimes were dubious or even violent or hateful (J. M. Burns, 1978). Transformational leadership also worked as a corrective to transactional theories of leadership in which leaders bartered with organizational members to achieve their ends by conceding to some organizational members' interests but did not attend to an underlying ethical or human dimension. Transactional theories were based on leaders exchanging rewards or administering punishments for following or not following their wishes. In what follows, we outline four main assumptions that serve as major contributions to transformational leadership theory: moral purpose, mutual and position interactions between leaders and followers, separating leadership from position, and treating leadership as a process.

One of the main contributions of transformational leadership is that it brought a decidedly ethical, values-based, or moral dimension to leadership that had been lacking in earlier theories. J. M. Burns (1978) suggested that if leaders did not have a moral or socially desirable purpose, they were not executing leadership. A second major departure from earlier theories is that the theory defined leadership as a mutual process based on an ethic of care for the follower. Many of the earlier theories of leadership did not articulate the type of relationship that should exist between leader and follower. Burns suggested that if the leadership process involves any type of exploitation of followers— even if effective and socially just ends are achieved—it does not constitute leadership. The interactions between leaders and followers need to be mutual and, ideally, result in the growth of followers. We believe these two assets of transformational leadership—moral purpose and mutual interactions—are incredibly important to address both the neoliberal and white supremacist contexts. Neoliberal leadership and leadership that upholds the project of

122   *Perspectives on Leadership Research and Practice*

white supremacy do not have any moral or socially desirable purposes as a necessary part of leadership, beyond an extremely narrow definition of economic viability and efficiency. Also, as is quite clear from the chapter on neoliberal leadership, organizational members (followers) are generally not treated with an ethic of care in the current leadership environment. In fact, it is quite the opposite. Both neoliberal and white supremacist leadership approaches actively dehumanize and exploit. And both leadership approaches, when taken in tandem, create unethical institutions like the one that exists today.

J. M. Burns (1978) originally considered transformational leadership hierarchical, with certain individuals as leaders and others as followers. He did not, however, necessarily identify the leader as an individual with a position of authority or formal power. His views of leadership left it possible for anyone to be a leader. Therefore, his approach opened the possibility for leadership to be considered nonhierarchical, which is another critical contribution of transformational leadership. As a result of Burns's work to open leadership roles to a more expansive group, subsequent studies began to look at the role of nonpositional leaders and how followers may move into leadership roles from time to time (Kezar & Lester, 2011; Pearce & Conger, 2003).

Burns also considered leadership a process of interaction between leaders and followers, and he stressed the importance of examining those interactions. The leader sets high standards and purposes for followers, engaging them through inspiration, exemplary practice, collaboration, and trust. Many earlier theories did not focus on the process and relationships, but instead treated leadership as a set of individual (and idealized) characteristics, traits, and behaviors. Burns's focus on process, in general, is a contribution to leadership theory. However, his specific focus on processes like collaboration and the development of trust forged new lines of inquiry into the interrelational aspects of leadership that happen over time.

Key Findings and Insights

Research on transformational leadership has unearthed critical insights, including a more defined list of characteristics for transformational leaders, its effectiveness in meeting outcomes such as organizational goals and follower satisfaction, and the applicability of transformational leadership in different cultural contexts and sectors. We highlight studies and findings of transformational leadership and explore specific findings relevant to higher education.

Studies of transformational leadership focus on the identification of characteristics and qualities of transformational leadership such as inspiration, trust, passion, and commitment (Bass, 1985; Kouzes & Posner, 2002). Perhaps one of the most cited articulations of transformational leadership is Kouzes and Posner's (2002), which identified five types of behaviors in transformational leadership: challenging the process (searching for opportunities and experimenting); inspiring a shared vision (motivating people toward a vision); enabling others to act (fostering collaboration and self-development); modeling the way (setting an example); and encouraging the heart (celebrating achievements). Over the past four decades, hundreds of studies have been conducted that articulate and describe these facets of transformational leadership (Dinh et al., 2014). And over time, transformational leadership studies have articulated features that show an expanded set of characteristics and actions that encourage and support transformational leadership, such as sharing power, being willing to learn from others, and being sensitive to each team member's needs for achievement and growth (Dinh et al, 2014). Some studies identify a focus on the need for followers to be transformed as part of transformational leadership, rather than the outcomes being the focus of transformation. For example, Bass (1990) proposed that transformational leadership is the process through which leaders broaden and elevate the interests of their followers, generate awareness and acceptance of the purposes and mission of the group, and motivate followers to look beyond their own self-interests for the good of the group (Bass & Stogdill, 1990).

Research on transformational leadership behaviors demonstrates that they are associated with leaders' effectiveness and lead to more satisfaction among followers than transactional leadership behaviors (Avolio & Bass, 1991; Sadeghi & Pihie, 2012; Zacharatos et al., 2000). Hundreds of primary studies and dozens of meta-analyses have consistently identified moderate to strong relationships between transformational leadership and outcomes such as performance, engagement, satisfaction, commitment, and turnover (e.g., DeRue et al., 2011; Judge & Piccolo, 2004; Lowe et al., 1996; Wang et al., 2011). Additionally, transformational leadership has been associated with a range of other outcomes including greater creativity among followers (Zacher & Johnson, 2015); cultural intelligence (Keung & Rockinson-Szapkiw, 2013); emotional intelligence (G. M. Mir & Abbasi, 2012); increased innovation (Owusu-Agyeman, 2019); organizational citizenship (Majeed et al., 2017); the

124 Perspectives on Leadership Research and Practice

ability to address resistance (McBride, 2010); spiritual intelligence and mindfulness (Gieseke, 2014); and resilience (Wasden, 2014), to name a few. There have been hundreds of studies examining positive outcomes of transformational leadership, making it one of the most robust leadership concepts.

Transformational leadership appears to be generalizable across different cultures. One effort that explored its transferability is the Global Leadership and Organizational Effectiveness Project, which examined transformational leadership behaviors and attitudes internationally across sixty-two cultures (Den Hartog et al., 1999). Part of the project was to study whether certain traits of transformational leadership transcend cultural contexts. Despite traditionally recognized social and cultural differences, the findings of this project supported the claim that certain attributes are universally associated with transformational leaders. In most cultures studied, leaders were identified as transformational if they exhibited the following qualities: encouraging, positive, motivational, confidence building, dynamic, risk taking, and possessing foresight. Importantly, countries differ in the extent to which leaders practice transformational leadership (L. Y. C. Leong & Fischer, 2011; Dickson et al., 2012). Other researchers investigated universal versus culturally contingent leadership attributes and found similar results. Dorfman et al. (1997) conducted a study in five countries in order to investigate which leadership attributes are universal and which are culturally contingent. The study, conducted in Japan, South Korea, Taiwan, Mexico, and the United States, identified leader supportiveness, contingent rewards (e.g., rewards based on meeting identified goals), and charisma as universally accepted, while participativeness, directedness, and contingent punishment (e.g., administering negative feedback in the form of reprimands, criticisms, or disapproval to employees who exhibit poor performance or undesirable behavior) were culturally specific. Research suggests that there is evidence for both universal and culturally contingent leader characteristics that should be taken into account when identifying successful leaders in different countries. Also, it appears that people may perceive transformational leadership similarly in different countries, but the outcomes may differ. For example, Holten et al. (2018) found no difference between native Danes and immigrants in their perception of transformational leadership, but they also found that transformational leadership is not a universal predictor of outcomes. It predicted none of the outcomes for immigrants, but it did predict change in job satisfaction and well-being for native Danes. Holten et al. hypothesized that immigrants face societal disadvantages that mitigate the positive impacts of transformational leadership.

Transformational leadership has been found relevant across sectors, including higher education. Studies of transformational leadership in higher education have found that leaders at different levels (e.g., presidents, deans, and provosts) use both transformational and transactional forms of leadership (Gmelch & Wolverton, 2002; Harrison, 2011; Kezar & Eckel, 2008). Studies have continuously found that using both approaches is effective for leading change and enhancing organizational functioning (Bensimon, 1993; Kezar & Eckel, 2007; Komives, 1991; Wolverton, 2002). Leaders identified a preference for transformational approaches but utilize transactional approaches to be successful within their environments (Kezar & Eckel, 2007). All of the researchers hypothesize that the hierarchical structure, reward system, and tenure and promotion processes in the higher education institution favor a transactional approach, even though many leaders prefer using transformational leadership (Bensimon, 1993; Kezar & Eckel, 2008; Komives, 1991; Wolverton, 2002).The studies do not explore the impact of the neoliberal context, but the trends outlined in chapter 3 suggest that transactional approaches will be favored over transformational ones, making the use of transformational leadership more challenging in the coming years.

In terms of outcomes, studies in higher education generally identify transformational leadership as an effective strategy to create change (Lo et al., 2010). Research also suggests that certain issues may require more transformational forms of leadership. For example, Aguirre and Martinez (2002) examined the role of leaders in diversifying college campuses and found that utilizing a more transformational view of leadership was more successful for leading diversity, equity, and inclusion efforts. Transformational leadership has also been identified as important for moving higher education out of the status quo and making many needed changes to increase equity and improve teaching and learning, technology, assessment, and other critical challenges facing higher education (Balwant, 2016; Harrison, 2011; Jyoti & Bhau, 2015; Kezar & Eckel, 2008).

A few studies have examined the actual usage of transformational leadership among higher education leaders and found that it is used with much the same frequency as other approaches to leadership, including passive approaches—in which leaders shirk their responsibilities and are indifferent toward their subordinates—and transactional approaches (Bodla & Nawaz, 2010). Studies have also explored the role of institutional context. For example, Bodla and Nawaz's (2010) study revealed that the faculty members in both public and private institutions were practicing transformational and passive or avoidant leadership styles to the same extent. On the other hand, the transactional leadership style was being practiced more frequently by faculty members in the private sector than by those in the public sector. More studies of contextual differences might shed more light on transformational leadership's potential versus other approaches within different sectors in higher education. Although transformational leadership is likely the most studied approach outside of higher education, its application in studies of higher education has not been as extensive.

Key Concepts

Transformational leadership added three key concepts that have expanded our understanding of leadership: ethics, social change, and empowerment. Here we review these concepts, as well as how the neoliberal environment and white supremacy have shaped and continue to shape them, essentially preventing these new concepts from entering mainstream leadership and meeting their potential. This chapter, in particular, extensively covers these key concepts because they have remained crucial in the evolution of leadership and theories. All three stem from central ideas offered by transformational leadership theories.

Ethics and Morality

Transformational leadership connects ethics to leadership by focusing on moral or socially desirable ends. Scholars working within this line of research continue to emphasize that leadership processes, interactions, and ends must all be grounded in an ethical or moral context (Kouzes & Posner, 2002; Rost, 1991). While there is not a specific ethical or moral lens guiding transformational leaders, different ideals have been presented over the years, including Robert K. Greenleaf's servant leadership (1998), in which a leader is focused on improving the environment for the people they are leading. The moral lens is leadership as stewardship and a sense of responsibility to and for stakeholders. Starratt (2004) suggested that three pillars guide leaders, an ethic of care, an ethic of justice, and an ethic of critique. Avolio and Gardner (2005) noted the importance of follower development as part of the ethical underpinning. Others have emphasized certain characteristics or behaviors that will lead to a moral end, such as integrity, honesty, or transparency (C. W. Stewart, 2019).

In higher education, the majority of the literature on the moral role of leadership in higher education is historical and written by college presidents (Hesburgh, 1994; S. J. Nelson, 2000; Vaughn, 1992). There is a body of literature that describes how current leadership challenges around diversity, community engagement, environmental issues, and globalization have an ethical dimension and require leaders to have experience with ethical decision-making. This literature emphasizes the importance of ethics and moral leadership because of the role higher education plays in society, its responsibility for the public good, and its tax-exempt status, as well as the fact that a university's lay board of governors is responsible to a host of stakeholders (Olscamp, 2003). Another study that highlighted the role of moral leadership is that by Wilcox and Ebbs (1992), which articulated a model of ethical decision-making to help inform the practices of successful leadership in higher education institutions and to provide a strong ethical base for leadership. They recommended that college and university leaders develop an ethos of ethics on campus. Typically, an ethical tone is not set by top leadership; the authors believe this missing tone affects leadership throughout the campus, diminishing the ethical dimension. Ethics are so important that they cannot be left up to individuals but must be integrated into the fabric of the institution—its structures, culture, and value system. Wilcox and Ebb articulated an approach for creating such a culture around ethics to guide leadership in higher education.

Within the increasingly neoliberal environment, we have seen a decline in literature about the moral role of leadership as well as the role of ethics in leadership's decision-making. In fact, there has been virtually no writing on the topic in the last three decades. Given that this was already a gap in our understanding of leadership, more attention to this area is needed. Downplaying moral arguments suggests that the interests of leadership are aligned with all organizational members, which tends to reinforce whiteness.

Social Change

Historically leadership has served the role of social control. From Plato to Machiavelli to modern military and business notions of leadership, the goal has been to maintain the status quo (H. S. Astin & Leland, 1991). And even when leaders have created change, it has often been quite conservative and focused on the interest of elites. Transformational theories of leadership were among the first to highlight social change as a goal for leadership within mainstream, traditional, white male approaches. Over the past four decades, critical theories of leadership have been instrumental to positing the role of social change for leadership. Critical theorists are much more likely to specifically describe the social changes they are focused on, including equity, justice, care, and compassion. As will be highlighted in future chapters, studies of women and people of color find that these types of specific social ends are a necessary component of leadership.

The focus on social change can be seen in several examples of higher education leadership. One model developed within the field of higher education that reflects the tenets of transformational leadership is the social change model of leadership development. The model is organized around seven core values beginning with the letter c, which are organized into three levels—individual values (consciousness of self, congruence, and commitment), group-process values (collaboration, common purpose, and controversy with civility), and community and societal values (citizenship) (H. S. Astin et al., 1996). The ultimate goal of the social change model is to alter the social world to make it a better place for oneself and others. The model underscores the work that needs to be done at the individual level to participate in a group process that is guided by specific values and is oriented toward broader social change. This model has also helped foster self-reflection about values and, like J. M. Burns's (1978) earlier work on transformational leadership, suggests a moral role for leaders. Leadership, as framed by the social change model, is explicitly engaged in furthering social equality, democracy, and justice. Dozens of studies have explored how college students and staff members on campus develop as social change leaders (Dugan, 2006a, 2006b; Dugan & Komives, 2010).

Another work that addresses transformational leadership is *Leadership Reconsidered: Engaging Higher Education in Social Change* (A. W. Astin & Astin, 2000), which argued for higher education leadership to more fully engage service to society and the processes of social change. The book applied the earlier research by H. S. Astin and Leland (1991) on women leaders on college campuses and the ways they lead to enact social change and utilize processes like empowerment, collaboration, and shared purpose. The book articulated how higher education leaders need to ground their day-to-day practice in the work of social change as well as encourage this activity among faculty, staff, and students. The authors identified the value ends of leadership as the following: to champion equity, social justice, and quality of life; to expand access and opportunity; to encourage respect for difference and diversity; to strengthen democracy, civic life, and civic responsibility; to promote cultural enrichment, creative expression, and intellectual honesty; and to foster the advancement of knowledge and personal freedom coupled with social responsibility (A. W. Astin & Astin, 2000, p. 11). The authors outlined five individual leadership characteristics and five group leadership behaviors that are essential for higher education leaders who wish to encourage this process of social change. The individual qualities are self-knowledge, authenticity and integrity, commitment, empathy, and competence. The five group behaviors are collaboration, identification of a shared purpose, disagreement with respect, division of labor, and creation of a respectful learning environment. To date, there have been no studies utilizing this framework to understand higher education leadership from a social change perspective, though Kezar et al. (2017) did describe how faculty and staff can support students in developing skills in leadership for social change.

There are also several researchers who have examined the role of leaders in social change, particularly women and people of color. Hart (2008) and Ardoin et al. (2019) documented the role of faculty and staff in grassroots organizing on campuses to develop more gender-friendly policies and practices. Kezar and Lester (2012) studied faculty and staff leaders who foster important grassroots social changes on campus, such as ones that address environmental and sustainability issues; diversity, equity, and inclusion; greater college access; student support; and improvements to the teaching and learning environment. They noted that most of these leaders tend to be women and people of color, which highlights how traditional leadership is reinforcing whiteness and patriarchy and demonstrates that new theories and approaches are needed to dismantle these approaches. Kezar and Lester (2012), Hart (2008), and Ardoin et al. (2019) identified sets of leadership strategies that parallel those often seen within the social movement literature, such as protest and demonstrations, as well as those used by tempered radicals, such as putting up posters for a social cause. Additionally, Kezar and Lester (2012) documented some new leadership strategies that are used by higher education activists, such as partnering with students and using educational spaces as forums for collective action. Santamaría (2014) illustrated the social change fostered by faculty and administrative leaders of color in addition to the novel social movement–oriented strategies they use. Sudbury & Okazawa-Rey (2009) demonstrated how faculty of color often lead change through their social justice–oriented scholarship (again a tactic that is novel and specific to higher education), which they then use to lead on specific issues on campus such as hiring diverse scholars, addressing campus climate, or encouraging sustainability.

Several of the leadership theories reviewed in this book focus on and elaborate on the importance of collaboration, networks, and partnering for leadership in social change, which is also central to transformational leadership and the social change model of leadership. J. M. Burns's (1978) emphasis on the mutual relationship between leader and follower opened up the door to the consideration of collaboration, which has been developed extensively within other theories of leadership. Transformational leadership theories make clear that desirable social ends cannot be achieved by the leader alone and must involve collaboration between leader and follower, which significantly alters the nature of leadership. In the processual leadership chapter, we will describe the way that collaboration has been pivotal to all more progressive forms of leadership that focus on process and collective action.

Today's environment, however, is moving higher education leadership toward social control again and away from social change and the public purposes of higher education. The trends within the Gig Academy work against collective action by fragmenting workers and making it difficult for them to meet and strategize toward collective action and grassroots leadership, which also reinforces whiteness because these efforts are often led by faculty and staff of color and women.

Empowerment

Empowerment is the practice of sharing power and enabling other constituents to act on issues they feel are important and relevant (H. S. Astin & Leland, 1991; Eddy & VanDerLinden, 2006; Hechanova & Cementina-Olpoc, 2013; Jyoti & Bhau, 2015; Komives et al., 1998; Rubin, 2002; Shakeshaft, 1999). A major contribution of the research on empowerment is that it helps to distinguish leadership from authority and hierarchy, expanding the unit of analysis for research and the way that people conceptualize leadership (Jordan et al., 2017). Because organizations have traditionally been structured to reinforce hierarchy, social control, and the concentration of power in positional leaders, empowerment and the sharing of power have not come easily (Shaver, 2004). Almost all of the extensions of transformational leadership note the importance of empowerment (H. S. Astin & Leland, 1991; Komives et al., 1998; Rubin, 2002). For example, the social change model of leadership emphasizes empowerment and working synergistically toward a common goal (H. S. Astin et al., 1996). This model articulates the central role of the leader and does not define the leader as someone in a position of power. Interdependence between different leaders and followers is central, and power is about energy, not control (Shaver, 2004). The leader is described as a facilitator who enables others to act collectively toward a goal. Empowerment is also emphasized in terms of leaders working together to help define the mutual goals of the group. The chain of influence proceeds between people instead of passing through the hierarchy, again emphasizing empowerment rather than hierarchical relations.

The majority of the literature on empowerment provides techniques and models for breaking down hierarchical structures through the delegation of authority, the creation of teams, and the destruction of political environments (H. S. Astin & Leland, 1991; Jordan et al., 2017; Komives et al., 1998). The importance of developing a culture of trust as a prominent strategy for ensuring empowerment is highlighted in the literature. If people do not trust one another, they are unlikely to feel that empowerment is authentic, and empowering others builds trust (Hechanova & Cementina-Olpoc, 2013; Komives et al., 1998). Many studies also emphasize that environments that foster democratic practices are linked to empowerment.

Early on, studies of leaders in higher education identified the central role of empowerment. Given the historical structures of shared governance, faculty expected to be empowered as a part of the leadership process (Birnbaum, 1992). Even the earliest studies found that shared leadership was extremely beneficial. For example, Birnbaum (1992) observed, "When leadership is

132   *Perspectives on Leadership Research and Practice*

shared, a college has multiple waves of sensing environmental change, checking for problems, and monitoring campus performance. Shared leadership is likely to provide a college with a more complex way of thinking" (p. 187). These early studies on higher education identified ways that leaders in positions of authority could create empowerment by encouraging and rewarding participation, collecting and disseminating data of interest to constituents, providing forums for constituents to talk together, and promoting a campus climate of openness. Through these processes, leaders in positions of authority are able to identify informal leaders whom they can empower to be part of a broader leadership process. The growth of literature on shared leadership—discussed later—also demonstrates and provides evidence for the importance of empowerment to successful leadership processes (Kezar & Holcombe, 2017).

Some research on higher education has also examined barriers to empowerment, particularly the role of power conditions and how they affect leadership processes. Kezar (2002) found that individuals' beliefs about leadership are affected by oppression they have experienced and that many individuals will not feel empowered or will have difficulty embracing an empowering environment if they have experienced environments that limit their power and influence in the past. Research on empowerment remains limited, and we need more studies on barriers to as well as successful models of empowerment.

Critiques

Several critiques have been lodged against transformational leadership theories, including how they still reinforce hierarchy and position, reinforce a divide between leaders and followers, leave the moral ends open to ambiguity, allow interactions to be defined by elites and thus do not lead to empowerment or mutuality, and how theories have not been explored nearly as extensively outside of white, westernized contexts (Dugan, 2017; Kezar et al., 2019).

While transformational leadership has the advantage of emphasizing ethics or moral purpose, social change, and positive and humanistic interactions including empowerment, it also reinforces dimensions of patriarchy and white supremacy through emphasis on a leader who is hierarchically positioned (the leader-follower dichotomy) to organizational members, and we know that white men tend to be in positions of power (Dugan, 2017). When those in traditional positions of power envision transformation, it typically reinforces the status quo rather than transformational ends. In addition, in today's neoliberal environment we have seen that when those in positions of power consider the outcomes of leadership, they tend to think in terms of return on investment and efficiency. Neoliberalism also focuses on the centralization of power and the elevation of individuals who tend to come from elite backgrounds, which means that the interests of other groups, including people of color, can often be left out by leadership.

As we look at the concepts of ethics and morality, the question that continues to arise is, Whose morals and whose ethics? And how can we ensure social change is aimed at equity and justice if this is not specified? Today's transformational leadership approaches are not able to address this critique, as they leave the ultimate purpose open-ended. Transformational leadership might better meet its goals if it were aligned with social movement theories and approaches to leadership that advance ends typically aligned with those marginalized in society and often support their interests (although conservative and unjust groups have also used social movement theories). Additionally, followers can be open to exploitation in some situations, such as when they are asked to align their personal values with the values of the team or organization. If the organization does not represent the interests of all of its followers, then the starting assumptions for transformational leadership can be problematic (Siangchokyoo et al., 2020).

Another critique is that the notion of humanistic interactions has typically been defined through the perspective of white men, and a needed corrective is to understand humanistic relations from the perspective of nonwhite people, women, and other traditionally marginalized groups. While transformational leadership has been found across cultural contexts, most of the cultures explored are white and hierarchical. Further, the concept of empowerment has been questioned because it is often those in positions of authority who make decisions on who is empowered. This allows for abuses to emerge, as there is no check on how leaders make decisions about empowerment and whether they would empower those whose interests are not aligned with their own. As we look at evolutions in transformational leadership, we address many of these critiques.

New Evolutions

Two new models have emerged in higher education that advance transformational theories of leadership: shared-equity leadership and leadership for liberation. These models serve as a corrective by breaking down the hierarchical orientation of transformational leadership theories. Both are grounded in the belief that leadership is nonhierarchical, process-based, and collaborative. Both evolutions move away from the language of *followers*, instead reframing individuals outside of formal leadership positions as *organizational community members*. These approaches are clear that equity, social justice, and liberation are the desired ends of leadership. Mutual interactions are reinforced by new values and principles (e.g., vulnerability, transparency, and fellowship) that are brought to leadership. Social change, ethics, and empowerment are more readily the outcome of these new approaches.

Next, we review in detail how these approaches challenge the neoliberal and white supremacist roots of transformational leadership theories.

Shared-Equity Leadership

A recent evolution of transformational leadership is shared-equity leadership (Kezar et al., 2021). The ultimate goal of shared-equity leadership is to dismantle inequitable structures and policies in order to advance and realize equity. This model of leadership directly designates the end goal, and all of the activities that are a part of the model help to advance that ultimate goal. Therefore, the strong focus on social change, as well as the specific articulation of the type of social change, is an evolution of the transformational model of leadership that better aligns it with the progressive goals outlined as important for future leadership that combats neoliberalism and white supremacy. The more that leadership research specifically examines and identifies leadership approaches that advance equity, justice, and public purposes, the more likely it is that our systems will change and leadership will serve as a progressive pathway forward.

Shared-equity leadership directly connects the aim of leadership with advancing the goals of equity, an ethical imperative of transformational leadership. The very explicit connection to equity and social justice aims in this model addresses the critique regarding whose interests are served in transformational leadership. Additionally, shared-equity leadership is inherently collaborative and inclusive, which builds from the relational emphasis in transformational leadership and also reinforces shared notions of leadership. The collective nature of shared-equity leadership and the equal relationships among the leadership collective emphasized in this model address the critique about hierarchy remaining in transformational leadership models. Participation in a collective leadership process requires that those involved are empowered and given authority to act in service of shared-equity goals. The values and practices in shared-equity leadership reflect the ethic of care and positive relationships that underscored early theories of transformational leadership. Yet the specific values and practices are more strongly aligned with the goals of meeting equity and advancing diversity and inclusion.

The shared-equity leadership approach has three main elements: (1) individuals who have undergone a *personal journey* toward critical consciousness of systemic power and oppression, cementing their commitment to equity; (2) *values* that are shared among members of the leadership team or group; and (3) a set of *practices* that leaders continually enact that enable them both to share leadership and to create more just and equitable conditions on their campuses. Shared-equity leadership requires a critical mass of leaders who have undergone a personal journey to critical consciousness of systemic oppression and who collectively embody the values and practices. Every individual does not have to embody every value and practice. Instead, when leaders work together in teams, or when leadership is distributed broadly throughout an organization, different individuals may bring expertise or skills in different areas.

The heart of shared-equity leadership is a personal journey toward critical consciousness of systemic oppression such as racism, sexism, and classism, which directly challenges whiteness as people examine their own privilege as well as oppression. Having leaders engage in personal transformation toward critical consciousness ensures leaders are not operating out of implicit white supremacy, as has happened with many transformational leaders who have not undergone their own personal transformations. Thus, transformational leadership is just as much about individual transformation as it is about altering organizational and societal structures. This model makes evident that one cannot transform external structures without personal transformation. This journey toward critical consciousness of oppression can occur in several different ways, and the model expands avenues for critical consciousness

136 Perspectives on Leadership Research and Practice

from earlier studies (Kezar et al., 2021). Many campus leaders have described how their personal experiences with exclusion and discrimination affected their commitment and passion to do equity leadership work, acknowledging the role of oppression in their lives and others'. Others shared stories about their professional background detailing years of training and learning that informed their desire to be social justice leaders. What this model emphasizes is that transformation is both personal change and external change happening in the social world. In this model, the two are linked, and individual transformation and an awareness of white supremacy and various other forms of oppression are part of the broader social transformation. This also builds from transformational leadership, which emphasizes organizational members' growth, but here the personal transformation is aligned not with broad and unspecified organizational values but with critical consciousness of oppressive systems.

Equity leaders operate with a particular set of values that animate their work: love and care, vulnerability, humility, transparency, courage, self-accountability, creativity and innovation, and comfort with being uncomfortable. Transformational leadership does not ground itself in specific values, so the values of shared-equity leadership provide an important foundation needed to do the work of personal, group, and social transformation for equity. By engaging specific values, transformational leadership is less likely to go off track and succumb to the forces of whiteness and neoliberalism. Additionally, these specific humanistic values address the critique that transformational leadership theories do not have reciprocal relationships.

In addition to holding these values, leaders also enact particular practices that embody shared-equity leadership. Practices are regular activities that leaders perform both individually and collectively to accomplish their equity goals. These include one foundational practice—centering systemically marginalized groups' needs—and five practice areas: communication, development, relationships, structure, and ones that challenge the status quo (fig. 5.1). The practices include setting expectations, building trust, cultivating positive relationships, diminishing hierarchy, welcoming disagreements and tensions, questioning, disrupting, using language intentionally, learning and helping others learn, hiring diverse leaders, creating rewards and incentives, modeling, and implementing new approaches to accountability. A few of these are part of transformational leadership (such as cultivating positive relationships,

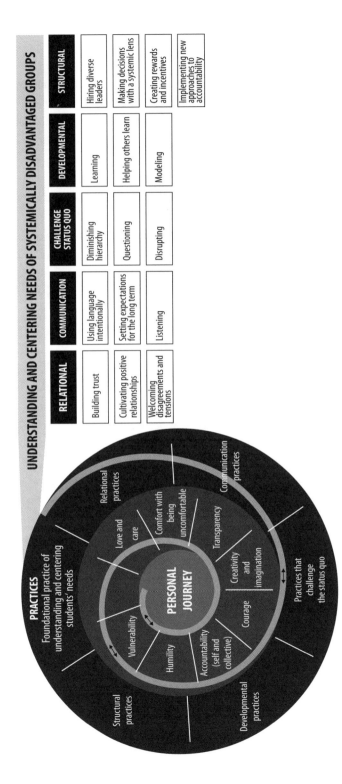

Figure 5.1 Shared-Equity Leadership. *Source:* Courtesy of Pullias Center for Higher Education, University of Southern California

138 *Perspectives on Leadership Research and Practice*

modeling, and helping others learn), and a few are part of authentic leadership theories (such as vulnerability), but many other practices seen as critical to shared-equity leadership are not identified in any other models of leadership, such as disrupting, questioning, and diminishing hierarchy. These practices address the critiques raised about transformational leadership theories reinforcing the status quo, and the practices of disrupting and questioning press transformational approaches to dismantling the status quo.

The elements in this model are not static and separate, nor are they part of a linear process with discrete steps. Some sort of personal journey toward critical consciousness is generally necessary for leaders who engage in shared-equity leadership, as the values and practices are all connected and interact with one another in a mutually reinforcing way. As noted earlier, this model makes evident that one cannot transform external structures without the personal transformation, so the work begins personally.

LEADERSHIP FOR LIBERATION

Another evolution of transformational leadership was offered by Harper and Kezar (2021), who provided an addendum to and critique of the social change model of leadership using critical race theory combined with Yosso's (2005) theory of community cultural wealth called "leadership for liberation." Harper and Kezar challenge whether the social change model addresses power, oppression, and the knowledge stakeholders bring from communities of color. Further, Harper and Kezar critiqued the social change model for overlooking the perspectives of racially minoritized individuals and how they experience the social world and leadership. They draw on Yosso (2005) for a counterargument that communities of color exist as spaces of wealth and therefore students (and faculty and staff) from communities of color come to formal education systems with an accumulation of knowledge and capital to help them succeed and persist in spaces not built with them in mind. Yosso identified forms of capital among racial and ethnic minorities that are often overlooked but serve as critical skill sets and knowledge that help these populations to succeed despite their location at the margins. Yosso outlined six forms of capital that compose community cultural wealth and are integrated as new values for the social change model of leadership: navigational capital, social capital, linguistic capital, aspirational capital, resistant capital, and familial capital.

Transformational Leadership Perspectives 139

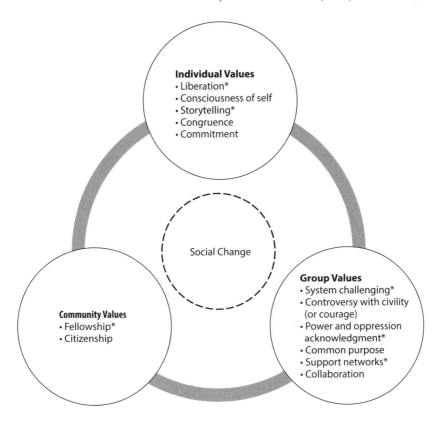

Figure 5.2 Leadership for Liberation / Social Change Model Integration (asterisk connotes leadership for liberation values). *Source:* Courtesy of Pullias Center for Higher Education, University of Southern California

Figure 5.2 provides an overview of all the new values and connects them to the existing values that make up the social change model.

Individual Values

Liberation. Liberation is an ongoing process in which one is in a constant state of becoming, and it should be the driving goal of the social change model. In other words, without liberation there is no meaningful social change. The social change model is built on the premise that everyone should see themselves as leaders regardless of the formal leadership position they hold. There is no direct value that gets at this, however. Liberation is an intimate matter, so it is situated in this expansion of the model as an individual

140 *Perspectives on Leadership Research and Practice*

process in which one begins to understand the values, beliefs, and experiences that make them who they are, but also asks critical questions regarding power and oppression (e.g., What identities afford me power? What identities label me as oppressed? What does my racial or ethnic identity have to do with individual or collective liberation?). The process of liberation is different from development of the consciousness of self-value because the latter does not capture the unshackling that racially minoritized students have to do in order to escape harmful messages and stereotypes projected onto them from society. Therefore, liberation derives from aspirational capital, as it concerns the ability to actively and authentically participate in leadership regardless of the real and perceived barriers the group or society may create.

Storytelling. Storytelling has the ability to illuminate the past, present, and future toward small- and large-scale change. Individual stories help us see the world and situations from other people's perspectives. Linguistic capital reflects the idea that racially minoritized students arrive at educational institutions with multiple language and communication skills that may deviate from those of the dominant culture. Strong and effective leaders should be able to tell unique, difficult, and inspiring stories in order to communicate to others their values and beliefs as individuals and to mobilize groups and stakeholders toward action. Storytelling is critical to creating a shared vision, as well as motivating and providing a persuasive message. Stories also help to provide clarity. Research shows that people are more likely to engage in change if a meaningful and relevant story is communicated to them—a storytelling canvas (Kernbach, 2018). When dealing with difficult issues and topics, students should be able to formulate a story that resonates. Storytelling is situated in this adaptation of the model as an individual tool because it has historically been used in communities of color and labeled a "vehicle by which voices from the margins are heard" (R. Reynolds & Mayweather, 2017, p. 288). Yet it is an individual tool that also has significance for the scope of the group and should be taught as a group tool as well. Sharing personal stories and creating a collective story can liberate individuals and unite a group as they work together as leaders toward change.

Group Values

System Challenging. System challenging focuses on denouncing and actively confronting oppressive systems, policies, and practices that prohibit real change. To actively challenge a system means to diverge from what society or those in positions of power view as normal or even acceptable. Ways to challenge systems include participating in sit-ins or protests and writing or signing demand letters. System challenging is an important element in this new iteration of the social change model because the original model privileges normative and dominant ways of enacting change that may not be deep or systemic. The social change model deviates from traditional leadership models and theories, so it is appropriate for there to be a tool that deviates from what are traditionally understood or accepted as tools for social change. Teaching students to challenge systems actively pushes against notions of white supremacy and helps them see that deep and systemic change occurs when you challenge oppressive and inequitable systems. Resistant capital fits into this value as it refers to knowledge and skills fostered through oppositional behavior. The social change model for leadership focuses on achieving change through shared processes that can perpetuate interest convergence and the loss-gain dichotomy. Many of the group values in the social change model for leadership are built around hegemonic behaviors such as controversy with civility and collaboration. Adopting a group tool of system challenging acknowledges, or values, that unconventional and creative methods and ideas are sometimes the only ways to achieve change. System challenging asks for group members to be tempered radicals (Kezar et al., 2011), working within the system but also finding ways around it to enact change.

Power and Oppression Acknowledgment. The acknowledgment of power and oppression is an extensive, intentional process in which the group works together to understand and eradicate power imbalances by sharing personal anecdotes and experiences to comprehend the social other. This group process arises from navigational capital, which refers to one's ability to navigate various social institutions, especially institutions not created with certain communities in mind. Therefore, a great deal of personal and group acknowledgment is needed in order to enact change in these spaces. In earlier sections, we illuminated the argument being made in critical leadership scholarship about the lack of discussion of power as it relates to the practice and teaching of leadership. Here, we posit that a true disservice is done if power and oppression are not explicitly called out in leadership processes and development opportunities. Power and oppression are always at play in leadership, as there is usually a person or group that has more power and a person or group that is experiencing less power, perhaps oppression. Encouraging an explicit acknowledgment of power dynamics ensures this aspect cannot be ignored. In acknowledging the dynamics of power and oppression in the room, together the group can raise questions about who speaks, ensure voice for all, think about the ways in which power dynamics shape leadership processes, and help leaders to call on support networks if they are not feeling comfortable.

Support Networks. The social change model for leadership reinforces the idea that leadership is relational and not positional. Thus, it seems natural that the model would also encourage people to lean on their support networks for guidance, support, and motivation to make influential change. Advancing support networks as a group tool allows for the group to confide in and find support in people outside the group who are actively working to create change. These support networks provide an unbiased, detached view of the problem, allowing group members to get different opinions about the issue, advice on how to tackle the issue, or just simple support in the challenging process of change. The concept of support networks comes directly from Yosso's social capital, which notes the importance of networks of people and community resources.

Community Value
Fellowship. Fellowship is the connectedness of a group or community beyond the problem they are trying to change. Familial capital embraces the idea that, through kinship ties, one learns the importance of maintaining a healthy connection to their community and its resources. Through fellowship, isolation is minimized, and relationships can be built outside the issue the group is trying to change. Presented as a community value, fellowship is a supplement to the value of citizenship, as there must be a level of comradeship to positively enact change. Fellowship also places a burden on those with privileged identities to see ways that members of a leadership team may feel disconnected and to rectify this isolation.

In addition to failing to acknowledge the capital of communities of color, the traditional social change model of leadership does not acknowledge power or systemic racism and oppression in society. In fact, oppression is often not directly discussed when describing leadership development theories and models more generally, which is why we explicitly focus on the issue in this book. While persuasion might be discussed as a manifestation of power, power is often not explicitly mentioned—particularly negative uses such as oppression. Without an explicit calling out of the role of power in leadership, power remains unproblematized. The model has been incorporated into a guide, *Leadership for Liberation* (Harper & Kezar, 2021).

Conclusion

In this chapter, we have reviewed the emergence and major assumptions of transformational leadership, which is part of a larger tradition of power and influence theories. We noted how transformational leadership provides an important turn in leadership research by highlighting the role of ethical processes and ends such as social change, mutual processes between leaders and followers, and processes that are rooted in empowerment and trust. We also highlighted two new evolutions—shared equity leadership and leadership for liberation—that challenge the status quo and push transformational leadership toward new ends. We conclude this chapter by revisiting the opening vignette.

Using shared-equity leadership, LeShaun can rethink his work to revise the service-learning program and illustrate how leadership can be a solution, not barrier. LeShaun realizes that he and his colleagues need some time to reflect on the program and its benefits and relationship to the community. He starts by gathering his colleagues to reflect on the feedback from the community and to challenge how their own whiteness is reflected in how they have set up the programming. He talks about his own experiences facing discrimination as a Black man in the community of curriculum that so often reflects white views, and suggests that the campus needs to consider how its own racism has played out in the service-learning program. They decide as a group that they need to better understand their community members without burdening them, as has been the tradition, and they need to challenge each other's views of the community. They search out newspaper articles, review websites, conduct observations, and do field trips into the community. They also start a reading group about whiteness within the student affairs division but invite service-learning faculty as well. They are excited that forty-six people sign up, and they create three reading groups to ensure good discussion and the individual journey work needed to better align their efforts with their aspirations. LeShaun kicks off each group by sharing his hopes and also care and love for each person's commitment to take on these personal changes. After six months, LeShaun asks community members if they will meet to jointly develop a new service-learning program with mutual goals and invites the vice president to attend the meeting to hear community voices firsthand. At the meeting, several faculty and staff are speaking too much, so he pulls them aside at a break and asks them to listen more and be humble in the setting. They end the day with a plan for ways to work together, learn from each other, and commit to better understanding community needs as they design the program going forward. The vice president who told LeShaun earlier that his ideas were not reasonable thanks him and says she has been inspired by his leadership and is rethinking other campus structures that lack equity.

In closing, we offer a summary of key takeaways for practice.

Traditional Theory

- Transformational leadership shows the potential for leadership to be a moral or ethical endeavor. It is a set of principles and practices that have been found to be relevant and effective across many different cultures and organizational settings. Asking yourself about the moral or ethical underpinnings of your leadership practice is an important step.
- While the behaviors and practices vary, some key transformational leadership behaviors are challenging the process (searching for opportunities and experimenting); inspiring a shared vision (motivating people toward a vision); enabling others to act (fostering collaboration and self-development); modeling the way (setting an example); and encouraging the heart (celebrating achievements).
- Leadership should be humanistic in orientation and create positive leader and follower relationships, celebrating accomplishments and modeling positive interactions. Studies demonstrate the value of such an approach for creating changes and improving organizational functioning.
- Leaders can change traditional hierarchical power structures and empower others, which is a key insight of transformational leadership theories.
- Collaboration is a central way to begin the process of empowerment. Leaders should foster more collective approaches to work, as well as creating and supporting mechanisms for leaders across campus to work together.

- Leaders who experiment and push boundaries can create social and organizational transformation.

New Evolutions

- Leadership should be more than experimental and should specifically challenge systems of oppression and create equity. This is more likely to occur when leaders name the transformational goals (social justice and equity) and adopt equity-mindedness (also see the chapter on cognitive leadership for more information on equity-mindedness).
- Leaders need to acknowledge existing power systems, actively dismantle hierarchies that prevent true empowerment, and create greater egalitarianism. When hierarchical power structures are left unattended to, transformation will likely not meet the equitable goals and aspirations of leaders.
- Questioning, disrupting systems, welcoming divergent views, and diminishing hierarchy are some practices that leaders need to engage in to alter existing systems of power.
- Leadership is a shared process of working toward equity as a collective, and transformation requires group action. Shared-equity leadership provides a model for collective action to pursue goals of equity within campuses.
- Personal transformation is as necessary as external transformation of organizations and systems, and leaders must engage in a personal journey toward critical consciousness of power and oppression.
- Leaders need to embrace a set of values that are quite different from those of traditional approaches to leadership by embodying vulnerability, love and care, comfort with being uncomfortable, and transparency. The work of personal transformation is pivotal to adopting these new values, which often have not been widely illustrated by leaders on campus.
- Frameworks that call out power and oppression and that take an asset-based approach to leaders from historically excluded groups can inform leadership perspectives and development so that values embedded in whiteness are not made normative and inculcated.

Discussion Questions

1. What are the goals and aspirations for your leadership? What changes are you trying to make? What roles do equity, social justice, and the dismantling of systems of power play in your goals?

2. What practices of transformational leadership do you engage in? How do others respond? Do you find yourself needing to use transactional leadership approaches? If so, when and why?

3. Humanistic interactions, empowerment, and collaboration are central to advancing transformational leadership. How is this represented in your leadership? Provide examples of when you have been humanistic and empowered and supported collaboration.

4. Have you undergone a journey toward critical consciousness of power and oppression? If not, how might you engage in such a process? If you have, where are you on this journey? What are your next steps (as this is an ever-evolving process)?

5. When have you utilized the practices of questioning, disrupting systems, welcoming divergent views, and diminishing hierarchy? If you are working alone, this can be risky. How might you create a shared leadership environment to support these practices?

6. Looking at the shared-equity leadership model, what values and practices would you say are best exemplified in your own leadership? What might you work on? Think about a team you are on. What values and practices are present there? How might you build the group's capacity?

7. As you consider leadership development, have you interrogated the values you use in working with other leaders? Have you considered how many skills and traits might be valuing whiteness? How might you challenge leadership development you do interpersonally as well as in formal programs on campus?

Chapter 6

Cognitive Leadership Perspectives

The presidential search committee of Green Valley State College (GVSC) has worked in secrecy for much of the fall term to recruit and screen candidates for the institutional leadership vacancy created by the unexpected resignation of the campus's top executive. Outgoing president Russ Thompson was recruited to run GVSC twelve years ago after a successful tenure as the CEO of a local health-care system. Credited with increasing the college's endowment through corporate partnerships, Thompson benefited from the respect and support of the GVSC Board of Trustees, who valued his projection of confidence and charisma along with his strong political connections to the state legislature. When Thompson announced he planned to step down at the end of the current academic year, gossip at the water coolers across campus quickly turned to whom the board would select to fill the chief executive role.

The GVSC Board of Trustees has retained the services of an executive search firm to facilitate the presidential search process. At the committee's first meeting, the firm's consultant attempts to help the committee reach consensus on the set of qualities and experiences they are looking for in the next GVSC leader. The conversation is highly contentious, with committee members from different campus constituencies expressing diverse leadership preferences. One contingent of the committee expresses a desire for the search firm to identify candidates with strong business and political ties in

148   *Perspectives on Leadership Research and Practice*

the state, along with a proven track record of managing large, complex organizations. It is clear they are looking for a leader to match the prototype established by Thompson. A second committee faction describes their ideal president as someone with strong academic roots, a collaborative approach to decision-making, an authentic communication style, a demonstrated commitment to educational access and equity, and the ability to motivate others through inspiration and mentoring. The consultant attempts to find common ground among the committee members but is unsuccessful. The members' disparate images (or prototypes) of the ideal GVSC president are a product of their experience and the cognitive processes (e.g., perception and information processing) that have formed their individual and collective leadership frameworks.

The committee ultimately invites two finalists to campus, one representing each of their respective leadership prototypes. The first to visit campus is Mark Simon, a white male in his mid-50s who built a national storage facility chain from the ground up and has just ended a twelve-year tenure as a state senator. The second candidate, Linda Martinez, is a Latina woman in her early 50s who proudly identifies as the daughter of immigrants and a first-generation college student. Martinez possesses more typical academic leadership credentials, including having assumed the role of provost at a Historically Black College in the neighboring city after rising through the faculty ranks and senior leadership roles within the school of health sciences. The GVSC board ultimately decides to hire Simon as the next president of GVSC, a decision that prompts Mary Stokes, the sole Black female GVSC trustee, to resign her position. In her letter of resignation, Stokes cites her objection to the raced and gendered leadership schemas used to evaluate the qualifications of Simon and Martinez, resulting in the devaluing of Martinez's leadership experience and style. Although Stokes's resignation garners local and national media attention, the controversy eventually dies down and Simon is inaugurated without incident.

Leadership selection controversies such as the one depicted in this opening vignette are frequently featured in higher education trade publications (Gluckman, 2019; Jaschik, 2012; Toppo, 2019). We open this chapter on cognitive approaches to understanding leadership with the GVSC vignette because the identification and evaluation of leaders and leadership are

Cognitive Leadership Perspectives   149

frequent focuses of cognitive leadership inquiry. The vignette illustrates how one's leadership schemas and prototypes (our mental images of ideal leaders) influence perceptions and evaluations of individuals holding or seeking formal leadership roles. The vignette also demonstrates how mental images of leadership rooted in biased (e.g., raced, gendered, classed, nationalist, or heteronormative) cognitive constructs result in discriminatory leader evaluations and decisions. Additionally, this vignette highlights the continued focus within the cognitive leadership perspective on positional authority and the formal leader-follower dynamic. As we will discuss later in the chapter, although perceivers (followers) play an important role in the identification and evaluation of leadership, this cognitive processing is still framed by a recognition of leadership as formal authority and positional influence.

As detailed in *Rethinking the "L" Word in Higher Education* (Kezar et al., 2006), cognitive approaches to understanding leadership received a great deal of attention within and beyond higher education in the late twentieth and early twenty-first centuries. Our contemporary literature analysis reveals waning interest among higher education leadership scholars; however, we have opted to include this strand of scholarship in the book to highlight its value for understanding the continued dominance of neoliberal and white supremacist leadership systems and structures within American higher education, as well as to explore its potential for dismantling these systems of oppression. We begin the chapter with a review of the historical roots of cognitive leadership perspectives along with a discussion of major assumptions and key research findings pertaining to implicit leadership theories, mental models, and organizational learning. After discussing critiques of existing cognitive leadership perspectives, we turn our attention to three emerging cognitive constructs that hold promise for advancing more socially just and inclusive leadership perspectives—wisdom, authentic leadership, and equity-minded leadership.

Definition and Emergence

Cognitive theories of leadership examine and explain the mental processes associated with leadership, including information processing, learning, sensemaking, and attribution. In recognition that leadership is an interpersonal process characterized by mutual influence, cognitive perspectives adopt a systems orientation (Lord & Emrich, 2001), shedding light on individual, dyadic, and collective cognitive processes influenced by societal and cultural beliefs (T. L. Lee & Fiske, 2008). Cognitive leadership perspectives are rooted in the disciplinary knowledge of cognitive psychology, social psychology, and neuroscience. This body of scholarship builds on foundational trait-, skill-, and behavior-based leadership theories, seeking to understand the (social) cognitive processes individuals and groups use to identify, interpret, and respond to the words and deeds of leaders (T. L. Lee & Fiske, 2008). While trait- and behavior-oriented scholars are interested in documenting universal and culturally specific characteristics and behaviors of successful leaders, cognitive leadership researchers seek to understand the function that information processing plays in shaping how and why individuals and groups perceive some traits and behaviors as markers of successful leadership and how these same individuals then draw on mental representations of leadership as sources of motivation and attribution of influence over organizational outcomes (Avolio et al., 2009; Thomas et al., 2013).

Consistent with its psychological disciplinary roots, cognitive leadership research is frequently informed by the principles and practices of postpositivism, with scholars using experimental and quasi-experimental designs to identify definitive, causal relationships between cognitive structures and leadership perceptions and judgments (Lord & Emrich, 2001). The influence of the social constructivist paradigm can be seen in those cognitive leadership studies that examine the role of culture, context, and experience in individual and collective meaning-making (e.g., Smerek, 2013). An appreciation of the complexity and ambiguity that characterize modern society highlights the potential influence of postmodernism in this body of work. For example, scholars have studied the value of cognitive complexity and flexible and adaptive mental structures for making meaning of ambiguous and contradictory information within complex internal and external organizational systems such as higher education (Da'as et al., 2018). On a related note, cognitive leadership perspectives that recognize leadership as a relational process reflect the evolution of leadership theory away from hierarchical, individual-centered notions of leadership; however, much of this scholarship continues to focus on the demarcation of leaders and followers. In recognition that some cognitive leadership scholars use the term *perceiver* when discussing the perspective of those typically described as followers or subordinates, we too use the terms *follower* and *perceiver* interchangeably throughout this chapter when describing those individuals who are the targets of influence by those in formal or informal leadership roles.

Major Assumptions and Contributions

The foundational assumptions of cognitive leadership perspectives address both the structure and content of leadership cognition. A key premise of this body of leadership theory is that information-processing constructs (e.g., schemas and prototypes) are important to how individuals and groups identify, interpret, and respond to leadership experiences (Dugan, 2017). As a result of engaging in the ongoing processes of observation, meaning-making, and action, individuals produce implicit, contextually sensitive mental representations they can access when challenged to interpret new leadership stimuli.

Building on Eden and Leviatan's (1975) observation that "leadership factors are in the mind of the respondent" (p. 741), many cognitive leadership scholars place the mental models of followers at the center of their research, examining how schemas, scripts, prototypes, exemplars, and implicit leadership theories influence follower perceptions of and responses to formal leaders (Avolio et al., 2009; Day & Antonakis, 2012; Forsyth & Nye, 2008; T. L. Lee & Fiske, 2008; Lord & Emrich, 2001; Thomas et al., 2013). Within this line of inquiry, it is recognized that the cognitive processing of observed leadership traits and behaviors, not the traits and actions themselves, influences how participants in the leadership process make sense of and interact with one another.

As noted earlier, cognitive leadership theories attend to both the content (beliefs and evaluations of self, others, and context) and structure (organization of information in the mind) of mental processes (Avolio et al., 2009). These cognitive processes are simultaneously stable and context sensitive. Specifically, research has shown that national and organizational culture, social beliefs, and contextual conditions (e.g., crisis) influence leadership cognitions (Lord & Emrich, 2001). Although the content of leadership cognitions is dynamic, scholars have found that mental representations of leadership are consistently organized around the core dimensions of warmth (interpersonal relations, trustworthiness, and sociability) and competence (intelligence and task accomplishment) (T. L. Lee & Fiske, 2008).

152 *Perspectives on Leadership Research and Practice*

Given the important function that leadership schemas and prototypes play in illustrating the foundational assumptions of cognitive leadership theory and their manifestations within higher education, we briefly review both of these constructs before turning our attention to significant cognitive leadership research findings and insights.

LEADERSHIP SCHEMAS

Leadership schemas are subconscious cognitive structures that organize prior knowledge at a broad, abstract level (Dugan, 2017). A defining feature of schemas, which are derived from experience as well as societal and cultural beliefs, is that they conceptualize the focal construct (e.g., leadership) as a coherent whole, rather than a collection of fragmented elements (T. L. Lee & Fiske, 2008). This detail is important, as it helps explain how individuals use broad, general schemas to make sense of complex phenomena, facilitating awareness of schema-consistent information and drawing one's attention to details that are not aligned with schematic expectations.

Within the context of higher education, faculty and staff often have a well-developed schema of presidential leadership, including expected traits (charismatic, good communication skills, and the ability to think strategically), attributes (academic background and experience as an administrator), behaviors (task and relationship oriented), and preferences (expectation of respect). Higher education professionals draw on the presidential leadership schema when processing their observations of a campus president, giving attention to observations that do not align with their leadership schema (e.g., lack of academic management experience) or assuming the leader possesses traits that have not been observed (e.g., integrity or good judgment). Once the individual has recognized the relevance of a particular schema (e.g., presidential leadership) for making sense of an experience, the individual enacts the corresponding cognitive script (associated set of behaviors). Establishing a connection between cognitive perspectives on leadership and transformational leadership (discussed in the previous chapter), Wofford et al. (1998) found that transformational and transactional leadership were characterized by different meaning-making schemas, which influenced the selection of different scripts (leadership behaviors).

Prototypes

Closely associated with the notion of leadership schemas are leadership prototypes. Both schemas and prototypes draw on social beliefs and personal experience to identify the expected traits and behaviors of leaders. Yet whereas schemas are unitary mental images of leadership (individuals either match or do not match the full range of attributes detailed in a schema), prototypes are conceptualized as fragmented mental representations that allow perceivers to evaluate others along multiple dimensions, recognizing some leaders as more or less typical based on how closely they align with the prototype (Dugan, 2017). If a perceiver's leader prototype includes the attributes of strong public speaking skills, excellent organization skills, male, and formal positional authority, the perceiver may recognize a female grassroots activist as a leader, although less prototypical, even though the activist does not possess all the characteristics associated with the leader prototype. Research on American leadership prototypes has revealed common prototypical traits (e.g., intelligence, kindness, honesty, and charisma) as well as embodied characteristics (e.g., height, weight, tone of voice, and facial structure) (Dinh & Lord, 2012). Contemporary scholars have recognized that prototypes, though originally conceptualized as static, are dynamic and influenced by the nature of the leadership challenge or environmental constraint (Avolio et al., 2009; Dugan, 2017). One's prototype for a higher education leader tasked with managing a crisis likely differs from the prototype one holds for corporate executives facilitating strategic change.

As illustrated in this review of major assumptions, cognitive leadership perspectives underscore the important role that perception, particularly the information-processing efforts of followers, plays in shaping leadership dynamics within and beyond higher education. Individuals interested in understanding and influencing leadership processes and organizational outcomes are encouraged to examine the leadership schemas and prototypes that inform the meaning-making and actions of key constituents. Additionally, this body of scholarship affirms the contextual nature of leadership, highlighting the influence of culture, social beliefs, and environmental conditions on the way we think about and enact leadership. This set of foundational assumptions frames the key cognitive leadership research findings synthesized in the next section.

Key Insights and Findings

Our review of significant cognitive leadership research insights is organized around three distinct strands of inquiry: implicit leadership theories, the framing of leadership with mental models, and leadership and learning. Although presented as discrete bodies of literature, these three approaches to studying leadership cognitions share an emphasis on individuals in formal leadership roles as well as the perceptions of those they seek to influence.

IMPLICIT LEADERSHIP THEORIES

Implicit leadership theories (ILTs) specify the traits, characteristics, and behaviors an individual expects to be exhibited by individuals who are categorized as leaders (Dugan, 2017; Forsyth & Nye, 2008; T. L. Lee & Fiske, 2008). According to the theory, which is described interchangeably as a recognition-based theory of leadership and leader categorization theory (Dugan, 2017; Thomas et al., 2013), individuals draw on their implicit (intuitive and typically unrecognized) leadership theories to evaluate the match between observations of a leader's (or potential leader's) traits and behaviors and their mental representations (schemas and prototypes) of leadership. A product of the perceiver's experience, ILTs are context and culturally dependent, with research documenting the influence of national culture and contextual conditions such as crisis on ILTs (Lord & Emrich, 2001). Although ILTs are dynamic, these mental representations of leadership are consistently organized along two dimensions—competence or task structure and interpersonal relationships (Forsyth & Nye, 2008). Perceivers use their ILTs to categorize individuals they encounter as leaders or nonleaders. Categorizing someone as a leader triggers the enactment of corresponding leadership scripts as well as expectations for the leader and one's interactions with them (T. L. Lee & Fiske, 2008). The closer the match between the perceiver's observations and their ILTs, the more favorably they will evaluate the leader even when the leader's performance may not be effective (Dugan, 2017; Junker & van Dick, 2014). Additionally, leaders who align their behaviors with a perceiver's ILTs benefit from higher perceiver ratings of collegiality, liking, popularity, and respect (Junker & van Dick, 2014). ILTs also influence the perceiver's organizational experiences. Specifically, alignment between a leader and the perceiver's ILTs has been shown to influence the perceiver's motivation, effort, satisfaction, attribution, organizational commitment, and well-being (Forsyth & Nye, 2008; Junker & van Dick, 2014; T. L. Lee & Fiske, 2008; Thomas et al., 2013). Accordingly, individuals seeking to influence others are motivated to project an image that aligns with the ILTs of perceivers (Lord & Emrich, 2001).

A tool of cognitive efficiency allowing individuals to process complex information quickly, ILTs can also serve as sources of distortion and bias in the process of leader recognition (Dugan, 2017). For example, ILTs rooted in unrecognized sexist, racist, and heteronormative assumptions regarding desirable leadership traits and behaviors may negatively influence the recognition and evaluation of individuals who do not conform to the perceiver's mental models of effective leaders (Dugan, 2017; Eagly & Chin, 2010; Forsyth & Nye, 2008; Lord & Emrich, 2001; Ospina & Foldy, 2009; Thomas et al., 2013). The white supremacist and sexist roots of leadership prototypes and ILTs are evident in research that documents how cognitive processes contribute to the formation of biased prototypes that discount the agentic leadership of female leaders (K. A. Scott & Brown, 2006) and frame whiteness as a central aspect of leadership prototypes, resulting in higher evaluation of white leaders compared with individuals from other racial groups (Festekjian et al., 2014; Rosette et al., 2008). Studies have also shown that the "whiteness equals leadership" prototype has been internalized by people of color, resulting in lower leadership aspirations among Asian Americans operating from the whiteness prototype (Festekjian et al., 2014) and higher evaluations of white leaders by Black, Latinx, and Asian individuals (Rosette et al., 2008). Additionally, Rosette and Livingston (2012) documented the intersectional nature of discriminatory leadership prototypes, finding that Black women were evaluated more negatively than Black men and white women in the context of organizational failure (these three groups were rated similarly, but lower than white men, in conditions of organizational success). Individuals with historically marginalized identities may be socialized or called on to adopt traits and behaviors that conform to biased ILTs or else face the negative consequences of exhibiting their authentic leadership style. In the vignette that opened this chapter, the subconscious nature of biased cognitions in the recruitment and hiring process means that "people can unknowingly discriminate by means of 'mindless' processes that operate beyond their conscious attentional focus, all the while thinking that they are

156 *Perspectives on Leadership Research and Practice*

merely choosing the best person for the job or otherwise acting in an unbiased manner" (Eagly & Chin, 2010, p. 217). Naming, examining, and disrupting biased leadership prototypes that inform hiring and promotion decisions may prove a valuable strategy for achieving the diversity and equity aims of higher education institutions.

FRAMING LEADERSHIP WITH MENTAL MODELS

In addition to ILTs and prototypes, another significant line of inquiry within cognitive leadership perspectives examines the influence of mental models and mindsets on leadership (H. H. Johnson, 2008). Specifically, numerous scholars have used Bolman and Deal's (2017) notion of cognitive frames to explore the ways in which individuals make sense of organizational life and exercise leadership in the resolution of organizational challenges (Birnbaum, 1992; Eddy, 2003; Kezar, Eckel, et al., 2008). Bolman and Deal (2017) described a cognitive frame as a "mental model—a set of ideas and assumptions—that you carry in your heart to help you understand and negotiate a particular 'territory'" (p. 12). Bolman and Deal have also used maps as a metaphor to illustrate the function of cognitive frames in meaning-making. In the context of higher education organizations, cognitive frames help an individual map a particular territory (department, division, institution, or ecosystem) so that they can effectively navigate organizational boundaries, relationships, rules, norms, and so on. A cognitive map of the University of California, Los Angeles, is likely of little value in making sense of organizational life at Alamance Community College in rural North Carolina given that these institutions are characterized by vastly different missions, organizational structures, demographics, and behavioral norms.

Bolman and Deal (2017) have identified four common cognitive frames: (1) the structural frame, rooted in scientific management theory, focuses attention on the social architecture of organizations, including organizational structure, rules, policies, and planning; (2) the human resource frame, anchored in the discipline of psychology, emphasizes the human needs and relationships embedded in organizational life; (3) the political frame draws on political science theories of scarce resources, conflict, and competition to understand the nature of power in organizations; and (4) the symbolic frame utilizes concepts from anthropology, dramaturgy, and institutional theory to help make meaning of organizational culture, including symbols, myths, and rituals. The key to effective leadership within the organizational frame model is to select the right frame or frames for addressing specific situations. For example, an organizational dilemma in which the technical quality of the decision is important is best addressed by attending to structural issues; however, in situations where conflict and scarce resources are significant concerns, political frame concepts and strategies might be more appropriate for analyzing and resolving the challenge. Given the complexity of modern, global organizations, such as institutions of higher education, most organizational processes and dilemmas could benefit from a multiframe analysis and action plan (Bolman & Deal, 2017; Kezar, Eckel, et al., 2008). Matching cognitive frames to organizational tasks or adopting a multiframe approach to dilemmas may be easier said than done given Bolman and Deal's (2017) assertion that individuals draw on preferred cognitive frames to process organizational observations. A leader with a strong human resource orientation may focus their attention on the interpersonal relationships embedded within the organization at the expense of attending to structural issues such as ambiguous policies or redundancy in task distribution. To help organizational members identify their preferred frames, Bolman and Deal have developed a quick frames self-rating scale (Bolman & Deal, 1988).

The concepts of cognitive frames and framing align with the social constructivist leadership paradigm, in which individuals develop personalized interpretations of situations based on their unique identities, experiences, and cognitive models (Capper, 2019). Individuals operating from different mental frames will derive different meanings from shared experiences and draw on these diverse interpretations when determining future actions. Additionally, scholars of mental frames recognize that organizational dynamics are complex and fluid, necessitating that leaders cultivate the capacity to draw on multiple frames to accurately interpret a situation and artfully respond. The postpositivist search for universal truths does not match the flexible and highly personal mental model framework.

A number of scholars have examined the role of cognitive frames in the context of higher education leadership, commonly focusing their attention on the cognitive frames used by college presidents (Bensimon, 1989; Birnbaum, 1992; Eddy, 2003; Kezar, Eckel, et al., 2008). A prime example of this body of scholarship is Birnbaum's (1992) five-year institutional leadership project, which examined the beliefs and assumptions of college presidents. Aligning with Bolman and Deal's (2017) four frames, Birnbaum found that presidents tended to use one of four frameworks to make sense of their work, despite the fact that institutional leaders were considered more effective when they displayed cognitive complexity and used multiple mental frames to analyze and address institutional challenges. In a similar line of inquiry, Bensimon (1989) noted that new institutional leaders and community college presidents were most likely to use one mental frame; however, experience seemed to foster wisdom, with more seasoned campus leaders demonstrating the capacity for multiframe analysis. Interested in exploring the relationship between cognitive frames and actions, Eddy (2003) examined the ways in which a community college leader's cognitive framing of institutional change efforts influenced the selection of change goals and strategies. The president with a visionary orientation to change utilized symbolic meaning-making and collegial relationships to foster commitment to and engagement in change efforts. By contrast, the community college president who adopted an operational (structural) approach to organizational change leveraged formal authority and rules to accomplish their goals. Kezar, Eckel, et al. (2008) also used cognitive framing to examine presidential efforts to facilitate change but focused their study on the specific change agenda of advancing campus diversity efforts. Their findings underscored the need for university presidents to look beyond the traditional structural frame strategies for change (e.g., strategic planning, new task forces, and resource allocation) and spend significantly more time and energy engaging in the human resource strategy of building "an interconnected web of activity" (p. 86) that fostered participation and commitment from a broad swath of campus and community stakeholders. Looking to investigate the influence of cognitive frames beyond the president's suite, higher education scholars have examined the extent to which cognitive framing of leadership differs by disciplinary orientation (humanities versus hard sciences; Kekale, 2001) and staff subcultures (Palestini, 1999). Differences in the preferred cognitive frames of disciplinary professionals (e.g., the collegial approach of humanities faculty contrasted with the structural orientation of STEM faculty) are important to consider given the significant role academic disciplines play in organizing higher education institutions and structuring formal leadership opportunities (e.g., department chair or dean).

Circling back to the cognitive perspective's recognition that leadership is a mutual-influence relationship in which information-processing patterns shape the meaning-making and actions of both perceivers and those seeking to exert influence, Birnbaum (1992) examined how the cognitive frames of perceivers influenced whom they identified as formal leaders. Not surprisingly, individuals who relied on a structural mental model of leadership recognized those in formal positions of authority as leaders, while those operating from a collegial or human resource frame identified leaders as those individuals they perceived as encouraging, relational, and strong teammates. Perceivers using a symbolic frame identified individuals who reflected the vision and values of the organization as leaders, and those situated in the political lens associated leadership with individuals who exerted influence and made things happen. This line of research affirmed that the perceiver's cognitive frames shape whom they identify as leaders and how they assess effectiveness. Returning to a point made earlier in our discussion of ILTs, current and aspiring higher education leaders who wish to be perceived as successful and effective are well served by matching their leadership approach to their constituents' mental models.

In recognition of research findings that demonstrate that cognitive complexity, the ability to analyze organizational dilemmas using multiple mental frames, increases leader efficacy, scholars have explored strategies for expanding the mental models individuals use to make meaning of and influence their organizational environments. H. H. Johnson (2008) drew on Jack Mezirow's transformative learning theory to make the case that "context-specific experiences that challenge existing meaning structures, and that force the learner to critically reflect on the assumptions underlying existing mental models, as well as develop new and more effective ways of dealing with the challenges being faced" (p. 86), are the most promising method for expanding one's mental models. Johnson called for leaders and aspiring leaders to fundamentally change their meaning-making structures, which will produce new and different ways of interpreting the environment, rather than merely adding new information (content) to existing mental models. Applying Mezirow's transformative learning process to the context of cognitive leadership development, Johnson called for structuring on-the-job, real-world experiences that foster disorientation, are characterized by professional tasks of increasing scope and responsibility, and provide structured opportunities for receiving feedback, reflecting on actions, and piloting new approaches. Johnson noted that, rather than waiting until individuals attain senior positions of authority, leaders should prepare new professionals for the cognitive complexity of leadership by engaging them in disorienting events early in their careers and sustaining this leadership development practice throughout their employment.

LEADERSHIP AND LEARNING

A third strand of inquiry and practice within cognitive perspectives of leadership is organizational learning, which encompasses individual- and shared-level changes in thought and action within the context of a specific organization (Parry, 2013). More specifically, Yukl (2009) described the foundational elements of organizational learning as "the discovery of relevant new knowledge, diffusion of this knowledge to people in the organization who need it, and application of the knowledge to improve internal processes and external adaptation" (p. 49). Although we also discuss organizational learning in the chaos and complexity chapter, we include a synthesis of relevant research in this chapter as well, in recognition that organizational learning theorists have spent considerable time and energy examining the ways in which formal leaders foster the organizational conditions that support or hinder individual and collective cognitive processes of learning (Berson et al., 2006; Parry, 2013). Given the important function organizational learning plays in performance, innovation, adaptation, and organizational survival (Berson et al., 2006; Heifetz, 1994; Wheatley, 1999; Yukl, 2009), higher education leadership scholars are well served to understand the underlying leadership principles and processes that advance learning in postsecondary institutions.

Scholars have identified four processes of organizational learning: intuiting, interpreting, integrating, and institutionalizing (Berson et al., 2006; Parry, 2013). A great deal of organizational learning scholarship focuses on the role formal leaders play in facilitating each of these processes. At the intuiting stage, formal leaders support learning by creating conditions that encourage members to question assumptions and traditional approaches to work, consider new perspectives in their efforts, cultivate new skills, and engage in experiments to test out new ideas (Berson et al., 2006; Parry, 2013; Yukl, 2009). In the interpreting process, leaders help organizational members make meaning of their new cognitive maps by guiding them through the process of framing knowledge and pointing their attention to certain aspects of the insight most relevant for the organization (Berson et al., 2006). The facilitation of communication and collaboration are also key learning-centered leadership behaviors. Through the establishment of communities of practice and other forms of social networking inside and outside the boundaries of the organization, formal leaders help translate individual knowledge to a shared understanding and collective learning during the interpreting and integrating processes (Berson et al., 2006; Parry, 2013; Yukl, 2009). As Parry (2013) noted, "Dialogue lies at the core of organizational learning. Without dialogue, individuals and groups cannot effectively exchange ideas or develop shared understanding" (p. 63). Finally, in the institutionalizing phase, formal leaders advance learning through the adoption of new or revised structures, policies, protocols, and so on that reflect the organization's new shared knowledge.

Organizational learning scholars view formal leaders as critical to the learning process given the central role they play in creating systems and incentives for the discovery, diffusion, and application of new knowledge and innovations (Yukl, 2009). Scholars seeking to identify the specific leadership qualities and styles that promote organizational learning have drawn on classic transformational leadership theory for inspiration and guidance. The transformational and charismatic leadership abilities of communicating vision and fostering shared commitment have been found to facilitate organizational learning (Berson et al., 2006); however, Yukl (2009) reminded readers that followers who hold charismatic and transformational leaders in too high a regard may find it difficult to challenge organizational assumptions, report failures, or innovate, given their belief that the formal leader already has a good solution.

Common obstacles to organizational learning include the placement of responsibility for innovation on the shoulders of the senior executive team; constraint placed on the flow of information in the interest of consolidating power or suppressing awareness of failure; the adoption of a highly differentiated organizational structure, which limits collaboration and information exchange; and conflict among organizational stakeholders (Yukl, 2009). Yukl contended that leaders at all levels of the organization can and should address these barriers to learning by explicitly and tangibly supporting innovation, experimentation, collaboration, flexibility, and continuous improvement, as well as by creating communication norms and operating structures that facilitate the open and honest exchange of information across units.

In this section we have reviewed three prominent strands of cognitive leadership research: ILTs, leadership mental models, and organizational learning. All three bodies of work have expanded our awareness of the cognitive processes, structures, and content framing leadership within and beyond higher education. Additionally, cognitive research insights have deepened our understanding of the mutual influence within leadership, as they often place the leader-follower dynamic at the center of inquiry—a feature of cognitive leadership perspectives that we revisit in the following discussion of critiques leveled against this leadership approach.

Critiques

Although cognitive leadership perspectives have shed valuable light on the mental processes (e.g., perception, interpretation, attribution, and learning) that shape leadership and facilitate organizational learning and success, this strand of inquiry is subject to critique for its continued focus on hierarchical leadership relationships and its noticeable silence on matters of social injustice and inequity (Capper, 2019). Additionally, more attention needs to be paid to understanding the ways that white supremacy, patriarchy, heteronormativity, and other oppressive ideologies shape cognitive perspectives of leadership (e.g., schemas and ILTs) that constrain the leadership opportunities of individuals with minoritized identities and contribute to hostile organizational environments. We expand on each of these critiques in this section.

Continued Prominence of the Formal Leader

Within the context of the evolution of leadership theory and research described in chapter 1, cognitive leadership perspectives align with the social constructivist recognition of leadership as a mutual process of influence shaped by context and culture. Many of the cognitive leadership perspectives featured in this chapter (e.g., ILTs and learning) are relational in nature, highlighting the interpersonal dynamics of cognition. For example, one's leadership schemas and ILTs are formed and revised by making meaning of social interactions. Despite the fact that cognitive perspectives conceptualize leadership as relational, much of this line of inquiry remains rooted in hierarchical notions of formal positional authority and dyadic (leader-follower) interactions (Dugan, 2017; Parry, 2013). Recall that a significant strand of organizational learning theory focuses on the specific qualities and behaviors of those in formal positions of authority. Positional leaders are charged with creating the organizational conditions that facilitate learning, including establishing a culture of open communication, risk-taking, and dialogue. Similarly, studies of the role mental models play in making sense of and addressing organizational challenges have centered on the experiences of senior leaders. This is particularly true within the field of higher education, where studies of the mental models and sensemaking of presidents dominate the literature base (Birnbaum, 1992; Eddy, 2003; Kezar, Eckel, et al., 2008; Smerek, 2013).

Positional leadership also remains a prominent aspect of dyad-centered leadership cognitions, such as ILTs and schemas, which examine the cognitive processes of perception, interpretation, and attribution. Perceiver cognitions are formed as a result of reflecting on interactions with formal leaders, and individuals seeking formal recognition as leaders are well served to align their behaviors with the ILTs of their target followers (Forsyth & Nye, 2008). Dugan (2017) did acknowledge that cognitive perspectives cede important influence to perceivers or followers, who can shape the behaviors of formal leaders seeking recognition and approval. Although there are some exceptions (e.g., Shondrick et al., 2010, explored the cognitive processes associated with nonhierarchical, shared leadership, and Kezar & Lester, 2011, studied grassroots leadership perspectives), cognitive leadership research and theory continues to maintain a scholarly focus on positional leadership, affirming the entrenched nature of traditional leadership perspectives.

Tools of Neoliberalism

A second line of critique leveled against cognitive leadership perspectives centers on the facade of neutrality that surrounds the conceptualization and application of mental models and organizational learning constructs. Foundational scholarship in both lines of inquiry (Berson et al., 2006; Bolman & Deal, 2017) is relatively silent on matters of (in)justice, offering little insight on the ways systemic oppression, marginalized social identities, privilege,

164 *Perspectives on Leadership Research and Practice*

and so on influence the cognitive process of learning and framing (Capper, 2019). On the contrary, organizational learning and cognitive frames are seen as tools of efficiency and productivity that can be used to achieve the neoliberal aims of capitalist organizations, including colleges and universities (Gonzalez et al., 2018). Cognitive leadership scholars and practitioners seek to identify the optimal conditions (e.g., organizational structures, lines of communication, policies, beliefs, and norms) for maximizing innovation, performance, and profit (Berson et al., 2006; Bolman & Deal, 2017). Bolman and Deal (2017) did identify the analysis of organizational conflict and power as central features of their political frame; however, their discussion of power is seemingly neutral, with the goal being to productively use power to achieve organizational goals, whatever they may be (Capper, 2019).

Although cognitive leadership perspectives can be used to advance equity aims (Kezar, Eckel, et al., 2008), the lack of explicit attention to issues of oppression and identity within the cognitive theories themselves is highly problematic. Gonzales et al. (2018) attempted to address this limitation by exploring how organizational theories, including those at the nexus of leadership and organizational behavior like learning and mental models, might be reimagined through the critical paradigm lens. For example, in their reimagination of scientific management theories that align with Bolman and Deal's (2017) structural frame, Gonzales et al. illustrated how critical concepts such as equity, justice, and radical humanism can be used to examine and disrupt neoliberal-driven labor conditions that oppress adjunct faculty (e.g., limited opportunities for engagement in shared governance structures, no compensation for student advising and mentoring efforts, and temporary contracts). Reframing labor practices as tools for facilitating employee economic emancipation rather than institutional profit will lead academic administrators to think and lead differently, resulting in the development of policies that nurture and reward adjunct faculty (e.g., renewable contracts and compensation for institutional service).

Understanding, Not Action

Dugan (2017) critiqued cognitive leadership research, particularly ILTs and prototypes, for perpetuating "willful blindness" (p. 79) and the abdication of responsibility for addressing the hegemonic impacts of biased leadership cognition. Dugan contended, "The theory is largely descriptive, documenting the potentially harmful effects of implicit prototypes, yet only minimal attention is directed at ways to mitigate negative impacts. What good does the recognition of implicit assumptions do without also offering insights on how to disrupt them? . . . The theory is certainly a step in the right direction in terms of naming implicit assumptions, but simply making the implicit explicit without framing what to do with that information leaves substantive change to chance" (p. 79). Extending his critique that cognitive leadership perspectives expand understanding but stop short of establishing calls to action (a function of their postpositivist and social constructivist roots), Dugan lamented that ILT research rarely addresses how leaders and followers should handle misalignment between leader traits and behaviors and perceiver ILTs. To the extent possible, should leaders modify their actions to match the ILTs of those they are seeking to lead, or should perceivers adapt their ILTs to match the specific style of those in formal leadership roles (and if so, how)? In either scenario, the process of seeking congruence between ILTs and leader behaviors necessitates an examination of privilege, power, and oppression, as researchers and practitioners wrestle with the implications of asking individuals with historically minoritized identities to conform to dominant (white, male, heteronormative) leadership prototypes or styles.

Congruent with our efforts to name and dismantle the white supremacist and neoliberal principles that perpetuate oppressive leadership perspectives, Dugan (2017) sought to reimagine or reconstruct ILT with a focus on action. The transparency of cognitive leadership perspectives with respect to documenting the nature and consequences of biased mental processes (schemas, prototypes, and ILTs) facilitates the reconstruction process, as the target of action (biased cognitions) is clearly named. Building on existing ILT and leadership prototype research, Dugan proposed three strategies for disrupting the social stratification that both guides and results in biased information processing. First, unconscious biased cognitions must be exposed and consciously examined through ongoing reflection and dialogue. We cannot change what we are not aware of. Second, Dugan maintained that structural changes (e.g., policies and protocols) must be adopted to address the structural consequences of hegemonic cognitions. Changes to hiring committee structures and protocols must be implemented to account for cognitive bias in candidate reviews and hiring decisions. This call to action

166   Perspectives on Leadership Research and Practice

aligns with Kendi's (2019) structural approach to antiracism efforts. Finally, Dugan advocated for personal and interpersonal approaches to cognitive leadership bias, using counterstories and empirical research findings to disrupt the biased ILT assumptions and prototypes. We return to Dugan's suggestions for reimagining ILT research in the final chapter of this book, where we map out a future higher education research agenda.

New Evolutions in Cognitive Leadership Perspectives

Building on the foundational cognitive leadership theories and principles introduced earlier in this chapter, this section highlights significant and emerging leadership concepts. Specifically, we review wisdom, authentic leadership, and equity-minded leadership.

Wisdom

Wisdom is an emerging cognitive leadership construct that holds promise for dismantling the white supremacist and neoliberal principles that frame and constrain contemporary higher education. Underscoring the potential for wise leadership to advance social justice aims, Kezar and Posselt (2020) identified wisdom in judgment as an essential element of their framework for equity and justice in higher education administration. Their notion of wisdom is situated in an emerging body of leadership and organizational studies literature that highlights the harmful implications of neoliberal-driven decisions that emphasize short-term profit and productivity at the expense of the collective good (Branson, 2009; B. McKenna et al., 2009; Yang, 2011). We situate this discussion of wisdom and leadership within the cognitive perspectives chapter given the important role that the cognitive processes of reflection, learning, and creativity play in developing wisdom and engaging in wise decision-making (Ardelt, 2004; Yang, 2011).

Kezar and Posselt's notion of wisdom draws on the foundational work of Sternberg (2003), who defined wisdom as the integration and application of intelligence and creativity toward the common good. At the heart of Sternberg's construction of wisdom is the principle of balance; wise leaders seek balance among (1) personal interests, the needs of others, and the interests of the broader context (e.g., geographic region); (2) short- and long-term considerations; and (3) the strategies of adapting to new environments, shaping existing environments, and selecting new environments. Wisdom challenges the short-term, self-interested decision-making frameworks that characterize neoliberalism, instead calling on leaders and leadership processes to consider the immediate and long-term consequences of decisions for others (with particular attention to those most marginalized and historically excluded) and the environment (Jakubik, 2021; Kezar & Posselt, 2020; Yang, 2011). This attention to the needs and interests of historically excluded groups is a critical aspect of wisdom and wise leadership (Nonaka & Takeuchi, 2011; Yang, 2011), necessitating that decision makers forge authentic relationships with a broad array of individuals so they can expand their understanding of and empathy for diverse perspectives and experiences. Kezar and Posselt (2020) also drew on Nussbaum's (2011) theory of justice rooted in full inclusion within society as a pathway for equality. Nussbaum's work connected wise decisions to ones that lead to full inclusion and that center fostering the capabilities of all people, again with particular attention to groups that have been historically excluded and marginalized.

It is important to note that, for Sternberg (2003), wisdom is not just a function of knowledge; creativity is needed to develop novel solutions to complex or new challenges, and a well-developed set of values is essential for making wise decisions that emphasize the common good over self-interest (Kezar & Posselt, 2020; Nonaka & Takeuchi, 2011). Drawing connections to the Japanese construct of *toku*, which values the pursuit of the common good and moral excellence, Nonaka and Takeuchi (2011) framed wisdom as practical, "experiential knowledge that enables people to make ethically sound judgments" (p. 60). Turning mainly to Japanese corporate culture for exemplars in how organizations can balance the pursuit of profit and harmony with society, Nonaka and Takeuchi highlighted six leadership abilities associated with fostering practical wisdom. Specifically, they contended that wise leaders are able to (1) quickly ascertain the essence of a situation, including its meaning and implications for others; (2) draw on their values frameworks to determine the common good and use these assessments to drive action; (3) create informal and formal learning opportunities that facilitate the exchange of information and the construction of shared purpose; (4) use stories and metaphors to clearly communicate their experiences and intuitive knowledge to other organizational members; (5) effectively leverage their power to create opportunities for those with diverse interests to connect and work toward a common goal; and (6) provide mentoring and apprenticeships in the interest of fostering the practical wisdom of others. Here in this list of abilities we see a strong connection between wisdom and the discussion of organizational learning presented earlier in this chapter.

Indigenous leadership perspectives offer meaningful insights on the nature and practice of wisdom within non-Western societies (Intezari et al., 2021; Julien et al., 2010; Kennedy et al., 2023; Rosile et al., 2018). Wisdom rooted in Indigenous values such as harmony with nature, stewardship, mentorship, humility, kinship, and an integrated understanding of wellness (including physical, spiritual, intellectual, and relational health) offers a promising pathway for contesting and dismantling neoliberalism and white supremacy. For example, Spiller et al.'s (2021) phenomenological examination of cultural wisdom as conceptualized and practiced by Māori managers in New Zealand presents a vision of wisdom that explicitly counters the neoliberal principles of profit, efficiency, and productivity with a leadership philosophy that frames authentic relationships, the cultivation of community, and civic responsibility as essential elements of organizational success. Similarly, Spiller et al. named and critiqued transactional constructions of diversity (i.e., compositional diversity as a tool for expanding consumer engagement, improving organizational outcomes, and generating revenue) and offered Indigenous wisdom as an alternative approach to diversity and inclusion that centers reciprocal relationships rooted in mutual respect and a recognition of the whole person (not just their contribution to organizational metrics). Here we see the potential for Indigenous notions of wisdom to counter the white supremacist notions of interest convergence that frame many institutional diversity efforts. We elaborate on Indigenous leadership in chapter 8 but felt it important to acknowledge the valuable role Indigenous wisdom theory and practice play in advancing equity-minded cognitive leadership perspectives.

Within the specific context of higher education leadership, several international scholars have studied wisdom. Yang (2014) examined how leadership learning fosters wisdom among Taiwanese higher education leaders, and Jakubik (2021) drew on case study data from fourteen Finnish universities to advance a compelling argument regarding the important work higher education institutions must do to bring about a wiser and better future. The key to achieving this vision of a better future, according to Jakubik (2021), is the transformation of higher education knowledge workers into wisdom workers and wise leaders who "(1) use reason and careful observations; (2) allow for non-rational and subjective elements when making decisions; (3) value humane and virtuous outcomes; (4) have practical actions oriented towards everyday life, including work, and (5) are articulate, understand the aesthetic dimension of their work, and seek the intrinsic personal and social rewards of contributing to a good life" (p. 22). The focus on valuing human and virtuous outcomes and the good life suggests that it will orient leaders to think about others' interests and a broader collective good that can further equity and social justice. Jakubik did not offer specific guidance on the types of experiences or conditions that facilitate the cultivation of wise higher education leaders; however, Janfada and Beckett's (2019) autoethnographic study shed light on aspects of a doctoral-level leadership class ("her seminar embraced practical activities which required embodied and performative actions and judgements; she also had to articulate her own way of leadership and therefore she owned it better"; p. 343) that served to foster phronesis (practical wisdom). Similarly, although not situated explicitly in the context of higher education, Gunnlaugson (2011) explored the potential for contemplative approaches to learning in groups and teams, including intersubjective mindfulness, Quaker discernment, and leading from presence, to foster collective wisdom and facilitate the development of shared leadership commitments.

We view studies of wisdom and wise leadership within higher education as a promising strand of inquiry for contesting the twin ideologies of white supremacy and neoliberalism. The emphasis within wise leadership on elevating collective interests, particularly those that have been historically excluded; bringing lived experience into decision-making; focusing on long-term and sustainable interests; and drawing on Indigenous ways of developing knowledge has the potential to demonstrate tangible pathways for challenging the primacy of profit maximization, efficiency, and the norms of whiteness as guiding forces within higher education. We elaborate on the transformative possibilities embedded within wisdom and wise leadership research in the final chapter of the book.

Authentic Leadership

A second emerging cognitive leadership concept is authentic leadership. Although authentic leadership is frequently discussed in the context of transformational leadership (Caza & Jackson, 2011), we have decided to situate our review of authentic leadership theory and research within the cognitive perspectives chapter because scholars and practitioners seeking to facilitate organizational learning have identified authentic leadership as a valuable strategy for creating the organizational conditions that promote "open, honest, balanced, congruent and transparent communication" (Parry, 2013, p. 63), a critical precursor to organizational learning.

Additionally, another strand of authentic leadership literature emphasizes the cognitive process of follower perception with respect to identifying authenticity in formal leaders; it is the follower's perception of the leader's alignment between espoused values and actions that leads to recognition as an authentic leader (Gardiner, 2015; Owusu-Bempah et al., 2014). Dugan (2017) presented an engaging and candid summary of authentic leadership theory, noting its increasing popularity and numerous limitations, including a lack of conceptual clarity and coherence. Specifically, Dugan asserted that the absence of a unifying definition of authentic leadership makes the construct difficult to examine empirically. Additionally, consistent with other cognitive leadership perspectives featured in this chapter, the theory of authentic leadership maintains a focus on formal leaders and the leader-follower dynamic. Critiques aside, the growing popularity of authentic leadership and its potential for fostering leadership characterized by the alignment of values and actions suggest it may play a valuable role in disrupting white supremacist and neoliberal principles and practices in higher education organizations.

Drawing on positive psychology and transformational leadership scholarship, authentic leaders are characterized as self-aware and balanced processors, skilled at self-regulation guided by an internalized sense of morality, and committed to relational transparency (Dugan, 2017; Gardner et al., 2005). Collectively, these authentic leadership characteristics result in leaders who have an accurate sense of their strengths, limitations, knowledge, and values; self-regulate their actions to ensure alignment with beliefs; and cultivate authentic relationships grounded in trust, candor, and a willingness to accept feedback (Avolio & Walumbwa, 2014; Gardner et al., 2005, 2011). Authentic leaders are who they say they are (a consistency that spans time and context), contributing to an organizational environment characterized by open dialogue and a willingness to try new ideas and learn from failure—the hallmarks of organizational learning (Mazutis & Slawinski, 2008). Additional authentic leadership outcomes include enhanced teamwork, follower satisfaction, and organizational citizenship behaviors (Dugan, 2017). Given our interest in leadership that advances equity, it is important to highlight the "fundamentally moral" (Dugan, 2017, p. 261) dimension of authentic leadership; authentic leaders are guided by an internal moral compass and seek to cultivate organizational environments that demonstrate a commitment to ethical decision-making.

Both transformational and authentic leadership emphasize dialogue; however, the aims of these organizational dialogues differ. Transformational leadership emphasizes discussion in the pursuit of consensus and commitment to organizational goals. Authentic leaders do not shy away from conflict, encouraging organizational conversations that examine difficult topics and the free exchange of ideas and concerns. By valuing and practicing open communication, authentic leaders establish an organizational culture that facilitates the discovery, exchange, and adoption of new knowledge as well as incorporates feedback and the lessons of failure into organizational norms and processes. The emphasis placed on transparency in authentic leadership can help to identify and dismantle neoliberal and white supremacy power structures. Authentic leaders can foster honest discussions of inequitable policies, practices, and outcomes and translate insights into action.

As noted by Dugan (2017), research on authentic leadership is characterized by a lack of conceptual clarity and coherent empirical findings. Much authentic leadership scholarship continues to be anchored in the tenets and methodologies of postpositivism, with studies seeking to measure authentic leadership traits and outcomes (Banks et al., 2016; Caza & Jackson, 2011; Hoch et al., 2018). Within the context of higher education, only a few scholars have examined authentic leadership beyond student leadership development. Owusu-Bempah et al. (2014) studied commonalities and differences in perceptions of authentic leadership in different countries (Ghana and New Zealand) and organizational sectors (higher education and nongovernmental

172 *Perspectives on Leadership Research and Practice*

organizations). The researchers found that university staff in both Ghana and New Zealand perceived authentic leadership as characterized by self-confidence and a commitment to empathizing with, encouraging, and supporting others in the organization, highlighting a dimension of authentic leadership in higher education that is not featured in the foundational literature (i.e., support for others). Additional research is needed to examine the nature and consistency of this authentic leadership characteristic across diverse postsecondary contexts in the United States.

Another line of authentic leadership inquiry seeks to understand the influence of graduate leadership education on authentic leadership identity development (Latta, 2021; Whitehall et al., 2021). Latta (2021) used a repertory grid method to study the ILTs of students enrolled in their first and last leadership core seminar, finding evidence that doctoral leadership education may facilitate the construction of leadership identities that center the authentic leadership principles of self-reflection, transparency, open-mindedness, and the acknowledgment of personal limitations. Similarly, Whitehall et al. (2021) found significant increases in the authentic leadership constructs of self-awareness and transparency (but not balanced process or internalized moral perspective) after students completed an online graduate leadership education program. More research is needed to understand how leadership development programs within and beyond graduate education foster the adoption of authentic leadership perspectives.

Finally, we highlight Gardiner's (2015) phenomenological study of authentic leadership based on data collected from ten senior women higher education leaders. For the women featured in Gardiner's study, authentic leadership was characterized by the formation of deep relationships with campus colleagues, the demonstration of compassion, and open communication as a vehicle for fostering trust. Potential barriers to authentic leadership included bureaucratic structures that focus attention on policy and protocols rather than building relationships, pressure to conform to institutional expectations, and situations that call for the performance of emotions (e.g., confidence) or the hiding of emotions (e.g., fear) in ways that do not align with one's authentic sense of self. The participants had differing views on whether compromise, a common senior leadership strategy, contradicted the ethical commitments of authentic leadership, with some seeing compromise as a necessary, pragmatic approach to leading conflict-laden organizations and others framing a decision to compromise core values as antithetical to authentic leadership. Similarly, "performing" the role of senior leader in ways that were at odds with one's preferences or emotions was seen by some women leaders as disingenuous and by others as a critical strategy for success. The structural and personal challenges highlighted in the study influenced the leaders' framing and enactment of ethical action, leading Gardiner to question the value of the authentic leadership framework for promoting ethical behavior in higher education leaders. The connection between authentic leadership and ethical decision-making in higher education is a potentially productive line of inquiry. Additionally, Gardiner's study, anchored within the social constructivist paradigm, significantly advances our knowledge of how "situated, embodied experiences influences our understanding of authentic leadership" (p. 7). Women in Gardiner's study spoke to the inextricable connection between social identities, prejudice, and authentic leadership. More research is needed to understand the lived experiences of authentic leadership within the context of higher education organizations, with a particular focus on individuals with historically marginalized and intersectional identities (e.g., those pertaining to race, class, and gender).

EQUITY-MINDED LEADERSHIP

Equity-minded leadership is a third emerging strand of cognitive approaches to leadership that holds promise for challenging neoliberal and white supremacist principles and practices within higher education institutions. Rooted in the recognition that faculty, staff, and students continue to experience inequities within higher education despite decades of well-intentioned interventions, equity-minded leadership seeks to "promote practitioner learning that brings about the major changes in institutional practices, routines, and culture needed to obtain equitable outcomes for historically marginalized and minoritized populations" (Malcom-Piqueux & Bensimon, 2017, p. 6). Cognitive processes such as reflecting, learning, changing schemas, and reframing are at the heart of equity-minded leadership (Bragg & McCambly, 2018; Felix et al., 2015; Malcom-Piqueux & Bensimon, 2017).

Cognitive schemas play an important role in framing how individuals interpret and seek to solve organizational challenges such as inequities in educational access and achievement, labor conditions, and so on (Bragg &

McCambly, 2018; Felix et al., 2015; Malcom-Piqueux & Bensimon, 2017). Deficit-oriented schemas place the blame for inequitable outcomes on historically underrepresented individuals and their upbringing (e.g., their motivations, behaviors, goals, and resiliency) (Felix et al., 2015; Malcom-Piqueux & Bensimon, 2017). An equity-minded schema shifts focus away from minoritized individuals and instead frames inequity as a consequence of institutional (in)actions (e.g., policies, practices, structures, and routines). In the absence of explicit attention and action, discriminatory practices rooted in deficit-oriented schemas will continue to run in the organizational background (like the operating system of a computer), perpetuating inequity and expanding the equity gap. Equity-minded leadership facilitates inquiry, reflection, and actions designed to identify and change problematic mental models and practices, rewriting the operating code that guides institutional activity.

Malcom-Piqueux and Bensimon (2017) identified five principles of equity-mindedness that frame a specific way of thinking about practice that has proved successful in reducing racial educational inequities. They described the equity mindset as "(1) race conscious, (2), institutionally focused, (3) evidence based, (4) systemically aware, and (5) action oriented" (p. 6). First, Malcom-Piqueux and Bensimon framed equity-minded higher education professionals as *race conscious* in that they explicitly and unapologetically shed a spotlight on racial inequities and resist commonplace efforts to use socioeconomic status as a more socially acceptable proxy for race. Kezar and Posselt (2020) took a more expansive view of equity-mindedness and noted that while race should be privileged in consideration in US contexts given the pernicious history of race relations, equity-mindedness must also address other systemic and intersecting oppressions, including those based on class, gender, sexual orientation, religion, and ability status.

In recognition that inequity is a product of structural discrimination rooted in historical, economic, sociocultural patterns of oppression, *institutionally focused* and *systemically aware* equity-minded change efforts seek to dismantle oppressive structures and systems and replace them with institutional practices that promote equitable outcomes. Equity-minded leadership is also characterized by a commitment to robust processes of practitioner inquiry and *evidence-based* interventions that align with the needs and goals of the local context (Felix et al., 2015). This work is informed by the aims and principles of the participatory inquiry paradigm presented in chapter 2.

Rather than identifying and implementing one-size-fits-all best practices, equity-minded professionals work in teams to examine disaggregated data and document inequity (e.g., graduation and transfer rates disaggregated by race) (McNair et al., 2020). Once racial and other forms of inequity have been identified, practitioner-researchers engage in a systemic process of inquiry to understand the institutional systems, policies, and practices that contribute to documented inequities (Felix et al., 2015; Malcom-Piqueux & Bensimon, 2017; McNair et al., 2020). It is through the process of inquiry and self-discovery that practitioners recognize their discriminatory mental models and develop the equity mindset that is essential for evaluating and (re)designing institutional structures that facilitate achievement of equity aims (Felix et al., 2015).

Finally, the equity mindset is *action oriented*. Equity-minded professionals identify and implement evidence-based interventions designed to eliminate documented equity gaps. For example, a department director who recognizes that discriminatory hiring protocols have resulted in the lack of any African American female finalists for the last three full-time vacancies in her department will act on this new insight, implementing data-driven changes to hiring practices such as the revision of search committee composition and training, candidate screening rubrics, and interview protocols that were identified as barriers to equity by the practitioner research team. Engagement in an ongoing monitoring of disaggregated data will let the equity-minded practitioner know if the interventions are working or need to be revised. Although professionals located throughout the organizational hierarchy can engage in activities framed by the five principles of equity-mindedness, individuals with formal leadership positions play a key role in advancing equity-oriented change through the exercise of positional authority to identify the reduction of inequities as an institutional priority, to appoint campus representatives to the inquiry team, to ensure disaggregated institutional data is produced and shared with members of the campus community, and to implement the evidence-driven interventions (McNair et al., 2020).

Even though equity-mindedness was not initially framed as a leadership theory or approach, leadership scholars have begun to explore the connections between equity-mindedness and leadership (Bragg & McCambly, 2017,

176   *Perspectives on Leadership Research and Practice*

2018). For example, Bragg and McCambly (2017, 2018) integrated insights from scholarship on equity-mindedness, adaptive leadership, and transformative leadership to frame their description of an equity-minded change leadership approach. Within this framework, equity-minded leaders located at all levels of the organization work to identify patterns of inequity, reflect on the role that systems and structures play in creating these patterns, and seek to restructure the organization via pro-equity strategies, all while situating these processes of reflection and action in broader social, historical, economic, and political contexts.

With respect to leading an effective equity change initiative, Kezar, Glenn, et al.'s (2008) case study research on the implementation of fourteen Equity Scorecard projects (an initiative of the University of Southern California Center for Urban Education that provides support for colleges and universities committed to addressing racial equity gaps in institutional outcomes) revealed six contextual conditions that influence equity interventions, including knowledge capacity, leadership, and institutional willingness to reflect. Campus leaders at all levels of the organization who are committed to advancing equity-oriented change would be well served to proactively attend to these contextual conditions, and Kezar et al. made a direct call to action for senior administrators to publicly support equity interventions via the dedication of financial and human resources and the integration of the change efforts into institutional planning documents.

Shifting from context to practices, Galloway and Ishimaru's (2015) proposed equity-oriented Interstate School Leaders Licensure Consortium standards and Theoharis's (2010) research on equity-oriented strategies of school principals offer meaningful scholarly insights on equity-minded leadership. Galloway and Ishimaru's equity leadership standards are (1) engaging in self-reflection and growth for equity, (2) developing organizational leadership for equity, (3) constructing and enacting an equity vision, (4) supervising for improvement in equitable teaching and learning, (5) fostering an equitable school culture, (6) collaborating with families and communities, (7) influencing the sociopolitical context, (8) allocating resources, (9) hiring and placing personnel, and (10) modeling. Similarly, the principals in Theoharis's study who had successfully disrupted educational injustices in their schools focused their efforts on staff recruitment, development, and empowerment; community engagement; cultivation of a welcoming school climate; and the dismantling of inequitable programs and structures. Although situated within the context of PK–12 school leadership standards, the equity leadership practices highlighted in these studies will likely translate well to higher education contexts.

Equity-minded leadership, authentic leadership, and leadership-related wisdom are three emerging cognition-oriented approaches to leadership that hold promise for dismantling the oppressive systems and structures of neoliberalism and white supremacy. Each of these approaches places justice and the public good at the center of leadership. Additionally, all three approaches rely on cognitive processes (e.g., information processing, reflection, learning, and framing) to explain the nature and impact of leadership. Higher education scholar-practitioners committed to creating more equitable and just learning environments would be well served to expand their understanding of and capacity for engaging in these leadership frameworks.

Conclusion

The aim of this chapter was to summarize foundational and emerging cognitive perspectives on leadership. Although Kezar et al. (2006) identified the cognitive leadership approach as gaining prominence in the late twentieth and early twenty-first centuries, our contemporary literature review finds continued interest in this leadership perspective in the broad leadership research community but muted engagement within the field of higher education. Higher education scholar-practitioners interested in advancing the understanding and practice of cognitive leadership theory, including constructs such as leadership schemas, prototypes, ILTs, and organizational learning, will need to wrestle with the critiques and limitations noted earlier in this chapter. How might research endeavors disrupt the continued cognitive focus on positional, hierarchical leader-follower dynamics? What does it look like to engage in equity-minded leadership that actively places racial and economic justice above the neoliberal aims of efficiency and profit? How might higher education professionals develop the scholarly insights and personal capacity needed to disrupt hegemonic norms and assumptions (effective leaders are white, male, tall, and charismatic) that dominate leadership prototypes and constrain the opportunities and evaluations of individuals who do not conform to these oppressive mental models? These are the pressing questions that must frame cognitive leadership inquiry and practice moving forward.

178 Perspectives on Leadership Research and Practice

Wisdom, equity-minded leadership, and authentic leadership are three emerging constructs within the cognitive leadership approach that hold promise for dismantling neoliberal and white supremacist structures and norms within higher education. We specifically encourage the pursuit of research that moves beyond postpositivist efforts to measure cognitive processes and outcomes and instead seeks to examine the lived experiences and implications of cognitive processes such as ILTs, learning, wisdom, and authenticity. We return to this emerging research agenda in the final chapter of the book.

In closing, we offer a summary of key takeaways for practice.

Traditional Theory

- Current and aspiring higher education leaders who seek to influence others are well served by aligning their words and behaviors with the implicit leadership theories (ILTs) and cognitive frames of those they seek to motivate. Efforts at alignment, however, need to consider power, privilege, and oppression with respect to the potentially biased nature of ILTs.
- Individuals seeking to advance equity within and beyond higher education must engage in structured reflection and dialogue on the biased cognitions (e.g., schemas, prototypes, and ILTs) that frame their decisions and interactions.
- Structural changes (e.g., policies and protocols) must be adopted to address the structural implications of hegemonic cognitions. For example, changes to hiring committee processes must be implemented to account for cognitive bias in hiring reviews.
- Individuals need to recognize and appropriately adapt to the cultural, social, and environmental conditions within which they are situated (i.e., perceptions of appropriate leadership behaviors for managing crisis differ from those perceived as necessary to facilitate innovation).
- Individuals and teams seeking to address complex challenges need to identify their dominant cognitive frames and then actively work to ensure multiple frames are used to analyze the issue and develop resolutions. Intentionally cultivating diverse teams that represent varied disciplines, professional roles, social identities, and so on is one strategy for ensuring cognitive complexity.

- To foster the cognitive complexity of current and aspiring leaders, managers need to engage staff in transformative learning experiences characterized by disorienting professional tasks that facilitate structured opportunities for reflection on action, feedback, and the piloting of new ideas.
- Creating the conditions that promote organizational learning (e.g., systems and incentives for the discovery, diffusion, and application of innovations) is a key responsibility of formal leaders.

New Evolutions

- Wise leaders (1) forge authentic relationships with a broad array of individuals in the interest of expanding understanding and empathy for diverse perspectives and experiences; (2) convey organizational vision through the use of stories, metaphors, and actions; (3) attend to balance among personal interests, organizational needs, and the public good; (4) consider the short- and long-term implications of their efforts; and (5) foster wisdom in others both within and beyond the organization through mentorship.
- Authentic leaders demonstrate self-awareness, self-regulation, relational transparency, and a coherent moral compass. These qualities can be fostered through engagement in intentional leadership development activities.
- Authentic leaders seeking to facilitate organizational learning demonstrate a commitment to the open exchange of ideas, constructive engagement with conflict, critical reflection on feedback, and support for testing new ideas and learning from failure.
- Engaging in equity-minded leadership requires identifying, reflecting on, and dismantling the deficit-oriented cognitive schemas that attribute the perpetuation of inequity to the characteristics of historically underrepresented individuals and groups.
- The collection and analysis of empirical data, disaggregated by social identities (e.g., those based on race, class, and gender), is a critical step in the cognitive processes of reflection and learning that are essential for dismantling the mental models that construct and sustain discriminatory policies and practices.

Discussion Questions

1. Eagly and Chin (2010) called attention to the mindless cognitive processes that result in the formation and application of biased leadership prototypes and implicit leadership theories. One strategy for reducing the potential harm of discriminatory leadership cognitions is to identify and critically examine them. Spend some time reflecting on your leadership prototypes and implicit leadership theories. What experiences have informed these cognitive processes? How might your implicit leadership theories and prototypes uphold white supremacist and neoliberal notions of effective leadership?

2. Complete the Bolman and Deal frame self-assessment survey (available at https://leebolman.com/wp-content/uploads/2021/02/Leadership-Orientations-2012.pdf) and reflect on your preferred frame orientation. How do you see your frame preferences informing the meaning you make of organizational life (what you attend to and consider important), your interpersonal interactions, and your approach to leadership?

3. What ideas do you have for studying the lived experience of cognitive leadership processes such as implicit leadership theories, wisdom, and authentic leadership? What questions are of interest to you? What methodologies seem most appropriate for examining these phenomena?

4. What equity-minded leadership principles or practices might you seek to enact in your daily leadership efforts? What actions will you take to cultivate these principles and practices? What support do you need from others to strengthen your equity mindset?

Chapter 7

Chaos and Complexity Leadership Perspectives

Leticia is an assistant director in the admissions office at Olive State University. To say her role has gotten challenging would be an understatement. Over the past year during the pandemic, she has had to alter her day-to-day work practices completely to adjust to changing conditions and new protocols. All of the admissions office's recruitment practices have been modified. They are no longer able to offer campus tours or visit high schools. Instead, they have begun offering an online module as a way for prospective students to visit campus and learn more about the university. Leticia worries that students in racially diverse school districts are not developing an awareness of Olive State. The process of reviewing applications has also changed, as the admissions staff cannot sit in the room together to discuss issues that arise. These changes have led Leticia to become worried about whether the office's recruitment and admissions processes are truly equitable this year. She is not sure that she and her colleagues are all working from the same assumptions, even though they are filling out the same rubric. When the admissions team works in person, they can help socialize each other to the meaning of the rubrics and deliberate as necessary. She raises her concerns about equity with the director, Shantell Young, and also mentions that she has heard complaints from several of the staff members. Shantell looks at her with exacerbation. She notes that they are dealing with innumerable challenges, and she does not have time to consider this

182   *Perspectives on Leadership Research and Practice*

issue. Leticia suggests that she could take the lead on addressing it if given the authority and could make decisions more locally with other admissions officers. A little begrudgingly, Shantell agrees—she is simply too overwhelmed. Leticia sets off to establish a problem-solving meeting with the staff and realizes that they will need to brainstorm and come up with a new way to do things.

In this chapter, we describe chaos and complexity leadership theory. The theory further captures the transformative nature of leadership and advocates for a networked, adaptive, and collaborative approach to engaging in the leadership process.

Definition and Emergence

Chaos theory has its roots in mathematics and the physical sciences (e.g., physics, astronomy, and chemistry). It emerged when scientists began to question existing scientific explanations that failed to consider the inevitable flow of time. These scientists, who eventually became chaos theorists and pioneers, explored the universe's unpredictability and attempted to find meaning in the unpredictability rather than make the universe conform to rationalistic principles (Lorenz, 1963; Ott et al., 1990). They referred to the systems they identified as nonlinear, chaotic, and complex. From the mid-1850s into the 1980s, scientists and mathematicians like meteorologist Edward Lorenz and physicist Robert May worked to advance chaos theory, eventually finding that there is a sense of order in apparent chaos and that order and chaos are, in fact, interwoven (Jackson, 2019).

A theory related to chaos is complexity theory, which extends chaos theory into social systems. Complexity theory is a newer and more expansive theory that shares some of the same ideas as chaos theory, but it emerged and developed as a distinct area of scientific study. P. M. Allen (2001) offered a straightforward definition of complexity theory, which is also often referred to as complexity science: "It is any system that has within itself a capacity to respond to its environment in more than one way. This means that it is not a mechanical system with a single trajectory, but has some internal possibilities of choice or response that it can bring into play" (p. 150). Thus, any situation can be viewed as a complex system, including but not limited to families, organizations, and cities. The relationship between chaos and complexity has been conceptualized as such: chaos theory is the scientific theory, and complexity theory relies on chaos theory's concepts (i.e., order and disorder, predictability and unpredictability) to achieve a broader, more far-reaching utility in other spaces (McMillan, 2004). For the purposes of this chapter, we use the term *chaos and complexity theory* to honor the original contributions of chaos theorists and other scientists.

As the context for leadership grew more complex, scholars began to search for new ways of understanding leadership that were more fitting for contemporary times and challenges. They looked to chaos theory to challenge earlier theories and approaches to leadership as an ordered process and focused on social control by individuals who adapted to contingencies. Scholars used the historical roots and concepts of chaos theory, coupled with the realities of our changing environments, to redefine leadership as an emergent event that requires adaptability and collaboration (Heifetz, 1994; Wheatley, 1999). Scholars believed chaos theory was perfect for the times because it challenged the simplicity of earlier leadership theories, such as contingency approaches in which leaders simply matched a leadership style to a given task or preference of other organizational members. Chaos and complexity leadership scholars, guided by postmodern and social constructivist paradigms, call attention to the ambiguous, ever-changing realities of organizations and recognize that individuals and organizations must abandon hierarchical structures and outdated organizational processes to thrive in the presence of chaos (K. E. Allen & Cherrey, 2000; J. S. Burns, 2002; Cutright, 2001; Heifetz, 1994; Wheatley, 1999). Simply put, chaos and complexity leadership theory challenges traditional notions of hierarchy and authority and places them in tension with decentralization, collaboration, flexibility, and the adaptability of structures and processes to argue that traditional notions of leadership predicated on authority and individuality stifle innovation and threaten the survival of organizations.

Major Assumptions and Contributions

Several assumptions undergird chaos and complexity theory. They include continuous organizational learning, experimentation, flexibility, systems-level thinking and acting, and collaboration. Context is also a thread that runs through chaos and complexity leadership and the key assumptions we detail in this section.

Organizational learning helps leaders become familiar with the system's intricacies, which is especially important if there exists a desire to change it. Scholars like Wheatley (1999) and Senge (1990) have argued that organizational learning helps leaders to craft, with others, a collective vision based on data, trends, patterns, external forces, and other key information about the organization. Chaos and complexity leadership insists that organizational learning is continuous because environments and context often change. Dialogue and encouraging interactions are central to supporting learning. In higher education, as it pertains to leading for equity and the public good, it becomes particularly important for leaders to talk with and involve marginalized groups to figure out how they make sense of and navigate the campus climate and what changes they would like to see (McNair et al., 2020). A depth of knowledge at the margins can help organizations transform and develop toward equitable ends. Wheatley (1999) argued that learning from a systems level, in particular, helps leaders see the interconnectedness of organizational life and discover "many things worthy of wonder" (p. 158).

Chaos and complexity leadership theory also assumes that experimentation is necessary in order for complex environments to thrive and survive. Experimentation *is* a way to learn. As a result, one of the most important responsibilities of leaders is to experiment with new ideas and solutions that both attempt to rectify problems and change whole systems (Heifetz, 1994; Wheatley, 1999). Wheatley (1999) noted that leaders in complex environments are and must be inventors. Chaos and complexity theorists argue that leaders should lean into the fluidity and unexpectedness of complex organizations and develop and implement safe-to-fail experiments that seek to improve and sustain organizational life (Briggs & Peat, 1989; Silsbee, 2018). Wheatley (1999) suggested, for example, experimenting with organizational charts that diminish hierarchies and instead illustrate the fluid patterns of relationships. In sum, experimentation helps leaders address the ever-changing realities of organizations that happen to operate within modern global societies. It is assumed that leaders will experiment and try their hand at creative solutions to the most vexing problems plaguing their respective organizations.

Along the same lines as experimentation, another key assumption regarding chaos and complexity leadership theory is that leadership must operate from a place of flexibility. Because systems are unpredictable and internal and external contextual factors ebb and flow, leadership requires flexibility and a willingness to (re)prioritize when necessary. Scholars like J. M. Burns (1978) and J. S. Burns (2002) have exposed how the practice of leadership has become primarily concerned with attempts to conquer and control an inherently complex and uncontrollable environment. Wheatley (1999) contended that by paying close attention to the leadership process, organizations can make themselves and their leadership processes "as resilient and flexible as a spider's web" (p. 155). Requiring organizations to abide by strict organizing principles and rules fosters conformity that prevents organizations from adapting and changing according to the needs and requirements of the system. Thus, flexibility becomes an essential pillar of chaos and complexity leadership that affords organizations the power to do (not to be confused with power over) what needs to be done to secure sustainable futures. In the opening vignette, Leticia is able to make changes to admissions and recruitment efforts because of her supervisor's willingness to move beyond authoritative leadership, giving Leticia an opening to engage in the leadership process. Also, Leticia notices that the COVID-19 pandemic is requiring a great amount of flexibility and change. Instead of using previous policies and protocols, Leticia embraces the chaos and complexity of the pandemic and attempts to adapt as necessary.

Both Wheatley (1999) and Heifetz (1994) argued that leadership must be acted on and observed from a systemic perspective. The systems perspective argues that problems are complex, dynamic, and interconnected through webs of relationships. Heifetz (1994) argued that one of the most essential behaviors for adaptive leaders operating in complex environments is to get on the balcony and purposefully observe and assess the system and the situations penetrating the system. He introduced the analogy of a dance floor to demonstrate how being in motion makes it difficult to observe systems. Instead, he posited, "to discern the larger patterns on the dance floor—to see who is dancing with whom, in what groups, in what location, and who is sitting out which kind of dance—we have to stop moving and get to the balcony" (Heifetz, 1994, p. 253). Heifetz and other chaos and complexity theorists have emphasized that leaders must understand that problems and threats have to be addressed from a systemic perspective. Problems and threats may seem isolated, but they have the ability to upend entire systems. Further, scholars argue that the activity of systems thinking must be enacted

186   Perspectives on Leadership Research and Practice

with multiple and diverse perspectives so that the system can be interpreted and reflected on from multiple angles (Heifetz, 1994; Meadows, 2008; Stacey et al., 2000; Wheatley, 1999). Chaos and complexity theorists are careful to warn leaders that systems can only be influenced, not controlled (K. E. Allen & Cherrey, 2000). They are steadfast in their assumption that complex organizations are instinctively uncontrollable. Leaders must instead focus on responding and adapting as necessary. For more on systems thinking, we recommend reading Ackoff (2006), Betts (1992), Ison (1999), and Shaked and Schechter (2020).

Lastly, chaos and complexity leadership theory asserts that leadership should be collaborative and attempt to break down traditional hierarchies—focusing instead on shared power, mutual influence, and the exchange of knowledge and ideas across all levels of the organization (Heifetz, 1994; Wheatley, 1999). Chaos and complexity scholars argue that hierarchies thwart the ability for strong relations to coalesce and, in turn, allow authority-based leadership to take priority (Cutright, 2001; Wheatley, 1999). The importance of networks and relationships surfaces through collaboration and this breaking down of hierarchies. Relationships and networks inside and outside the organization are integral to cultivating and maintaining leadership activity in a chaotic and complex environment. Wheatley (1999) criticized hierarchical and disparate systems and advocated for stronger relations in leadership by noting, "The organization of a living system bears no resemblance to organization charts. Life uses networks; we still rely on boxes. But even as we draw our boxes, people are ignoring them and organizing as life does, through networks of relationships" (p. 144). Here, Wheatley is advocating for leaving behind the notion of hierarchies and replacing it with interdependent relationships, collaboration, and a place where we all become concerned with and invested in the direction of organizational life and the maintenance of a fair and just system.

Key Findings and Insights

Considerable research has been done on chaos and complexity leadership that offers key insights for scholars and leaders alike. Overall, researchers have consistently identified that taking complexity into account improves the effectiveness of leaders and the success of organizations (Heifetz & Linsky, 2002). Scholars still believe that chaos and complexity leadership remains undertheorized and understudied (Dugan, 2017; Osborn et al., 2002). Because measuring and studying complexity is difficult (Dugan, 2017), multiple research approaches have been used, but even fewer studies have successfully detached traditional hierarchical leadership from chaos and complexity leadership theory.

Chaos and complexity leadership theory is widely utilized and theorized in organizational science and management literature. Scholars contend that seeing problems and causes as patterns helps leaders implement coordinated interventions, which drives thoughtful systemic change (Cavaleri & Sterman, 1997; Jackson, 1991, 2016; Stroh, 2015). Some of the most popular and well-cited studies on chaos and complexity leadership in management are case studies and ethnographies of large corporations (e.g., Emery & Thorsrud, 1976; Gyllenhammer, 1977; Hill, 1971). These studies, among others, highlight the importance of feedback loops for helping organizations learn and adjust or, in some cases, remain in a somewhat steady state (Ackoff, 2010; Morecroft & Sterman, 1994; Randers, 1980; Warren, 2004). Feedback loops are useful in organizations because systems tend to be unpredictable. With feedback loops, organizations can better adapt to challenges as necessary and broaden leadership participation to include others' perspectives.

The few quantitative studies on chaos and complexity have been primarily focused on prediction and statistical significance associated with complexity. Streufert and Nogami (1989) sought to measure the complexity of managerial behavior and effectiveness using numeric measures. Study participants were assessed using structural measurement techniques that attached numerical value to complex traits and tasks, including breadth, high-level strategic planning, and simple activities. Managers' performance on these tasks correlated meaningfully with complexity leadership. Streufert and Nogami found that managers who scored highly in addressing unstable situations scored higher in leadership complexity than those who performed more efficiently in less chaotic and complex scenarios. These findings indicate the ability to predict how well leaders will perform and adapt to various structural and environmental complexities. The study, however, is limited in its predictive capacity and lacks external validity and practical application.

In the higher education leadership literature, some of the key findings about chaos and complexity leadership theory place emphasis on a shared vision (e.g., Kezar, 2004), detail the multidimensional and fragile relationships with both on-campus and off-campus stakeholders (e.g., S. J. Marshall, 2018), discuss the benefit of listening to the voices and perspectives of marginalized groups (e.g., Cooper & Ideta, 1994), and promote transcendence across boundaries and institutional norms (e.g., Love & Estanek, 2004). Unpredictable and chameleonic crises such as the 2008 recession and the COVID-19 pandemic have also contributed some key insights about adaptive leadership in higher education (e.g., Son et al., 2020). We detail a few studies and perspectives in the forthcoming paragraphs.

Several studies of higher education leaders have emphasized the importance of a shared vision to deal with present-day complexities. A shared vision provides a sense of purpose and coherence to organizational activities and often sets priorities (Farmer et al., 1998; Roueche et al., 2014). Cultivating a shared vision requires teaching new faculty and staff institutional missions and values (Kezar, 2004) and constantly centering student learning and student success (McNair et al., 2016; Papish, 1999). The presence of neoliberalism and white supremacy, however, often threatens any sincere notion of "shared" vision within the higher education context, as corporate and white interests implicitly focus faculty, staff, and administrators on supporting neoliberal agendas. Even perceived shared visions of student learning and student success are rooted in market values instead of the public good.

Higher education scholars have linked the collaborative nature and benefit of chaos and complexity leadership to notions of neoliberalism and white supremacy. They note that because neoliberalism and white supremacy are active elements of our complex and ever-changing world and institutions, identification of *whom* leaders collaborate with and *for what reasons* they collaborate helps to unearth important insights. Leaders often collaborate with or are answerable to external stakeholders (e.g., government agencies, foundations, accreditors, and policymakers). Higher education scholars have likened this relationship to a "dangling carrot," as external stakeholders hold money or resources (the carrot) in front of leaders and institutions in an effort to get them to advance their own interests (Beerkens & Udam, 2017; S. J. Marshall, 2018; Smythe, 2017), thus creating a fragile and dependent relationship between the two. External stakeholders often exert the ability to influence higher education priorities, and research has shown that external interests can create both friction and opportunities (Jongbloed et al.,

2008; Trow, 1996). As noted in earlier chapters, external stakeholders and groups tend to hold neoliberal and white supremacist values that are reinforced and amplified as they exchange resources for compliance with a certain way of operating. For example, particular state and system metrics often reinforce the priority of producing *workers* who are prepared for the corporate world (Giroux, 2015). And these metrics and priorities are greatly affected by state and political contexts (e.g., California may have a focus on equity and student success, whereas Florida may be more interested in banning critical race theory in classrooms). What this means is that leaders must attend to, be answerable to, and at minimum consider the different priorities of stakeholders that are enforced and mediated by state and local actors and political contexts. This particular insight illuminates complicated relationships among states, political actors, and contexts that animate chaos and complexity leadership.

Higher education scholars who write about notions of chaos and complexity leadership also discuss the importance of listening to historically silenced voices and perspectives. Cooper and Ideta (1994) conducted a qualitative study of women and minoritized higher education leaders, examining their perspectives on how to enact leadership in a complex and multicultural world. Leaders in complex environments spend more time listening and gathering information from individuals on the margins before making decisions. In addition, these leaders saw the value of different voices and perspectives in their institutions. Some leaders collected these voices and perspectives to effect a shift in power from the privileged to those groups that have been systematically disadvantaged (Cooper & Ideta, 1994). Leaders made sense of various voices instead of acting on the authority or voices and perspectives of only a few. These leaders were also committed to protecting groups in the organization that had been disempowered and silenced by domination. For example, contingent faculty, who have extremely high teaching loads, became a focus for these leaders as they tried to find ways to balance the institutional demands on this group. Leaders also listened more to students, especially student groups that have been historically disenfranchised and ignored (e.g., Black students and LGBTQ+ students).

Scholars like Love and Estanek (2004) have also been influenced by chaos and complexity theory, arguing that student affairs administrators should radically rethink their work and what it means to lead in the presence of chaos. Love and Estanek advanced a leadership framework that is built on trust, comfort with ambiguity, grassroots activism, learning, and authentic relationships. They argued that leadership should be guided by the belief that everyone in the organization can and should engage in leadership regardless of their position. An essential part of rethinking student affairs and leadership, Love and Estanek argued, is learning how to (1) value dualisms (e.g., exhibiting "both-and" thinking rather than "either-or" cognitive frames); (2) demonstrate paradigm transcendence (e.g., accept the coexistence of multiple views and understand that each view is informed by context); (3) recognize connectedness as a defining feature of organizational life (e.g., student needs are or *should be* connected to college or university operations and initiatives); and (4) embrace paradox (e.g., diversity, equity, and inclusion [DEI] programming is important, but students of color need and want more deep and meaningful programming that goes beyond "the celebration of difference"). Their framework considers notions of chaos and complexity leadership theory, especially collaboration and the breaking down of hierarchies. Their framework also embraces the chaotic and complex nature of organizational life by understanding and considering multiple perspectives and valuing dualisms.

Lastly, higher education scholars have begun documenting, perhaps unconsciously, a key insight that is becoming strikingly apparent in higher education contexts: that is, in moments of crises, the aspirational tenets of chaos and complexity leadership theory (i.e., collaboration, flexibility, and adaptability) are abandoned. Research from the 2008 recession supports the argument that economic crises lead many higher education institutions to feel insecure about their future (S. Davis, 2015; Skinner, 2010). This fear and ambiguity frequently lead to an abandonment of more collective and collaborative notions of leadership and reinforcement of bureaucratic, hierarchical notions of leadership in which one or a select few leaders make decisions. When this is coupled with neoliberalism and white supremacy, the most vulnerable and most marginalized (e.g., contingent faculty, racially minoritized students, and support workers) ended up deeply affected and inconvenienced. The context and overall environment of higher education were and continue to be pivotal to understanding why notions of chaos and complexity leadership theory may be abandoned in times of crisis. With the ongoing privatization of higher education and decreased state funding, leaders are tasked to find workarounds to these complex economic issues that crises exacerbate, and to do so in an expeditious manner (Gigliotti, 2019). As a result, many revert to habits of hierarchy and control rather than adopting the very approaches that would have them successfully address unstable and complex environments. A small subset of COVID-19 studies have also supported this insight, showcasing how institutions have made quick and irrational decisions to bring campus community members back in person during a surge of positive cases, without demonstrating care for mental health or physical health concerns or even consulting other campus community members about their wants and needs (e.g., Kelchen et al., 2021; J. Marshall et al., 2020; Son et al., 2020). While more studies about the effects of COVID-19 on higher education leadership undoubtedly will emerge in the coming years, it remains concerning that so few studies have utilized chaos and complexity leadership theory to study day-to-day leadership processes in higher education.

Critiques

Chaos and complexity leadership theory is not without critique. The theory remains undertheorized and rather difficult to theorize because of its many intricacies. Dugan (2017) noted that it struggles to move from the theory-building to the empirical stage because "the ability to study the concept requires a different set of research design approaches than are typically used in the dominant leadership literature" (p. 282). We have yet to expand our theoretical, methodological, and epistemological toolbox to adequately study and practice chaos and complexity leadership. We have also departed from the original, scientific key concepts detailed in chaos science theory (i.e., strange attractors and the butterfly effect—for more information on these, we suggest reading Gleick, 1987). Few leadership studies that use chaos and complexity theory call back to scientific concepts that undergird chaos theory.

Another critique is that scholars present complex systems as neutral (Fenwick, 2010; Koopmans & Stamovlasis, 2016). As a result, they also perpetuate the notion that leadership is a neutral, apolitical activity and process carried out by objective individuals, which reinforces the postpositivist paradigm that chaos and complexity theory intentionally attempts to move away from. In chaos and complexity leadership, leaders can play an active role in fortifying and reinforcing notions of neoliberalism and whiteness (and white supremacy). To counter this, leaders must be cognizant of how the system benefits from and reacts to the presence of neoliberalism and whiteness. It would be advantageous for leaders to also imagine their campuses in the absence of neoliberalism and whiteness. At present, chaos and complexity leadership theory is silent on notions of neoliberalism and whiteness. Further research is needed to expand chaos and complexity leadership to account for neoliberal and white supremacist realities in contemporary sectors like higher education. It would also be advantageous to explore how neoliberalism and white supremacy run counter to chaos and complexity leadership theory and further promote rigidity instead of equitable and just fluidity. In racist and neoliberal regimes, organizations and the leadership process become more about trying to control the uncontrollable instead of embracing the chaos.

There is also a lack of theoretical constructs embedded in chaos and complexity leadership theory that address and consider power relations, politics, and responsibility (Tourish, 2018). This gap produces clashing interests and the incessant presence of hierarchy and bureaucracy, which presents a real problem when higher education institutions are faced with pressures to advance equity, justice, and the public good.

Popularized theories about chaos and complexity leadership have actually reasserted notions of neoliberalism and white supremacy. In 2007, Uhl-Bien et al. published their influential paper, "Complexity Leadership Theory: Shifting Leadership from the Industrial Age to the Knowledge Era." To date, it has been cited over two thousand times. In their paper, Uhl-Bien et al. introduced the complexity leadership theory model, which argues that complex adaptive systems require three types of leadership: (1) leadership that is grounded in bureaucracy, hierarchy, and control (administrative leadership); (2) leadership that is optimistic about change and interested in creative problem-solving and organizational learning (enabling leadership); and (3) leadership that is focused on emergent, informal adaptive dynamics throughout the organization (adaptive leadership). Complex leadership theory argues that all three types of leadership are both needed and entangled. In fact, Uhl-Bien et al. argued that leadership only exists in, and is a function of, the interactions among these three types of leaders. When hierarchy is maintained, the other, emergent forms of leadership are less able to challenge existing power structures and make radical changes. Uhl-Bien et al. tried to position hierarchical leadership as necessary practice in organizations, which, in turn, fortifies notions of neoliberalism and white supremacy that rely on hierarchy and excess of power to maintain legitimacy.

New Evolutions

Despite the reassertion of neoliberalism and white supremacy in complexity leadership theory, we have also seen a few more promising evolutions of chaos and complexity leadership theory. Scholars looking to strengthen chaos and complexity leadership theories have done so through the lens of advancing racial equity and challenging dominant and oppressive systems. In this section, we chronicle a new evolution in the field of higher education, the weaver-leader framework (Fries-Britt et al., 2020). Additionally, we discuss abolitionist leadership (R. S. Harvey, 2021), which comes out of the K–12 literature but is sure to gain traction in higher education in the coming years. We also consider critical systems thinking (Pak & Ravitch, 2021a) as a way to alter our contemporary systems toward equity and justice.

Like the evolutions we discussed in the transformational leadership chapter, these evolutions of chaos and complexity leadership theory designate specific end goals toward which leadership should work. All of these evolutions rectify one prevalent critique of chaotic and complex systems, which is that these systems can be adaptable to neoliberal and white supremacist ends (Fenwick, 2010). These new evolutions, instead, are clear that leadership should be a collaborative and networked process with power-sharing aimed toward equitable and liberatory ends. These evolutions also attempt to add new assumptions to chaos and complexity theory, such as overcommunication and engaging contradictions, just to name a few.

Weaver-Leader Framework

The weaver-leader framework connects thoughtful leadership activities including overcommunicating, setting and sharing expectations, and building relationships, all in an effort to create common ground and advance a shared vision toward racial equity work with input from those who have historically been excluded (Fries-Britt et al., 2020). The framework advocates for

194 *Perspectives on Leadership Research and Practice*

a networked approach to leadership, especially after racial crises (the researchers studied the 2015 racial crisis at the University of Missouri as a case), arguing that campuses benefit from collectively working together and thinking together about a path forward, minimizing hierarchy and hierarchical power relations along the way. The networks are cross-disciplinary, diverse, and inclusive. The framework also makes the case for acknowledging fragmented system elements and weaving them together as a way to move toward equity and justice (e.g., people, policies, and behaviors). The weaver-leader framework builds on and evolves complexity leadership theory by offering new processes (actively working with stakeholder communities and actively listening) to counter neoliberalism and whiteness in the aftermath of racial crises and the rebuilding that must occur in their wake. Elements of the framework such as building networks, actively working with stakeholder communities, actively listening, and overcommunicating work against whiteness and neoliberalism, broadening the leadership process and allowing more stakeholders into the process. For the University of Missouri, strengthening networks and communication channels proved to be helpful in ensuring everyone had the same access to information, resisting neoliberal and white supremacist notions that conspire against transparency. Fries-Britt et al. (2020) argued for expanding shared governance structures and bringing more voices into decision-making processes as a way to make the leadership process more networked and collaborative.

In addition, Fries-Britt et al. (2020) posited that the weaver-leader is adaptive—setting up structures for learning and deliberation in the healing and reconciliation process. Fries-Britt et al. gave leadership activities a means to an end by explicitly stating their significance in advancing racial equity. The framework advances our main argument in this book, that leadership can be a pathway to equity and justice if done with others and with the right intention. Major assumptions like collaboration, flexibility, continuous organizational learning, and systems-level thinking are present in this framework.

Fries-Britt et al. (2020) wrote, "Weavers are able to see beyond the fractured views and envision a time when there is more common ground across the campus" (p. 4). To create a shared vision for DEI work on campus, leaders must imagine beyond the present and embrace imagination and experimentation, another key assumption that undergirds chaos and complexity theory. Weaver-leaders tap into their imagination while embracing the tension and complexity in the moments following a racial crisis. They understand that DEI issues will not be solved quickly, but instead take their time and work collectively to make substantive progress toward realizing their DEI goals. Further, Fries-Britt et al. asserted that leaders must intentionally and actively communicate, set expectations, and build relationships. These tenets capture the major assumptions that undergird chaos and complexity theory, such as collaboration and flexibility. We further explore the tenets of the weaver-leader framework in the subsequent paragraphs.

Whereas communication is important, Fries-Britt et al. (2020) noted that *over*communication is even more crucial. This critical tenet of the framework stresses that leaders must communicate progress as it is made, share approaches taken, and prioritize personalized forms of communication. Fries-Britt et al. noted that overcommunicating keeps everyone informed and helps to build the relationships needed to heal and recover from racial crises. They also posited that weaver-leaders must be comfortable sharing incomplete information. This prevents rumors from circulating around campus and in networked circles. Overcommunication ensures that individuals across campus are included in the healing and reconciliation process. It is a tenet that helps to disrupt whiteness and neoliberalism, leaving the door open for community members to demand accountability and transparency in the rebuilding phase.

Additionally, setting and sharing expectations is crucial in the weaver-leader framework. According to the framework, expectations can and will change as new issues and emotions arise, and this understanding is supported by major assumptions of chaos and complexity theory like flexibility and experimentation. Fries-Britt et al. (2020) noted that the complex environment of higher education calls for managing different expectations and accepting nonlinear and uneven progress because different changes require different stakeholders and some changes take more time due to bureaucracy and governance structures. Generally, setting and sharing expectations is pivotal to creating a campus that cares deeply about racial equity.

The last tenet of the weaver-leader framework is relationship building. Relationship building is a vital process for recovering from racial crises on

196 *Perspectives on Leadership Research and Practice*

campus. Fries-Britt et al. (2020) noted that leaders should prioritize making broad connections, hosting open forums, having meetings with key campus constituents, and being on the ground to connect with students. Relationship building is also a tenet in the work of Heifetz (1994) and Wheatley (1999), as they both stressed the importance of viewing leadership as a relational process.

Abolitionist Leadership

In his book *Abolitionist Leadership in Schools: Undoing Systemic Injustice through Communally Conscious Education*, R. S. Harvey (2021) offered K–12 leaders insights about and approaches to advancing equity and engaging in abolitionist leadership. Harvey argued that institutions like education are doing more harm than good to students of color and are inadequately educating students about the facts of our nation (e.g., settler colonialism, slavery and the afterlife of slavery, and the dehumanizing effects of capitalism). Harvey asserted that in order for education to be the site of liberation and endless possibilities, it must be led by abolitionists. He described an abolitionist as "a passionately human, radically moral, no less divine freedom conspirator who embodies (or is consumed by) the principles of collective community power, the transformative justice of love, the universal emancipation of all oppressed people, the dismantling of subjugating social systems, and the practice of imagining and pursuing a new world, a new way, and a new witness" (p. 18). Harvey directly addressed the contested nature of leadership as an apolitical and neutral process and activity. Instead, he firmly argued for an abolitionist stance, leadership objective, and leader identity. Harvey, along with other scholars who also study abolitionist leadership (e.g., Gray et al., 2021), invited contemporary leaders to break free of plantation leadership logics and principles (see chapter 4 in this book) and to instead work to advance education toward the liberation of oppressive systems and systematically oppressed and disadvantaged people. R. S. Harvey (2021) named nine rhythms to abolitionist leadership that help to further construct the abolitionist leadership framework: (1) students are humans, not property; (2) people and place are mutually beneficial; (3) institutionalized academic exploitation should be abolished; (4) imagination cannot be policed; (5) racism and white supremacy in classrooms must be rejected; (6) complex, multifaceted histories should be embraced; (7) the grip of oppression can be loosened by engaging in healing and humanizing actions and exercise; (8) relationships should be deepened to challenge forms of domination and oppression; and (9) hope is invented every day. These nine rhythms are essential to abolitionist leadership and are meant to be acted out every day. Central to these rhythms are acts of resistance and embracing the contradictions that come with the process of tearing down one system to build another.

The abolitionist leadership framework embraces major assumptions of chaos and complexity leadership theory such as experimentation, flexibility, and systems-level thinking. An example that captures all three of these assumptions is that of the "human-first" approach. R. S. Harvey (2021) advocated for K–12 leaders to experiment with this approach, in which "schools, and school leaders . . . exercise [their] strategic imagination on how to plan with humans in mind and how to ensure that the humans within the community have the resources and tools required to continue advancing the community" (p. 105). He juxtaposed the "human-first" approach with the techno-neoliberal approach of minimizing people and tasks and leveraging technology to enhance the individual human experience and save, in this case, school district money. The human-first approach requires a great deal of flexibility and comfort with uncertainty, as humans are constantly being (re)defined by their contexts and situations. Harvey also argued that the human-first approach helps to deepen care and requires leaders to think about the people within the system of K–12 education and how they are affected by the "technology-first" way of thinking that animates much of the K–12 education space. Harvey offered an invitation for leaders to submit to abolitionist leadership praxis, in which humans and their full beings are always considered in leadership activities such as strategic planning. Harvey noted and accepted that the human experience is ever changing, meaning that abolitionist leaders must adapt accordingly.

R. S. Harvey (2021) pointed to the need to engage contradictions—the space in between reality and the imaginary and aspirational. Harvey, and other abolitionists and activists (see Hale, 2008; Purnell, 2021), acknowledged that revolutionary breakthroughs and systemic changes derive from the recognition of contradictions apparent in our psyches, society, and institutions. Harvey argued that we must embrace that contradiction and let such contradictions animate collective leadership efforts. Harvey also offered abolition as

198   Perspectives on Leadership Research and Practice

a lens to observe the system as a whole. Viewing the system in this way requires an "acknowledgement, and naming, of the identity/ies of the ones shaping, managing, and assessing accountability, which directly influences the level to which oppression and racism operate" (R. S. Harvey, 2021, pp. 180–181). Here, Harvey once again evolved chaos and complexity leadership by paying close attention to who has the most power and authority to operate systems and to take identity into account, especially in bureaucratic systems like education. Lastly, Harvey added to concepts of organizational learning to move beyond quantitative data and statistics to more contextual information such as history as a crucial component of understanding systems.

Having an abolitionist approach requires the experimentation and imagination noted as central to complexity theory. Harvey's abolitionist approach is future oriented in nature, calling for leaders to think about the past, present, and future simultaneously. A future where racism and domination do not exist requires thinking about our world in wholly new ways, breaking from current ways of operating and being within institutions.

Critical Systems Thinking

Senge (1990) defined systems thinking as "a discipline for seeing wholes. It is a framework for interrelationships rather than things, for seeing patterns of change rather than static snapshots" (p. 68). To take it a step further, *critical* systems thinking attempts to draw connections between how and to what effect power, identity, and oppressive logics and ideologies come to characterize and influence systems (Ortegón-Monroy, 2003). Critical systems thinking maintains all of the traditional ideas and concepts that undergird systems thinking (see Meadows, 2008, and Stroh, 2015, for more on systems thinking) but applies a critical overlay to understand and challenge oppressive and dominant systems.

There is a consensus among scholars that reflection is important in understanding and challenging oppressive and dominant systems (Duncan-Andrade & Morrell, 2008; Pak & Ravitch, 2021a). The Annie E. Casey Foundation (2014) offered several questions meant to be asked and reflected on in community with various stakeholders to "see the system" (p. 8):

1. What are the racial inequities, barriers, or negative outcomes involved in the problem being examined? Who is burdened most and who benefits most?

2. What institutions are involved? What unfair policies and/or practices are involved?
3. What social conditions or determinants contribute to the problem? What other compounding dynamics are involved (such as income or gender inequities)?
4. How did things get this way, and what are some of the cumulative impacts?
5. What can be learned from prior efforts to solve the problem or change the system?
6. What strategies could result in systemic change and advance equitable solutions?

These questions, and the notion of reflection, push the organizational learning assumption that undergirds chaos and complexity leadership theory. Instead of simply learning about the organization's mission and vision regarding equity and social justice, critical systems thinking, and more specifically the reflection component, challenges those across the organizational hierarchy to ask themselves questions and offer answers from their unique purview. This individual reflection exposes who has access to what information and why and, further, who has the ability to expose the lack of transparency apparent in the organization. On a more positive note, this individual reflection activity can help broaden participation in the leadership process and foster more collaboration.

Pak and Ravitch (2021b) also replied to Dugan's (2017) critique of chaos and complexity theory and the lack of adequate methods to study chaos and complexity leadership by offering some applied research methods, such as transect walks, photovoice, empathy interviews, oral histories, systems mapping, and affinity mapping, to get a more nuanced understanding of systems and how people are deliberately disadvantaged by them.

Conclusion

This chapter sought to outline the basics of chaos and complexity leadership theory. We traced the emergence and offered a definition of chaos and complexity theory. Furthermore, we offered a number of key insights and studies that have relied on the theory over the years. We then mapped out critiques of the theory and highlighted some new evolutions to it that help to solidify the theory as worthy of study and use in empirical research and practice,

Perspectives on Leadership Research and Practice

paying particular attention to the ways the new evolutions seek to challenge neoliberalism, whiteness, and other oppressive systems. This chapter shows that leadership can be a pathway to equity and justice; however, we must first eradicate some of the structures and beliefs that continue to cement hierarchy and other traditional notions of leadership in organizational life.

In closing, we offer a summary of key takeaways for practice.

Traditional Theory

- Leadership should be a process that is flexible and adaptable because of the chaotic and complex nature of our environment and its organizations.
- Leaders should always look for ways to challenge and dismantle hierarchies and other notions of bureaucracy, as hierarchies can serve as barriers to equity and public-good missions and goals.
- Organizational learning should be embedded in the leadership process and a continuous endeavor—organizations are constantly changing, and new information and insights are always emerging.
- Leaders should consider experimentation as a way to keep organizations afloat in unpredictable and changing times. Innovation is key in chaos and complexity leadership.
- The realities of the system and how the system will respond are important considerations for leaders to ponder and use to help guide their decisions.
- In times of crisis, leaders tend to pull away from the progressive and collaborative elements of chaos and complexity leadership and instead embrace traditional, hierarchical notions of leadership.
- The leadership process should center on relationships and networks. Responsibility regarding leadership processes should be shared.

New Evolutions

- Leaders need to overcommunicate in times of uncertainty and chaos and allow a shared vision and subsequent expectations to guide leadership processes.
- Leaders in higher education must see students as humans, not property, and make decisions with them in mind.
- Leaders should embrace an abolitionist stance and mindset as ways to create new and progressive paths forward and challenge notions of oppression.

- Leaders must break free of the neoliberal and white supremacist shackles placed on their imaginations and constantly question how they are operating within oppressive and dehumanizing logics and frames.
- Individual and collective reflection are important aspects of the leadership process and a key way to "see the system."

Discussion Questions

1. How might Leticia use an abolitionist leadership framework to advance equity in her role in the admissions office?
2. We briefly discussed how the concepts that undergird chaos theory in math and the sciences are notably missing from leadership theory. Take some time to familiarize yourself with the concepts of strange attractors and the butterfly effect, then try your hand at sharing some examples of these concepts in contemporary higher education. Consider how you might work to address these problems by relying on chaos and complexity leadership theory.
3. Why do you think there is resistance to notions of chaos and complexity leadership in higher education?

Chapter 8

Cultural Leadership Perspectives

In the chapter 6 opening vignette, we introduced Linda Martinez, a finalist for the presidential vacancy at Green Valley State College. As you may recall, Linda is a Latina woman in her early 50s who identifies as the daughter of immigrants and a first-generation college student. Before assuming her current role as the provost at a Historically Black College (HBCU) in the southern United States, she followed a traditional academic leadership pathway, rising through the ranks of the professoriate to serve as chair in a department of public health at a large, predominantly white research university. She then transitioned to the role of dean at the same HBCU where she now serves as chief academic officer. In preparation for her Green Valley State College presidential interview, Linda sits down at her desk to write out some notes on her leadership philosophy and style.

Linda has given considerable thought to her leadership journey as a result of participating in a leadership institute sponsored by a national association for public health scholars. The aim of the program is to expand the pipeline of women of color into public health leadership roles. The institute's curriculum is guided by the principles of applied critical leadership (Santamaría & Santamaría, 2012), an emerging cultural approach to leadership rooted in critical race theory (CRT) that views the cultural knowledge, skills, and dispositions of individuals from historically marginalized communities as strengths that uniquely position these leaders to bring about equity-oriented change. Workshop activities and reflective writing practices have helped Linda recognize the ways her race, ethnicity, gender, socioeconomic class, immigration status, and other salient social identities have shaped her leadership experiences and approach to facilitating change. Examining her leadership journey through a CRT lens has shed light on the systemic oppression (organizational policies and practices anchored in the norms of white supremacy, patriarchy, and capitalism) that has limited her access to leadership opportunities as a female faculty member of color and incentivized the adoption of a leadership style that mirrored that of her successful white male colleagues.

In addition to helping Linda recognize how her intersectional social identities influence her leadership style, the institute curriculum also examines the interdependent relationship between leadership and organizational culture. Linda and her leadership mentor, a seasoned Black female president of a local community college, have engaged in numerous discussions regarding the need for higher education leaders to understand the role they play in shaping organizational culture as well as how organizational culture shapes their approach to leadership. Having held academic leadership roles at both a predominantly white research institution and a comprehensive master's HBCU, Linda recognizes the distinct cultural norms that characterize both institutional types and frequently reflects on how she has adapted her leadership approach since arriving at the HBCU, shifting from a hierarchical model of authority and decentralized decision-making to a leadership style characterized by collaboration, open communication, and consensus-based decisions.

As Linda wraps up her interview preparations, she reflects on the valuable lessons she has gained from her participation in the leadership institute. She feels prepared and excited to share her unique leadership journey and style with the Green Valley campus stakeholders, an approach guided by the principles of cultural leadership perspectives.

In this chapter, we build on the brief introduction to cultural leadership embodied by Linda's story, providing a detailed overview of traditional concepts and new developments in cultural leadership theories and practices.

204 *Perspectives on Leadership Research and Practice*

You may note this chapter is a bit longer than the preceding ones, reflecting the significant growth in this line of leadership research since Kezar et al. (2006) conducted their review. This extended discussion of cultural leadership also reflects the promise this approach holds for contesting and dismantling the twin ideologies of neoliberalism and white supremacy. Before synthesizing new research insights and implications for practice, we review the definitions, emergence, major assumptions, and contributions of cultural approaches to leadership. The chapter also includes a summary of criticisms leveled against this body of work, as well as an examination of evolutions in cultural leadership. We close the chapter with a summary of key points and discussion questions intended to spark individual reflection and group dialogue.

Definitions and Emergence

In contrast to postpositivist leadership frameworks, which seek to identify universal leadership traits or the essential aspects of the leader-follower dynamic, cultural leadership perspectives recognize that leadership processes are situated within complex sociocultural systems and thus reflect the influence of history, identity, context, and culture (Alvesson, 2011; Kezar et al., 2006). Guided by constructivist, critical, and participatory paradigm assumptions, cultural leadership theorists examine how culturally and contextually specific conditions (e.g., values, beliefs, norms, and rituals) and intersectional social identities (e.g., race and ethnicity, gender, and nationality) inform leadership perspectives and behaviors. This strand of leadership inquiry also considers the ways in which systemic oppression rooted in racism, sexism, heteronormativity, and so on shapes and constrains the leadership experiences of individuals and groups. Contemporary evolutions in cultural leadership theories, including the expansion of Indigenous leadership perspectives (McCall, 2020; Newenham-Kahindi & Stevens, 2021; Spiller et al., 2020; Voyageur et al., 2015) and the development of applied critical leadership (Santamaría & Santamaría, 2015) and other culturally responsive leadership models (Pak & Ravitch, 2021a), honor the lived experience, unique wisdom, and positive attributes that historically marginalized individuals and communities draw on while engaging in leadership endeavors that seek to advance equity and social justice. Kezar et al. (2006) noted that cultural leadership perspectives were rising in prominence in the early twenty-first century, and this body of scholarship has continued to expand in recent years (Alvesson, 2011; Pak & Ravitch, 2021a; Santamaría & Santamaría, 2015, 2016a).

J. M. Burns's (1978) examination of transformational leadership and the emphasis he placed on the role of values and purpose in shaping leadership processes have been credited with paving the way for cultural leadership perspectives (Kezar et al., 2006), shifting attention away from the search for universal leadership truths and instead recognizing that leadership is a constructed phenomenon rooted in local values and shared meaning. Cultural perspectives are also rooted in and build on previous studies of context and leadership. Classic contingency theories such as path-goal theory and Fiedler's contingency model revealed the influence of contextual conditions related to task, social dynamics, and time on leadership processes, and contemporary contextual and cultural leadership scholars have extended this line of inquiry (Oc, 2018). Drawing on Johns's (2006) categorical framework for context, which details the influence of omnibus contextual factors (broad dynamics such as national culture, organizational type, or societal or organizational events such as the pandemic) and discrete contextual conditions (e.g., task or physical environment characteristics) on leadership, Oc (2018) synthesized contemporary contextual leadership scholarship that underscores the important role that multiple levels of context play in shaping leadership processes and outcomes. Although both processual and cultural leadership perspectives examine the influence of context within leadership, developing a deep understanding of leadership processes is the primary focus within processual leadership, while cultural leadership scholars seek to understand the relationship of mutual influence between contextual conditions like organizational values or nationality and leadership.

Under the broad umbrella of cultural leadership perspectives, a number of subfields exist, including studies examining the intersection of organizational culture and leadership; leadership perspectives rooted in national culture; and explorations of the ways in which social identities influence leadership perceptions, experiences, and behaviors. In the next section, we provide a snapshot of contemporary cultural approaches to leadership, highlighting foundational assumptions and the major contributions of this

Major Assumptions and Contributions

Alvesson (2011) identified three prominent perspectives on the relationship between leadership and culture. The first emphasizes leadership as local cultural understanding, reflecting shared beliefs about power, influence, human behavior, interpersonal relationships, and so on. Operating from this perspective, researchers investigate how members of a specific culture (e.g., a society, an organization, or an occupation) talk about and enact leadership beliefs, seeking to identify shared meanings that maintain and reproduce local culture. Within the context of higher education, researchers operating from this perspective aim to understand how leadership discourses and actions reflect the culture of a campus as a whole or distinctive subcultures (e.g., an academic department or professional roles).

The second cultural leadership perspective identified by Alvesson (2011) examines the active role culture plays in shaping leadership. Rather than exploring conceptualizations of leadership as a reflection of culture, this strand of inquiry seeks to understand how shared values, beliefs, and norms regarding what is perceived as legitimate leadership discourse and behavior guide and constrain the actions of those who seek influence within a culture. Here we see a connection to research on implicit leadership theories and prototypes reviewed in the chapter on cognitive approaches to leadership. As discussed in chapter 6, implicit leadership theories specify the traits, characteristics, and behaviors expected to be exhibited by individuals who are categorized as leaders (Dugan, 2017; Forsyth & Nye, 2008; Lee & Fiske, 2008). Implicit leadership theories are rooted in specific cultures and contexts. Accordingly, individuals seeking to exert influence within a particular culture are wise to align their actions with expected behaviors (Lord & Emrich, 2001). Failure to conform to the culture's leadership norms is likely to result in limited influence or negative perceptions of one's leadership competencies (Dugan, 2017; Junker & van Dick, 2014). Within the context of higher education, extensive leadership selection and socialization processes focus on communicating cultural norms to prospective and emerging leaders. Individuals who conform to organizational values and behavioral expectations are rewarded with influence; those who fail to adapt to cultural cues regarding leadership may experience resistance and short tenures in office.

Alvesson's (2011) third cultural leadership perspective sheds light on the role leadership, particularly organizational founders and formal leaders (Schein, 2010), plays in shaping organizational culture. In this strand of inquiry, scholars seek to understand how leaders establish and convey cultural values, beliefs, and norms in the early days of an organization or facilitate cultural change when existing shared beliefs and patterns of behavior no longer meet organizational needs. Scholars also examine the role leadership processes and leaders play in reproducing and maintaining culture in the face of constant change (e.g., staff turnover, new technologies). Alvesson was critical of Schein's (2010) and others' preoccupation with the influence of the formal leader on the establishment and communication of organizational culture, and he noted that a diverse array of contextual and cultural factors shape human actions and perceptions, including societal, occupational, and generational cultures. Alvesson (2011) advocated dedicating less scholarly attention to the culture-shaping efforts of positional leaders and instead spending more time seeking to understand "leadership as the adaptation, mechanical reproduction, reinforcement, creative variation and/or rejuvenation of dominating cultural orientations in organizations" (p. 161).

In addition to advancing understanding of the relationship between culture and leadership, cultural leadership scholars have explored and explained the influence of social identities (particularly race, ethnicity, gender, sexual orientation, and nationality) on leadership experiences and processes. These researchers have identified shared approaches to leadership rooted in social identities (e.g., Bordas, 2012, identifies a set of multicultural leadership values commonly held by Latinx, African American, and American Indian communities) and highlighted the significance of intersectional minoritized identities in leadership experiences (e.g., calling attention to the unique barriers confronted by Black women administrators) (Agosto & Roland, 2018; Breslin et al., 2017; Chance, 2022). This line of inquiry has also illustrated the ways in which normative (i.e., gendered, heteronormative, neoliberal, and white supremacist) leadership assumptions and beliefs perpetuate discrimination and oppression (Carli & Eagly, 2016; H. Liu, 2019; Lugg & Tooms,

208   *Perspectives on Leadership Research and Practice*

2010). Rather than exclusively framing leaders with minoritized identities as the targets of oppression, scholars examining the relationship between social identities and leadership have also documented the positive attributes fostered as a result of successfully navigating identity-based leadership challenges (e.g., resilience, collaborative style, and the ability to manage uncertainty) (Chan et al., 2021; Chance, 2022; Coon, 2001; C. Lee, 2020; Santamaría & Santamaría, 2012, 2015).

A foundational assumption undergirding all cultural approaches to leadership is that it is critical for individuals engaged in leadership to recognize and reflect on the cultural influences (history, values, norms, rituals, traditions, identities, etc.) that shape their leadership beliefs, as well as to cultivate the capacity to accurately interpret and adapt to diverse leadership contexts and cultures (Ayman & Korabik, 2010). A keen ability to observe and make sense of one's cultural surroundings and engage in perspective taking are critical cultural leadership competencies.

The contributions of cultural theory are quite significant. Leadership is seen in a much broader perspective as part of the human condition and a vital part of any culture. In addition to opening up new areas of leadership inquiry, such as values, symbols of meaning, and social identities, cultural approaches have also provided a temporal perspective to leadership research, recognizing the importance of the history of a society or organization to the leadership process.

Key Insights and Findings

Numerous studies have examined the relationship between various cultural constructs (e.g., values, race, or gender) and the leadership process, demonstrating that culture is indeed a very significant component of leadership. This section highlights the ways that leadership research from a cultural perspective has evolved in recent years, taking new directions in the study of organizational culture, social identities, and cross-cultural issues. Table 8.1 provides a summary of the distinct yet overlapping strands of cultural leadership discussed in this section.

Leadership and Organizational Culture

As mentioned earlier, the emergence of values as an important leadership construct can be attributed to the rising prominence of research on cultural

Cultural Leadership Perspectives　209

Table 8.1　Cultural leadership perspectives

Theme	Foundational research
The role that formal and informal leaders play in **shaping culture and meaning-making** in their groups and organizations	J. M. Burns's (1978) influential work on transformational leadership highlighted the central role leaders play in conveying purpose and values to organizational members. Schein (2010) underscored the significant influence formal leaders and other individuals play in shaping organizational core beliefs and culture.
Influence of **social identities** on leadership perceptions, experiences, and behaviors	A diverse array of scholars have examined the influence of social identities on leadership. Focal identities include race and ethnicity (Bordas, 2012), gender (Eddy et al., 2017; Madsen, 2008), sexual identity (Fassinger et al., 2010; Lugg & Tooms, 2010; Pryor, 2021), ability (Roberson et al., 2021), and intersectional identities (D. R. Davis & Maldonado, 2015; Menchaca et al., 2016; Montas-Hunter, 2012).
Similarities and differences in leadership perspectives across diverse **national cultures**	The GLOBE study (House et al., 2004) and similar projects seek to reveal universally adopted and culturally specific leadership characteristics through the analysis of data collected in diverse national contexts (see Dorfman et al., 2012; Hofstede, 1994; Hofstede et al. 2010; G. S. Martin et al., 2013; Oc et al., 2015).
Culturally relevant leadership that explicitly values the cultural knowledge of individuals from historically oppressed communities and views their unique experiences and perspectives as strengths in efforts to advance equity	Santamaría and Santamaría's (2011, 2016b) applied critical leadership is a strengths-based model of leadership rooted in transformational leadership, critical race theory, and critical multiculturalism developed to understand and celebrate the leadership practices of individuals who identify with multiple historically oppressed social groups.
Indigenous leadership principles and practice rooted in Indigenous ways of knowing	Indigenous leadership scholarship examines the shared values and commitments anchored in Indigenous ways of knowing that emphasize service to the community, collective wisdom, connections to ancestors and nature, and the importance of storytelling (McCall, 2020; Minthorn & Chávez, 2015b; Spiller et al., 2020).

leadership. As with culture, many definitions and interpretations of values exist, and values can be manifested in multiple ways throughout an organization (e.g., mission statements, ethical codes, or reward structures). Building on the assumption introduced earlier that leaders actively shape organizational culture, researchers have investigated the role leaders' values play in the construction of culture. In *Organizational Culture and Leadership*, Schein (2010) drew on years of research with some of America's most well-known organizations to inform his argument that leaders' values underpin most organizational cultures. He described culture as being multifaceted and consisting of three key layers. In the first layer, the one closest to the surface, are visible organizational behaviors and practices. Underlying those behaviors in the second layer are espoused values that represent organizational philosophies and understandings. The third and deepest layer of culture consists of values and core beliefs that construct the philosophies represented by organizational actions. It is at this level, the deepest source of organizational ideologies, that leaders' values are most influential. Schein explained that when groups and cultures are first created, they adopt the thoughts, beliefs, and assumptions of certain individuals. Those individuals, who are often later identified as leaders, play a central role in determining the philosophies and subsequent actions of an organization and its constituents. One example from higher education is the founding members of a college or university. The core principles that guide an institutional mission are frequently the direct results of one key individual and their beliefs and values. In many instances these values are passed on for centuries without being questioned. A second and more important example involves organizational change. It is often the case organizational change cannot take place effectively unless the change is compatible with leaders' values and beliefs (Schein, 2010).

Within the context of higher education, Bergquist and Pawlak's (2008) *Engaging the Six Cultures of the Academy* is a common reference for understanding the relationship between leadership and organizational culture. Bergquist and Pawlak identified six common cultures within American and Canadian colleges and universities (collegial culture, managerial culture, developmental culture, the culture of advocacy, the virtual culture, and the tangible culture) and argued that effective leaders do not seek to "change or mold a culture to meet one's own needs; rather, [they] must determine how to work with and use the strengths and resources of the existing organizational culture" in order to achieve desired goals (p. x). Building on Bergquist and Pawlak's call for leaders to align their leadership practices with the organizational cultures in which they are situated, Latta (2020) developed a conceptual framework for matching specific leadership theories and their corresponding notions of power and influence with each of the six academic cultures. For example, Latta suggested that leaders operating within a collegial culture would be well served to draw on authentic and shared leadership theories, characterized by commitments to collaboration, consultation, and the formation of coalitions. By contrast, leaders operating within a managerial culture characterized by the values of efficiency and competence should consider enacting hierarchical and contingent leadership theories.

Leadership and Social Identities

A second prominent strand of cultural leadership inquiry examines the influence of social identities on leadership beliefs, practices, and opportunities. Contemporary scholars have been particularly interested in expanding understanding of the gender and racial dynamics that frame and constrain leadership experiences within and beyond higher education. Additionally, leadership scholars have begun to explore the influence of sexual orientation on leadership, although this line of inquiry is still rather new. Finally, examinations of leadership through the lens of intersectionality, which were featured in Kezar et al.'s (2006) overview of cultural leadership perspectives, have continued to gain prominence in recent years. Collectively, this body of work and these lines of leadership inquiry hold tremendous promise for identifying and dismantling patriarchal, heteronormative, and white supremacist systems and structures that perpetuate oppression and subvert efforts to create more equitable postsecondary learning environments.

Gender and Leadership

With respect to cultural research on gender and leadership, recent scholarship continues to build on lines of inquiry initiated in the late twentieth century, including ones that examine gender-based differences in leadership approaches and motivations (H. S. Astin & Leland, 1991; Bensimon & Neumann, 1993; Dahlvig & Longman, 2021; Eddy et al., 2017; Herrera et al., 2012; Ibarra et al., 2013; Kezar, 2000, 2002). With few exceptions (Eddy et al., 2017; Fassinger et al., 2010), this work continues to frame gender as a binary construct, documenting that cisgender women's leadership is associated with a more participatory, relational, and interpersonal style and with power and influence strategies that emphasize reciprocity and collectivity (Herrera et al., 2012). Moreover, women leaders tend to conceptualize leadership as collective rather than individualistic, emphasize responsibility toward others and the empowerment of others to act in the organization, and deemphasize hierarchical relationships (Dahlvig & Longman, 2021).

Gendered perspectives on and experiences with leadership are illustrated in recent autoethnographic and narrative studies that examine the personal biographies and professional journeys of women higher education administrators, particularly women of color (D. R. Davis & Maldonado, 2015; Madsen, 2008; Menchaca et al., 2016; Montas-Hunter, 2012). For example, Menchaca et al. (2016) used CRT, LatCrit, and feminist critical race theory (FemCrit) to examine the leadership journeys of senior Latina administrators, highlighting the significance of strong supportive mothers, fervent faith, humble beginnings, mentors, and intelligence. Another line of contemporary inquiry examines the gendered nature of leadership discourse (Eddy & Khwaja, 2019; Khwaja, 2017). Readers interested in taking a deep dive into women's leadership research and practice will appreciate the breadth and depth of insights shared in several edited collections on the topic (Chin et al., 2007; Eddy et al., 2017; Kellerman & Rhode, 2007; Longman & Madsen, 2014). In addition to documenting gender-based leadership differences with respect to values and behaviors, numerous scholars have examined the cultural (macro), organizational (meso), and individual (micro) factors that perpetuate gender-based leadership inequities within and beyond higher education (Dahlvig & Longman, 2021; Eddy et al., 2017). We summarize these important scholarly insights next.

Oppressive cultural assumptions and structural barriers cement and perpetuate gender-based differences in access to power, resulting in seemingly intractable gender gaps in educational attainment, economic participation, and empowerment (World Economic Forum, 2017). Within the context of higher education leadership, the underrepresentation of women in senior-level leadership roles (Catalyst, 2016; Eddy et al., 2017; H. L. Johnson, 2017) is particularly vexing given the fact that women earn the majority of postsecondary degrees in the United States (H. L. Johnson, 2017), leadership development programs targeting women have proliferated in recent years (Madsen et al., 2012; Teague & Bobby, 2014), and numerous scholars have documented the expanded recognition and effectiveness of collaborative and empowering approaches to leadership more frequently demonstrated by women (Eagly & Carli, 2007; Eagly & Johannesen-Schmidt, 2001; Kezar, 2014).

In 2013, bell hooks identified white supremacist capitalist patriarchy as a root cause of sustained gender inequity, and a number of scholars within and beyond higher education have examined the ways these oppressive ideologies serve to undermine the leadership ambitions and efforts of women

(Eddy et al., 2017). Drawing on the imagery of glass ceilings, sticky floors, and labyrinths (Carli & Eagly, 2016), researchers have conceptualized and documented the multiple layers of obstacles women encounter on their leadership journeys (Carli & Eagly, 2016; Dahlvig & Longman, 2021). At the societal level, scholars have examined how deep-seated cultural beliefs regarding gender hierarchy, roles, and stereotypes (women as subordinate caregivers; men as dominant, achievement-driven leaders) constrain women's opportunities, choices, and perceptions of leadership competence (Blair-Loy et al., 2015; Catalyst, 2007; Chin, 2011; Dahlvig & Longman, 2021; Diehl & Dzubinski, 2016; Keohane, 2014). For example, Eagly and Karau (2002) developed role congruity theory to explain how firmly entrenched gender roles that associate successful leadership with masculine qualities negatively influence women's leadership aspirations and experiences. Women are incentivized to align their behaviors with prescribed gender roles, potentially limiting access to leadership opportunities, or face criticism for exhibiting behaviors typically associated with masculine leadership approaches. Within the context of higher education leadership, Eddy and Cox (2008) found evidence that role congruity theory shaped the leadership experiences of female community college presidents. Evidence also exists that gendered leadership stereotypes influence evaluations of women's leadership performance and preferences for male supervision (Chin, 2011; Heilman, 2012; Powell, 2011). The internalization of negative gender stereotypes may lead women to temper their leadership aspirations or doubt their competence (Keohane, 2014). The negative consequences of rigid gender norms transcend cultural and national borders, with scholars documenting similar patterns of oppression in Western, African, and Asian societies (Hofstede et al., 2010; Odhiambo, 2011; White & Bagilhole, 2012; Zhao & Jones, 2017).

At the meso (organizational) level, leadership scholars identify the masculine cultural norms (e.g., hierarchy, competition, individualism, and prestige-seeking behavior) that characterize higher education institutions as significant barriers to women seeking and attaining influential leadership roles (Bornstein, 2008; Chin, 2011; Eddy & Cox, 2008; Eddy & Ward, 2017; Kezar, 2014; L. G. Sullivan, 2009; D. F. Wood, 2009). Oppressive cultural norms are institutionalized in policies and practices (hiring and promotion protocols, family care and leave policies, etc.) that limit access and support for women leaders. These meso-level barriers have been documented in higher education institutions across the globe, including Kenya (Odhiambo, 2011), Tanzania (Nyoni et al., 2017), Scandinavia (Seierstad & Healy, 2012), the United Kingdom, and Australia (Burkinshaw & White, 2017; White & Bagilhole, 2012). Additionally, L. D. Paris et al.'s (2009) cross-cultural research demonstrated that industry culture (e.g., telecommunications or finance) had a significant influence on leadership prototypes, underscoring the need for cultural leadership theorists to attend to multiple layers of culture—macro, meso, and micro.

The individual and internal dynamics (micro-level factors) that shape women's leadership and may perpetuate gender inequities in higher education leadership have been the subject of inquiry in recent years (Helgesen & Johnson, 2010; Ibarra et al., 2013; Kellerman & Rhode, 2014). Research has documented gendered differences in motivations for seeking leadership (women seek leadership as a means to advance shared goals, make a difference, or fulfill a duty to care for others; Dahlvig & Longman, 2014; Henningsen et al., 2022; Ibarra et al., 2013; Keohane, 2014), gendered patterns in how women evaluate the costs and benefits of pursuing leadership (Hewlett, 2014), and the role of internalized gendered stereotypes (male equals leadership) in undermining women's self-perception of their leadership potential (Ibarra et al., 2013; Keohane, 2014; Koenig et al., 2011). Additionally, scholars have highlighted the important role that social validation, the relational process of others recognizing one's leadership potential, plays in adopting a leadership identity (DeRue & Ashford, 2010). Women who have not been recognized as (potential) sources of leadership within their higher education organization may be reluctant to self-identify as a leader and seek out formal influence opportunities. This strand of micro-level leadership scholarship offers meaningful insights on how those interested in advancing women's higher education leadership may approach this work, including intentionally attending to issues of motivation and purpose as well as creating mentoring, coaching, or peer support programs that provide aspiring women leaders with social validation (Lafreniere & Longman, 2008; Longman et al., 2019).

Scholars interested in advancing understanding of the intersectional influences of culture and gender on leadership were called on by Eagly (2015), McNae and Vali (2015), and Do and Brennan (2015) to refrain from using a Western feminist ideological lens—or what Eagly (2015) described as

Western, educated, industrialized, rich, and democratic (WEIRD) values and norms—when seeking to understand how women make sense of and enact leadership. Scholars must seek to understand and frame leadership within culturally situated notions of power, social roles, dress, speech, and so on. Next, we synthesize contemporary scholarship that centers race and ethnicity in the study and practice of leadership.

RACE, ETHNICITY, AND LEADERSHIP

Ospina and Foldy (2009) offered a compelling argument for the expansion of leadership theory and research that center race and ethnicity. Specifically, they contended that the continued centrality of race and ethnicity in modern society necessitates a deeper understanding of the influence race and ethnicity have on leadership perceptions, actions, and outcomes. Additionally, leadership studies centered on race and ethnicity have the potential to shed light on the ways power is leveraged in leadership, not just as an individual tool of influence but as a systemic force of institutionalized oppression or equity-oriented transformation. Ospina and Foldy also argued that leadership studies that place race and ethnicity at the center of inquiry offer meaningful insights not just on the "special case" of leadership as practiced by individuals with historically minoritized identities but on the broader nature of resistance, empowerment, and agency, processes that are essential to dismantling the dominant ideologies of neoliberalism and white supremacy. In this section we review several strands of scholarship that advance understanding of the ways leadership beliefs and racial and ethnic identities influence each other, including studies situated within CRT, research on the leadership styles and experiences of specific racial and ethnic groups, the influence of institutional type on the experiences of leaders of color, and constructions of race within educational leadership programs.

As in studies of biased perceptions of women's leadership (Blair-Loy et al., 2015; Chin, 2011; Diehl & Dzubinski, 2016; Heilman, 2012; Keohane, 2014; Longman, 2021; Powell, 2011), scholars have examined the influence of bias, racism, and stereotyping on both the opportunities afforded leaders of color and the evaluation of their leadership abilities (Eagly & Chin, 2010; Ospina & Foldy, 2009; Sanchez-Hucles & Davis, 2010; Wolfe & Dilworth, 2015). Ospina and Foldy (2009) critiqued this body of literature for continuing to frame the influence of race on leaders as an individual-level phenomenon, rather than examining the ways in which the systemic forces of white supremacy influence leadership processes. Additionally, they expressed frustration that leaders of color are typically framed as passive recipients of biased leadership perceptions rather than active agents of resistance. The recent expansion of leadership studies rooted in CRT (e.g., Santamaría & Santamaría, 2012, 2016b), including those that examine the manifestations of white supremacy in leadership, have begun to address the criticisms leveled by Ospina and Foldy.

Leadership inquiry framed by the aims and tenets of CRT has gained prominence in recent years, with scholars drawing on the CRT principles of the permanence of racism, interest convergence, whiteness as property, counternarratives, the critique of liberalism, the legitimacy of experiential knowledge, and intersectionality to understand the influence of race and racism on leadership as well as examine leadership practices centered on eliminating racial inequity (Alemán, 2009a; Amiot et al., 2020; J. Blackmore, 2010; Capper, 2015; Giles, 2010; Gooden, 2012; Ladkin & Patrick, 2022; H. Liu, 2019; H. Liu & Baker, 2016; Menchaca et al., 2016; Parker & Villalpando, 2007; Santamaría & Santamaría, 2012, 2016b; Wolfe & Dilworth, 2015). Examples of this scholarship within the field of higher education include Menchaca et al.'s (2016) application of LatCrit (Latino/a critical race theory), counterstorytelling, and feminist theories to analyze the leadership journeys of two senior Latina administrators and Wolfe and Dilworth's (2015) critical race analysis of forty years of scholarship on the experiences of African American higher education administrators at predominantly white institutions. Wolfe and Dilworth illustrated how the higher education administrator role came to be framed as whiteness property, contributing to the institutionalization of disparities between African American administrators and their white counterparts.

Contemporary leadership scholars continue to explore how racial and ethnic identities influence leadership beliefs, practices, and experiences, a prominent strand of scholarship that was noted in Kezar et al. (2006). Specifically, researchers have examined the distinctive leadership experiences and styles of Indigenous and American Indian peoples (Fitzgerald, 2006; Krumm & Johnson, 2011; Minthorn & Chávez, 2015b; Stull & Gasman, 2017), Asian Americans (Akutagawa, 2013; Burris et al., 2013; Chan et al.,

2021; Gündemir et al., 2019; Kawahara et al., 2013; Neilson & Suyemoto, 2009), African Americans (Arday, 2018; Bower & Wolverton, 2009; D. R. Davis & Maldonado, 2015; Dowdy & Hamilton, 2012; Giles, 2010; Gooden, 2012; Reed & Evans, 2008; Roberts et al., 2019; Townsend, 2021), and Latinx individuals (Alemán, 2009a, 2009b; Burmicky, 2021; Guajardo et al., 2019; Gutierrez et al., 2002; Menchaca et al., 2016; Montas-Hunter, 2012; Muñoz, 2009; Rodríguez et al., 2016, 2018).

An example of a study that seeks to highlight shared leadership values and approaches rooted in a particular racial identity is Giles's (2010) historical analysis of the African American leadership values (e.g., collectivist ethos and spirituality rooted in racial uplift) exemplified in the life and work of Howard W. Thurman, a Baptist minister and dean of chapel in the 1930s and 1940s. Similarly, Kawahara et al.'s (2013) study of fourteen Asian American leaders revealed patterns of having a strong work ethic, adopting a group orientation, collaborating, focusing on excellence, and leading in response to the urging of others. In *Salsa, Soul, and Spirit: Leadership for a Multicultural Age*, Bordas (2012) drew on and integrated leadership values commonly exhibited within Latino, African American, and American Indian communities (spirituality, communal responsibility, collective activism, generosity, and intergenerational leadership) to inform a model of multicultural leadership that fosters inclusion and "encourages diverse people to actively engage, contribute, and tap their potential" (p. 27).

The influence of institutional type and racial identities has also emerged as a popular line of inquiry with scholars examining the lived experiences of leaders of color at predominantly white institutions (Townsend, 2021; Wolfe & Dilworth, 2015), minority-serving institutions (Freeman & Gasman, 2014; Nichols, 2004; Palmer et al., 2018), and community colleges (Burmicky, 2021; Gutierrez et al., 2002; Muñoz, 2009). For instance, in a national study of Latina community college administrators (Muñoz, 2009), participants described several common experiences on their pathways to leadership, highlighting the strong role culture and family play in shaping their value systems and internal motivations, earning academic credentials, engaging in professional leadership development programs (for example, the National Community College Hispanic Council Leadership Fellows Program), and receiving strong mentorship. Taking a slightly different angle but still centering the relationship between context and racial (and gender) identity, Townsend's (2021) phenomenological study of five African American women in leadership roles at predominantly white institutions revealed the ways in which identity politics (e.g., microaggressions, the extra workload and scrutiny often framed as a Black tax, and constraints on the presentation of their authentic selves as expressed through attire, hairstyles, speech, tone, etc.) shaped the women's leadership experiences and contributed to organizational departures. Predominantly white institutions seeking to retain talented African American women leaders (emerging and seasoned) would be well served to consider structural changes that address the identity politics highlighted in Townsend's study (e.g., more equitable university service expectations, expanded bias awareness and intervention training, and cluster hires).

Beyond institutional type, scholars of race and educational leadership have spent considerable time examining the ways in which race is constructed and experienced within educational leadership preparation programs and the potential for these spaces to cultivate a cadre of educational leaders committed and prepared to engage in transformative, equity-minded leadership (Akutagawa, 2013; Boske, 2010; Gooden & Dantley, 2012; Leon, 2005; Quezada & Martinez, 2021; Rodríguez et al., 2018). Pedagogical practices that have demonstrated promise for fostering inclusive leadership learning environments include adopting a curriculum rooted in critical theoretical perspectives, fostering critical self-reflection, engaging explicitly with race across the curriculum, and conducting a strengths-based analysis of cultural values and experiences (Akutagawa, 2013; Carpenter & Diem, 2013; Gooden & Dantley, 2012; Zarate & Mendoza, 2020).

Finally, in their synthesis of studies that explore the influence of race and ethnicity on the enactment of leadership, Espino and Foldy (2009) called attention to a particular strand of research in which leaders of color recognize their racial and ethnic identities as a resource and source of strength and agency in their navigation of organizational spaces steeped in the norms of white supremacy. This strand of inquiry has indeed gained prominence (Chan et al., 2021; Chance, 2022; Eagly & Chin, 2010; Santamaría & Santamaría, 2016b). We will return to the conceptualization of marginalized identities as sources of strength and empowerment later in the chapter in our discussion of Santamaría and Santamaría's (2016b) applied critical leadership model.

Cultural Leadership Perspectives   219

Sexual Orientation and Leadership

In contrast to the expansive body of literature examining the mutual influence between gender and leadership and race and ethnicity and leadership, there is a limited but growing understanding of the ways in which LGBTQ+ social identities shape leadership experiences (Fassinger et al., 2010; Jourian & Simmons, 2017; C. Lee, 2020, 2021; Lugg & Tooms, 2010; Pryor, 2021; Renn, 2007; Renn & Bilodeau, 2005; Sumara, 2021). Fassinger et al. (2010) attempted to address the LGBTQ+ leadership knowledge gap by proposing an affirmative multidimensional LGBTQ+ leadership paradigm aligned with contemporary leadership approaches that emphasize collaboration, inclusion, nonhierarchical notions of leadership, and the influence of social identities on the leadership experiences of historically marginalized communities. Drawing on extant LGBTQ+ and gender scholarship, including Renn's (2007) and Renn and Bilodeau's (2005) studies of LGBTQ+ student leadership, Fassinger et al. (2010) suggested that LGBTQ+ leadership is informed by sexual orientation (in particular, disclosure of LGBTQ+ identity within professional contexts), gender orientation (a dimension that recognizes that beliefs and attitudes about sexual orientation are gendered), and situation (conceptualized as the sexual orientation worldviews of the group engaged in the leadership process). Building on previous scholarship documenting the strong influence of follower perceptions and experiences within the leader-follower relationship (this literature is reviewed in the chapter on cognitive leadership perspectives), Fassinger et al. (2010) suggested that the experiences of LGBTQ+ leaders is significantly shaped by the composition of the group engaged in the leadership process (predominantly heterosexual, predominantly LGBTQ+, or mixed). Finally, Fassinger et al. acknowledged that LGBTQ+ leadership is situated within the broader contextual dimensions of stigma and marginalization enacted at the cultural, societal, and individual levels.

Rather than framing cultural and organizational marginalization as solely an obstacle to LGBTQ+ leadership, Fassinger et al. (2010) contended that marginalization "may also increase the effectiveness of LGBT people in a variety of contexts, including leadership roles. Learning to cope with the stresses related to marginalization may actually catalyze certain kinds of skill development that aid LGBT individuals in leadership roles" (p. 206). For example, the openly gay and lesbian leaders studied by Coon (2001) articulated a relationship between their sexual orientation and effective leadership practices such as challenging the status quo, facilitating collaboration, fostering a shared vision, and demonstrating integrity. Similarly, C. Lee (2021) found that the strategies LGBTQ+ teacher leaders used to negotiate heteronormative work environments fostered five leadership attributes essential for contesting the influence of neoliberalism: "sensitivity to the inclusion of others; connecting with others and building teams; emotional intelligence; managing uncertainty and stressful situations; and courage and risk-taking" (p. 96).

Within the context of higher education leadership theory and research, most examinations of LGTBQ leadership have centered the student experience (Jourian & Simmons, 2017; R. A. Miller & Vaccaro, 2016; Renn, 2007; Renn & Bilodeau, 2005). A few contemporary scholars have explored the themes of LGBTQ+ leadership among university staff and administrators (C. Lee, 2021; Pryor, 2021; Sumara, 2021). For example, Pryor (2021) has developed a model of queer activist leadership that examines the positional and grassroots leadership efforts of campus staff dedicated to advancing LGBTQ+ equity. Extending Kezar and Lester's (2011) individual, group, and organizational grassroots leadership dimensions (see our chapter on processual leadership perspectives), Pryor's model explores the influence of queer identities, queer leadership strategies, and queer policies and practices on the leadership experiences of queer activists. Pryor's analysis of campus leadership through a queer epistemological lens illuminates meaningful pathways for identifying and dismantling heterogendered institutional norms that perpetuate oppression. One such pathway may be the establishment of LGBTQ+-specific university leadership development programs. Building on the demonstrated success of the United Kingdom's first LGBTQ+ school leadership program, C. Lee (2021) offered a compelling case for designing university leadership development initiatives that provide LGBTQ+ individuals a safe space to explore and cultivate leadership rooted in their authentic selves. Such programs will expand the pipeline of transformative higher education leaders capable of fostering inclusive organizational environments that work to dismantle the twin forces of neoliberalism and white supremacy.

Emerging Social Identity Leadership Research

Although the area is not as fully developed as the lines of social identity research synthesized in previous sections, contemporary cultural leadership scholars have begun to explore the influence of disability and social class on leadership. In this section, we highlight key findings from this body of research.

Leadership scholars have examined the ways in which physical disability and neurodiversity shape leadership experience beyond the academy, but this line of research is missing from studies situated within higher education (Emira et al., 2018; Hurley-Hanson & Giannantonio, 2017; Luria et al., 2014; Roberson et al., 2021). A promising framework that merits exploration within the context of higher education is Roberson et al.'s (2021) conceptual model of neurodiversity characteristics, leadership behavior, and outcomes. Rooted in critical disability theory, the model explains how cognitive characteristics associated with neurodiversity (e.g., sensitivity and attention to detail and the ability to recognize patterns) may align with task-based leadership behaviors (e.g., the search for and use of information in problem-solving) resulting in positive leadership outcomes (e.g., perceived leader effectiveness). The model also identifies those conditions that support the emergence and development of neurodiverse leaders, including complex environments and novel situations. As already mentioned, scholarship on leadership and disability is nearly nonexistent within higher education research (Emira et al., 2018; Tupling & Outhwaite, 2017). One exception is Emira et al.'s (2018) study of the leadership challenges and experiences of eighteen staff at an English university who disclosed their disabled status to the institution. Emira et al. found that over half of the participants were engaged in formal and informal leadership activities, but these individuals faced both organizational (e.g., staff resistance) and personal barriers (e.g., low aspiration). Higher education leadership scholars seeking to foster more equitable and inclusive organizational environments would be well served to expand research and theory on leadership from a critical disability perspective.

The relationship between social class and leadership is another line of inquiry that merits attention within and beyond the academy (Ardoin & Guthrie, 2021a; S. R. Martin et al., 2017). S. R. Martin et al. (2017) offered a concise synthesis of research on the topic, citing evidence that "those from higher social classes appear more likely to emerge as leaders due in part to their enhanced self-confidence and independent relational orientation, and may engage in leadership processes differently than those from lower social classes" (p. 49). Martin et al. concluded their literature review with a call for additional inquiry on the relationship between social class and leadership, including developing a deeper understanding of how social class influences leadership attributions, enactment of leadership in informal roles, and leader effectiveness. Few scholars have examined the way social class influences leadership within postsecondary settings. The exception is a 2021 issue of *New Directions for Student Leadership* edited by Ardoin and Guthrie that examined "leadership learning through the lens of social class." In their introduction to the volume, Ardoin and Guthrie (2021b) reminded readers that social class encompasses much more than socioeconomic status. To understand the relationship of mutual influence between social class and leadership, scholars must consider how diverse forms of capital (i.e., cultural, social, linguistic, familial, academic, aspirational, navigational, and resistance) shape leadership learning, opportunities, and experiences.

INTERSECTIONALITY AND LEADERSHIP

In contrast to Kezar et al.'s (2006) observation of limited scholarship on the overlapping influences of social identities within leadership, intersectional leadership research has gained prominence in recent years (Agosto & Roland, 2018; Breslin et al., 2017; Chance, 2022; D. R. Davis & Maldonado, 2015; Dowdy & Hamilton, 2012; Fitzgerald, 2006; N. N. Johnson & Fournillier, 2022; Menchaca et al., 2016; Montas-Hunter, 2012; Reed & Evans, 2008; Rosette et al., 2016; Sanchez-Hucles & Davis, 2010; Townsend, 2021). This strand of inquiry seeks to examine the leadership experiences of individuals who hold multiple marginalized identities (e.g., ones based on race, class, gender, sexual orientation, or religion), in recognition that positionality influences leadership beliefs and behaviors (Kezar 2000, 2002).

Breslin et al.'s (2017) review of public administration leadership scholarship from 1992 to 2017 provided an overview of diverse approaches to conceptualizing intersectionality as well as revealed a narrow focus in the literature on examining the leadership experiences of women of color. This trend is also apparent in contemporary intersectional leadership research situated within higher education. Specifically, scholars have examined the adversity (e.g., tokenism, discrimination and microaggressions, and limited role models) and resilience that characterize the leadership experiences of Black women (Bower & Wolverton, 2009; Chance, 2022; Davis & Maldonado, 2015; Dowdy & Hamilton, 2012; Townsend, 2021) and Latina (Menchaca et al.,

2016; Montas-Hunter, 2012; Muñoz, 2009) higher education leaders. These examinations of the intersectional influences of race and gender on leadership offer important insights that can be translated into action directed at advancing and supporting women of color as they engage in leadership processes (e.g., establishing mentoring and networking programs, offering professional development programs that address the unique experiences of women of color, or requiring training programs that shed light on the nature of racial and gender bias in higher education leadership). Yet the limited focus on racial and gender identities within intersectional leadership scholarship continues to minimize and marginalize the experiences of leaders navigating other dimensions of social inequality, including sexuality, class, disability, and age. We return to this limitation later in the chapter in our discussion of critiques of the cultural leadership perspective.

Cross-Cultural Leadership

The understanding of cross-cultural leadership was significantly advanced through the efforts of an international team of researchers affiliated with the Global Leadership and Organizational Behavior Effectiveness project (House et al., 2004), a postpositivist effort to measure and predict the influence of specific cultural variables, such as future orientation, assertiveness, and uncertainty avoidance, on leadership beliefs and behaviors. Interest and engagement in cross-cultural leadership research have increased with the emergence of a global economy characterized by the vast and rapid exchange of goods, labor, and knowledge across national borders. Both scholars and business executives were motivated to better understand national differences in leadership beliefs and practices given the growing size of the expatriate workforce charged with navigating cross-cultural interactions in the foreign outposts of their global employers. Much of this work has focused on generating lists of culturally specific dos and don'ts that global executives can follow to avoid offending workers and customers in the local context.

Contemporary cross-cultural leadership research remains rooted in the foundational principles advanced by Geert Hofstede, a Dutch scholar who defined culture as "the collective programming of the mind which distinguishes the members of one group or category from another" (Hofstede, 1994, p. 1). Hofstede's primary focus was national culture, which he asserted individuals learn at an early age and which, given its deep psychological roots, exerts a stronger influence on leadership behavior than organizational culture does (Guthey & Jackson, 2011). Drawing on survey data collected in the early 1970s from one hundred thousand IBM employees in sixty-six countries, Hofstede identified four value dimensions that can be used to compare leadership beliefs in forty-nine national cultures. The first dimension is individualism and collectivism, or the degree to which a culture values self-interested action or prioritizes attending to the good of the social group. The second dimension—hierarchy, status, and power distance—describes national cultural beliefs about the distribution of power and influence. In high power-distance cultures, individuals accept the unequal distribution of power among organizational members, whereas in low power-distance cultures, organizational members expect leaders to display a participatory leadership approach. Uncertainty avoidance is the third culture dimension and describes national differences in the extent to which societies rely on formal rules and norms to minimize the impact of ambiguity. The masculinity-femininity dimension characterizes masculine national cultures as valuing the traits of assertiveness and toughness and feminine cultures as rooted in the values of positive social relationships and quality of life. In later research, Hofstede added a fifth national culture dimension—long- versus short-term orientation—which captured differences in how societies conceptualized truth (in long-term cultures, truth is relative; in short-term cultures, truth is absolute) and approached the future (long-term cultures value saving, whereas short-term cultures live for the moment).

Hofstede's traditional power- and influence-oriented cultural dimensions continue to hold a place of prominence in contemporary cross-cultural leadership research (Guthey & Jackson, 2011); however, other scholars have examined alternative cross-cultural dimensions of relevance to leadership. Specifically, Hall (1990) described cultural differences in communication patterns between high-context languages (e.g., Japanese), which call for more subtle and indirect communication norms, and low-context languages such as German and English, which favor direct and clear communication. Schwartz (1999) distinguished between "mastery cultures," which value achievement-oriented and competitive leaders who will manipulate the environment as needed to ensure the accomplishment of goals, and "harmony cultures," which emphasize a holistic approach to leadership that seeks integration with the natural environment. Much of the cross-cultural leadership research is situated in North America and has been conducted by North American researchers, who are most certainly influenced by the particular sociopolitical and historical context of the United States, which includes an emphasis on individual, heroic leadership.

Studies have applied findings from cultural and social leadership research to develop instruments for measuring leaders' cross-cultural knowledge to enhance leadership development programs and activities (McCauley & Van Velsor, 2004). They observe that assessment of and feedback on leaders' performance (usually in the form of surveys) are themselves affected by cultural norms about whether one can be open and honest with coworkers; the notion of criticizing is foreign in some cultures, and trust is often lacking in others. Because psychology, the discipline that develops the surveys, and survey methodology are considered more Western approaches, scholars also suggest creating forms of development that fit better in the cultural context—for example, journaling. An important first step is for leaders to read about and become aware of cultural differences in their beliefs and behaviors so that they can act more appropriately in the context. Leaders are encouraged to learn the art of perspective taking, which involves listening to and absorbing information skillfully, recognizing that other people may view a situation differently, understanding that other people's assumptions may be different, and accepting the limitations of one's own point of view.

Critiques

In this section we present three distinct critiques of contemporary cultural leadership perspectives. Specifically, we highlight the ways in which this body of scholarship is characterized by (1) limited conceptualizations and examinations of power and oppression, (2) a rigid and colonial framing of national culture, and (3) a dominant focus on race and gender with respect to understanding the influence of (intersectional) social identities on leadership approaches and processes. Fortunately, cultural leadership scholars are beginning to address these criticisms. Accordingly, we highlight promising new developments as relevant.

Limited Conceptualizations of Power

The recognition and examination of power (its nature, its manifestations, and its role as a tool of oppression) are precursors to understanding and dismantling the twin ideologies of neoliberalism and white supremacy within higher education. Unfortunately, contemporary cultural leadership scholarship frequently ignores the role of power in leadership (Breslin et al., 2017; Riad, 2011) or adopts a "normative apolitical" stance that frames power as a natural element within the dualistic relationship between leaders (superior power) and followers (R. Gordon, 2011). Schein's (2010) analysis of the important role formal leaders play in shaping organizational culture exemplifies the individualized approach to understanding power. More recently, Lumby (2019) examined the role of power in higher education institutions in the United Kingdom by interviewing eighteen institutional leaders, exploring how these individuals made sense of power, exercised power, and observed power in the course of their leadership work. Similar to Schein's, Lumby's conceptualization of power is a function of individual meaning-making and action. Ospina and Foldy (2009) critiqued contemporary constructions of power that center the individual. Their particular concern is situated within studies of race and leadership that continue to frame the influence of identity on leadership as an individual-level phenomenon, rather than a function of the systemic power exercised via white supremacist norms and structures.

Answering this common critique of contemporary cultural leadership perspectives, Riad (2011) offered an alternative perspective on power—power rooted in and shaped by culture and context—that holds promise for shedding light on the systemic nature of power, oppression, and pathways to liberation. Riad argued, "Leadership is not independent of the power relations within a given cultural context. These [power relations] shape how 'leadership' comes to be 'known': both how it is defined (what the concept includes/excludes), and how it is identified (in certain individuals over others)" (p. 831). Rather than recognizing power as an individual possession or dyadic exchange, Riad framed power (and leadership) as embedded in cultural systems. These systems determine the boundaries of inclusion (acceptable leadership behaviors, beliefs, identities, etc.) and exclusion (behaviors, beliefs, identities deemed inappropriate, etc.) through the establishment and enforcement of normative policies, structures, and practices. Here we see an alignment between Riad's notion of culturally situated power and the call to examine systemic power and racism embedded in the tenets of CRT.

Importantly, Riad (2011) viewed cultural systems of power as fluid, not fixed. Thus, leadership theory, research, and practice seeking to foster more equitable and socially just higher education environments are well served to focus their attention on identifying and dismantling oppressive systems of power (not individual leadership actions) within specific cultural contexts (e.g., an institution, a division, or a department). Studies that explore the ways race and gender influence leadership experiences and processes have certainly highlighted the cultural norms and assumptions that constrain opportunities and perpetuate discrimination among women and leaders of color; however, the frequent focus on the lived experiences of individuals rather than systems of power as the unit of analysis has resulted in limited opportunities to understand the nature and efficacy of system-level interventions.

RIGID AND COLONIAL CONCEPTUALIZATIONS OF NATIONAL CULTURE

Some scholars critique Hofstede's work and similar cross-cultural research efforts for their deterministic framing of national culture (Osland et al. 2000) and the unidirectional focus on examining how cultural constraints influence leadership beliefs and behaviors, as opposed to recognizing the relationship of mutual influence that exists between national culture and leadership (Guthey & Jackson, 2011). Another strand of critique, this one situated in a postmodern and postcolonial perspective, challenges the notion and aims of objective cross-cultural research and calls on cross-cultural researchers to reflexively examine the colonial cultural politics that shape constructions of foreign "others" (Ailon, 2008, 2009). Ailon (2008, 2009) and other scholars who advocate for moving beyond postpositivist efforts to predict and generalize national influences on leadership make the case for adopting a constructivist lens and examining culture from within through ethnographic or other culturally immersive methodologies. In these studies, national cultural identity is not a fixed, predictable set of preferences and behaviors; rather, it is a fluid and symbolic construct that is strategically adapted to meet diverse and shifting needs. This constructivist perspective also recognizes that individuals living and working in the modern era of globalization will shape and be shaped by cultural influences that are not bounded by rigid national borders but instead reflect the overlapping, interwoven, and ever-evolving cultures produced through global travel, migration, and social interaction.

Dominant Focus on Race and Gender

A third critique leveled against contemporary cultural leadership scholarship is the dominant focus on race and gender in studies seeking to understand the ways social identities and leadership influence each other (Breslin et al., 2017). Knowledge of the challenges, approaches, and strengths that characterize the leadership experiences of cisgender women and individuals with minoritized racial identities has expanded in recent years; however, as noted in the synthesis of research on social identities and leadership, a number of social identities historically associated with economic, social, educational, and political marginalization and discrimination remain underdeveloped in the cultural leadership literature, particularly studies situated within higher education. As evidenced in our discussion of emerging social identity leadership inquiry, scholars are beginning to address these knowledge gaps with respect to disability and social class, but this is an area ripe for substantive expansion.

Returning to a critique introduced earlier in the chapter, we also highlight the need for expanded constructions of gender in contemporary cultural leadership research and practice. Despite the proliferation of trans* theory and research within the discipline of higher education and beyond (Nicolazzo, 2017), contemporary leadership studies in higher education continue to frame gender as a binary construct, focusing almost exclusively on the leadership experiences of cisgender women. Eddy et al. (2017) presented a compelling argument for disrupting binary constructions of gender, shedding light on the systems and structures of power that preserve normative (oppressive, exclusionary) gender roles and expectations within higher education institutions. Scholars who seek to advance understanding of the ways leadership shapes and is shaped by gender would be well served to adopt a critical orientation, conceptualizing gender as a continuum, not a fixed category, and seeking to understand how individuals across the gender continuum experience, resist, and dismantle oppressive gender leadership norms.

The intersectional leadership research synthesized earlier in the chapter clearly illustrates that leadership is shaped by multiple and fluid identities (multiple standpoints or positionalities) rather than essentialist or singular identities (such as gender). The strong relationship between positionality and leadership underscores the need for cultural leadership scholars to expand beyond race and fixed gender binaries in their efforts to better understand the ways in which social identities shape leadership experiences. Having identified meaningful gaps in contemporary cultural leadership perspectives, we next turn to new developments in this body of scholarship that are actively seeking to dismantle the oppressive systems of neoliberalism and white supremacy.

New Evolutions

In this section, we review three new evolutions in cultural approaches to leadership: (1) expanded studies of whiteness and white supremacy in educational leadership, (2) applied critical leadership, and (3) Indigenous leadership perspectives. All three build on the foundational principles of cultural leadership, honoring the influence of history, identity, context, and culture on leadership processes and relationships. Individually and collectively, these three strands of cultural leadership hold promise for shedding light on tangible strategies for establishing more socially just and inclusive higher education organizations.

WHITENESS AND LEADERSHIP

Recognizing that the manifestations and implications of whiteness and white supremacy are undertheorized in leadership studies broadly and educational leadership more specifically (R. L. Allen & Liou, 2019; Evatt-Young & Bryson, 2021; H. Liu, 2019; Tanner & Welton, 2021), contemporary scholars are drawing on CRT tenets, particularly whiteness as property, and anti-racism epistemologies to interrogate and dismantle normative leadership discourses and practices rooted in whiteness (Amiot et al., 2020; Blackmore, 2010; H. Liu, 2019; Salisbury et al., 2020; Tanner & Welton, 2021). H. Liu (2019) offered a particularly compelling description of white supremacist leadership norms and suggested two anti-racist praxes that may prove useful in tearing down systems of oppression: redoing whiteness and abolishing whiteness. As described by Liu, "redoing whiteness requires us to reflexively interrogate the practices of whiteness and reinvent ways of doing whiteness differently" (p. 105). Specific strategies for redoing whiteness include naming the racial identities of all leaders, not just leaders of color; engaging in counterstorytelling; and resisting the imperial tendency to take center stage in efforts to advance the inclusion of historically marginalized communities.

With respect to abolishing whiteness, Liu explains, "abolitionists believe that when those aligned with being white defect from this identification, they become free to realise themselves as other things, such as workers, youth, women, or any other self-definition they wish to explore" (p. 108). Although abolitionists recognize it is impossible to completely eschew the privileges of one's white identity, they believe that actively seeking to denounce whiteness is a pathway toward constructing a new humanity.

Within the context of higher education, Evatt-Young and Bryson's (2021) critical phenomenological study of ten white higher education administrators and the role their racial identity plays in making meaning of campus racial equity efforts is a prime example of critical whiteness leadership inquiry. Building on observations regarding the deeply entrenched nature of whiteness in higher education leadership norms and practices (e.g., whiteness as niceness and whiteness as professionalism), Evatt-Young and Bryson offered five recommendations for cultivating anti-racist leadership practices among white higher education administrators. First, white anti-racist higher education leaders must intentionally examine racial biases, assumptions, and power dynamics and their implications for perpetuating or disrupting racial inequities (here we see a connection to the equity-minded leadership discussed in chapter 6). Second, anti-racist leaders must address representation and the overwhelming presence of whiteness across all levels of the university, but especially senior administrative roles, through strategic changes in campus hiring processes. Third, leaders must interrogate white supremacist power dynamics embedded in constructions of "professionalism," including decision-making processes, communication norms, and policies. Fourth, white administrators must take personal responsibility for naming and challenging the "whiteness as niceness" norms that inform constructions of collegiality and teamwork framed as color-blind approaches to a harmonious work environment but that actually work to minimize opportunities for authentic and meaningful dialogues on race and racism. Finally, white anti-racist leaders must seek to develop authentic relationships with people of color characterized by humility, deep self-awareness, active listening, personal accountability, and a demonstrated commitment to collaborative action. In addition to framing research on whiteness and anti-racist leadership practices, CRT also plays a prominent role in the model of applied critical leadership described in the next section.

Applied Critical Leadership

Culturally responsive leadership theories and practices are another evolution in cultural leadership perspectives that hold promise for disrupting the institutionalization of inequity in postsecondary organizations. Culturally responsive leadership is a theory and set of educational leadership practices "that take into consideration race, ethnicity, language, culture, and gender" and are characterized by efforts to foster a critical consciousness among stakeholders (students, faculty, and administrators), enactment of culturally inclusive pedagogies that honor the values and cultural knowledge of diverse students, and a commitment to creating inclusive organizational structures that empower individuals and communities historically underrepresented and commonly silenced within postsecondary institutions (Santamaría & Santamaría, 2016b, p. 3). In this section, we highlight one example of culturally responsive leadership, Santamaría and Santamaría's (2016b) model of applied critical leadership, which has been examined and applied in the higher education context.

Applied critical leadership is a strengths-based model of leadership rooted in transformational leadership, CRT, and critical multiculturalism that was developed to understand and celebrate the leadership practices of individuals who identify with multiple historically oppressed social identities. Santamaría and Santamaría (2016b) developed the theory on the premise that "when leaders of color, otherwise marginalized individuals, or those who may choose to practice leadership through a CRT lens, make leadership decisions, they reflect and draw upon positive attributes of their identities and life experiences within their societal locality," resulting in leadership approaches and behaviors that are "more responsive to social justice, educational equity, and educational change for the greater good of all learners, teachers, and educational stakeholders involved" (pp. 5–6). It is in the connections that applied critical leaders make between changes in the way they are thinking about educational leadership (framing their intersectional identities as unique sources of strength, a notion counter to traditional leadership theory) and changes in their leadership actions that the promise of tangible, equity-oriented change lives.

Santamaría and Santamaría (2012) make a point to acknowledge that applied critical leadership can be practiced by both educational leaders with marginalized identities (those based on race, class, language, ability, gender, etc.) and leaders who identify as white or who benefit from societal privilege. The common theoretical thread connecting these disparate groups is a commitment to examining and practicing educational leadership through the lens of CRT. The centrality of CRT to the study and practice of applied critical leadership is evident in this definition advanced by Santamaría and Santamaría (2012): "Applied critical leadership is the emancipatory practice of choosing to address educational issues and challenges using a critical race perspective to enact context-specific change in response to power, domination, access, and achievement imbalances, resulting in improved academic achievement for learners at every academic level of institutional schooling in the U.S." (p. 7). It is the explicit adoption of a CRT perspective within educational leadership practice that facilitates a shift from well-meaning but misguided calls for change based on "sterile and very politically correct" deficit-based assessments of educational inequity (Santamaría & Santamaría, 2012, p. 9) to an applied critical leadership framework that recognizes and leverages the strengths cultivated by individuals and communities that navigate and confront systemic racism and other forms of oppression on a daily basis.

A foundational dimension of applied critical leadership theory is a commitment to action, including engagement in micro patterns (daily practices) aimed at dismantling systemic oppression and advancing equity. In their text *Applied Critical Leadership in Education*, Santamaría and Santamaría (2012) presented multiple applied critical leadership case studies, detailing the specific strategies and values enacted by the focal educational leaders. To illustrate applied critical leadership in higher education, Santamaría and Santamaría presented the case of Mona, "a self-assured Latina woman of Mexican descent" who is "one of four Associate Vice Presidents . . . of Academic Affairs and the Dean of Undergraduate Research at a midsized university in Southern California" (p. 120). In their case analysis, Santamaría and Santamaría described Mona's successful efforts to leverage the assets embedded in her social identities (strong family connections, inspirational role models of political engagement, and active spiritual practice) and enact her values (e.g., transparency, forgiveness, and collaboration) in an applied critical leadership practice that disrupts negative social stereotypes of Latina women and advances educational equity. Linking Mona's activities to the tenets of CRT and LatCrit, Santamaría and Santamaría pointed to Mona's use of storytelling to share culturally relevant knowledge rooted in her personal experience as well as her spiritual and mindful approaches to leadership (e.g., starting the workday with yoga and meditation) as examples of micro patterns and behaviors that result in a materially different, culturally relevant approach to leadership that fosters tangible positive change.

Empirical investigations of applied critical leadership (Santamaría, 2014; Santamaría & Jean-Marie, 2014; Santamaría & Santamaría, 2015, 2016b; Santamaría, Santamaría, & Dam, 2014; Santamaría, Santamaría, Webber, & Pearson, 2014), primarily guided by case study methodology and the CRT approach to counterstorytelling, have generated a set of nine applied critical leadership characteristics observed consistently across educational levels (K–12 to postsecondary), leadership positions (elementary school principal, school psychologist, academic dean, etc.), and national borders (research has been conducted in Australia, New Zealand, and the United States):

1. Willingness to *initiate and engage in critical conversations* with individuals and groups even when the topic was not popular for the greater good of the whole group (e.g., ageism, institutional racism, affirmative action, LGBTQ-ism);

2. Willingness to *choose to assume a CRT or critical lens* in order to consider multiple perspectives of critical issues;

3. Use of *consensus building as the preferred strategy for decision-making*; consciousness of "stereotype threat" or fulfilling negative stereotypes associated with their group, working hard to dispel negative stereotypes for groups with whom they identify;

4. Feeling for the *need to make empirical contributions* and, thus, add authentic research-based information to academic discourse regarding underserved groups;

5. Feeling for the *need to honor all members of their constituencies* (e.g., staff, parents, community members);

6. Tendency to *lead by example to meet an unresolved educational need* or challenge *for the purpose of giving back* to the marginalized community with which they identified and that also served to support their own academic journeys;

7. Feeling that it was *their responsibility to bring critical issues* with regard to race, ethnicity, gender, and class *to their constituents for resolution*. If they

234   *Perspectives on Leadership Research and Practice*

didn't address issues around race, language, gender, and power, critical issues would not be brought to surface;

8. Feeling for the *need to build trust when working with mainstream constituents* or partners, or others who do not share an affinity for issues related to educational equity;

9. Led by what they call "spirit" or practice a variation of servant leadership, where *expression of leadership practices may be classified as transformative,* servant leadership for those who work ultimately to serve the greater good. (Santamaría & Santamaría, 2016b, p. 7)

Santamaría and Santamaría's (2016a) edited volume, *Culturally Responsive Leadership in Higher Education*, presented a collection of chapters that illustrated how higher education leaders specifically operationalize these nine characteristics in daily practice. This is a must-read text for higher education researchers and professionals interested in adopting the applied critical leadership framework in their work.

Indigenous Leadership

Although Indigenous leadership philosophy and practice are not new (indeed, Indigenous forms of leadership can be traced back for millennia; Spiller et al., 2020), we frame this body of work as a new evolution in cultural leadership perspectives given the increased attention it has garnered within the last fifteen years and the powerful counternarrative that Indigenous leadership offers in opposition to traditional hierarchical, individual-power-centered notions of leadership rooted in white supremacy and neoliberalism. At the outset of this discussion, it is imperative to acknowledge the importance of specific cultural context when studying Indigenous leadership perspectives. Aboriginal, Indigenous, First Nation, and American Indian peoples in the colonized nation-states of Africa, Asia, Australia, New Zealand, and North and South America are not monolithic communities. Distinct cultural contexts (history, geography, language, customs, etc.) coupled with unique colonization experiences and tribal politics shape diverse Indigenous leadership perspectives (Sandefur & Deloria, 2018). Yet a review of Indigenous leadership scholarship does suggest a set of shared values and commitments anchored in Indigenous ways of knowing that emphasize service to the community, collective wisdom, connections to ancestors and nature, and the importance of storytelling (McCall, 2020; Spiller et al., 2020). In this section, we synthesize research on Indigenous leadership principles and practices, noting the ways this cultural approach to leadership disrupts traditional notions of purpose, power, and time.

Nearly all Indigenous leadership sources consulted for this chapter identified a collectivist orientation as a foundational dimension of Indigenous leadership (McCall, 2020; Minthorn & Chávez, 2015a; Rosile et al., 2018; Sandefur & Deloria, 2018; Spiller et al., 2020; Warner & Grint, 2006). The collectivist nature of Indigenous leadership has a significant influence on the aims of leadership processes. A commitment to serving the community (which encompasses the natural environment) is the primary motivation for engaging in leadership (McCall, 2020; Rosile et al., 2018; Spiller et al., 2020). The Indigenous notion of serving as a form of being (Minthorn & Chávez, 2015a) represents a stark contrast with the self-interested drivers of neoliberal leadership that prioritize profit and efficiency over community needs.

Beyond purpose, the collectivist orientation of Indigenous leadership also influences perspectives on knowledge. Indigenous leadership is rooted in Indigenous ways of knowing that emphasize collective forms of knowledge that are passed down from generation to generation and embedded in relationships that encompass humans, nature, and the cosmos (Minthorn & Chávez, 2015a; Spiller et al., 2020). In contrast to linear models of neoliberal leadership that focus on rational (individual) progress toward a better material future, Indigenous leadership adopts a temporal and spatial orientation that connects the past, present, and future and is deeply embedded in the natural ecosystem (Sandefur & Deloria, 2018). Spiller et al. (2020) drew on Indigenous connections to ancestors and the natural environment to distinguish collective Māori (Indigenous people of New Zealand) leadership concepts from the contemporary collective leadership principles that have gained prominence in recent years (see chapter 9 on processual leadership approaches). Although both mainstream collective leadership theories and Indigenous leadership principles emphasize the importance of relationships in the leadership process, Indigenous leadership is rooted in the "the notion of developing a kinship culture where leadership is seen as movement through time, with each generation of leaders seeking to grow and enhance the collective toward intergenerational, interdependent flourishing" (Spiller et al., 2020, p. 533).

The collective orientation of Indigenous leadership is also associated with decentralized notions of power and authority (Rosile et al., 2018; Sandefur & Deloria, 2018). In alignment with the recognition of multiple social roles and needs within the tribe (e.g., governing, teaching, and leading ceremonies), "different people move through different positions as leaders. . . . This diffusion requires a more flexible posture on authority, which shifts situationally across a range of individuals" (Sandefur & Deloria, 2018, p. 130). In addition to facilitating the adoption of an intergenerational perspective on the timing of leadership, the collective orientation of Indigenous leadership can also inform a consensus approach to decision-making, which values input and agreement over quick and efficient decisions (Sandefur & Deloria, 2018).

The significant role that stories and storytelling play in Indigenous leadership is also connected to the deeply relational nature of Indigenous knowledge beliefs (McCall, 2020; Minthorn & Chávez, 2015a; Spiller et al., 2020). The wisdom of ancestors, elders, and nature is passed down from generation to generation through song, parables, stories, and carvings (Spiller et al., 2020). These stories may be nonlinear in nature (a narrative style aligned with Indigenous perspectives on the interconnections of past, present, and future) and reflect an indirect communication style that draws on metaphors and animal imagery to communicate insights (Julien et al., 2010). Creating opportunities for intergenerational storytelling, both as a form of daily leadership practice and as a research methodology (e.g., narrative inquiry, counterstorytelling, testimonio, autoethnography, or photovoice), is one way contemporary higher education leadership scholar-practitioners may draw on Indigenous leadership principles to guide the development of more inclusive and culturally relevant leadership perspectives.

Within the field of higher education, studies of Indigenous leadership have predominantly centered the stories and experiences of Indigenous institutional leaders within Australia, Canada, New Zealand, and the United States (Minthorn & Chávez, 2015b; Povey et al., 2021, 2022) and the nature of leadership at Tribal Colleges and Universities in the United States (Krumm & Johnson, 2011; Stull & Gasman, 2017). The Walan Mayiny: Indigenous Leadership in Higher Education project is a multiyear research endeavor funded by the Australian Research Council that seeks to examine the professional roles, impacts, and challenges experienced by senior Indigenous administrators in Australian, Canadian, New Zealand, and American higher education institutions (Coates et al., 2021, 2022; Povey et al., 2022). Findings from the project identify organizational structures and policies rooted in neoliberalism and racism as significant barriers to achieving transformational objectives; however, participating senior Indigenous leaders shared their success stories as well, highlighting the increased visibility and resources of Indigenous studies, the hiring of new Indigenous faculty, and the adoption of more consensus-oriented approaches to decision-making. Participants in the Walan Mayiny project identify systemic changes in exclusionary hiring practices and governance structures as necessary conditions for realizing the transformative agenda of Indigenous leadership.

Minthorn and Chávez's (2015b) *Indigenous Leadership in Higher Education* also offered a significant contribution to contemporary knowledge of Indigenous leadership principles and practices within postsecondary institutions. Drawing on an analysis of twenty-two Indigenous higher education leaders' autoethnographies, Minthorn and Chávez (2015a) presented an Indigenous leadership model comprising four dimensions: (1) who we are, (2) what we strive to embody, (3) what is known, and (4) what we do. Minthorn and Chávez (2015a) elaborated on each dimension, utilizing participant quotes to illustrate subthemes. For example, in the "what we strive to embody" dimension, the authors named "wisdom, activism, courage, strength, generosity, humility with confidence, cultural competence, balance, spirituality [and] discernment" as foundational Indigenous leadership characteristics and values (Minthorn & Chávez, 2015a, p. 9). In "what is known," Minthorn and Chávez (2015a) highlighted the importance of intergenerational learning and the past-present-future orientation when they stated, "We are of Those who Come Before, Those We are With, and Those Who Came After Us [sic]" (p. 9). In the final chapter of *Indigenous Leadership in Higher Education*, Minthorn and Chávez (2015c) presented a set of concrete strategies for transforming higher education. The recommendations are organized into six areas of transformation. Table 8.2 identifies the six categories and provides a sample of corresponding strategies.

Higher education leaders and teams seeking to draw on Indigenous leadership principles to foster more culturally inclusive leadership processes and practices would be well served to review the organizational dynamics ripe for transformation (e.g., curriculum and budgeting processes) and adopt one or more of the strategies described by Minthorn and Chávez (2015c). Doing

238   Perspectives on Leadership Research and Practice

Table 8.2   Indigenous perspectives on transforming higher education

Areas for transformation	Strategies
Approaches and philosophies	• Transform to a culturally strengths-based philosophy of education that draws from Indigenous educational systems of knowledge and wisdom. • Develop systems that continuously serve the needs of all.
Working with students	• Tell students about their strengths and gifts and that you believe in them. • Integrate Indigenous ways of doing and being into leadership expectations and activities for all students.
Relational strategies	• Create prominent roles for elders. • Lead through stories.
Academics	• Promote and advocate Indigenous scholarship, language studies, and education.
Personnel, planning, and policy	• Plan and budget strategically to implement change for the betterment of Indigenous Peoples.
Structural development	• Create specific spaces for cultural gathering, refuge, and empowerment.

Source: Adapted from table 24.1, "Transforming Higher Education," in Minthorn & Chávez (2015c), pp. 246–247.

so is likely to result in the facilitation of a leadership culture that reflects values of humility, reciprocity, respect, altruism, cultural authenticity, and a temporal orientation that honors the past, present, and future (Haar et al., 2019; McCall, 2020; Sandefur & Deloria, 2018), values common within Indigenous communities and that directly contest the self-centered and individualistic principles characteristic of neoliberalism and white supremacy.

Conclusion

Cultural approaches to leadership were highlighted as a prominent strand of theory and practice by Kezar et al. (2006), and this body of work has continued to garner extensive attention in the twenty-first century. Although distinct strands of inquiry exist under the broad umbrella of cultural leadership perspectives (e.g., organizational culture, social identities, and national culture), cultural scholars share a common interest in understanding the ways history, identity, context, and multiple layers of culture (macro, meso, and micro) shape leadership beliefs, experiences, and behaviors. Existing and emerging cultural leadership perspectives hold tremendous promise for identifying broad strategies and daily leadership practices that may be effective in resisting and dismantling systems of oppression rooted in neoliberalism and white supremacy. Explorations of the intersectional nature of identity, culture, and leadership have shed light on cultural factors that constrain the leadership opportunities and experiences of individuals from historically marginalized communities. Importantly, cultural leadership research has also documented the ways individuals and communities can leverage the unique cultural knowledge and skills cultivated through efforts to navigate and resist systemic oppression as tools for transformational change. Cultural leadership perspectives rooted in CRT and Indigenous principles demonstrate the power of critical consciousness, collective wisdom, a commitment to serving others, and the articulation of counterstories for constructing inclusive and socially just higher education organizations. Building on these important insights, we suggest promising new directions for cultural leadership research and practice in chapter 10.

In closing, we offer a summary of key takeaways for practice.

Traditional Theory

- Cultural leadership perspectives recognize that leadership processes are situated within complex sociocultural systems and thus reflect the influence of history, identity, context, and culture.
- Cultural leadership theorists examine how culturally and contextually specific conditions (e.g., values, beliefs, norms, and rituals) and intersectional social identities (e.g., race and ethnicity, gender, and nationality) inform leadership perspectives and behaviors.
- Cultural leadership approaches consider the ways in which systemic oppression rooted in racism, sexism, heteronormativity, and so on shapes and constrains the leadership experiences of individuals and groups.
- There are three common perspectives on the relationship between leadership and culture (Alvesson, 2011): (1) leadership is a shared local cultural understanding (i.e., beliefs about leadership reflect shared values about power and interpersonal relationships); (2) cultural norms, beliefs, values, and so on

240   *Perspectives on Leadership Research and Practice*

serve to frame and determine what is perceived as legitimate leadership within a specific cultural context; and (3) leadership (organizational founders and formal leaders) plays an active role in shaping organizational culture.

- Contemporary research on gender and leadership continues to document that cisgender women's leadership is associated with a more participatory, relational, and interpersonal style and with power and influence strategies that emphasize reciprocity and collectivity.
- Gender-based differences and inequities in leadership are shaped by cultural (macro), organizational (meso), and individual (micro) factors.
- Contemporary leadership scholars have documented distinctive leadership experiences and styles among Indigenous and American Indian peoples, Asian Americans, African Americans, and Latinx individuals.
- Critical race theory principles (e.g., the permanence of racism, interest convergence, whiteness as property, counternarratives, the critique of liberalism, the legitimacy of experiential knowledge, and intersectionality) have been used to understand the influence of race and racism on leadership as well as examine leadership practices centered on eliminating racial inequity.
- Leadership processes, experiences, beliefs, and styles are influenced by intersectional social identities. Additional research is needed to expand understanding of the relationship between social identities and leadership, particularly social identities beyond race and gender (e.g., those pertaining to social class, disability, spirituality or religion, LGBTQ+, and age).

New Evolutions

- Critical race theory tenets, particularly whiteness as property, and anti-racism epistemologies are useful for examining and dismantling normative leadership discourses and practices rooted in whiteness.
- Anti-racist practices focused on dismantling white supremacist leadership norms and discourses include (1) intentionally examining racial biases, assumptions, and power dynamics; (2) engaging in strategic hiring practices focused on fostering greater racial representation across all levels of the institution; and (3) disrupting normative discourses that uphold whiteness as the standard for niceness, professionalism, communication, and so on.

- Indigenous leadership perspectives are characterized by an emphasis on service to the community, collective wisdom, connections to ancestors and nature, and the importance of storytelling.
- Leaders practicing applied critical leadership who have historically marginalized identities or those who choose to adopt a critical race perspective enact a more culturally responsive and inclusive leadership approach as a result of drawing on their unique cultural knowledge, experiences, and attributes.

Discussion Questions

1. Reflect on your experiences with the three layers of culture described by Schein (2010). What personal and organizational leadership insights arise from this cultural analysis (e.g., observable behaviors, espoused values, or core beliefs)?
2. Identify the cultural (macro), organizational (meso), and individual (micro) factors that have shaped your leadership journey. What factors have created opportunities? What factors have limited opportunities? How have these factors shaped your approach to leadership (beliefs, behaviors, etc.)?
3. In what ways do your social identities influence your approach to leadership?
4. Reflecting on your current or previous organizational contexts, what examples of white supremacist power dynamics can you identify (communication norms, decision-making processes, etc.)? How might you draw on critical race theory principles to make meaning of and dismantle these dynamics?
5. In the Critiques section, we highlight three substantive knowledge gaps within contemporary cultural leadership perspectives. Select one critique and draft two to three research questions that would serve to expand understanding of this cultural leadership topic.
6. How might you incorporate the Indigenous leadership principles of service to the community, collective wisdom, connections to ancestors and nature, and the importance of storytelling in your leadership practice?
7. Which of the applied critical leadership characteristics are embedded in your approach to leadership? Which of these characteristics have you observed in others? What challenges do you foresee when engaging in applied critical leadership? How might you overcome these challenges?

Chapter 9

Processual Leadership Perspectives

As a Hispanic-Serving Institution, Harbor Community College's student body is approximately 56% Latinx. It fought long and hard to establish both a Pride Center for LGBTQ+ campus community members and a Latinx Cultural Center. At the start of the summer, the staff of both centers are notified that they will have to join together to create one large multicultural center for the upcoming academic school year. In addition to the organizational merger, several staff positions are being cut, meaning there will be less full-time staff to carry out programs and initiatives. The vice president for student life attributes the changes to budget restrictions stemming from the COVID-19 pandemic. To make matters worse, the Pride Center is also notified that their office space is being reallocated to the Division of Advancement, which needs office space for a new associate vice president of annual giving and associate vice president for alumni relations. As they rush to implement the organizational merger, Pride Center and Latinx Cultural Center students and staff worry that these changes will prevent them from adequately providing programming and holistic support for students. Students and staff are also deeply concerned that senior-level administrators are not prioritizing the needs of Latinx or LGBTQ+ campus community members.

Deeply hurt by the merger and loss of space, students organize a sit-in at the president's office. The students partner with professional staff members

Marisol (program coordinator, Pride Center) and Hector (assistant director, Latinx Cultural Center) to organize, strategize, and devise a plan of action to save their space and jobs. Unsure of how to help students maneuver protests and enact the change they desire, Marisol and Hector search for frameworks and concepts to guide them as they fulfill their roles as advocates and coconspirators.

The students and staff at Harbor Community College are uniquely positioned and would find it beneficial to enact processual leadership perspectives to save the Latinx and LGBTQ+ student spaces. In this chapter, we synthesize contemporary knowledge regarding processual leadership perspectives—including their emergence, key insights, and new developments—in the interest of illustrating how higher education professionals might draw on these frameworks and concepts to contest the influence of neoliberalism and white supremacy.

Definition and Emergence

Processual leadership emerges from the field of process studies, which was popularized by philosophers Alfred North Whitehead (1929) and Henri Bergson (1946). It draws on the disciplines of anthropology, political science, and sociology, which share a focus on process, structures, and context as central to understanding human behavior (Cronshaw, 2012; Fiedler, 1997; M. Wood, 2005). Processual theories identify how leadership happens over time, involves complex interactions of people and events, and exists within multiple layers of context—breaking from individualistic definitions of leadership focused on a set of traits, behaviors, or influence strategies (Antonakis et al., 2003; Pettigrew, 1997; Tourish, 2014).

The emergence of processual leadership can be seen as an advancement of contingency and situational theories of leadership, which also focus on leadership as taking place within a context but are instead rooted in a postpositivist orientation that seeks to match specific situations and leadership styles (Kezar et al., 2006). In contrast, processual theories are grounded in social constructivism, which frames situations not as objective realities to which leaders must respond but rather as unfolding processes that are created and interpreted by multiple people in a particular setting. Processual leadership is conceptualized from the presumption that "process *is the* concrete reality of things" (D. R. Griffin, 1986, p. 6, original emphasis). Process theoretical perspectives and studies document interrelatedness and the notion that the world—its people and institutions—is in a constant state of (re)construction and becoming (Chia, 2002; Nayak, 2008; Rescher, 1996). In this fashion, processual leadership shifts attention away from the study of individual-level leadership traits and behaviors and instead directs focus toward the events, activities, and choices—the processes—that compose leadership (Endres & Weibler, 2016; Langley, 1999; Ruben & Gigliotti, 2016; M. Wood, 2005; Yukl, 1999).

Major Assumptions and Contributions

A number of major assumptions underlie processual leadership theory. Those assumptions include the following: (1) meaning emerges as a result of participation in the leadership process, (2) contexts significantly influence leadership processes, and (3) temporality is an important dimension of processual leadership. We detail these assumptions in this section.

As noted earlier, processual leadership theories are grounded in social constructivism. Thus, a major assumption that undergirds processual leadership is that meaning emerges as a result of participation in the leadership process, which is constantly constructed, deconstructed, and reconstructed among organizational members (Fairhurst, 2008; Fairhurst & Grant, 2010; Tourish, 2014). The multiple meanings and constant (re)construction of meaning showcase the complexity and richness evident in the leadership process, which challenges earlier approaches to leadership that posit leadership as a fixed reality and as narrowly embodied in individual behavior (Alvesson, 1996). Here again, processual leadership challenges the popularized notion that leadership can be reduced to an individual.

Processual leadership also places great significance on context—political context, interpersonal context, organizational context, and global context (Dawson, 1994; Dunphy & Stace, 1992; Pettigrew, 1997). There is a consensus among processual leadership theorists that any shift in context can greatly affect an organization and the leadership process. Contextual conditions are the drivers and shapers of leadership and change (Dawson 1994, 2019; Parry, 1998; Pettigrew, 1985, 1997). Accordingly, processual leadership perspectives contest the notion of a one-size-fits-all model of effective leadership. Rather, interpretations of leadership efficacy are a function of specific contextual conditions and needs as well as the identities and experiences (e.g., race, class, and socioeconomic background) of those engaged in the leadership process (Dawson, 1994; Pettigrew et al., 2001).

A third major assumption of processual leadership perspectives is the temporal nature of leadership. In processual leadership, the process itself is centered and studied, making obvious the need to consider the past, present, and future, as well as the cyclical, universal, particular, closed, and open-ended temporal orientations of leadership (Dawson, 1994, 2019; Orlikowski & Yates, 2002). Research on higher education and other organizational environments has captured these alternative temporal orientations (e.g., Bennett & Burke, 2018; Dodd et al., 2013; Griesbach & Grand, 2013; Reinecke & Ansari, 2017). For example, Okello et al. (2021) suggested that we consider the embodiment of time—our feelings tied to single events (past and present), the notion of singularity (ongoing state), and how they all work to construct or shape our imagined futures and forge a path to getting there.

Collectively, these three processual leadership assumptions hold significant implications for the study of leadership. Scholars like Dawson (2019) have described studying processual leadership as developing a motion picture, a far more complex inquiry process than that of studies that aim to produce static snapshots of leadership through surveys or brief interviews. Van de Ven and Huber (1990) found that studies that seek to capture and detail processes over time require different data collection approaches (e.g., longitudinal field research methods or interviews *and* focus groups). Dawson (2019) argued that the central reason for qualitative longitudinal research designs is to collect contextual and temporal data by using numerous collection techniques over an extended period of time. This allows new and multiple perspectives to emerge regarding the leadership process. Scholars who have utilized qualitative longitudinal research designs for the study of process have highlighted their benefits and their ability to capture data that would not otherwise be captured using traditional qualitative research designs (e.g., Dawson, 1994; Francis & Sinclair, 2003; Pettigrew, 1997; Ropo et al., 1997; Tuttle, 1997). Areas of focus might include the sequencing of tasks, a series of events, or the evolution of crises and organizational responses. Additionally, processual leadership theorists argue that it is advantageous for researchers to study the leadership process as it happens ("reality in-flight") instead of after it happens (retrospective) (Dawson, 2019). Thus, the prolonged observation and engagement that are characteristic of ethnographic and extended case study methodologies are better suited for illustrating how context and temporality shape the leadership process.

In addition to expanding insights regarding diverse approaches to the study of leadership, processual perspectives have advanced our understanding of how multiple and intersecting contextual conditions (e.g., history, culture, societal trends, political dynamics, and economic circumstances) shape leadership experiences and interpretations. Relatedly, processual approaches have shifted attention away from individual leaders and the search for universal leadership characteristics and behaviors in favor of leadership frameworks that recognize the influence of diverse perspectives and contextualized meaning-making. The result has been the development and practice of more complex and nuanced forms of leadership that honor time and space.

As with other social constructivist–anchored leadership perspectives reviewed in this book, processual theories are not inherently equity oriented. Processual leadership approaches can be used to advance neoliberal and racist organizational aims. The key to leveraging processual perspectives to advance equity and social justice goals is to focus on identifying, resisting, and dismantling neoliberal and racist processes embedded in leadership and organizational life.

Key Findings and Insights

Operationalizing the assumptions just described, studies of processual leadership have expanded our understanding of the conditions, outcomes, benefits, and challenges associated with adopting processual leadership perspectives. In this section, we synthesize key processual leadership research findings and insights, organizing the discussion by specific strands of inquiry: the influence of context on leadership processes, and collective leadership approaches.

The Influence of Context on Leadership Processes

Studies of context have demonstrated that leaders socially construct context and have identified key contextual features that shape leadership processes. In the specific context of higher education, the loosely joined and bureaucratic structures of higher education create a culture that shapes leadership processes and the ability to scale and create changes. Different sectors of higher education require distinctive leadership approaches, and the complexity of goals makes communication and consensus on change challenging. In general, these studies point to the value of leaders aligning their efforts to be attentive and responsive to contextual elements. This does not always mean leaders must alter their approach to align with the context, as changes may require challenging or altering the context instead, especially as it relates to issues of white supremacy and neoliberalism discussed throughout this book. But studies consistently find that a lack of awareness of context can lead to challenges and failure for leaders, as they will not be prepared to navigate these spaces (Kezar, 2018).

Studies on the leadership process demonstrate that individuals uniquely develop understandings of context as part of the leadership process and that relationships shape those interpretations (Dawson, 1994; Neumann, 1995; Osborn et al., 2002; Parry, 1998; Pettigrew, 1997; Pettigrew et al., 2001; Vine et al., 2008). Some scholars have even begun to think through the interplay between internal contextual variables (i.e., organizational culture, history, and the political process) and external conditions (i.e., business and legitimacy concerns) with respect to shaping leadership processes (e.g., Koivunen, 2007; Shamir & Howell, 1999; Wood & Dibben, 2015). For example, in his early work on the evolution of Imperial Chemical Industries amid changing social, political, and economic environments, Pettigrew (1985) offered a multilevel analysis of different contextual variables and conditions such as socioeconomic influence on organizational group behavior to understand how processes are "both constrained by structures and shape structures . . . both in catching reality in flight and in embeddedness" (p. 37). Guided by this insight, Pettigrew found that fixation on the status quo, a lack of vision, and the absence of leadership were key contextual factors that affected Imperial Chemical Industries' ability to change with the times. In higher education, scholars have identified how various layers of context within institutions (e.g., long histories; various subunits; numerous processes, structures, and practices; and constantly shifting cultures and climates) and external to the institution (e.g., multiple campuses being part of a state system or consortia of colleges, state or federal political policy influences, local and regional economies, and social forces and politics) shape leadership processes (Kezar, 2018).

The context of colleges and universities is shaped simultaneously by bureaucracy and by a loosely joined structure, which affects processual leadership (Birnbaum, 1988; W. R. Scott, 2015; Weick, 1976). The loosely joined structure affords autonomy to individual offices, departments, and divisions. Bureaucracy, on the other hand, shapes a more top-down leadership context. One study examined campus efforts to provide more equitable graduate education and found that the loosely joined structure made it difficult to scale equitable change across the university and its STEM community; changes remained localized (Posselt et al., 2017). Studies of campuses that use matrix structures that connect the more bureaucratic parts of campus with loosely joined departments to initiate change found that they were better able to achieve scale and diffusion of changes (Kezar et al., 2021).

Different sectors of higher education (e.g., community colleges, liberal arts colleges, public state universities, and religious institutions) are animated by their own unique hierarchies, politics, and constraints, which require them to utilize distinctive leadership approaches. For example, Boggs and McPhail (2016) wrote about how community colleges differ from four-year institutions because they have different missions and functions (e.g., trade preparation, transfer function, and dual enrollment) and thus must involve different stakeholders, such as high school counselors and four-year institution partners, in their leadership processes. Doing so allows community colleges to maintain crucial partnerships and strengthen transfer programs and dual enrollment. Small liberal arts colleges have fewer constraints and administrative obstacles than some public state universities, which allows them to be more responsive to changing conditions, as evidenced by an ethnographic case study of Keuka College in New York (Bonvillian & Murphy, 1996). The lack of constraints birthed new possibilities at Keuka, where the president was able to mobilize the entire campus to tackle changes in the face of adversity. Partly due to the unique institutional context, the president was able to engage in collective leadership approaches, a point we consider in the section that follows.

COLLECTIVE LEADERSHIP

Because process is a focus in processual theories, studies have identified the importance of people working together and illustrated how leadership is distributed among individuals as well as their interactions. This phenomenon became known as collective leadership. Consistent with processual leadership's emphasis on the multiple stakeholders who create and make meaning of leadership processes, collective leadership shifts attention from the leader-follower binary and instead emphasizes the diverse individuals involved throughout the organization in nonhierarchical, collaborative, and mutually beneficial leadership relationships (Pearce & Conger, 2003).

Three forms of collective leadership are most common: shared, team, and distributed. In some cases, the terms *shared*, *team*, and *distributed* are used interchangeably. What often separates these different types of "shared" leadership is the unit of analysis. For distributed leadership, the unit of analysis is the organization as an entire entity (Gronn, 2002; Spillane & Diamond, 2007). For team leadership, the unit of analysis is the team (Day et al., 2006). According to Zhu et al. (2018), the unit of analysis for shared leadership is also the team. The unit of analysis is important because it provides additional information about how these different types of shared leadership are studied and understood.

Collective leadership has been associated with dozens of positive outcomes, including increased confidence at both the individual and group levels; increased trust among team members; increased social integration, problem-solving quality, and cognitive complexity in decisions; greater organizational citizenship behavior; positive team performance or increased effectiveness; and, in educational settings, changes in organizational processes and structures that in turn led to improvements in student learning (Holcombe et al., 2021; Kezar & Holcombe, 2017; Pearce & Conger, 2003). Many of these studies and others suggest that collective leadership is especially beneficial in complex environments that require frequent adaptations (Feyerherm, 1994; Pearce & Sims, 2002; Pearce, 2004).

Generally, research has shown that women and certain cultural groups (e.g., Native Americans and African Americans) demonstrate a preference for distributed or team leadership (H. S. Astin & Leland, 1991; Kezar, 2000, 2002; Kezar & Moriarty, 2000; Rhode, 2003). The adoption of shared leadership practices and processes may be an essential step toward dismantling neoliberalism and white supremacy in leadership by cultivating inclusive organizational environments that tap into the unique perspectives and experiences of historically marginalized social groups. As noted in

250   *Perspectives on Leadership Research and Practice*

the transformational leadership chapter, shared-equity leadership (Kezar et al., 2021) illustrates how shared approaches can dismantle white supremacy by foregrounding the voices of marginalized groups within leadership processes.

In recognition of the nuanced conceptual differences that frame shared, team, and distributed leadership, we first synthesize key insights of shared leadership, then provide overviews of team and distributed leadership. We also discuss grassroots leadership and social movements as collective forms of leadership whereby individuals work as a collective to enact social change and challenge hierarchies and oppressive systems.

SHARED LEADERSHIP

Like other processual leadership approaches, shared leadership emerged out of studies of leadership as a complex process in which the contributions of many people were identified and valued. Shared leadership helps organizations to create an infrastructure in which everyone benefits from the leadership of multiple people (Kezar & Holcombe, 2017). To this end, shared leadership is enhanced and supported by engaging with the perspectives of diverse individuals through professional development, relationship building, increased access to information, and team-based work (Kezar & Holcombe, 2017; Pearce & Conger, 2003). Shared leadership is included in virtually every new leadership model, such as adaptive leadership (Heifetz, 1994), leadership for complexity (Wheatley, 1999), systems leadership (K. E. Allen & Cherrey, 2000), connective leadership (Lipman-Blumen, 1996), and situated cognition practice (Spillane et al., 2006). All these new models are focused on how leadership best operates in a complex environment, and shared leadership emerges as a central concept for managing and addressing complexity. As noted earlier, processual leadership in higher education has typically been studied in terms of leadership teams, but that is changing and studies of more distributed models are being conducted (e.g., Bolden et al., 2009; S. Jones, 2014; S. Jones et al., 2017; Menon, 2005; White-Lewis, 2022).

Research on shared leadership identifies ways that contextual conditions can support the development of effective shared leadership, including through team selection and socialization, facilitation, team empowerment, delegated authority and autonomy, shared purpose, accountability structures, resources, and support (Kezar & Holcombe, 2017). A detailed and nuanced interrogation of shared leadership is beyond the scope of this book; however, we recommend *Shared Leadership: Reframing the Hows and Whys of Leadership* by Pearce and Conger (2003) as an introduction and background and *Shared Leadership in Higher Education: A Framework and Models for Responding to a Changing World*, an edited volume by Holcombe et al. (2021), for detailed reviews of shared leadership in the higher education setting.

Leadership Teams

Team leadership inquiry and practice focus on the processes that guide team decision-making and outcomes. Team leadership is different from shared and distributed leadership because it focuses on a defined group rather than a broad process across an institution, as is typical of shared leadership.

Higher education scholars have pointed out that the notion of leadership and followership is unnecessary in a well-trained and diverse team that recognizes that each person has valuable expertise and perspectives to provide in any leadership process (Kouzes & Posner, 2003; Lucas, 1994). Bensimon and Neumann (1993) were among the first higher education researchers to focus on leadership as a team-oriented, collective process in their study of presidential cabinets. Their study identified the different key roles that people can play on teams to make them more effective (e.g., task monitor, emotional monitor, and synthesizer), as well as organizational conditions that support team effectiveness. Bensimon and Neumann also outlined the challenges and obstacles that leadership teams can face in conducting their work. Grounded in critical and social constructivist paradigms, their work acknowledged the influence of multiple perspectives on team leadership processes, viewed team conflict as inevitable and healthy, and framed the goals of team leadership to be more humanistic and relational in nature rather than narrowly focused on efficiency and effectiveness, which happen to be defining elements of neoliberalism. Although Bensimon and Neumann's research was focused on presidential cabinets, it elucidated the key insight that teams throughout colleges and universities make better decisions than individual decision makers.

Higher education research has continued to find that teams are an effective mechanism for helping campuses develop cognitively complex decisions (H. S. Astin & Leland, 1991; Branson et al., 2016; Bryman, 2007; Kezar, 1998). Although described in detail in the chapter on transformational leadership, the social change model of leadership development (H. S. Astin et al., 1996) can also be characterized as a processual leadership approach that recognizes the value of teams and engagement in collective leadership processes (e.g., collaboration, controversy with civility, and establishing a shared purpose) for advancing social change.

Within the broader topic of team leadership, contemporary scholars have examined the nature and efficacy of virtual team leadership processes (Horila & Siitonen, 2020; Maduka et al., 2018; Zhang & Fjermestad, 2006). Virtual team leadership has been popularized more recently because of the COVID-19 pandemic. It "is typically not under the control of any one person, but is expressed through the interplay of team members and technology" (Zigurs, 2003, p. 348). In virtual teams, leadership roles shift among team members depending on the specific objectives and tasks in that particular moment in the team's life cycle. Meaning is created as a result of the relationship between team members, the tasks at hand, and the mediating force of technology. Business and management scholars have made it clear that virtual teams—and, as a result, virtual team leadership—are a necessity in today's global and changing world (Colfax et al., 2009; Dimitrov, 2018; Lipnak & Stamps, 2000).

Virtual team leadership pays particular attention to temporal stability (e.g., how long teams will be virtual), membership structure (e.g., who is involved in the team and for how long, stability), level of distribution (e.g., how spread out the team is geographically), and technologies used (e.g., videoconferencing or instant messaging). Research on virtual teams explores how the leadership process is acted out virtually, the role technology plays in the leadership process, and how teams maintain efficiency and morale in virtual spaces (Horila & Siitonen, 2020; Maduka et al., 2018; Zhang & Fjermestad, 2006).

Technologically mediated communication and virtuality in teamwork have, together, produced a new set of required skills for engaging in the leadership process, including relationship-building skills (e.g., establishing trust and motivating team members virtually), technical skills (e.g., how to use videoconferencing software), and communication skills (e.g., emotional intelligence and team interaction styles) (Eberly et al., 2013; Hambley et al., 2007; Roy, 2012). Leaders often have to put in more effort to ensure the leadership process runs smoothly and efficiently because of the different barriers and challenges presented by virtuality.

Processual Leadership Perspectives   253

DISTRIBUTED LEADERSHIP

Leadership scholars within and beyond higher education are also exploring distributed leadership. The terms *team leadership* and *distributed leadership* are sometimes used interchangeably, but distributed leadership is distinctly focused on "leadership dispersed across multiple organization levels or even organizational boundaries" and typically involves more individuals in leadership processes than teams (Kezar & Holcombe, 2017, p. 6). Research on distributed leadership that exists beyond higher education has focused primarily on *how* and *when* leadership can be distributed. Distribution can be formal or informal (MacBeath et al., 2004; Spillane, 2006) or even spontaneous (Gronn, 2002). Yet empirical findings about distributed leadership are far from conclusive, and its benefit remains largely unknown. Scholars like A. Harris (2009) and Leithwood and Mascall (2008) have noted that a significant relationship has yet to be identified between distributed leadership and performance outcomes. And especially in the presence of hierarchy and even bureaucracy, it remains unclear what exactly is being distributed (e.g., power, accountability, or decision-making).

Studies of distributed leadership within higher education have highlighted both the promise of this perspective for enhancing organizational performance and the challenge of implementing distributed leadership models that move from rhetoric to authentic action (Bolden et al., 2009; Joslyn, 2018; Lizier et al., 2022). General insights on distributed leadership in higher education suggest that it helps move away from hierarchical models of leadership to more inclusive styles (Hartley, 2010; Kezar, 2001). The context of the academic enterprise (i.e., loosely structured) also makes distributed leadership a promising approach, especially when considering the democratic characteristics that guide the vision of higher education (Joslyn, 2018). Institutions such as the University of Richmond and Kingsborough Community College use distributed leadership to advance diversity, equity, and inclusion goals and increase student success, showing distributed leadership's promise in practice (Holcombe et al., 2021).

Lizier et al.'s (2022) case study of distributed leadership in an Australian university found that a lack of clarity in distributed leadership definitions, purposes, and objectives undermined implementation of the distributed leadership framework. The structure was also ambiguous, in some cases resembling traditional leadership hierarchies. Lizier et al. also found that individuals' positions within the organizational hierarchy and their level of trust in the distributed leadership process influenced their perceptions of distributed leadership. Similarly, Bolden et al.'s (2009) study of faculty and staff perspectives on distributed leadership within twelve UK universities found that many faculty and staff still perceived hierarchical leadership as dominant within their campus contexts despite espoused distributed leadership commitments. When distributed leadership was authentically adopted, however, faculty and staff attributed numerous positive outcomes to it, including improved teamwork, enhanced communication, and heightened responsiveness to student concerns. A common theme in studies of distributed leadership within higher education is the need to intentionally and transparently address issues of power, authority, and hierarchy in the design and implementation of distributed leadership processes.

Grassroots Leadership

Aligned with processual leadership's emphasis on the various individuals who are part of leadership, studies began to explore grassroots efforts. These studies featured organizational and community members operating without formal power and authority as they participated in leadership processes that fostered change (Kezar & Lester, 2011). In some cases, grassroots leaders develop and advocate for moral and ethical changes that would not otherwise be developed or advocated for by top-down leaders. Grassroots leadership is noninstitutionalized, meaning grassroots leaders often have to create their own networks, systems, and structures for sustainable change (Kezar & Lester, 2011; Spillane & Diamond, 2007). In higher education, grassroots leaders are faculty, staff, and students who act as agents of change and work collectively to alter their campuses. The grassroots leaders whom Kezar and Lester (2011) studied were actively working against white supremacy and neoliberalism in the change agendas they adopted. But Kezar and Lester's research also showed how neoliberalism shaped grassroots efforts by reducing the power of shared governance on campus, making contingent faculty easily subject to dismal working conditions and precarity, and outsourcing staff roles, making it challenging for them to engage in collective leadership, for example. In recognition of neoliberalism's dominant influence within higher education, some grassroots leaders have leveraged neoliberal strategies such as seeking to align with students or alumni who have market power, securing external funds, and appealing to institutional desires for prestige or revenue generation in order to navigate campus resistance and advance their change efforts.

Grassroots leadership is animated by a number of activities and tactics such as consciousness-raising, organizing, mobilizing, strategizing, and engaging in direct action, many of which are absent from the dominant leadership research and which reflect the influence of social movement theories on grassroots leadership (Kezar et al., 2011). Grassroots leaders tend to also use activities and tactics that appear in the dominant leadership research as well, such as vision building. But grassroots leaders are likely to use the vision-building strategy differently from a college president—for example, by creating vision collectively and integrating a broad set of interests. While grassroots leadership can be entirely independent of more top-down efforts, there has also been research that explores grassroots leaders as partners with senior administrators in change processes. This shift from grassroots to more shared leadership models over time reflects the fragility of grassroots leadership and the desire to foster sustainable change (Kezar & Lester, 2011). Additionally, it is important to note power and oppression are actively explored within grassroots leadership making it among the few processual approaches that explicitly name power conditions and the ways grassroots leaders are subject to these forces in the workplace, ranging from being fired or demoted, to being silenced or controlled, or harassed with microaggressions. Strategies for building the grassroots leadership capacity of higher education professionals include mentoring, providing course releases, or sending faculty or staff to conferences where they can network with other change agents.

Higher education scholars have continued to demonstrate the possibilities of grassroots leadership as a way to advance equity and social justice. One example is Hughes's (2018) study on the sources of resilience utilized by grassroots faculty and staff as they fought for a more positive LGBTQ+ campus climate at a Catholic university. Similarly, Broadhurst et al. (2018) explored narratives of student affairs staff attempting to create change for LGBTQ+ students in the South.

SOCIAL MOVEMENTS: COALITIONS, ALLIANCES, AND NETWORKS

In addition to grassroots leadership emerging as a central focus for processual theories, social movements have also been a focal point (Meyerson, 2008; Morris & Staggenborg, 2004). Social movements involve distributed groups of actors who typically do not have the positional power to change a system (Weber & King, 2014). One key avenue for doing so is through coalitions and alliances. These are groups that agree to work together—from planning to action—in an effort to build consensus, advocate for change, and achieve goals. Coalitions and alliances are often strategic, taking the strengths and assets of individuals to weave together a dynamic and powerful group eager to enact change and bring about awareness of an issue or issues (Bystydzienski & Schacht, 2001). These coalitions and alliances are often built across differences and must be not only created but maintained (Bandy & Smith, 2005).

Coalition and alliance work spans several movements, including the LGBTQ+ (D'Emilio, 1983), women's (S. Gilmore, 2008), environmental (Litcherman, 1995; Murphy, 2005), civil rights (Mantler, 2013), and labor movements (Dray, 2011). Often, there are numerous coalitions and alliances working toward the same goal, but belief systems, priorities and actions, and epistemological and ontological stances keep them separate and distinct and can sometimes make cross-coalitional or cross-alliance action difficult. An example that illustrates this tension is that of police reform and abolition. There are coalitions and alliances that seek to simply reform the police state, and there are those that are working tirelessly to abolish it. Collaboration across these coalitions and alliances may prove to be difficult because the belief systems are different, yet the issue of excessive police power remains the reason that both groups were formed to begin with.

Higher education scholars have explored social movements and to a lesser extent the alliances and coalitions that often emerge within them. Studies of social movements have found that current events related to social injustice and oppression both on and off campus mobilize students, faculty, and staff to engage in acts of protest and resistance (Dache, 2019; Morgan & Davis, 2019; Stokes & Davis, 2022). In addition, social movements are using a variety of strategies to mobilize and enact changes such as formal protests, petitions, rallies, letter writing, and social media campaigns (Barnhardt,

2014; Byrne et al., 2021; Cabrera et al., 2017). Findings from these studies have also noted that activists engaged in social movements see and understand higher education as both oppressive and liberatory, which shapes their perceptions of social issues, the campus context, and leadership processes (Baker & Blisett, 2018; Linder et al., 2019; Museus, 2022).

General notions of collaboration and collective action have been well studied in higher education and have proved to be successful in enacting change. These studies have suggested that collaboration and collective action with different groups on campus help foster student growth and development, challenge top-down status quo notions of leadership to achieve equitable outcomes, and support interdisciplinarity and the breaking down of silos (M. Harris, 2010; Kezar & Maxey, 2014). Kezar and Lester (2009) noted the importance of networks, rewards, and resources to sustain collaboration and collective action and establish them as a necessary part of leadership processes in higher education. Coalitions and alliances are supported by collaboration and collective action. Only a handful of studies in higher education focus on and name coalitions specifically, and this is an important area for future research. In these studies, scholars have found that coalitions that gather students, faculty, staff, and administrators together tend to link agendas, align messages, and organize resistance across numerous groups (Kezar, 2005). Coalitions and alliances in higher education tend to bring together different marginalized and oppressed groups. Studies of cross-racial alliances have shown that when different racial groups come together to create an alliance to fight oppression on campus, they must attend to conflict and tensions that arise from stereotypes and unlearn the competition mindset that arises from both real and perceived resource scarcity (Literte, 2011; Rhoads et al., 2005; Tawa et al., 2016). Working together across struggles has greater implications for advancing equity and social justice and dismantling oppressive systems.

In this section, we have reviewed several leadership theories and concepts rooted in the assumptions of processual leadership. Collectively this body of work shifts attention away from individual, hierarchical notions of leadership, shedding light instead on the nature of collective engagement in leadership processes that extend across time and are contextually dependent. Although the highlighted processual leadership perspectives are not explicitly guided by equity and social justice aims, processual leadership research does highlight the value embedded in broad participation in leadership and pays close attention to the ways in which a variety of perspectives, from both inside and outside the organization, can help leaders meet goals and priorities. But these theories are not without drawbacks and limitations, which we explore next.

Critiques

Our critique of processual leadership is organized around two themes. The first is the absence of an explicit consideration of power and oppression in leadership processes. The second is the methodological challenges associated with studying complex leadership processes.

Processual leadership focuses on the notion that the leadership process is defined by relations to and interactions with others (M. Wood, 2005), yet it does not always consider how power and oppressive systems, structures, and ideologies operate explicitly in such interactions (Bolden, 2009; Joslyn, 2018; Lizier et al., 2022). Some exceptions to this critique include explorations of grassroots leadership and social movement coalitions and alliances, which inform some of the new evolutions we review later in the chapter. Processual leadership approaches could benefit from intentionally exploring power and oppression in the contexts, environments, and systems (e.g., neoliberalism, white supremacy, and equity) studied. For example, if a leadership team is tethered to neoliberalism and primarily interested in return on investment, notions of neoliberalism will animate the entire process, from how the team is composed to who is able to speak, say what, and when. The individuals on the team who are interested in advancing equity and the public good for marginalized individuals will be shut out of the leadership process or actively silenced. Leadership processes are inherently guided by people's commitment to certain systems, structures, and ideologies, and processual leadership should capture this. Additionally, research has shown that explicitly attending to issues of power, hierarchy, and trust in the design and facilitation of distributed leadership will likely contribute to more positive perceptions of and engagement in this processual leadership approach (Bolden, 2009; Lizier et al., 2022).

Even though process theorists have advocated for studying the leadership process as it happens (Dawson, 2019), there are challenges and barriers that make studying processual leadership difficult. These include access, navigation of administrative and institutional red tape, and the need for lengthy, sustained fieldwork. Researchers interested in studying the leadership process as it happens may struggle to gain access to the necessary site and the people, especially high-level professionals, involved in the leadership process. As a result of the need for scholars to go through the institutional review board process, researchers may not be able to quickly and efficiently enter the site and begin their investigation. There may also be significant red tape for researchers to navigate; by the time they are able to enter the site, the leadership process may be further along than initially anticipated. Furthermore, studying leadership from a processual standpoint requires lengthy, sustained fieldwork to produce detailed and contextualized accounts (Bate, 1997). Thus, researchers must have the time and resources (especially financial) to study the leadership process in the ways that processual leadership theory requires (i.e., ethnographic inquiry). In sum, studying leadership from a processual perspective is time consuming and resource dependent. This creates challenges for scholars who are chained by their institution's neoliberal metrics of merit, productivity, and success (e.g., number of publications or amount of grant money secured).

New Evolutions

The new evolutions to processual leadership we outline in this section begin to address some of the stated critiques, problems, and issues. Importantly, these new evolutions are clear in their commitment to dismantle oppressive systems and include systematically disadvantaged perspectives in the leadership process. In this section, we highlight a new concept (transformative storytelling), a new model (design for equity in higher education), and a new field of study (critical social movements studies) that have the potential to greatly influence research on processual leadership.

TRANSFORMATIVE STORYTELLING

In the edited volume *Critical Leadership Praxis for Educational and Social Change*, contributing authors Colket et al. (2021) wrote about transformative storytelling as critical praxis for educational leaders interested in advancing social change. They observed, "Stories can strengthen the connections within a network of individuals while they collaborate to create educational experiences that are culturally sustaining (Alim & Paris, 2017), liberatory

(Freire, 1970; hooks, 1994), and ultimately more equitable" (p. 101). Framing storytelling as a relational act characterized by dialogue between the storyteller and listener that creates opportunities for collective meaning-making, transformative storytelling evolves processual leadership by highlighting the power of storytelling to disrupt hierarchical power structures and build meaningful, collaborative relationships with colleagues engaged in shared or grassroots leadership processes that are focused on establishing more equitable learning environments.

In addition, when stories are shared beyond the borders of campus through public media campaigns, community organizing, and so on, transformative storytelling advances processual leadership by looping "less than likely stakeholders," such as surrounding residential neighbors and local business owners, into the leadership process so that change can be mutually beneficial for both institutions and local communities.

Transformative storytelling emerged from the works of scholars such as Paulo Freire, Tara Yosso, Daniel Solórzano, bell hooks, Gloria Ladson-Billings, and Kimberlé Crenshaw who championed the use of stories as a critical means of humanizing the historically dehumanized and opening up opportunities for actualizing their liberation. Transformative storytelling disrupts the white and neoliberal gaze by decentering normative narratives of oppression and empowering storytellers to share personal narratives that "talk back" (hooks, 1990) to those who have been responsible for the creation and maintenance of an oppressive and dehumanizing social order. These counterstories allow for healing and for new possibilities of change and liberation to emerge (Solórzano & Yosso, 2002).

Within the context of higher education, opportunities to share and learn from personal stories that counter and dismantle racist, sexist, heteronormative, and other narratives raise the individual and collective consciousness of leadership process participants, contributing to more culturally inclusive and equitable decisions, policies, and practices. Speaking specifically about the potential for storytelling to transform curriculum and pedagogy, Colket et al. (2021) asserted that when educators listen to the stories of their students' lives and learning experiences, they are better positioned to engage in culturally relevant teaching and learning practices that honor diverse cultures, language, and literacies. The same can be said for the power of storytelling to inform culturally relevant higher education leadership processes.

The temporal nature of processual leadership also aligns with the conceptualization and practice of transformative storytelling. Colket et al. (2021) encouraged educational leaders to recognize stories as "dynamic, ongoing, generative, and reflective of multiple/shifting realities" (p. 104). As such, storytelling is not a one-time event but rather should be folded into ongoing leadership processes and organizational culture to allow opportunities for participants to retell and reshape their stories to reflect evolving conditions and new understandings. Strategies for infusing transformative storytelling into leadership processes include asking participants to write and share autobiographies (the autobiographies could be broad or narrowly focused on a particular issue like college access), collecting oral histories, inviting participants to visually depict powerful experiences of relevance to the focal topic (drawing concepts can challenge deeper thinking and learning), and facilitating the periodic creation and sharing of three-word, six-word, or one-sentence stories (Colket et al., 2021) that challenge participants to concisely articulate their evolving understanding of the situation. The common aim across these storytelling strategies that can be initiated or repeated at multiple points throughout leadership processes is to create opportunities to share and learn from diverse perspectives.

Although we view transformative storytelling as a powerful evolution of processual leadership that has the potential to advance equity aims within higher education, it is important to note that stories can also be used as weapons against historically marginalized individuals and communities. Sharing stories can be (re)traumatizing for individuals who are called on to share vivid details of their oppression. In addition, stories can be manipulated, co-opted, or commodified for the purposes of advancing neoliberal and white supremacist objectives. For example, consider how the stories of students of color are commodified in institutional marketing materials or used to evaluate resilience in competitive admissions processes. Colket et al. (2021 insisted that, to avoid perpetuating oppression, leaders must be "be critically aware of how, why, and to what end [they] ask students and teachers [and community members] to share their stories, and how those stories are then used" (p. 104). Here, Colket et al. (2021) situated intentionality as a critical element of transformative storytelling. Overall, transformative storytelling has the potential to extend processual leadership in ways that foster greater freedom and liberation by creating spaces for leadership participants to share and learn from the experiences of diverse collaborators as well as construct and reshape narratives that convey the lessons learned as a result of participating in equity-oriented leadership processes.

Design for Equity in Higher Education Model

Another important evolution for the higher education context is the design for equity in higher education (DEHE) model, which is a collective leadership approach that emphasizes a specific process—liberatory design thinking (LDT). LDT, which was created to center and empower historically marginalized groups in design processes that develop changes for campus, involves collective action and is very explicit about process steps to guide such leadership efforts. It has seven phases:

1. Notice—developing awareness of values, identity, biases, and assumptions that affect the design process and product.
2. Empathize—understanding the experiences, emotions, and motivations of those you are designing for.
3. Define—developing a point of view about the needs of those you are designing for by narrowing information down and clearly defining the problem.
4. Ideate—generating as many solutions to a problem as possible.
5. Prototype—developing artifacts and experiences to elicit feedback.
6. Test—receiving feedback and improving ideas and prototypes.
7. Reflect—reflecting on actions, emotions, and insights from the design process.

LDT also involves liberatory mindsets such as the following:

- Strive for self-awareness—acknowledging and challenging assumptions about ourselves for a more equitable design process.
- Focus on human values—getting to know those you are working with and for on a human level through codesign, observation, and immersion.
- Build relational trust—investing in relationships across differences, honoring stories, and tending to emotions.
- Share, don't sell—practicing transparency in process and nonattachment to ideas in the ideating and prototyping phases.

LDT foregrounds equity by disrupting the status quo processes that have historically guided the creation of policies and practices in organizations. It requires designers to be cognizant of power imbalances and self-aware of their identities, positionality, and assumptions. Furthermore, designers must obtain a robust understanding of the group they are building for, which requires them to observe, interview, and deeply understand the experiences of the target population. Designers are tasked to listen with intentionality and with an open heart.

Culver et al. (2021) modified LDT for use by higher education leaders in solving problems and inequities in the unique campus environment. To do so, they add new phases such as "organize" and "get buy-in" to capture the importance of design team formation and the widespread role of political will in organization. While a detailed review of the model is beyond the scope of this book, figure 9.1 visualizes the DEHE model in its entirety. We also recommend reading Culver et al.'s (2021) supplemental guide for practice to get a better understanding of how to apply the model in higher education.

The DEHE model evolves processual leadership theories by intentionally centering marginalized groups that policies and practices are being designed for and including them both on the design team and in the design thinking

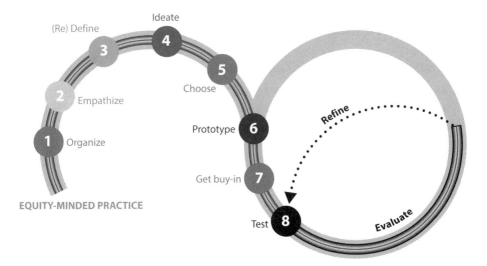

Figure 9.1 Design for Equity in Higher Education. *Source:* Courtesy of Pullias Center for Higher Education, University of Southern California

process. These individuals (who are typically excluded from decision-making) serve as a check and balance at every stage of the leadership process, from ideating to prototyping and testing. In addition, the DEHE model takes seriously not only team formation but the political moment that opens a policy window for equitable change to occur. This is a particularly important advancement in processual leadership, as it illustrates how political moments and policy windows both constrain and enable the leadership process. The model can also address neoliberalism and white supremacy by focusing on the need to dismantle existing oppressive systems and create new ones in its place.

CRITICAL SOCIAL MOVEMENTS STUDIES FRAMEWORK

Museus and Sifuentez (2021) proposed the critical social movements (CSM) studies framework as a more robust lens to study social movement dynamics in higher education. Social movement theory and critical theory make up CSM studies. Museus and Sifuentez argued that research on social movements must be rooted in a systemic analysis that considers the intersection of hegemony, institutions, and social movements, which social movement theory and critical theory do not sufficiently capture. Their argument and subsequent contribution advanced processual leadership by focusing on constraining macro-systems such as neoliberalism and white supremacy. How these macro-systems constrain grassroots leadership efforts is central to CSM.

Whereas higher education scholars tend to use social movement theory and critical theory to understand leaders' experiences with enacting social change and envision how institutions can better support these leaders, CSM studies place deliberate emphasis on power, oppression, and researcher accountability. The theory thus "transcend[s] generating knowledge for its own sake and is grounded in explicit commitments to social justice" (Museus & Sifuentez, 2021, p. 288).

To this end, Museus and Sifuentez (2021) offered the CSM framework with considerations for assessing grassroots movements in higher education:

1. *Foster critical agency:* CSM is committed to generating knowledge that can help develop leaders' critical agency, one's capacity to effect change. There are three elements to critical agency: (1) critical consciousness (awareness

of societal ills), (2) agency (change is possible, and individuals and collectives can effect change), and (3) urgency (moving quickly to join movements and create change).

2. *Utilize catalytic approaches:* CSM is against objectivity and neutrality and is morally committed to social justice. CSM can contribute to the transformation of individuals and systems. To do so, scholars engage in continuous reflexivity, reciprocal engagement with communities, and the dissemination of knowledge to effect social change.

3. *Cultivate solidarity in social justice movements:* Social cohesion across identities and communities makes collective action possible and sustainable. The task for researchers is to understand how social movements can cultivate forms of solidarity that enhance leadership efforts.

4. *Bolster social justice movement resources:* CSM studies engage in research that helps cultivate more robust social justice movement resources, including networks, organizations, and media tools that support collective leadership.

5. *Enhance efficacy of social justice movement strategies and tactics:* CSM studies seek to advance knowledge about whether, to what extent, and how social movements lead to concrete outcomes that advance equity and liberation goals. CSM studies are also interested in the manner in which social movements may create unintended consequences for organizers and for organizations.

6. *Expose how systems constrain movements:* CSM perspectives are concerned with exposing how power structures resist and attempt to shut down social justice movements. CSM scholars should especially focus on neoliberalism and white supremacy.

Transformative storytelling, the DEHE model, and CSM studies have the potential to revolutionize the study and practice of processual leadership. Each of these approaches considers the systems, structures, and ideologies in which leadership processes are embedded and begins charting a path toward equitable and liberatory change.

Conclusion

The aim of this chapter was to summarize foundational and emerging processual perspectives on leadership. Our review of the literature highlights the many insights processual leadership has to offer; however, the presence of neoliberalism and white supremacy in higher education and other organizational settings prevents the adoption of more equity-oriented processual perspectives. New evolutions to these perspectives begin to more explicitly call out systems, structures, and ideologies that pose threats to authentically implementing processual leadership approaches. These evolutions are careful to advocate policies, practices, and research that place greater emphasis on the leadership process while simultaneously challenging and dismantling neoliberalism and white supremacy.

In closing, we offer a summary of key takeaways for practice.

Traditional Theory

- Processual leadership perspectives shift the focus of leadership theory and practice from individuals (leaders and followers) to leadership processes that are socially constructed, are context bound, and evolve over time.
- Leaders should pay close attention to and be aware of the multiple contexts (international, national, organizational, social, political, economic, and virtual) in which the leadership process is occurring.
- Leadership should be collaborative and mutually beneficial and influential.
- Leadership that is shared is beneficial for meeting the multiple goals of leadership, including equity.
- Leaders should make deliberate attempts to partner with student activists, community organizations, and other grassroots leaders to enhance the leadership process and enact change.
- Grassroots leaders benefit from using specific strategies that fit within higher education settings and can learn about particular obstacles and challenges they will need to navigate on neoliberal campuses.

New Evolutions

- Storytelling is an essential practice that can yield transformative results for organizations and help deepen relationships.
- Leaders can benefit from liberatory design thinking and should prioritize carefully organizing design teams, getting buy-in, leveraging political will, and being equity-minded as they seek to develop new practices and policies that are rooted in systemic change and the public good.

- Leaders should find ways to build solidarity across a variety of issues affecting different aspects of the campus community and help create agency and empower others to act.
- Critical social movement studies encourage the researcher to participate in critical continuous reflection while remaining answerable and account-able to the social justice cause and the social movement group, not the institution.

Discussion Questions

1. Revisit this chapter's opening vignette. What insights from processual leadership (both traditional approaches and new evolutions) might prove useful in guiding efforts to contest the merger of the cultural centers and staff layoffs?
2. How might you apply the design for equity in higher education model to the opening vignette?
3. How might you study the problem in the opening vignette using a critical social movements studies approach?
4. What are your experiences with collective leadership? What benefits or challenges have you encountered while engaged in process-oriented leadership?
5. What challenges do you imagine running into while doing processual leadership research? How might you go about addressing these challenges?

PART III / Leadership for Liberation

Chapter 10

Looking to the Future of Leadership Practice and Research

In this final chapter, we summarize ideas for orienting leadership practice toward dismantling whiteness and neoliberalism with the aim of advancing liberation and equity within higher education organizations. We also introduce new ideas for researching leadership that reflect the concepts we have discussed throughout the book. This chapter is a call to leaders and researchers to fundamentally reframe conceptualizations of leadership. The four case studies presented in the appendix provide opportunities to consider what it looks like to pursue future directions in leadership research and practice.

In 2006, Kezar et al. called for more studies that used critical and postmodern paradigms. Since then, we have seen a modest expansion in paradigms used to frame leadership research but not a relinquishing of neoliberal and white supremacist ideologies that serve to preserve and advance hierarchical, individual-centered constructions of leadership. In general, we have not seen dramatic changes in the nature of insights across the areas of transformational, cognitive, complexity and chaos, and processual leadership or team and shared approaches. Within cultural perspectives on leadership, scholars exploring the relationship between social identities and leadership have increasingly turned to the critical paradigm to frame their work, including adopting critical race theories and methodologies to shed light on the ways in which the

272   *Leadership for Liberation*

leadership opportunities and experiences of individuals with minoritized identities are constrained within higher education organizations. Unfortunately, much like the other leadership approaches synthesized in this book, cultural perspectives have not sufficiently expanded their work to include an explicit examination and interrogation of power as it relates to leadership. We have seen some research on several areas that Kezar et al. noted should receive more attention, including social movement theories and grassroots leadership, social identity and leadership, team and shared leadership, leadership processes, leadership and learning, and how campus context shapes leadership. But there is much more work still to be done to change leadership beliefs and practices, and research will play a central role in developing new ways of thinking about and practicing leadership.

Future Directions for Leadership Practice

While we have alluded to implications for practice throughout the book, in this concluding chapter we summarize some of the key ideas for reconsidering leadership practice that are embedded in notions that challenge white supremacy and neoliberalism and move toward equity, social justice, and liberation.

OPERATING UNDER A "PEOPLE OVER PROFIT" PRINCIPLE

In order to move beyond white supremacy and neoliberalism, leaders and leadership processes need to refrain from operating under a "profit over people" principle and instead enact a commitment to "people over profit." A focus on the liberation and humanization of systemically disadvantaged people must replace capitalist and white supremacist notions of ownership and revenue generation. Many of the new evolutions in leadership reviewed in this book begin moving us toward more human-centered practices; however, adopting new approaches to leadership is likely insufficient to bring about the transformational changes required to dismantle systemic forces of oppression that are deeply entrenched in postsecondary educational institutions. Instead, higher education professionals must embrace an unwavering commitment to centering people—their needs, wants, desires, and freedom—in tandem with utilizing new leadership models and practices. As noted earlier in the book, too often leaders and leadership processes are concerned with maintaining legitimacy and ensuring leaders and organizations

Looking to the Future of Leadership Practice and Research 273

are accountable to neoliberal and white supremacist interests. The "people over profit" principle, in practice, breaks free of these oppressive frames and helps birth new possibilities for leadership and campus life. Adopting the leadership processes described in this chapter will help organizations operationalize a "people over profit" value system and facilitate achievement of equitable outcomes for students, staff, faculty, and community members.

FOSTERING EQUITY-MINDEDNESS: BREAKING THE STATUS QUO, WHITE GAZE, AND HIDDEN AGENDA

Because our systems are set up to reinforce anti-Blackness and other systemic inequalities, leaders and leadership processes need to begin with an active investigation of how actions, policies, and structures might be reinforcing discrimination. Those seeking to influence change need to question every aspect of the system: Who are the leaders on campus? Do they represent the community in terms of race, gender, income, ethnicity, and other key social identities? What criteria are used to choose leaders? How are leadership roles defined (e.g., raising revenues or supporting racial equity policies on campus)? How are leadership priorities determined? How do decisions get made? Whose values and interests are represented by the goals and outcomes of a leadership process? How do people interact as part of the leadership process?

Shared-equity leadership (Kezar et al., 2021) and equity-mindedness (Malcom-Piqueux & Bensimon, 2017) hold promise for challenging neoliberal and white supremacist principles and practices within higher education institutions. Equity-mindedness is developed when leaders expose patterns of inequity and acknowledge how historical circumstances give rise to present-day systems of oppression and discrimination. Equity-minded professionals are race and identity conscious and aware of the social and historical context of exclusionary practices in American higher education and worldwide. This approach to leadership also involves challenging traditional assumptions and recognizing biases, stereotypes, and deficit thinking within routine decisions and practices.

Equity leadership takes a systemic perspective to explore how educational systems have perpetuated inequalities and how systems can be redesigned in ways that create equity. Equity leadership practices include reflection, learning, changing schemas, and reframing. An equity-minded schema shifts focus away from blaming minoritized individuals and instead frames

274   *Leadership for Liberation*

inequity as a product of institutional actions, policies, practices, structures, and routines. As outlined in chapter 6, equity-minded leadership is (1) race conscious, (2), institutionally focused, (3) evidence based, (4) systemically aware, and (5) action oriented. Readers interested in adopting an equity-minded approach to leadership are encouraged to review equity-minded action guides, case studies, and practitioner reflections (Bensimon & Malcom, 2012; Felix et al., 2015; McNair et al., 2020), carefully considering the ways these principles and tools might be applied in one's local context.

Aiming for Wisdom in Decision-Making and Leadership Practice

Studies of equity leadership practice underscore the importance of learning and reflection, which are also connected to notions of wisdom. The emphasis on wisdom reflects a deep tradition in Indigenous leadership of advocating for knowledge developed through experience and insight, not just abstract learning and scientific approaches (Cajete, 2016). Wisdom captures the complex, systemic, and holistic nature of lived experience, along with the emotional currents and physical embodiments often left out of scientific approaches that favor the mind and narrow versions of rationality. Leaders orient their learning and reflection toward wisdom as they make decisions rooted in experiential knowledge. Additionally, as noted in chapter 6, wisdom challenges the short-term, self-interested decision-making frameworks that characterize neoliberalism and capitalism, instead calling on leaders and leadership processes to consider the immediate and long-term consequences of decisions for others and the environment (Jakubik, 2021; Kezar & Posselt, 2020; Yang, 2011). Higher education professionals seeking to cultivate wisdom within personal and organizational decisions should strive for balance among (1) personal interests, the needs of others, and the interests of the broader context (e.g., geographic region); (2) short- and long-term considerations; and (3) the strategies of adapting to new environments, shaping existing environments, and selecting new environments (Sternberg, 2003). These wise practices, when applied in pursuit of social justice aims, are likely to foster leadership processes that disrupt the norms of neoliberalism and white supremacy by honoring the interests and experiences of those historically excluded from power.

Establishing Transparency

One important step for dismantling the influence of white supremacy and neoliberalism in higher education is adopting greater transparency in leadership processes. Campus leadership often lacks transparency around numerous facets of leadership, including goals and priorities, budget, who is selected for engagement in leadership processes and why, who has authority for processes, and other key decisions that affect the entire campus community. Creating structures in which transparency is foundational can help to identify systemic inequalities and promote a more inclusive leadership process and campus environment. For example, campus leaders can make a more explicit effort to openly share how they go about choosing a new college president, or even how they decide who serves on faculty hiring and promotion committees. Rationales for decisions and priorities should be shared openly. It is much more difficult to be complicit in white supremacy and hidden agendas if transparency is actively practiced.

Relinquishing and Acknowledging Power

Power and authority are at the heart of white supremacy and neoliberalism. As long as certain people are vested with more power, and there are no checks on that power, it will be difficult, if not impossible, to make progress on a leadership future that is not embedded in these oppressive ideologies. Those who have power need to be willing to share it, especially with people like local community members, marginalized staff, faculty, and students. Empowerment efforts aimed at dismantling white supremacy and other systemic inequalities will not work unless accompanied by a radical restructuring of power.

Relinquishing power involves both acknowledging that power imbalances exist and calling out examples of oppression that have occurred so that these issues can be corrected. Without an open discussion of such power dynamics, leadership processes will continue to reinforce systemic inequalities. For example, many campuses bring together different stakeholders on committees and task forces, but the individuals sitting around the table have very different amounts of power. Members with less power and prestige may find it challenging to voice their perspectives if power differentials are not

276   *Leadership for Liberation*

acknowledged and steps are not actively taken to share power and empower others.

Centering Liberation, Social Justice, and Humanization

A clear theme throughout the book is that most contemporary leadership scholarship has not had a clear compass aimed at guiding actions toward liberation, social justice, and humanization, instead adopting a broader and less confrontational focus on ethics and morality in general. Unless leadership is actively redirected toward liberatory aims, toxic behaviors such as exploitation, bullying, harassment, and discrimination will continue unabated, along with the sweeping dismissal of academic values such as academic freedom and shared governance (Flaherty, 2022a, 2022b).

Centering liberation and social justice requires a different set of values and practices. The shared-equity leadership model articulates some of these new values, such as love, humility, courage, and creativity. Models of leadership that promote an equitable future are grounded in distinctive values that leaders need to exhibit day to day. Furthermore, the shared-equity leadership model (Kezar et al., 2021) describes the importance of practices that challenge the status quo of inequity, such as disrupting and questioning toward liberation, as well as the importance of communication and relationships for rehumanizing leadership. Focusing on models such as leadership for liberation (Harper & Kezar, 2021) or leadership approaches focused on social justice (see Kezar & Posselt, 2020) can help center these ideas in the work of leaders.

Engaging Both Personal and Organizational Work

Studies of concepts such as shared-equity leadership (Kezar et al., 2021) demonstrate that leaders will be less likely to gain equity-minded competence if they do not undertake a personal journey toward critical consciousness. Studies of the impact of social identities on leadership also suggest the importance of understanding how our own backgrounds shape how we lead (see chapter 8 for a review of social identity and leadership research). Therefore, leaders must do personal work in order to be equity-minded. Organizations are made of people, so if individuals are not transformed, organizations are unlikely to transform.

Yet at the same time, organizations need to be restructured to support equity leadership. This must be a collective effort that involves the expertise of people across important leadership spheres of campus. Understanding the inextricable link between individual transformation and organizational transformation is another insight from recent leadership scholarship. Higher education professionals need to recognize that efforts at both the personal and organizational levels are needed to advance equity and social justice goals and to dismantle oppressive systems.

Advocating for New Leadership Processes

Traditional approaches to leading and managing campuses, such as strategic planning, summits, task forces, and the like, have not produced a more equitable environment. Part of the problem is that we need new approaches that have equity and liberation built into the processes of campus operations. Adopting an equity mindset but working through traditional campus structures and operations is unlikely to bring about equitable results. In the preceding chapters, we reviewed examples of new leadership processes including liberatory design thinking, the abolitionist framework, critical systems thinking, equity-minded leadership, Indigenous leadership, shared-equity leadership, transformative systems thinking, and the weaver-leader framework. Higher education professionals seeking to dismantle entrenched systems of neoliberalism and white supremacy must commit to approaching and facilitating the work of leadership differently. The case studies in the appendix provide readers with multiple opportunities to imagine translating transformative leadership processes into action. Reading and reflecting on these case studies with a leadership team can spark meaningful conversations within the group regarding the possibility of adopting one or more of these new leadership processes within their own collective work.

Reevaluating White Leadership Approaches

Styles or approaches to leadership rooted in whiteness and neoliberalism—namely, niceness and professionalism—need to be interrogated and problematized in leadership practice. These taken-for-granted concepts and mechanisms play an important role in ordering institutions like higher education and thus create barriers to systemic change.

Niceness serves as a way to evade important conversations about equity, social justice, race, and racism (Alemán, 2009b; Castagno, 2014). Contemporary leaders in higher education who hope to maintain identities as good, nice, and efficacious and remain in good standing with powerful and elite stakeholders dance along a path of niceness that often involves evoking color-blind and neutral stances and attempting to find common ground with other integral stakeholders who may not share the same goals or objectives (Liera, 2020; Villarreal et al., 2019). Niceness is a concept and mechanism that shows up frequently in collaborative approaches to leadership. Thus, it is important for leaders to consider the ways niceness presents itself in these spaces, and make intentional efforts to disrupt it so that systemic progress can be made.

Professionalism is another concept and mechanism worth reevaluating. It is a tool of social control that is used by dominant racial groups and people in power to gatekeep, maintain the status quo, and preserve boundaries. Like niceness, actions and behaviors under the cloak of professionalism almost seamlessly prevent transformative and systemic change (Pechenkina & Liu, 2018). Often, instead of changing systems (and individual actions and behaviors) toward an equity and justice focus, leaders rely on oppressive norms of professionalism to resolve conflicts that threaten their interests and ability to preserve power (Frye et al., 2020). Organizations and leaders attempt to provide strict guidelines for the socialization and behavior of individuals in organizational life in an effort to promote uniformity and civility. For example, white people and other members of dominant groups often police the emotions of others under the banner of maintaining professionalism, asking people of color to suppress their real emotions around issues of race, racism, and societal injustice. Professionalism leaves little room for adaptability or resistance to dominant systems. Leaders must reevaluate their relationship with professionalism and act in ways that challenge these norms and socialization practices.

Having synthesized several lessons for practice gleaned from our review of contemporary leadership literature, we now turn our attention to future directions in leadership theory and research. We contend that leadership scholars, in order to transform higher education leadership processes with the intent of bringing about more socially just and equitable organizations, must focus their attention on new topics (e.g., power and white supremacy) as well as adopt a wider set of methodologies that center the voices and experiences of historically marginalized individuals and communities (e.g., photovoice and counterstorytelling).

Future Directions in Leadership Theory and Research

In this section we describe a set of new directions in leadership inquiry that may serve as the foundation of a higher education leadership research agenda focused on cultivating inclusive and equitable organizational environments. As we have argued throughout the book, we believe that challenging neoliberalism and white supremacy is the most important and pressing area for new directions in leadership research, so we start with it.

There are a variety of areas for future research on neoliberalism's reconfiguration of academic leadership and its reinforcement of whiteness and white supremacy. The first area of interrogation should be the criteria used to hire leaders and how these criteria reflect neoliberal principles and norms of whiteness. For example, the criteria that governing boards use to hire presidents would be an important area for exploration using this lens. Also, the promotion of faculty and staff into administrative and leadership roles should be explored for the degree to which these selection processes are also dominated by the ideologies of neoliberalism and white supremacy. While higher education has emerging research about biases and faculty hiring (e.g., Liera, 2020; Sensoy & DiAngelo, 2017; White-Lewis, 2020), there has not been the same attention to the hiring up and promotion of administrative leaders. We revisit the need to expand and reimagine studies of higher education recruitment and hiring processes in the cognitive research agenda discussed later in this chapter. Additionally, there are limited studies on the extent to which public-good principles are in conflict with the neoliberal principles that drive contemporary leader behaviors; this is another area ripe for future inquiry.

The centralization of power that has occurred in recent years, with executive leaders controlling decision-making, budgets, and policymaking, should continue to be explored, especially as we emerge from the pandemic and as future crises occur. Making leaders aware of the impact of centralized power, which has not been positive in responses to the COVID-19 pandemic, might help them to reassess this neoliberal urge. Also, other manifestations of this power centralization are important to document. While the focus has been on governing boards and presidents, the centralization of

280   *Leadership for Liberation*

power is also likely occurring with deans and those at other levels of leadership. We have some data about the impacts of this centralization, but continued studies of its impact will help us understand the overall magnitude.

It is important to better understand how neoliberalism and whiteness are penetrating different positional leadership roles on campus. There are scant studies of neoliberalism in student affairs, institutional research, business and finance, and other fields, and much of the work that has been conducted has been on faculty or senior leaders. It would be useful to understand the way that leaders are being shaped by neoliberalism and whiteness in many other roles, positions, and units.

Another critical topic to explore is the outcomes of neoliberal leadership, which, as we noted in chapter 3, focuses on a corporatized and market-based form of influence. There are very limited studies about how neoliberalism is affecting campuses in terms of lowering morale, increasing bullying, decreasing community, dehumanizing employees, and decreasing innovation. Yet these studies are few in number and it is likely that all of the outcomes are not documented. Researchers also have little understanding of whether neoliberal leadership outcomes differ by institutional type, mission, student body, or other contextual conditions. A deeper understanding of how these outcomes emerge in different contexts and across varying communities is needed.

There have been virtually no studies that link leadership approaches to campuses meeting their missions or the equity and social justice goals described in the book. Comparison studies of very different institutions using different leadership processes might be an effective way to explore these linkages. For example, a researcher could compare and contrast the equity outcomes of an institution guided by neoliberal values and processes with the outcomes of a campus enacting a shared-equity approach to leadership. Some of the main priorities of higher education, such as student success, effective teaching, and high-quality research, have not been studied in relation to campus leadership. Examining the relationship between the main activities and priorities of higher education and different leadership processes or styles can help to shed light on the implications of current leadership practices.

Researchers can disrupt white supremacy in research by shifting the lens of study. Too often, studies focus primarily on leaders in positions of power

Looking to the Future of Leadership Practice and Research   281

and authority, which may lead to findings, claims, and recommendations for research and practice that reinforce the status quo and keep whiteness intact. Researchers should spend more time focusing their inquisitive eye on historically obscured and marginalized groups that also engage in leadership practices on campus, such as coalitions and activist groups. A few examples of such studies were profiled in this book (e.g., those on grassroots leadership in chapter 9). Scholars should also find ways to engage in more participatory approaches to research that are mutually beneficial for the researcher, the field, and the participants. In participatory approaches, findings are shared in open forums that encourage dialogue between the researcher and the community. Here, whiteness is challenged, and so are the norms around knowledge production and dissemination. We will revisit the recommendation for more participatory forms of research in the discussion of new directions in leadership research methodologies later in this chapter.

Researchers can also disrupt white supremacy in research by participating in acts of refusal. Tuck and Yang (2014) noted that not all communities, processes, and human beings need to be researched. And if they are researched, they should be researched toward their empowerment and liberation and not in ways that help reproduce the institution and its pursuit of power and wealth. Thus, researchers must walk a fine line and make conscious decisions about whom and how they research; this is precisely where researchers in higher education can engage or refuse acts of white supremacy. Researchers can disrupt white supremacy by looking for the "code beneath the code" (Tuck & Yang, 2014, p. 812) when analyzing their findings— "Who gets to know? Who gets known? Where is knowledge kept, and kept legitimated? What knowledge is desirable? Who profits? Who loses/pays/ gives something away? Who is coerced, empowered, appointed to give away knowledge?" (p. 812). These questions are especially relevant to studies on the leadership process in higher education. For example, when studying how COVID-19 affected leadership processes in higher education, researchers should consider how, if at all, the institution and people involved in the leadership process were privileged and reaped benefits, and what this means for the system and ideology of white supremacy. By asking these questions and configuring ways to refuse, researchers can unearth new realities and complexities and forge new possibilities for a type of leadership that is unshackled from whiteness and white supremacy. They may also find impossibilities—ways

282   *Leadership for Liberation*

that leadership cannot and will not change. These, too, are important and birth thoughtful and searing critiques of the university, its leaders, and its leadership processes.

Having introduced broad themes we see as ripe for investigation in the interest of identifying and dismantling the influences of neoliberalism and white supremacy within higher education leadership, we now turn our attention to possibilities for inquiry associated with each of the leadership approaches featured in the book. We begin with transformational leadership.

TRANSFORMATIONAL LEADERSHIP

Transformational leadership is one of the areas that has received the most attention in higher education research. But there are still several aspects that would benefit from further study.

One of the concepts related to social change is the public purpose of leadership, and even though this is a central element in transformational leadership, there has been very little research on it. In chapter 3 we discussed how neoliberalism has eroded a commitment to the public good, and we see emphasizing the transformational focus of leadership as a way to recommit to and reorient leadership to broader values and purposes than currently advanced. Kezar and Lester (2011) identified how faculty and staff grassroots leaders on college campuses typically engage in work that serves the public good, focusing on poverty, environmentalism, climate change, sustainability, access to public resources, and homelessness, among other key issues. Yet leadership in higher education is generally not connected to the public good. A Google Scholar search for leadership and the public or common good only brings up a handful of articles. Even though transformational leadership suggests this link, it is not being explored in the research, and neoliberalism is making it difficult, if not impossible, to enact in practice.

Relatedly, there is a dearth of research on the connections between ethical or moral processes or ends and leadership in the higher education context. Whether leadership processes are executed in humanistic ways is rarely examined and needs far more attention, as do the end goals of leadership. If the impacts or ends of leadership are not defined, it can continue to support neoliberal and white supremacist ends. We have little understanding of what transformational leadership looks like outside hierarchical structures. The shared-equity leadership model starts to move in this direction, and other studies that identify nonhierarchical models of shared leadership would be beneficial. For example, how do groups come to consensus around equity goals? How do they negotiate priorities? Social movement literature can inform and frame such studies.

Understanding the role of context is critical to advancing transformational leadership. For example, we need studies about how neoliberalism challenges and compromises transformational leadership. Studies about institutional differences in higher education suggest we need to explore whether and why certain institutions face more challenges to enacting transformational leadership, as well as potential ways to navigate such challenges.

And we have limited understanding of avenues leaders can use to help encourage personal growth among collaborators involved in transformational leadership processes. In shared-equity leadership (Kezar et al., 2021), modeling emerges as a key process. There are many ways that such growth can occur, and more knowledge of these would help advance the goals of transformational leadership. Additionally, there is little research on empowerment that takes a more critical perspective toward the examination of how leaders empower certain organizational members who support whiteness and the neoliberal agenda but not those who challenge neoliberalism and white supremacy. It is likely that, in a neoliberal environment that fosters the centralization power and authority, empowerment is not frequent and is not a high priority.

Cognitive Leadership

In the conclusion to chapter 6, we posed a number of questions that might frame future directions in cognitive leadership inquiry and practice: How might research endeavors disrupt the continued cognitive focus on positional, hierarchical leader-follower dynamics? What does it look like to engage in equity-minded leadership that actively places racial and economic justice above the neoliberal aims of efficiency and profit? How might we develop the scholarly insights and personal capacity needed to disrupt hegemonic norms and assumptions (effective leaders are white, male, tall, and charismatic) that dominate leadership prototypes and limit the opportunities and evaluations of individuals who do not conform to these oppressive mental models? These questions and similar lines of inquiry are intended to guide the development of cognitive leadership theories and practices that dismantle the neoliberal and white supremacist psychic prisons (Kezar & Posselt, 2020) that currently frame and constrain higher education leadership.

As described in chapter 6, cognitive approaches to studying leadership remain rooted in hierarchical and dyadic (leader-follower) constructions of leadership that frequently center the experiences and interests of senior leaders, a group that remains overwhelming white and male (Crandall et al., 2017). In the interest of disrupting patriarchal and white supremacist leadership norms, more research is needed on the leadership cognitions of diverse higher education professionals situated in all levels and divisions of the organization. Aligning with the cognitive approach's recognition that leadership is a relational, cultural, and contextual phenomenon, researchers need to move beyond their preoccupation with top-down leadership relationships and shift attention to the cognitive processes that frame and are influenced by shared and team leadership experiences as well as peer-to-peer interactions. For example, a researcher interested in disrupting hierarchical, dyadic leadership constructions might decide against a more traditional study of how new academic deans adapt their behavior to align with the implicit leadership theories of faculty and instead examine how members of an administrative assistant employee resource group draw on their leadership schemas and mental models to make meaning of the collaborative leadership experience and how their lived experience of the staff collective (re)shapes their implicit leadership theories. Decentering white male positional leaders in studies of leadership cognition and meaning-making is an important first step toward advancing a more equity-minded cognitive leadership approach.

Additionally, researchers must engage in efforts to better understand the role white supremacy, patriarchy, heteronormativity, and other oppressive ideologies play in shaping cognitive processes, such as implicit leadership theories, that constrain the leadership opportunities of individuals with minoritized identities and contribute to hostile organizational environments. Narrative and autoethnographic studies (particularly ones with a longitudinal design) would be useful for examining ideological influences on leadership cognitions at the individual level. For example, researchers might draw on theoretical constructions of whiteness and white supremacy, critical race theory, queer theory, or critical feminist perspectives in a narrative study of

Looking to the Future of Leadership Practice and Research 285

entry-level higher education professionals to understand the influence of oppressive ideologies on leadership cognitions at the start of one's career. They could then interview these individuals at regular intervals to see if and how their leadership beliefs evolve over time. Critical case studies and ethnographies of leadership processes (e.g., hiring committees or strategic planning) would shed light on the way oppressive cognitive leadership perspectives influence individual behaviors, collective processes, and organizational outcomes.

A third potential pathway for disrupting the neoliberal and white supremacist anchors of cognitive leadership research is to eschew neutrality in studies of cognitive processes such as organizational learning and meaning-making with mental models (Bolman & Deal, 2017). Rather than conceptualizing these cognitive processes as neutral tools for achieving organizational outcomes, scholars situated in the critical paradigm might examine the ways organizational learning processes and mental models are used to advance neoliberal principles and priorities such as efficiency, productivity, entrepreneurialism, and capitalism. Explicitly engaging constructs such as power, privilege, oppression, and the public good in studies of organizational learning and cognitive framing would productively disrupt dominant neoliberal and white supremacist knowledge regimes. Here again, critical case studies, ethnographies, and participatory inquiry are promising research designs.

Even when cognitive research does document the presence and discriminatory consequences of biased leadership cognitions, these studies often stop short of mapping out the personal, interpersonal, and structural actions that can and should be taken to alter oppressive leadership schemas and prototypes (Dugan, 2017). More research is needed on the pedagogies, actions, experiences (individual and shared), and structural initiatives (e.g., policies and protocols) that are effective in identifying and dismantling discriminatory cognitive processes as well as forging an equity-oriented mindset. Participatory action research projects that engage stakeholders in structured and cyclical processes of reflection, action, data collection, and analysis are likely to shed light on meaningful steps that individuals and higher education organizations can take to foster more inclusive leadership cognitions that, in turn, will produce more inclusive and equitable outcomes. Scholar-practitioners interested in pursuing this line of inquiry would be well served

286   *Leadership for Liberation*

to review the methodologies and achievements highlighted in research on equity-minded leadership (Felix et al., 2015).

Authentic leadership is another strand of cognitive leadership that could benefit from additional inquiry. In addition to addressing Dugan's (2017) critique that authentic leadership lacks conceptual clarity and empirical coherence, contemporary scholars might seek to investigate the tensions between ethical decision-making and authentic leadership revealed in Gardiner's (2015) study of senior women higher education leaders. Additionally, Gardiner highlighted the situated and embodied nature of authentic leadership. More research is needed to understand the lived experiences of authentic leadership within the context of higher education organizations, with specific attention given to intersectionality and the possibilities and constraints of authentic leadership.

Finally, wise leadership is a cognitive leadership construct that merits additional attention. Research on the nature and practice of wise leadership might explore the conditions that foster wisdom among higher education professionals working at all levels of the organization, as well as the organizational and leadership characteristics that facilitate the exercise of wisdom in decision-making related to critical higher education issues (e.g., access and inclusion, sustainability, and community partnerships). Case studies and ethnographies of individuals and organizations identified as demonstrating wisdom would provide valuable insight into the daily habits of mind and action that facilitate wise decision-making that prioritizes the common good over profit.

Chaos and Complexity Leadership

Chaos and complexity leadership theory can benefit greatly from new theoretical contributions. Some of the major assumptions and contributions (e.g., flexibility and experimentation) that undergird chaos and complexity theory are strained when held simultaneously with hierarchical constructions of leadership. This signals the strong hold that hierarchical notions of leadership have on scholars and leaders alike. Scholars can meaningfully counteract this by extending complexity leadership theory (Uhl-Bien at al., 2007) in ways that remove the hierarchical elements of the theory and bring to the fore the more ambitious and collaborative insights presented by Heifetz (1994) and Wheatley (1999). Scholars who heed this call can, for example, revisit some of the scientific concepts of chaos theory, such as strange attractors and the butterfly effect, and operationalize them for the leadership context.

More empirical research should be conducted on the ways state, local, and national crises—literal moments of chaos and complexity—affect how leadership is enacted. In our review of key studies, we featured a few scholars who have investigated this very issue in relation to the COVID-19 pandemic and even the 2008 recession. We encourage scholars to continue designing similar studies and empirically investigate these issues with a specific focus on different campus contexts. What can be learned from times of crisis can also inform ways to be adaptive more generally.

There is very little new research from a chaos and complexity approach that moves leadership toward explicitly equity-oriented and liberation ends. We recommend the abolitionist framework as a particularly strong approach for moving the theoretical perspective in this direction. This framework likely will spur the development of more models such as the weaver-leader framework as guides for ways leaders can navigate complexity and move toward liberatory ends.

Scholars should employ a different set of tools in their studies of chaos and complexity leadership. As noted in chapter 7, looking at leadership from a systemic level requires different research methods and even an expansion of whom scholars interact with and learn from during the research process. Methods such as empathy interviews and oral histories allow scholars to connect with both people who are a part of and those who are affected by the leadership process and subsequent decisions. Scholars who are interested in studies of chaos and complexity leadership should be open to a variety of methodological approaches and data collection methods that allow a whole and nuanced understanding to emerge, as our typical methods tend to fragment reality rather than gather a wholistic picture, and complexity cannot be captured through many of our traditional methods.

CULTURAL LEADERSHIP

As noted in chapter 8, cultural approaches to leadership have received a great deal of attention in recent years, with a particular focus on examining the influence of race and gender on leadership. Numerous researchers have documented the ways in which racial and gender identities shape leadership beliefs, practices, and opportunities. Emerging strands of social identity leadership inquiry have shed light on the influence of sexual orientation, social class, and disability on leadership within higher education organizations. Collectively this body of work has advanced understanding of the intersectional nature of opportunity and oppression within postsecondary leadership; however, significant blind spots, questions, and knowledge gaps remain.

At the beginning of this section on new directions in leadership theory and research, we advocated for expanding inquiry into the manifestations and implications of whiteness and white supremacy in higher education leadership. In chapter 8, we identified this research as an important and productive line of inquiry within cultural leadership perspectives. In addition to examining representations of white supremacy in individual leadership beliefs and practices, a focus that will generate individual-level insights and interventions, we recommend scholars adopt an organizational level of analysis that explores how the values, norms, and tacit assumptions of white supremacy are embedded and operationalized through campus culture and discourse (stories, metaphors, rituals and ceremonies, policies, etc.). For example, a researcher might examine how an institution's organizational saga (Clark, 1972) communicates and reinforces normative leadership expectations rooted in white supremacy.

Beyond calling for an expansion of cultural studies of whiteness and leadership, the review of contemporary social identity leadership research presented in chapter 8 also highlighted several other social identities that merit additional exploration. For example, we encourage higher education leadership scholars to draw on trans* theory and research to frame studies that conceptualize gender as a continuum, rather than a fixed binary, and seek to understand how individuals across the gender continuum experience, resist, and dismantle oppressive gendered leadership norms, roles, and expectations. Additionally, more research is needed to understand how social class influences leadership processes and identities within higher education settings guided by the principles of neoliberal ideology (education as a private good, profit over people, etc.). Although not explicitly situated within the field of higher education, S. R. Martin et al. (2017) offered a compelling call for developing a deeper understanding of how social class influences lead-

Looking to the Future of Leadership Practice and Research 289

ership attributions, enactment of leadership roles, and perceptions of leader effectiveness. To this list we add examining how social class shapes leadership selection processes at all levels of the organization, not just governing boards and presidents. Also, Ardoin and Guthrie (2021b) highlighted a need for higher education leadership scholars to examine how diverse forms of capital (i.e., cultural, social, linguistic, familial, academic, aspirational, navigational, and resistance) shape leadership learning, opportunities, and experiences.

Gender and social class are certainly not the only social identities that could benefit from expanded research and theorizing. Scholars interested in examining the relationship between identity and leadership can build on the strong research base that has shed valuable light on the leadership experiences of cisgender women and individuals with historically marginalized racial and ethnic identities. Future lines of inquiry should seek to deepen understanding of the ways ability, sexual orientation, religion and spirituality, and nationality influence leadership beliefs, behaviors, and opportunities. Although we name nationality as an important social identity that merits additional attention within cultural leadership inquiry, we agree with Ailon's (2008, 2009) call to avoid research that perpetuates rigid and colonial constructions of national identity. Instead, scholars should seek to understand how the fluid and interdependent forces of economic, political, and cultural globalization (e.g., migration, social media, and global commerce) shape the leadership perspectives of higher education professionals located around the globe.

As discussed in chapter 8, the intersectional nature of the relationship between identity and leadership has been well documented. New directions in cultural leadership perspectives must extend this line of inquiry, exploring how intersectional social identities beyond race and gender shape the leadership experiences and approaches of higher education professionals. Such studies will generate powerful insights that can inform the expansion of identity-conscious leadership development and support programs that address the unique challenges and strengths of diverse higher education leaders. Recognizing the important role that context and culture play in shaping leadership, we would also like to see more studies examine how context (institutional type, organizational mission, academic culture, administrative unit, academic discipline, etc.) shapes the leadership style and experiences of individuals with one or more historically marginalized social identities.

Throughout the book, we have argued that new approaches to understanding and exercising power are essential for dismantling the twin ideologies of white supremacy and neoliberalism. Within cultural leadership perspectives, researchers can contribute to new ways of conceptualizing power by shifting their focus from individual-level influences on organizational culture (i.e., the power of founders and chief executives to shape culture) and leadership experiences (e.g., race as an individual-level factor) toward studies that seek to identify and understand the influence of systemic power rooted in particular historical, political, economic, national, and social conditions (Riad, 2011). For example, scholars interested in understanding how systemic power serves to advance or thwart an equity-oriented change initiative within a department might focus their attention on the ideologies, knowledge regimes, discourses, norms, and so on that frame constructions of leadership within the particular context, rather than adopting an individual-level unit of analysis that centers the lived experiences of department members.

Finally, in chapter 8 we highlight Indigenous leadership perspectives and applied critical leadership as new evolutions in cultural approaches to leadership that hold promise for contesting and dismantling neoliberalism and white supremacy within higher education. Although both Indigenous leadership and applied critical leadership theory have been studied extensively within and beyond higher education, there is still much to learn. Specifically, we are interested in understanding if and how the characteristics of applied critical leadership (e.g., adopting a critical race theory perspective, leading by example, and honoring all constituencies) can be adopted and enacted at the team or organizational level. Applied critical leadership emphasizes the importance of micropractices (daily, routine actions) that contest oppression and advance equity (e.g., adopting transparency in decision-making or engaging in daily meditations to promote mindfulness). How might colleagues interested in adopting an applied critical leadership approach in their unit scale up the notion of individual micropractices? This type of project lends itself well to participatory action research in which scholar-practitioners study and learn from their efforts to adopt a new organizational model of leadership. Similar types of studies are needed to understand the nature and efficacy of enacting Indigenous leadership principles and practices (collective orientation, relational knowledge, decentralized perspective on authority, etc.) in organizational settings not affiliated with Indigenous communities. How might non-Indigenous higher education professionals ethically and authentically draw on Indigenous principles to guide leadership processes and organizational transformation efforts? Cultural approaches to leadership have garnered significant attention in recent years. We expect this trend to continue in the next wave of leadership theory and research and believe this strand of scholarship holds tremendous promise for guiding efforts to bring about more equitable and socially just higher education organizations.

Processual Leadership

Future theoretical and empirical contributions on processual leadership should be advanced alongside critical organizational theories such as critical social movement theories and concepts such as grassroots leadership and coalitions and alliances. Theories of racialized organizations (Ray, 2019) and gendered organizations (Acker, 1990) provide meaningful insights and perspectives on why organizations like higher education maintain investments in inequality and how this profoundly affects the ways leaders shape their leadership processes and distribute seemingly limited resources. These critical organizational theories are a nice attendant to processual leadership since leadership happens in context. These theories provide a macro understanding of organizations and can help scholars and leaders alike understand how their context-specific leadership processes are shaped by macro forces. These individuals will then be better equipped to reimagine the leadership process toward equitable and liberatory ends.

When possible, researchers should attempt to study the leadership process as it happens. The benefit of this approach is that the researcher will receive real-time reactions and information as the process unfolds. This is rather difficult to do without the proper access, but it is worth it if the researcher can get ahead of the leadership process and become embedded in the environment before the process begins. For example, processual leadership could be an interesting frame for a study on the transition between college presidents. Here, the researcher can situate themselves on campus in the months before the president departs and in the months after the new president is installed. This would make for an interesting study on the leadership process in transition.

Future empirical contributions to processual leadership should focus on the struggle and solidarity movements that have become increasingly prevalent across higher education, such as graduate student labor organizing and Black and Asian student solidarity movements. Unions, coalitions, alliances, and other collectives are fascinating sites where processual leadership can be used as a frame to critically understand the change process and how complex it can be. Collective movements are also particularly interesting forums where power, constraint, and agency are defined and mediated by the structures and ideologies of contemporary colleges and universities, including neoliberalism and white supremacy.

Many of the theories and new evolutions reviewed so far in this book have great promise. They also have some noteworthy critiques. One issue we were aware of while writing this book is that existing theories of leadership are themselves embedded in traditions of whiteness and neoliberalism, so the way forward may be best served by breaking completely free of them and developing wholly new ones or adopting theories (e.g., critical race theory or colonial theories) that have been created with the intent of achieving equity, social justice, and liberation. Another approach is to meld various theories in creative and groundbreaking ways but with the aim of shedding the problematic ideologies of theories while preserving the redeeming aspects. Dugan (2017) used a similar but different approach in his book that reexamined traditional leadership theories.

New Theories of Leadership

This section highlights interdisciplinary or transdisciplinary leadership theories that do not fit neatly within any of the specific theory traditions featured in earlier chapters. The following list is not exhaustive but provides some examples for how leadership scholars might move beyond dominant theory traditions toward new multitheory approaches.

OTHERWISE POSSIBILITIES

We offer religious and Black studies scholar Ashon Crawley's (2016) idea of otherwise possibilities as a potential new way to reimagine leadership within the higher education context. In the simplest terms, the otherwise is "something or anything else; something to the contrary" (T. L. King et al., 2020, p. 8). Crawley has been one of the major contributors to the theory of the "otherwise," positing that the otherwise is mainly about disrupting normative practices and ways of being that have only served white supremacist and settler-colonial desires. Crawley (2016) reminded us that the exercise of otherwise possibility requires "thinking and desiring more than what we have, knowing we already have enough to produce flourishing in the world" (p. 9). A pivotal part of crafting the otherwise is identifying those possibilities that are buried beneath the powerful structures of white supremacy, settler colonialism, and the state. Crawley argues, in nearly all of his scholarly contributions, that fields and disciplines like Black studies and Native studies or theology and philosophy have missed key opportunities to stand in solidarity with each other. These fields and disciplines instead succumb to neoliberal pressures to stand on their own and represent themselves as worthy of study and worthy of existing within the bounds of the academy. To this end, Crawley's work on the otherwise seeks to marry the perspectives and ethos of fields and disciplines by exposing their interdependence as a way to produce otherwise possibilities.

What does this look like for leadership in theory and in practice? In the broadest sense, it means marrying different theories and concepts within leadership and beyond to produce a new set of relations built on different ideologies and practices. This otherwise leadership should move away from neoliberalism and white supremacy and should be careful not to reproduce the inequality that manifests from these structures. Crawley's theoretical contribution of the otherwise does not ignore systems of oppression such as neoliberalism and white supremacy. Instead, it reminds us about their presence and demands that leaders do more than enact and reproduce such violence and suffering. In the presence of the otherwise, leaders should find ways for campus community members to enjoy pleasantries, experience joy, and embrace their full humanity without the fear of overwhelming forces robbing and exploiting them. The practice of the otherwise is explicitly antithetical to what we do and have now.

294   *Leadership for Liberation*

A part of the task for researchers looking to study otherwise possibilities in leadership is to weave together a tapestry of what otherwise leadership looks like in a given context. It asks a different set of questions:

- Who was involved?
- What fields, disciplines, and traditions did they pull from?
- In what ways were leaders' relationships to systems, structures, and ideologies dealt with and interrogated?

Otherwise possibilities in leadership look different in various contexts, so each study of the otherwise will vastly differ. Researchers seeking to study the otherwise must also have an understanding of different fields and be able to identify and trace present-day actions to field- and discipline-specific underpinnings and historical moments. From each context emerges a new and unique leadership model that may or may not be applicable to other environments. Since leadership is multidisciplinary and research tends to draw from many fields, it is an ideal fit for such a theory. Leadership research will likely continue to orient toward these more expansive multidisciplinary approaches.

Transformative Leadership

As just mentioned, future research on leadership will likely move beyond the more singular approaches reflected in the theories outlined in this book. A recent evolution of a multitheory leadership approach is transformative leadership (Pak & Ravitch, 2021a), which is not to be confused with *transformational* leadership. Transformational leadership (reviewed in chapter 5) focuses on individual leader characteristics in relationship to followers. Transformative leadership, on the other hand, directly links the goals of leadership to equity, inclusion, and social justice, as has been called for throughout this book, as well as practices that lead to such transformation. As Pak & Ravitch (2021b) noted, "Transformative leadership requires leaders to continuously reflect on their own biases and goals, understand how power and privilege operate, appreciate the intra-diversity of cultural groups and the values of cultural differences, form cross cultural alliances, see and confront inequities that manifest in school settings, and possess the moral courage to actively and collaboratively work toward social transformation" (p. 6).

Looking to the Future of Leadership Practice and Research   295

Transformative leadership theory entails a critical leadership praxis model aimed at dismantling systems of power—that is the very transformation at the heart of the theory. The theory describes four domains of change that are necessary within this praxis model: personal, interpersonal, organizational, and system-level transformations. Transforming the self involves critical self-reflection by individual leaders on social identities, power, privilege, implicit bias, and racial literacy. Without critical consciousness, leaders are unable to engage the other levels of transformation. At the interpersonal level, leaders work to transform educators by providing mechanisms through which they can become compassionate, competent, and critically conscious educators. At the organizational level, leaders develop critical intersectional inclusivity in organizations by utilizing ethnographic methods to interrogate and then change organizational culture and learning mechanisms. And lastly, leaders can transform systems by critically analyzing systemic, colonizing policies and practices. This type of multitheory leadership draws from cognitive theories in exploring critical consciousness and individual mindset changes. But it also draws on chaos and complexity theory in exploring the way broader systems and organizations need to be changed, and on critical systems theory in its focus on learning and adaptability and its emphasis on the dynamic nature of leadership and changes.

Trauma-Informed Leadership

Trauma-informed leadership is another approach that draws on multiple theories and acknowledges the way oppressive systems (neoliberalism and white supremacy) create harm. Importantly, this approach also provides a corrective to this harm and a path to liberation and away from the cycle of oppression. Trauma-informed leadership involves an awareness of how oppression in society and systems creates pain and suffering. Leaders need to respond to this mechanism by bringing compassion, sensitivity, and new skills that can help alleviate the suffering. Given the power and oppression built into our systems and unprocessed emotions, trauma-informed leadership will play a central role in future work in leadership. In one example that can help show its application and promise, Kezar and Fries-Britt (2018) documented how leaders can use a collective trauma framework to help campuses recover from racial incidents. The collective trauma framework has three component parts: (1) actively listening, (2) speaking from the heart, and (3) acting with. Active listening is a structured form of listening and responding that focuses the attention on the speaker and improves mutual understanding without debate or judgment. This involves honest communication from leaders, free from political spin. Speaking from the heart means invoking and responding to emotions. The third element of overcoming collective trauma, "acting with," allows leaders to move forward by directly engaging with community, particularly the community members most affected by the traumatic events. Acting with requires leaders to move in a measured way that deeply connects to community members as the campus actively listens to inform its strategy for moving forward.

Trauma-informed leadership utilizes transformational leadership theories in invoking the role of leaders to care for other organizational members. It also involves cognitive theories in its emphasis on leaders being able to truly listen and change their mindsets by being open to feedback in new ways. Also, speaking from the heart relates to issues of framing often described in cognitive theories and authentic leadership theories in their focus on being honest and vulnerable. Trauma-informed leadership also reflects processual leadership in its emphasis on acting with and being oriented toward leaders working with a broad community over time to address trauma, which is a long-term and involved process. The emphasis on time and how trauma is historical and current helps provide the dimension of temporality to leadership studies.

New Directions in Leadership Research Methodologies

In addition to rethinking the focus of leadership theory and research in the interest of advancing liberatory ends, we contend it is also important to reconsider *how* we go about studying leadership phenomena and processes. The central premise of this section is that the way we choose to study leadership moving forward has important consequences for what we can come to know (Carducci, 2017; Pasque & Carducci, 2015). While traditional qualitative and quantitative research designs have expanded our understanding of higher education leadership in meaningful ways, continued reliance on traditional research methodologies (e.g., quasi-experimental, basic qualitative, narrative, and case study) and methods (e.g., surveys, elite interviews, and observation) will likely (re)produce knowledge similar to what we already have. Young and Lopéz (2011) offered a compelling argument in favor of rethinking reliance on traditional leadership theories and processes of inquiry:

> There is a circular relationship between the tools of inquiry we use and our commonly accepted ideas of what we know or need to know. . . . By expanding our theoretical and methodological lenses to include perspectives that stand outside traditional discursive configurations, we will not only create an opportunity to expose the field to different understandings of leadership and organizational phenomena, but also disrupt our taken-for-granted assumptions of what leadership is, what it can be, and what purposes it ultimately serves. (pp. 235–236)

Unfortunately, despite our observation that the critical paradigm has gained prominence within the higher education leadership research community, as evidenced by the number of published studies featured in this book that name the critical paradigm or center critical leadership topics (e.g., social identities, oppression, collective action, or grassroots change), we found that the methodologies and methods guiding contemporary leadership data collection, analysis, and representation processes remain fairly traditional. Critical and participatory methodologies such as critical participatory action research, performance ethnography, and arts-based inquiry (e.g., photovoice), which engage research participants in the processes of inquiry and disrupt majoritarian narratives of leadership, have not been widely adopted by higher education leadership scholars. One exception to this claim is the small segment of researchers who draw on the principles and practices of critical race theory and counterstorytelling to examine the leadership experiences of historically marginalized individuals. Additionally, we did not find many examples of researchers describing intentional engagement with research participants after the conclusion of the study, suggesting a limited commitment to helping participants translate leadership research findings into transformative action in the local context (Shields, 2012). Reliance on traditional research processes that utilize standard data collection practices and maintain separation between inquiry and advocacy will continue to generate leadership knowledge that upholds the oppressive status quo and cultivates educational leaders who are ill-equipped to address and overturn the systemic oppression that characterizes American colleges and universities. We have already highlighted how future studies of higher education leadership

298   *Leadership for Liberation*

might center new theories of leadership that reflect multitheory perspectives guided by social justice aims. Now it is time to explore what it might look like to develop a higher education leadership research agenda guided by the principles and practices of critical and participatory methodologies.

Although participatory methodologies have not been broadly used to study leadership in higher education, they are frequently used in many other fields as a way to center the needs of the most marginalized populations (S. R. Jones et al., 2022). Participatory methods, as described in chapter 2 (participatory paradigm), entail involving members of communities affected by an educational issue in the research process. Participatory approaches can create a sense of critical consciousness and empowerment among various actors in higher education to challenge neoliberalism and white supremacy. The approach helps uncover the hidden systems operating to subjugate or discriminate against groups within systems and offers approaches to move beyond them through creative problem-solving. Photovoice, a research design that blends the methodological principles of participatory action research and visual inquiry, may offer a particularly powerful means of generating novel and significant insights on the manifestations and meaning of neoliberalism and white supremacy within higher education. Kortegast et al. (2019) explained how participant-generated visual methodologies such as photovoice, which engage coresearchers (participants) in the creation, analysis, and presentation of visual images that reflect experiences of a phenomenon or process (e.g., leadership), serve to uncover tacit knowledge of the focal topic, facilitate examination of meaning-making, create a space for reflective consciousness, and disrupt the power dynamics within the inquiry process. Gonzales and Rincones (2013) also highlight the value of visual methodologies to capture and examine the emotional dimensions of leadership. Scholars seeking to develop a deep, experiential understanding of the ways in which oppression, empowerment, and advocacy are enacted within higher education leadership processes while simultaneously contributing to organizational transformation efforts (what Shields, 2012, described as critical advocacy research) should consider photovoice and other participatory action research designs.

A methodology related to participatory action research that has also been sparsely adopted in higher education leadership inquiry but holds promise for informing future research is decolonization. Decolonization involves applying perspectives and frameworks that question the status quo of society and its reproduction in educational settings. Decolonization begins by critiquing existing systems of power, dominance, and oppression. But it also requires the consideration of alternative approaches that help reconstruct a new system of education. Part of the work of the leaders as well as the study of leadership is to build more equitable and inclusive educational spaces. Decolonization involves the practice of reflection on the underlying assumptions of systems. It draws on Freire's (1970) notion of the practice of continuous cycling through theory, action, and reflection on educational practice, which is also the basis for participatory methods. Jacobs and Clonan-Roy (2021) described how they develop gender- and queer-inclusive cultures within school settings by engaging in a decolonization intervention with school leaders that involves sessions of presenting theory, guided reflection, and reexamination of practice. The last step is taking awareness about inequitable systems and developing approaches to disrupt the systems. Action or participatory research is typical within the decolonization approach, as is seen with the Jacobs and Clonan-Roy example. Other approaches, however, take more of a historical perspective in which they look at the evolution of a particular phenomenon over time and demonstrate how systems of power were prevalent in its development, in order to help educational practitioners see these systems.

An underutilized method that is particularly well suited to critically explore power and privilege within leadership is critical organizational ethnography. The method is devoted to transforming inequitable conditions within organizations and is emancipatory in its goals and focus (Jerolmack & Khan, 2017). Within this methodology, the researcher gathers observational data to understand cultural contexts and, using a critical lens, links data to wider social structures and systems of power. Data about practices are used to critique organizational practices and provide the basis for organizational learning. In studying leadership, critical organizational ethnography examines the degree to which leaders' stated beliefs, assumptions, and artifacts (e.g., mission/vision statements, job descriptions, strategic plans) privilege the identities, experiences, and rights of dominant groups while maintaining the oppression of nondominant groups (Gaggiotti et al., 2017; Pedersen & Humle, 2016).

300   *Leadership for Liberation*

The field of future studies also has a number of methodologies to consider, such as backcasting and scenario planning. Future studies is a field that attempts to understand "the roots and consequences of each of the manifold images of the future that exist in people's minds and in support of people's actions" (Dator, 2002, p. 7). Backcasting is a method that asks individuals to remember historical events and trends that helped create the present and will surely help construct the future. Scenario planning is a participatory method in which individuals imagine and create multiple—possible, preferable, and probable—scenarios and configure ways to arrive at or subvert these scenarios. Future studies has a repertoire of theories, methods, and tools to imagine various futures by actively taking into account and tapping into the past and the present and our imaginations of the future. In light of the emphasis throughout this book on leaders being able to reimagine new futures and be creative, future studies is a ripe area to draw on for rethinking leadership in the coming decades. For further reading on future studies, we suggest *Advancing Futures*, edited by Dator (2002), and the two-volume *Foundations of Futures Studies*, by W. Bell (2003, 2004).

Rather than present a lengthy list of research methodologies that hold promise for challenging "taken-for-granted assumptions of what leadership is, what it can be, and what purposes it ultimately serves" (Young & Lopéz, 2011, pp. 235–236), this discussion of new directions in leadership research methodologies serves to highlight the nature of inquiry principles and practices that have the potential to generate leadership knowledge of use in bringing about transformational, equity-oriented change. It is our hope that an increasing number of leadership studies moving forward will be characterized by collaborative research that disrupts traditional power dynamics; establishes connections between past, present, and future conditions; allows for in-depth examinations of culture and context; fosters consciousness of power; and sparks action, given that we see these inquiry principles as foundational to liberatory leadership research and practice.

Conclusion

Our review of contemporary leadership research has convinced us of the need to directly name and interrogate the ways white supremacy and neoliberalism remain a powerful force in higher education leadership and are actively operating to co-opt efforts toward seemingly socially just and equitable advances in leadership. The only hope for changing this direction is constant and vigilant interrogation—critical self-reflection along one's journey as a leadership practitioner or scholar. We hope that we have achieved our goal in naming the challenge (whiteness and neoliberalism) and offering up viable alternatives for liberatory forms of leadership practice and research.

Discussion Questions

1. Select two new directions for leadership practices featured in this chapter and reflect on what it would look like to enact these practices in your current higher education role. What challenges do you foresee? What support will you need? How might you go about securing or creating this support?

2. Identify a leadership challenge confronting your organization and analyze this issue using one of the transdisciplinary theories (e.g., trauma-informed leadership theory) described in this chapter. What questions does the theory raise? What insights does the analysis reveal? What course of action is suggested by your analysis?

3. Select a recently published higher education leadership study and consider the extent to which the featured research project aligns with the leadership research agenda mapped out in this chapter. In what ways does the study sustain or disrupt traditional constructions of leadership rooted in neoliberalism and white supremacy?

4. After reviewing the suggested new directions in leadership theory and research, write a brief research purpose statement along with at least two guiding research questions that might frame a study designed to address one or more of the knowledge gaps, blind spots, or inquiry areas highlighted in this chapter.

Appendix: Case Studies

1. Merger at Cañada College

Cañada College, a well-respected liberal arts institution, is experiencing a tremendous existential threat. For the past three years enrollment has declined, and the school's small endowment took a significant hit during the recent stock market decline. Additionally, like many campuses across the country, Cañada has found that as national racial demographics shifted, so too did the college's student body. Within the last decade, the college has transitioned from serving mostly white middle-class students to serving mostly first-generation, racialized minority students with high financial aid need. In order to meet enrollment goals, the institution has been offering much larger tuition discounts than in the past. Initially, administrators thought they would only need to provide these deep discounts for a few years, but this enrollment strategy has now been in place for a decade, placing Cañada in financial jeopardy. The president and her leadership team have tried expanding programs and pursuing other student populations, but they have not been able to achieve the scale needed to foster financial stability. Cañada's senior leadership team, working with the board of trustees, recently identified merging with another school as one possible strategy for addressing the campus's financial woes. There is a large research university in the neighboring town—Oilbaron University—that is looking to acquire property to accommodate the expansion of its high-demand and financially lucrative health science programs. Having read about Cañada's problems in the local paper, Oilbaron's chancellor approaches the senior administration at Cañada with the idea of a merger. Although the leaders of both schools agree to hold off on announcing the prospect of a merger given the tentative nature of the negotiations, rumors about the impending closure of Cañada begin to circulate.

Cañada faculty, staff, and administrators across various units are troubled by the discussion of a merger with Oilbaron. While the tentative agreement

304   *Appendix*

published in a campus press release speaks about mutual benefits and preservation of the Cañada mission, Oilbaron has a reputation of placing money above values. In direct opposition to Cañada's liberal arts mission, Oilbaron recently announced the elimination of three humanities majors due to low enrollment. The Cañada faculty senate sets time aside at their biweekly meeting for discussion of the proposed merger, with a majority of senators opposing the Oilbaron partnership. Despite months of debate and critique, nothing tangible comes out of the senate to counter the merger.

Student groups also begin to meet and voice concerns that the proposed merger will destroy the Cañada community and undermine their academic success. Oilbaron is a highly selective institution, unlikely to maintain Cañada's commitment to educational opportunity within local communities of color. The students recognize that they may not have enough power to capture the attention of decision makers, so they begin contemplating whom they might form an alliance with in order to ensure the student perspective is fully considered in merger discussions. Zania, an African American senior sociology major who identifies as gender nonconforming, remembers reading about a large donation from an alumnus who is very passionate about Cañada. Zania suggests that the student groups reach out to this alumnus to see if he would be willing to speak out against the merger. Zania has no idea if this person will even respond, but it is worth a try. Ruben Hayes (a Latinx alumnus) is quite touched to receive a message from Zania. He is very worried about Cañada's financial viability and is eager to participate in efforts focused on ensuring the school's survival as a standalone institution. Ruben suggests to Zania that they first identify prominent individuals and groups likely to shape the merger decision and then convene a meeting of these individuals with the aim of organizing collective action. Ruben contacts other prominent alumni and institutional donors and invites them to participate. He also reaches out to faculty and staff who have expressed concern. Zania and Ruben identify local businesses and nonprofits that work closely with the school as another set of organizations with a vested interest in the outcome of the proposed merger. Ruben and Zania cast a wide net for potential supporters, inviting all with a stake in the college's survival to join the Save Cañada College Collective. In the interest of gaining a deeper understanding of the college's challenges and developing evidence-based solutions, the collective requests financial and enrollment data from the administration. Unfortunately, their requests for information are denied given that Cañada is a private institution and these records are not open to the public.

The collective's information requests place their resistance efforts on the radar of the senior administration and board of trustees. Cañada's president and board chair send a joint statement to the local newspaper and various community organizations detailing the benefits of the merger and their concern about a misguided activist group that probably has good intentions but could jeopardize the school's future and survival if they do not support the merger. In addition, the president and board chair contend the resistance efforts have the potential to limit the educational opportunities available to Cañada's most vulnerable student populations. Specifically, they describe how the education that students are getting at Cañada would be enhanced by affiliation with Oilbaron University due to its healthy resources and robust academic programs. In an interview with a journalist, one of the board members explains how the proposed merger aligns with Cañada's mission, values, and tradition of supporting students of color, suggesting that the collective's resistance efforts are racist and counter to the college's culture of progress. Zania and Ruben are completely mystified by the characterization of their activism as racist given that their primary focus is on preserving educational access for Cañada's diverse student body, access that is threatened by the revenue-oriented and prestige-seeking priorities of Oilbaron.

In response to the arguments advanced by Cañada's leadership team, Zania and Ruben change tactics, shifting away from a data-driven advocacy approach with campus stakeholders and opting instead to take their case directly to the public and community. They appeal to board members directly, give speeches across town, and ask alumni and prominent community supporters to write letters to the local paper. Zania and Ruben come up with slogans to communicate their cause—"Oilbaron stop treading on Cañada" and "Support an enlightened education, not marketization." Faculty and staff work with students to organize sit-ins calling for an end to the merger.

Frustrated by growing support for the Save Cañada College Collective, the board begins to fight back, meeting with local government officials to warn them that, without their help, the school might collapse, with devastating consequences for the town's economy. Campus leaders also tap alumni, reaching out to those who have been receptive to the benefits of the merger.

Even though the pro-merger alumni group is relatively small, the campus leaders convince government agencies that there are an equal number of pro- and anti-merger alumni. These merger-aligned alumni are wealthy and powerful, donating funds to sponsor visits to institutions that have successfully merged with neighboring schools. The pro-merger group also introduces local officials to powerful foundations that want to help support the initiative as well.

Several Cañada administrators seeking to defuse tension within the campus and local community suggest that a few board members sit down with the Save Cañada College Collective in the interest of opening up a productive dialogue. The board chair rejects this suggestion, telling the administrators that if they are not aligned with the merger strategy, they are free to quit. In addition, the chair reminds the administrators that the new institution will be looking for people to fire when the merger happens, given that there will be fewer administrative roles in the streamlined organization. The board chair clearly insinuates that those administrators who oppose the merger will likely be the first let go. In the end, the merger occurs. Zania, Ruben, and their collective are devastated. Within eighteen months of the merger, Cañada College closes and a third of the faculty and staff are notified their positions are being eliminated.

Theoretical Analysis

This case demonstrates the influence of neoliberal market principles on university governance decisions and leadership behaviors. The reputation of Oilbaron University for prioritizing revenue potential and market proximity (e.g., the expansion of high-demand and lucrative health care programs) is reminiscent of the neoliberal tradition. In addition, the proposed merger between Oilbaron University and Cañada College is rooted in the logics of white supremacy and colonization, which justify taking over the land of an organization dedicated to the education and empowerment of students of color. The board members' actions clearly reflect the whiteness-as-property principle, which assumes all assets are subject to ownership and consumption by those in positions of (white) power. The board certainly wields power and privilege in their access to foundations and high-level government officials. Additionally, the board is using whiteness tactics such as impression management to garner support for their position, labeling the Save Cañada

College Collective as misguided and racist and reaching out to the press and local communities strategically to promote their perspective. The board and pro-merger administrators also display anti-Blackness in the ways they communicate little regard for the fate of displaced Cañada students. Additionally, the influence of the white gaze is evident in the way merger advocates characterize the education provided by Cañada as subpar in comparison to the education offered to students at the predominantly white Oilbaron University.

In addition to illustrating manifestations of neoliberalism and white supremacy, this case also demonstrates the possibility and value of drawing on multiple leadership perspectives to advance organizational aims. Both the Save Cañada College Collective and the Cañada Board of Trustees engage in team or shared leadership, leveraging networks to try to increase their influence, persuasion, and power. We also see both leadership groups utilizing concepts from complexity and chaos leadership perspectives, including adaptability and deviation from traditional hierarchy in favor of utilizing networks and systems thinking.

The Save Cañada College Collective reflects critical social movements theories, which highlight the importance of engaging in critical reflection, fostering solidarity, and exposing the ways power systems operate to oppress others. More specifically, the collective is a prime example of how grassroots groups can draw on bottom-up leadership strategies (e.g., raising consciousness, mobilizing people, and garnering resources) to advance a movement toward change. Zania, Ruben, and the other members of the collective are also demonstrating culturally responsive principles and practices associated with applied critical leadership. The preservation of educational access and advancement of educational equity are the twin aims driving the collective's resistance to the merger. Ruben and Zania are drawing on the strengths derived from their minoritized social identities and life experiences to engage in leadership efforts characterized by consensus building, leading by example in service of giving back to marginalized communities, a willingness to raise tough questions regarding racial inequities, and a commitment to empowering all stakeholders to participate in transformational change work. Processual leadership perspectives are also useful for making sense of this case. Both those advocating for the merger and those seeking to preserve Cañada's independence are benefiting from awareness of macro conditions

308   *Appendix*

(e.g., shifting demographics and labor demands), careful analysis of the socially constructed leadership dilemma, a willingness to restrategize in response to altered dynamics, and an understanding of how diverse perceptions of the merger might influence change processes and outcomes.

The Save Cañada College Collective and Cañada board are also drawing on the cognitive leadership construct of mental models to make sense of the situation and guide their leadership efforts. Both groups are engaging in actions that reflect a multiframe leadership approach, including utilizing symbols, slogans, and stories to communicate their vision for change and engaging in the political strategies of recognizing multiple sources of power and building coalitions among diverse constituencies with overlapping interests. The board member's characterization of the collective's efforts as racist is a particularly pernicious use of the symbolic frame to protect white supremacy. The board member is leveraging the cultural symbols of institutional history, mission, and traditions to reframe the merger as a pathway toward progress and inclusion for historically marginalized students, a symbolic argument contested by those who oppose the merger. The Save Cañada College Collective is operating from a human resource frame that values authentic relationships and the empowerment of Cañada faculty, staff, and students, while the board of trustees is attending to the structural dynamics of the merger, including identifying the most cost-efficient and productive staffing patterns. Additionally, the Save Cañada College Collective appears to be operating from an equity-minded cognitive leadership orientation, seeking access to institutional data in hope of understanding the differential impact of the merger on students of color. Unfortunately, the collective's data-gathering efforts are blocked, highlighting the challenges grassroots leaders may face in accessing information managed by organizational members with a vested interest in maintaining the inequitable status quo.

Both groups are deploying transformational leadership approaches of moral persuasion; yet the Save Cañada College Collective is guided more by transformational leadership in that they have an ethical or moral end, seek to care for and empower individuals throughout their group, and are working to create a shared vision. Additionally, the collective reflects the values and practices of shared-equity leadership, including courage, creativity, and trust building. The collective also demonstrates authentic leadership through their transparency, honesty, and openness regarding their goals, values, and direction as well as their commitment to acting with integrity. By contrast, Cañada board members display a lack of transformational or authentic leadership dispositions, showing little care for administrators in their threats to fire those who question decisions.

The case study of the Cañada College and Oilbaron University merger illustrates the active contestation between leadership approaches rooted in whiteness, white supremacy, and neoliberalism and a diverse array of leadership perspectives that can be drawn on to disrupt systemic oppression and create more equitable and socially just higher education organizations. Although the Save Cañada College Collective was not successful in preventing the merger, a realistic outcome given the entrenched nature of neoliberalism and white supremacy within contemporary society, participants in the resistance movement strengthened their individual and collective capacities to engage in future equity-oriented leadership endeavors. This case also illustrates that contemporary leadership perspectives such as shared leadership, chaos and complexity, and cognitive framing can be leveraged to maintain as well as disrupt oppression. In addition to examining the specific leadership approaches exhibited by higher education professionals, teams, and networks, scholar-practitioners must also interrogate the aims of individual and organizational actions in order to discern whether the efforts will serve to sustain or dismantle white supremacy and neoliberalism.

Discussion Questions

1. Based on your analysis of this case and the diverse leadership approaches presented in this book, what recommendations do you have for individuals and groups seeking to stop campus mergers? What could the Save Cañada College Collective have done differently?

2. What other ways do you see whiteness and neoliberalism manifested in this case?

3. Are there other cultural leadership theories or concepts that either group could have used to advance its aims?

4. Staff engagement in merger advocacy or resistance efforts is not addressed in this case. What leadership theories and concepts might entry- or midlevel staff adopt in the interest of advancing their merger preferences?

5. If you were to design a study of the Cañada College merger, what theories and methodologies might you use to frame the research project?

2. Rethinking Technology at Chumash State

Chumash State is a minority-serving institution that has found itself in a challenging position. The board of trustees has been worried about declining tuition revenue and slow growth in regional enrollment. To address these concerns, the board recommended that many of Chumash's programs and courses be moved to an online platform in the hope of raising enrollment among part- and full-time employees of local businesses. Campus leaders have been trying to execute the directive of the board but have encountered numerous challenges. Specifically, they have found that online courses are not as inexpensive as the board initially thought. They have presented this evidence to the board, but the trustees are unwilling to waver on their directive. Board members retort that costs will go down over time and that the campus needs to consider its long-term sustainability. Leaders throughout campus feel as though they are keeping the long-term interests of the campus in mind, and they just cannot see eye to eye with the board.

In addition to the cost issues, there are also real concerns that the move to online education is not beneficial to student retention and graduation, let alone the quality of their experiences. There are a lot of first-generation (72%) and racially minoritized (65%) students at Chumash State, and leaders on campus are aware that these populations are not always given equitable resources to perform well in the online environment. Faculty leaders have shared the difficulties of creating engagement in online programs. Staff leaders have raised concerns about lowering retention rates in online courses, describing how many students find the new learning environment challenging. Not all students are struggling, however; adult learners have reported increased satisfaction with their academic experiences. Administrative leaders in various units have noted limitations with the existing online tools, but the institution does not have the funds needed to move to another technology platform. Campus leaders realize that the board is trying to help them adapt to external pressures, but they are not sure the board directive is going in the right direction and serving students adequately. Furthermore, campus leaders wish that the board had sought their input or listened to their views in adapting to these very complex challenges. Given their distance from the day-to-day operations of the faculty and staff, board members are unable to develop a full understanding of the financial, technical, and human resource demands associated with the shift to online instruction. The board has dismissed faculty and staff reports regarding student challenges with a suggestion to offer better orientation to students in online courses.

Jorge is a faculty member in engineering at Chumash State. He has contacted several other faculty and staff across campus in the interest of starting an informal group that tries to solve the issues that are making it so challenging for students to learn online. Jorge is connected with computer science colleagues across the country and shares with the working group that he is reached out to them for some advice. Although the external guidance will be helpful, Jorge knows he really needs to hear from Chumash faculty, staff, and students about all the challenges they are encountering so the working group can develop solutions that will truly address the specific concerns of Chumash stakeholders. Jorge also recognizes that faculty and staff are quite demoralized. He starts the first meeting with the working group by asking how people are doing and how their students feel; he spends adequate time doing this. For months now, Chumash faculty and staff have felt they have been running in circles, and someone asking them how they are feeling is quite refreshing—several people cry through their responses.

Jorge notes that the group will need to listen to everybody's perspective to develop inclusive solutions. He helps people see how their work is important to ensure students get a quality and equitable education. People across campus begin to share their ideas, and Jorge realizes that the problems are more multifaceted than he thought. He remembers that one of his engineering faculty colleagues is particularly interested in and strong at systems thinking; Jorge brings this individual into the working group's next meeting to help map all the issues that need to be considered. Belinda from institutional research says she will bring in some of the most recent data to help inform their systems map. It is clear from the mapping activity that certain faculty, staff, and units are suffering more due to a lack of technical knowledge and even some resistance to technology. Real disagreements emerge within the working group about whether the technology system can be reworked or should be abandoned. Some of the individuals in the group begin to get impatient with Jorge's relational focus. They acknowledge that he has helped develop a shared vision, but they really worry whether the group will be able to come up with useful solutions in time. Jorge senses this

312   *Appendix*

tension and raises it for the group to consider. Some group members begin to defend Jorge and lash out at the individuals raising concerns. Jorge points out that different perspectives are welcome and that he appreciates their support. But he wants the group to wrestle with this tension between coming up with quicker but imperfect solutions and spending more time wrestling with the problem.

Jorge starts the next meeting with dedicated group processing time focused on developing principles for working together. While nothing is definitive, the group identifies three possible scenarios for moving forward that they believe will be better than the current system. Jorge realizes that whatever solutions they come up with to address the online education dilemma, the working group will run into problems if the administrative leadership and board do not engage their ideas. He contacts a local journalist and says he has a story about student dropouts on campus. Jorge leaks information to the journalist, who promises him anonymity. The story gets picked up by a much larger paper, and the board is pressured for answers by local legislatures, parents, alumni, and other interested parties. The board calls an emergency meeting, and the president shares with trustees that a team on campus has been working to develop innovative ideas for rethinking their reliance on online learning but also cutting costs and achieving scale. The board says they are ready to hear the ideas.

Theoretical Analysis

First, this case showcases plantation leadership where the board is exerting white supremacy and foisting technology and an inferior education on students. These actions happen to follow neoliberal principles of revenue generation, growth, and scarcity. The board's inability to think holistically and systematically in ways that benefit students, staff, and faculty ends up supporting the institution and its legitimacy and relevance—a key element of plantation leadership. In addition, Jorge's strategic leak of information in some ways allows the board to enact notions of impression management, as they are concerned with how the public will perceive the institution. The leak helps the working group's demands and suggestions gain more attention from senior leadership. Thus, one can also observe the interest convergence element of plantation leadership.

2. Rethinking Technology at Chumash State   313

This case also exemplifies many aspects of chaos and complexity leadership theories, in which external circumstances provide an adaptive challenge for leaders. The issue is complicated by a board that is not embracing any of the tenets of complexity leadership, such as demonstrating a willingness to bring in local knowledge, exhibiting openness to learning, maintaining flexibility, or valuing experimentation. Jorge does the opposite—he actively seeks out local knowledge from his faculty and staff colleagues and forms a working group that can learn and adapt together.

Jorge also demonstrates transformational leadership by expressing care and concern for the group that has experienced difficulties. He also reminds them of the ethical and moral ends of their work—student success—and helps create a shared vision for their work. Finally, he empowers faculty and staff members to be part of the problem-solving and helps to develop a shared vision for their work. Jorge's leadership reflects shared-equity leadership approaches, including humility, vulnerability, transparency, and comfort with discomfort (values) and relational, communication, and structural practices.

The case also demonstrates cultural leadership perspectives by showing how the cultural context—being a minority-serving institution—affects the leadership challenge. Jorge and others on campus are aware of the racial inequities that could result from the administration's decisions. On the other hand, the administration is ignorant of this key consideration. It makes poor decisions partly based on its lack of attention to cultural issues and understanding of the history and traditions of a minority-serving institution. Jorge is also very cognizant of disciplinary and role differences that represent different cultures on campus and their interpretation of the issues and approach to leadership. He is savvy in engaging differences rather than stifling conflict that can lead to problems later and result in unintended inequities over time when voices and perspectives are suppressed.

Cognitive leadership perspectives are illustrated in his focus on being equity-minded and ensuring the most marginalized groups have a voice. Jorge displays wisdom in his focus on long-term outcomes for the campus and bringing together all interested parties to inform the decision. His focus on systems thinking and learning more about the technical challenge is representative of cognitive perspectives on leadership. And one can also see his attention to disciplinary and role differences as a way to understand the different schemas that groups hold and that need to be navigated to address the leadership challenge.

Jorge's leadership also reflects processual approaches to leadership in building the leadership team to address the technology challenge. Jorge uses his understanding of the importance of the leadership process to focus on group dynamics and relationships. He devotes time to building solid relationships with the group and addressing the group tensions and different perspectives that can often derail leadership processes. He makes time for the group to process their differences and also offers them approaches to working together. Jorge can be seen through these many approaches as a weaver-leader—helping create expectations within the group, pulling together diverse perspectives, and navigating inevitable conflict toward a greater good. Jorge's leadership also reflects processual leadership in his effort to reach out to other campus contacts to help solve the leadership challenge and his attention to the many campus perspectives and stakeholders he brings for the group to consider. Jorge's reaching out to the journalist and being cognizant of the need to change the board's perspective also reflect processual theories of change that foreground external sources and contexts that can be brought to bear on leadership challenges. Lastly, Jorge utilizes future studies methods like scenario planning to get the leadership team to think about charting a better, more equitable path for the institution and its mission of student success.

Discussion Questions

1. How would you recommend that the working group present their ideas to the board? What leadership approaches would you lean into?
2. To what extent does the group need to be concerned about how plantation leadership, neoliberalism, and whiteness might continue to play out moving forward?
3. What other theories seem most relevant to understanding this leadership process?
4. How might you design a study to explore the interplay of the board's leadership and Jorge and his team's leadership? How might you study whiteness and neoliberalism in this case?

3. New Program and Leadership Process at Webster University

Webster University is a rural regional public institution in the heart of Illinois, and student activism is at the heart of the university. Recently, student activists have organized to create the Black Studies and Radical Political Thought academic program after recognizing a significant gap in academic offerings and increased student interest in the field of Black studies. Student activists worked with senior-level administrators to advocate for the program and suggested the appointment of Joy Davis, a Black woman and professor of political science, as director of the Black Studies and Radical Political Thought program. They were eager to have Joy lead the program because of her past activism efforts, her commitment to mentorship and student success, and her dedication to the field. Joy was very humbled that student activists suggested her appointment, and she graciously accepted. As part of her new appointment, university leaders tasked her with hiring three tenure-track faculty members and two non-tenure-track faculty members. She was also assigned to develop three courses to start the program, with the new faculty members helping to build out the rest of the curriculum later. Joy was grateful for all the institutional support and financial backing, but she was only one person. As part of her activism efforts, she learned the importance of working with the community and considering the perspectives of those you are helping to build for. Joy asked the group of student activists who organized to create the new program to serve on both hiring and curriculum committees, much to the dismay of other university leaders. They believed that the student activists' jobs were done and that they needed to focus on their academic success. University leaders believed the committee should comprise faculty, staff, and senior leaders. Joy stood firm in her desire to have students on the committee and resisted university leadership's recommendation. She even went as far as to ask each student representative to bring a friend onto the committee. The faculty hiring and curriculum committees consisted of Joy, six students, and two other colleagues from the university. Joy would pay committee members for their time.

The faculty hiring committee created interview protocols almost entirely from scratch, composed and edited the job descriptions, and worked with university leaders to figure out budgets for salaries. Students who would

316   *Appendix*

eventually transition into the Black Studies and Radical Political Thought program were deeply involved in each aspect of the hiring process and even led the planning for the on-campus interview day for top candidates. Joy provided students the agency and autonomy to help and play active roles in each step of the process. The curriculum committee crowdsourced syllabi from peer institutions and spoke with faculty from different institutions to configure Webster's unique course offerings. The curriculum committee also worked to find opportunities for cross-departmental collaboration, identifying courses that could be cross-listed while paying special attention to the departments that Webster University had identified as at risk for elimination—namely, the Philosophy and History Departments. Students were encouraged to take the lead in speaking with faculty from different institutions and different departments. Joy encouraged this as a way for students to network and build relationships. She encouraged committee members to collaborate, think through and experiment with new and exciting ideas, and just relish in this creative leadership process and endeavor.

The faculty hiring committee used new technology to conduct screening interviews—a software called HireVue that allows candidates to answer interview questions in a video format, which also allows committee members to review responses on their own time. The committee was also able to brainstorm requests that they knew successful candidates would ask for, such as guaranteed office space, course releases, and relocation assistance. Thus, the committee was ready to answer those questions during the interview instead of waiting for candidates to try to negotiate them in their contracts. This sped up the hiring process. The curriculum committee identified core course offerings and worked with the History and Philosophy Departments to find ways to collaborate, increase enrollment, and draw traffic to these departments and their course offerings.

Fast-forward a year and the Black Studies and Radical Political Thought Department is thriving. They have hired two new assistant professors, Marlon Stevens and Jessica Braithwright, and two adjunct faculty members who teach on a contingent basis, Belinda Waite and Claudia Johnson. Each thoroughly enjoyed and appreciated the hiring process and is eager to get involved in the process as the program expands. Two of the four core courses offered during the school year are being taught in collaboration with philosophy

3. New Program and Leadership Process at Webster University   317

and history professors and are cross-listed and filled. The adjunct faculty members can also submit elective course proposals to Joy. The students who served on each committee are now happily taking the courses with the faculty they helped choose. University leadership is pleased with the results of the committee process and is eager to use it as a model for future faculty hiring and curriculum development processes.

Theoretical Analysis

First, this case captures plantation leadership in action through the senior leaders' initial thoughts, actions, and behaviors at Webster. They agree to the creation of the Black Studies and Radical Political Thought program and the appointment of Joy Davis. Still, they seek to control who is involved in committee processes, which could have detrimental effects on the program's success. With a critical lens, one could argue that this is a quintessential illustration of impression management (seeking to *look* progressive and radical but trying to control the situation *underneath the surface*). The Webster administration also seems to have investments in neoliberalism because of its desire to control the committee's composition toward its interests so the program will not end up being "too radical" in its thinking. If it were to have its way and exclude students from the committee, Webster's administration would likely encourage Joy to compose the committee of people with varying degrees of investment in the legitimization of the institution. Courses could have easily swayed toward neoliberal market values and not been as creative or enticing for prospective students and faculty. We also see neoliberalism in the case with the mention of "at-risk for elimination" departments like Philosophy and History. The neoliberal framing is subverted, however, when Joy makes conscious efforts to collaborate with these departments and their faculty and use the new program to direct additional enrollments and revenues their way, creating collective success instead of neoliberal competition.

The committee is composed and carried out in a way that is true to processual leadership. Joy embraces leadership as a process by using shared leadership approaches and ensuring that students who will eventually enroll in classes in the program are meaningfully involved in each committee. Further, the case exemplifies transformational leadership approaches to support others in the leadership process and empowerment. The outcomes for students

318   *Appendix*

who are a part of the committee process are especially transformative, allowing them to observe often-hidden processes of the university (i.e., how universities determine salaries for faculty hires and budgeting) so that they can continue their activist endeavors with key insights and information about how colleges and universities work. These insights are imperative when working to change institutions toward equity and justice. Joy also empowers students to play an active role in the leadership process by giving them the opportunity to plan parts of the on-campus interview day and help create interview protocols.

The case also places a spotlight on cultural leadership perspectives. The committee—its composition, desires, and outcomes—is particularly attuned to both race (i.e., a *Black* studies program and a Black woman overseeing the new program) and the institutional culture (i.e., student activism being at the heart of the institution). Taking both into account, Joy is best able to create a program that meets student activists' demands and interests while staying true to the Black studies tradition, which is unapologetically concerned with the history and future of Black people and Black culture. Chaos and complexity leadership perspectives are also deeply embedded in this case. Joys encourages the committee to experiment with new and exciting interview methods and technologies, curriculum design, and course offerings. She asks committee members to crowdsource documents to help get started but encourages adaptation and experimentation.

Lastly, Joy resists Webster senior leaders' limiting schemas and prototypes (cognitive theories) about who should be involved in the leadership process and why. Their leadership schemas and prototypes and Joy's are distinct and incompatible. Webster senior leaders assume a traditional, hierarchical approach to leadership, seeking to pad the committee with people of power and influence. Joy sees students as relevant and necessary partners in the leadership process and fights to include them. The latter approach helps make the new program pertinent to students. Joy understands that student activists and their peers have unique perspectives to offer, and she seeks to invite and respect their insights in the creation of the program. She sees students as leaders and equal partners in the leadership process and even pays them accordingly. She also represents authentic leadership characteristics by staying committed to and acting congruently with the equity and social justice values she was hired to represent.

Discussion Questions

1. In what ways could Webster senior leaders penetrate the new Black Studies and Radical Political Thought program with notions of whiteness and neoliberalism? How can the committee work, in a continuous manner, to subvert this?
2. What new evolutions from the various leadership theories reviewed in this book could further improve and transform this leadership process? How?
3. As a researcher, how would you go about creating a study to explore this leadership process and challenge further?

4. Addressing Student Success at Westgate Community College

Westgate Community College is located in an urban area and serves a college student population that is largely first generation and racially minoritized. The college has been trying to improve its graduation rates, which fall around 12%. Westgate has tried various support programs, but nothing has positively shifted student degree completion trends. Naomi has been hired as the vice president for student success, a new position on campus. An immigrant and first-generation college student, Naomi has been working in student support roles for fifteen years. The campus leadership recognizes that it needs to make progress, as none of its efforts have been successful thus far. It believes hiring someone with expertise and new ideas might be helpful to move the college's trends onward and upward.

Naomi starts her tenure by gathering information about the institution's previous student success initiatives and efforts. She also speaks to key individuals who have been involved with planning efforts to increase student success, including members of the student retention task force and student success committee, as well as other groups and individuals actively engaged in student success work over the years. Rather quickly, she realizes that almost all of Westgate's efforts have been focused on support programs for students outside the classroom. She knows that student surveys document that most of their students work, have families, and spend minimal time on campus. This makes her pause, as she realizes outside classroom support will be very limited in impact, and that is where the campus has been focusing the most attention. Thus, she explores the classroom space, paying close attention to the data on faculty demographics and campus engagement. Naomi realizes that 80% of the faculty are adjuncts with a very loose affiliation with the institution and limited to no knowledge about the student body or the student success initiatives. She decides to drop in on a few classes and speak to the adjunct faculty afterward to understand their perspective on students and their roles. The faculty describe the challenge of teaching courses where they have little information about the overall academic program and students' backgrounds. The instructors recognize that students are not passing their classes at the rate they would hope but are unsure of what support mechanisms exist for students and how to connect students with appropri-

4. Addressing Student Success at Westgate Community College 321

ate resources or integrate campus success programs into their courses. When Naomi asks administrators about support for adjunct faculty members and how they are connected to the student success initiative, they all look puzzled and say that adjuncts do not need any support, given that most have been teaching at Westgate for years. And when she asked about the potential of hiring more full-time faculty to strengthen connections between the classroom and academic support programs, administrators described funding shifts to support programs aimed at student success and to construct new buildings. There is not money in the budget for hiring full-time salaried instructors.

Naomi also recognizes that many of the former and existing support programs approach students from a deficit perspective and have faulty assumptions about students' needs and interests. The development of multiple programs to address deficit students is a sign of this assumption. Still, her conversations manifest descriptions of students as "poor writers and thinkers" and "lazy and lacking engagement and interest in learning." It is also clear that although many people have been involved with committee work, these participants believe their activities and responsibilities are completed when summary reports are submitted to administration; few people say student success is a part of their day-to-day work.

But through her conversations with faculty and staff involved with the various initiatives, Naomi identifies a set of unconventional thinkers who have been considering other approaches to student success but have had difficulty gaining traction for their ideas with senior administrators. Many of these individuals are people of color, particularly women of color. Over the years, they have been silenced, so they no longer bother to share observations and recommendations. Instead, they opt to share best practices and interventions with each other. Naomi lets them know she is interested in their ideas and wants to support them. In fact, she starts an informal group called the Wise Sisters. They meet for lunch regularly, and now that they have a connection to the administration, they begin to feel empowered and connected to the campus again.

After six months of research and conversation, Naomi meets with the president's cabinet to share her insights. She asserts that the campus needs to restart its student success work, but these efforts must be guided by new assumptions, principles, and goals. Westgate needs to adopt an asset-based, classroom-centered programming model that instills a commitment to student success across the work of all employees. While senior administrators are initially concerned she might offend people, they concede that Naomi can do this work and that her ideas are worth exploring.

Naomi asks to convene an unconference—a meeting format with no strict agenda and in which creativity is utilized to break down traditional assumptions. She insists that adjuncts be invited and paid to attend the event, and that their attendance count toward merit pay for the year. And before the unconference, Naomi and the Wise Sisters plan to host a webinar series called "Exorcizing Deficit and Racist Thinking from Our Student Success Work." In this set of conversations, she will call into question the approach taken in the last decade as a prelude to the new student success framework she intends to promote. The series highlights the ideas developed by the Wise Sisters and brings in one sister every two weeks to share novel ideas. The unconference starts with a series of provocations to think anew. Specifically, Naomi begins the event with students reading poems that express their hopes for what a new campus environment might look like. The entire room is overflowing with emotions when the students finish their readings. There is a standing ovation at the end of the first day. After three days of unstructured brainstorming, a set of ideas emerges with a whole new approach to student success grounded in meeting students where they are at—in the classroom. These ideas include much greater support for adjunct faculty; a shift to hiring 15% more full-time faculty over the next five years; a one-stop-shop support program so that students do not need to go from office to office; streamlined course offerings and better ties between courses and majors; training for staff and faculty about the students as well as more ongoing data collection about student backgrounds and needs; partnerships with local four-year colleges and employers that regularly come to recruit and meet with students and aid in their next steps; and an accountability plan to ensure that changes are making a difference to graduation rates. And to many people's surprise, it is the adjunct faculty who develop the most profound ideas for change.

Theoretical Analysis

This scenario underscores the fact that white supremacy encourages faculty, administrators, and staff to take a deficit view of students, particularly students of color (anti-Blackness), low-income students, and others who have been oppressed in society. Unless leaders are willing to challenge the perspectives and viewpoints of their colleagues, these will remain embedded within our institutions. Naomi recognizes that she needs to challenge as well as educate her colleagues. She also identifies the neoliberal trends of hiring adjuncts and following the Gig Academy model. Throughout the case, her work identifying leadership barriers within her campus context is critical to her efforts to move toward more liberatory ends.

Naomi acts as a transformational leader by inspiring her colleagues, particularly in the unconference event where students read their poems, but also through her empowerment of the Wise Sisters. Her focus on a new, equitable future for students also reflects the social change emphasis evident in transformational leadership perspectives, where leaders help others see a different future outside today's status quo. She also helps shape a shared vision for the future through her moral persuasion, various learning activities, and discussion. Her approach of working with others to expand and create a critical mass of individuals focused on supporting students equitably reflects shared-equity leadership. Her identification of the Wise Sisters group reflects her interest in ensuring her decisions are informed by others intentionally, that her mental models are interrogated, and that she continues to focus on a broad set of collective interests, which reflects wisdom.

Her analysis of the campus context through her systems thinking reflects chaos and complexity theories of leadership. In addition, her unconference reflects chaos and complexity leadership perspectives by challenging the existing system, and it represents a call to rethink primary assumptions that can result in new systems. She also confronts the current system of professionalism and niceness within the presidential cabinet. Naomi helps them see a very different way to lead that is both confrontational and inspirational.

Naomi seeks out data and information as she enters the campus, reflecting cognitive leadership theories. She also seeks out the perspectives and voices of many individuals, particularly overlooked groups such as the adjunct faculty who work closely with students and thus hold key information related to the student success issue. Her challenge of cognitive biases such as deficit-oriented framing of student abilities, anti-Blackness, and lack of systems thinking among faculty and staff demonstrates cognitive leadership theories. We also see her focus on understanding faculty's, staff's, and

324   *Appendix*

administrators' mental models (deficit thinking) through her meetings with various groups to challenge their thinking and bring them aboard her new approach to student success. She recognizes that to be an effective leader, she needs to comprehend the perspectives of others, particularly their hidden or underlying assumptions. And we see her interest in helping campus members learn by challenging their deficit perspectives and setting up key learning opportunities like the webinar series and the unconference. She meets with and challenges administrators about their decisions, particularly their lack of support for adjuncts and unwillingness to hire more full-time faculty. This emphasis on learning is a core approach to cognitive strategies of leadership.

Naomi's ability to identify the interplay of race, gender, and social class stems from her facility in being a leader who exhibits cultural perspectives of leadership. Throughout the case, we see her awareness of the lived experiences and realities of women and people of color spring her into action, which drives her to support and uplift the distinctive and insightful perspectives of the Wise Sisters. Naomi's cultural approach is to draw from much more diverse voices to inform her leadership decisions, a technique that Westgate's leaders have not historically utilized.

Throughout the case, we see processual leadership unfolding in numerous ways. First, processual leadership perspectives are evident in the recognition from Westgate leaders that they need a new approach to student success that must be guided by collective action. This process is animated by Naomi's actions and interactions with faculty, staff, and students— particularly the Wise Sisters, student leaders, and adjunct faculty—and her drive to utilize the unconference format. She also engages with the campus context in a meaningful way and as a means to carefully shape the process toward a new student success approach. Naomi carefully identifies allies on campus and connects with people, such as the Wise Sisters, who are already doing interesting work from a grassroots perspective; this reflects tenets from shared leadership and critical social movements theory. The unconference involves transformative storytelling as a vehicle for creating a new culture on campus and a more equitable future. The steps that guide her work with the Wise Sisters reflect many phases and mindsets in the design for equity in higher education model, as she freely ideates and centers the needs of historically marginalized groups to create a new solution for Westgate's poor student success rates.

Discussion Questions

1. What do you see as the major leadership hurdles ahead for Westgate? How might the leadership perspectives you have learned help you to identify such challenges?
2. Using processual leadership theories, what external forces or circumstances could shape their implementation of the plan? How might the design for equity in higher education model mitigate these challenges?
3. How might whiteness or neoliberalism play out in the leadership process going forward?
4. How might you use cultural theories to examine the leadership of the Wise Sisters? Student leaders?

References

Acker, J. (1990). Hierarchies, jobs, bodies: A theory of gendered organizations. *Gender and Society, 49*(2), 139–158. https://doi.org/10.1177/089124390004002002

Ackoff, R. L. (2006). Why few organizations adopt systems thinking. *Systems Research and Behavioral Science, 23*(5), 705–708. https://doi.org/10.1002/sres.791

Ackoff, R. L. (2010). *Systems thinking for curious managers.* Triarchy Press.

Aggarwal, U. (2016). The ideological architecture of whiteness as property in educational policy. *Educational Policy, 30*(1), 128–152. https://doi.org/10.1177/0895904815616486

Agosto, V., & Roland, E. (2018). Intersectionality and educational leadership: A critical review. *Review of Research in Education, 42*(1), 255–285. https://doi.org/10.3102/0091732X18762433

Aguirre, A., & Martinez, R. (2002). Leadership practices and diversity in higher education: Transitional and transformational frameworks. *Journal of Leadership Studies, 8*(3), 53–62. https://doi.org/10.1177/107179190200800305

Ahmed, S. (2007). A phenomenology of whiteness. *Feminist Theory, 8*(2), 149–168. https://doi.org/10.1177/1464700107078139

Ailon, G. (2008). Mirror, mirror on the wall: Culture's consequences in a value test of its own design. *Academy of Management Review, 33*(4), 885–904. https://doi.org/10.2307/20159451

Ailon, G. (2009). A reply to Geert Hofstede. *Academy of Management Review, 34*(3), 571–573. https://doi.org/10.5465/amr.2009.40633815

Akutagawa, L. (2013). Breaking stereotypes: An Asian American's view of leadership development. *Asian American Journal of Psychology, 4*(4), 277–284. https://doi.org/10.1037/a0035390

Alemán, E., Jr. (2009a). Latcrit educational leadership and advocacy: Struggling over whiteness as property in Texas school finance. *Equity & Excellence in Education, 42*(2), 183–201. https://doi.org/10.1080/10665680902744246

Alemán, E., Jr. (2009b). Through the prism of critical race theory: Niceness and Latina/o leadership in the politics of education. *Journal of Latinos & Education, 8*(4), 290–311. https://doi.org/10.1080/15348430902973351

Alexander, M. (2010). *The new Jim Crow: Mass incarceration in the age of colorblindness.* New Press.

328 References

Allen, K. E., & Cherrey, C. (2000). *Systemic leadership: Enriching the meaning of our work*. University Press of America.

Allen, P. M. (2001). A complex systems approach to learning in adaptive networks. *International Journal of Innovation Management, 5*(2), 149–180. https://doi.org/10.1142/s1363919601000035x

Allen, R. L., & Liou, D. D. (2019). Managing whiteness: The call for educational leadership to breach the contractual expectations of white supremacy. *Urban Education, 54*(5), 677–705. https://doi.org/10.1177/0042085918783819

Alvesson, M. (1996). Leadership studies: From procedure and abstraction to reflexivity and situation. *Leadership Quarterly, 7*(4), 455–485. https://doi.org/10.1016/s1048-9843(96)90002-8

Alvesson, M. (2011). Leadership and organizational culture. In A. Bryman, D. Collinson, K. Grint, B. Jackson, & M. Uhl-Bien (Eds.), *The SAGE handbook of leadership* (pp. 151–164). SAGE.

Alvesson, M., & Deetz, S. A. (2006). Critical theory and postmodernism approaches to organizational studies. In S. R. Clegg, C. Hardy, T. B. Lawrence, & W. R. Nord (Eds.), *The SAGE handbook of organization studies* (2nd ed., pp. 255–283). SAGE.

American Association of University Professors. (2021). *Special report: COVID-19 and academic governance*. https://www.aaup.org/report/covid-19-and-academic-governance

American Council on Education. (2023). *American college president study*. https://www.acenet.edu/Research-Insights/Pages/American-College-President-Study.aspx

Amiot, M. N., Mayer-Glenn, J., & Parker, L. (2020). Applied critical race theory: Educational leadership actions for student equity. *Race, Ethnicity and Education, 23*(2), 200–220. https://doi.org/10.1080/13613324.2019.1599342

Anderson, G. (2020, November 12). Strength in numbers. *Inside Higher Ed*. https://www.insidehighered.com/news/2020/11/12/liberal-arts-college-presidents-create-diversity-and-inclusion-alliance

Anderson, G. L., & Middleton, E. B. (2014). LeaderPAR: A participatory action research framework for school and community leadership. In I. Bogotch & C. Shields (Eds.), *International handbook of educational leadership and social (in)justice* (Vol. 29, pp. 275–287). Springer.

Annie E. Casey Foundation. (2014). *Embracing equity: 7 steps to advance and embed race equity and inclusion within your organization*.

Antonakis, J., Avolio, B. J., & Sivasubramaniam, N. (2003). Context and leadership: An examination of the nine-factor full-range leadership theory using the Multifactor Leadership Questionnaire. *Leadership Quarterly, 14*(3), 261–295. https://doi.org/10.1016/s1048-9843(03)00030-4

Anzaldúa, G. (1987). *Borderlands / La frontera: The new mestiza*. Aunt Lute Books.

Applebaum, B. (2010). *Being white, being good: White complicity, white moral responsibility, and social justice pedagogy.* Lexington Books.

Ardelt, M. (2004). Wisdom as expert knowledge system: A critical review of a contemporary operationalization of an ancient concept. *Human Development, 47*(5), 257–285. https://doi.org/10.1159/000079154

Ardoin, S., Broadhurst, C., Locke, L., & Johnson, J. (2019). Peacemakers and rabble rousers: Women leaders as activists in higher education. *Journal of Women and Gender in Higher Education, 12*(1), 35–53. https://doi.org/10.1080/19407882.2019.1565868

Ardoin, S., & Guthrie, K. L. (Eds.). (2021a). Leadership learning through the lens of social class [Special issue]. *New Directions for Student Leadership, 2021*(169).

Ardoin, S., & Guthrie, K. L. (2021b). Leadership learning through the lens of social class. *New Directions for Student Leadership, 2021*(169), 7–11.

Arnold, N. W., & Crawford, E. R. (2014). Metaphors of leadership and spatialized practice. *International Journal of Leadership in Education, 17*(3), 257–285. https://doi.org/10.1080/13603124.2013.835449

Astin, A. W., & Astin, H. S. (2000). *Leadership reconsidered: Engaging higher education in social change.* Kellogg Foundation.

Astin, H. S., Astin, A. W., Boatsman, K., Bonous-Hammarth, M., Chambers, T., & Goldberg, S. (1996). *A social change model of leadership development: Guidebook* (Version III). Higher Education Research Institute, University of California, Los Angeles. http://www.heri.ucla.edu/PDFs/pubs/ASocialChangeModelofLeadership Development.pdf

Astin, H. S., & Leland, C. (1991). *Women of influence, women of vision: A cross-generational study of leaders and social change.* Jossey-Bass.

Avolio, B. J., & Bass, B. M. (1991). *The full range leadership development programs: Basic and advanced manuals.* Bass, Avolio Associates.

Avolio, B. J., & Gardner, W. L. (2005). Authentic leadership development: Getting to the root of positive forms of leadership. *Leadership Quarterly, 16*(3), 315–338. https://doi.org/10.1016/j.leaqua.2005.03.001

Avolio, B. J., & Walumbwa, F. O. (2014). Authentic leadership theory, research, and practice: Steps taken and steps that remain. In D. V. Day (Ed.), *Oxford handbook of leadership and organizations* (pp. 351–356). Oxford University Press.

Avolio, B. J., Walumbwa, F. O., & Weber, T. J. (2009). Leadership: Current theories, research, and future directions. *Annual Review of Psychology, 60*, 429–449.

Avolio, B. J., & Yammarino, F. J. (Eds.). (2013). *Transformational and charismatic leadership: The road ahead* (10th anniversary ed.). Emerald.

Ayman, R., & Korabik, K. (2010). Leadership: Why gender and culture matter. *American Psychologist, 65*(3), 157–170. https://doi.org/10.1037/a0018806

330 References

Baber, L. D. (2015). Considering the interest-convergence dilemma in STEM education. *Review of Higher Education, 38*(2), 251–270. https://doi.org/10.1353/rhe.2015.0004

Bacharier, G. (2020, July 28). Curators approve merger of UM System president and MU chancellor. *Inside Higher Ed.* https://www.columbiamissourian.com/news/higher_education/curators-approve-merger-of-um-system-president-and-mu-chancellor/article_4aec502a-d0fa-11ea-a0bb-ffed478a4c68.html

Baker, D. J., & Blissett, R. S. L. (2017). Beyond the incident: Institutional predictors of student collective action. *Journal of Higher Education, 89*(2), 184–207. https://doi.org/10.1080/00221546.2017.1368815

Ball, S. J. (2012). Show me the money! Neoliberalism at work in education. *FORUM, 54*(1), 23–28. https://doi.org/10.2304/forum.2012.54.1.23

Balwant, P. T. (2016). Transformational instructor-leadership in higher education teaching: A meta-analytic review and research agenda. *Journal of Leadership Studies, 9*(4), 20–42. https://doi.org/10.1002/jls.21423

Bandy, J., & Smith, J. (2005). *Coalitions across borders: Transnational protest and the neoliberal order.* Rowman & Littlefield.

Banks, G. C., McCauley, K. D., Gardner, W. L., & Guler, C. E. (2016). A meta-analytic review of authentic and transformational leadership: A test for redundancy. *Leadership Quarterly, 27*(4), 634–652. https://doi.org/10.1016/j.leaqua.2016.02.006

Barnhardt, C. L. (2014). Campus-based organizing: Tactical repertoires of contemporary student movements. *New Directions for Higher Education, 2014*(167), 43–58. https://doi.org/10.1002/he.20104

Bass, B. M. (1985). *Leadership and performance beyond expectations.* Free Press.

Bass, B. M. (1990). From transactional to transformational leadership: Learning to share the vision. *Organizational Dynamics, 18*(3), 19–31. https://doi.org/10.1016/0090-2616(90)90061-S

Bass, B. M., & Stogdill, R. M. (1990). *Bass & Stogdill's handbook of leadership: Theory, research, and managerial applications.* Simon and Schuster.

Bate, S. P. (1997). Whatever happened to organizational anthropology? A review of the field of organizational ethnography and anthropological studies. *Human Relations, 50*(9),1147–1175. https://doi.org/10.1177/001872679705000905

Beerkens, M., & Udam, M. (2017). Stakeholders in higher education quality assurance: Richness in diversity? *Higher Education Policy, 30*(3), 341–359. https://doi.org/10.1057/s41307-016-0032-6

Bell, D. A. (1980). *Brown v. Board of Education* and the interest convergence dilemma. *Harvard Law Review, 93*(3), 518–533. https://doi.org/10.2307/1340546

Bell, D. A. (1992). *Faces at the bottom of the well: The permanence of racism.* Basic Books.

Bell, W. (2003). *Foundations of futures studies: History, purposes, and knowledge.* Routledge.

Bell, W. (2004). *Foundations of futures studies: Values, objectivity, and the good society.* Routledge.

Bennett, A., & Burke, P. J. (2018). Re/conceptualising time and temporality: An exploration of time in higher education. *Discourse: Studies in the Cultural Politics of Education, 39*(6), 913–925. https://doi.org/10.1080/01596306.2017.1312285

Bensimon, E. M. (1989). The meaning of "good presidential leadership": A frame analysis. *Review of Higher Education, 12*(2), 107–123. https://doi.org/10.1353/rhe.1989.0024

Bensimon, E. M. (1993). New presidents' initial actions: Transactional and transformational leadership. *Journal for Higher Education Management, 8*(2), 5–17.

Bensimon, E. M., & Malcom, L. (2012). *Confronting equity issues on campus: Implementing the equity scorecard in theory and practice.* Stylus.

Bensimon, E. M., & Neumann, A. (1993). *Redesigning collegiate leadership.* Johns Hopkins University Press.

Bensimon, E. M., Neumann, A., & Birnbaum, R. (1989). *Making sense of administrative leadership: The "L" word in higher education* (ASHE-ERIC Higher Education Report 1). School of Education, George Washington University.

Bensimon, E. M., Polkinhorne, D. E., Bauman, G. L, & Vallejo, E. (2004). Doing research that makes a difference. *Journal of Higher Education, 75*(1), 104–126.

Bergson, H. (1946). *The creative mind: An introduction to metaphysics.* Wisdom Library.

Bergquist, W. H., & Pawlak, K. (2008). *Engaging the six cultures of the academy.* Wiley.

Berrey, E. (2015). *The enigma of diversity: The language of race and the limits of racial justice.* University of Chicago Press.

Berson, Y., Nemanich, L. A., Waldman, D. A., Galvin, B. M., & Keller, R. T. (2006). Leadership and organizational learning: A multiple levels perspective. *Leadership Quarterly, 17*(6), 577–594. https://doi.org/10.1016/j.leaqua.2006.10.003

Bertrand, M. (2018). Youth participatory action research and possibilities for students of color in educational leadership. *Education Administration Quarterly, 54*(3), 366–395. https://doi.org/10.1177/0013161x18761344

Betts, F. (1992). How systems thinking applies to education. *Educational Leadership, 50*(3), 38–41.

Birnbaum, R. (1988). *How colleges work.* Jossey-Bass.

Birnbaum, R. (1992). *How academic leadership works: Understanding success and failure in the college presidency.* Jossey-Bass.

Blackmore, J. (2010). "The other within": Race/gender disruptions to the professional learning of white educational leaders. *International Journal of Leadership in Education, 13*(1), 45–61. https://doi.org/10.1080/13603120903242931

Blackmore, J. (2014). Gender and the problematics of academic disenchantment and disengagement with leadership. *Higher Education Research & Development, 33*(1), 86–99. https://doi.org/10.1080/07294360.2013.864616

Blackmore, J., Sánchez-Moreno, M., & Sawers, N. (2015). Globalised re/gendering of the academy and leadership. *Gender and Education, 27*(3), iii–vii. https://doi.org/10.1080/09540253.2015.1028738

Blackmore, P., & Kandiko, C. B. (2011). Motivation in academic life: A prestige economy. *Research in Post-Compulsory Education, 16*(4), 399–411. https://doi.org/10.1080/13596748.2011.626971

Blair-Loy, M., Hochschild, A., Pugh, A. J., Williams, J. C., & Hartmann, H. (2015). Stability and transformation in gender, work, and family: Insights from the second shift for the next quarter century. *Community, Work & Family, 18*(4), 435–454. https://doi.org/10.1080/13668803.2015.1080664

Blaisdell, B. (2021). Counternarrative as strategy: Embedding critical race theory to develop an antiracist school identity. *International Journal of Qualitative Studies in Education*, 1–21. https://doi.org/10.1080/09518398.2021.1942299

Bledsoe, C. L., Dowd, A. C., & Ward, L. W. M. (2020). Silence is complicity: Why every college leader should know the history of lynching. *Change: The Magazine of Higher Learning, 52*(2), 22–25. https://doi.org/10.1080/00091383.2020.1732755

Bleiklie, I. (1998). Justifying the evaluative state: New public management ideals in higher education. *European Journal of Education, 33*(3), 299–316. http://www.jstor.org/stable/1503585

Bleiklie, I. (2005). Academic leadership and emerging knowledge regimes. In M. Kogan (Ed.), *Governing knowledge* (pp. 189–211). Springer.

Bodla, M. A., & Nawaz, M. M. (2010). Comparative study of full range leadership model among faculty members in public and private sector higher education institutes and universities. *International Journal of Business and Management, 5*(4), 208–214. http://doi.org/10.5539/ijbm.v5n4p208

Body, D. (2019, March 19). *Worse off than when they enrolled: The consequences of for-profit colleges for people of color.* Aspen Institute, Family Finance. https://www.aspeninstitute.org/blog-posts/worse-off-than-when-they-enrolled-the-consequence-of-for-profit-colleges-for-people-of-color/

Boggs, G. R., & McPhail, C. J. (2016). *Practical leadership in community colleges: Navigating today's challenges.* John Wiley & Sons.

Boggs, G. R., & McPhail, C. J. (Eds.). (2019). *Team leadership in community colleges.* Stylus.

Bok, D. (2003). *Universities in the marketplace: The commercialization of higher education.* Princeton University Press.

Bolden, R., Petrov, G., & Gosling, J. (2009). Distributed leadership in higher education: Rhetoric and reality. *Educational Management Administration & Leadership, 37*(2), 257–277. https://doi.org/10.1177/1741143208100301

Bolman, L. G., & Deal, T. E. (1984). *Modern approaches to understanding and managing organizations.* Jossey-Bass.

Bolman, L. G., & Deal, T. E. (1988). *Leadership orientations.* https://leebolman.com/wp-content/uploads/2021/02/Leadership-Orientations-2012.pdf

Bolman, L. G., & Deal, T. E. (2017). *Reframing organizations: Artistry, choice, and leadership* (6th ed.). Jossey-Bass.

Bondi, S. (2012). Students and institutions protecting whiteness as property: A critical race theory analysis of student affairs preparation. *Journal of Student Affairs Research and Practice, 49*(4), 397–414. https://doi.org/10.1515/jsarp-2012-6381

Bonilla-Silva, E. (2001). *White supremacy and racism in the post-civil rights era.* Lynne Rienner Publishers.

Bonilla-Silva, E. (2006). *Racism without racists: Color-blind racism and the persistence of racial inequality in the United States.* Rowman & Littlefield.

Bordas, J. (2012). *Salsa, soul, and spirit: Leadership for a multicultural age.* Berrett-Koehler.

Bornstein, A. (2008). Women and the college presidency. In J. Glazer-Raymo (Ed.), *Unfinished agendas: New and continuing gender challenges in higher education* (pp. 162–184). Johns Hopkins University Press.

Boske, C. A. (2010). "I wonder if they had ever seen a Black man before?" Grappling with issues of race and racism in our own backyard. *Journal of Research on Leadership Education, 5*(7), 248–275. https://doi.org/10.1177/194277511000500701

Bower, B. L., & Wolverton, M. (2009). *Answering the call: African American women in higher education leadership.* Stylus.

Bowman, N. (2009). Dreamweavers: Tribal College presidents build institutions bridging two worlds. *Tribal College Journal of American Indian Higher Education, 20*(4), 12–18.

Bragg, D., & McCambly, H. (2017). *Using "adaptive equity-minded leadership" to bring about large-scale change.* Bragg & Associates. http://www.dev.sbctc.edu/resources /documents/colleges-staff/programs-services/student-success-center/student -success-resource-center/debra-bragg-equity-minded-leadership-2017.pdf

Bragg, D., & McCambly, H. (2018). *Equity-minded change leadership.* Bragg and Associates. http://www.solano.edu/president/2021/equitymindedchangeleadershi pbraggmccambly.pdf

Branson, C. M. (2009). *Leadership for an age of wisdom.* Springer.

Branson, C. M., Franken, M., & Penney, D. (2016). Middle leadership in higher education. *Educational Management Administration & Leadership, 44*(1), 128–145. https://doi.org/10.1177/1741143214558575

Breslin, R. A., Pandey, S., & Riccucci, N. M. (2017). Intersectionality in public leadership research: A review and future research agenda. *Review of Public Personnel Administration, 37*(2), 160–182. https://doi.org/10.1177/0734371X17697118

Bridgeforth, J. C. (2021). This isn't who we are: A critical discourse analysis of school and district leaders' responses to racial violence. *Journal of School Leadership, 31*(1–2), 85–106. https://doi.org/10.1177/1052684621992760

Briggs, J., & Peat, F. D. (1989). *Turbulent mirror: An illustrated guide to chaos theory and the science of wholeness.* HarperCollins.

Broadhurst, C., Martin, G., Hoffshire, M., & Takewell, W. (2018). "Bumpin' up against people and their beliefs": Narratives of student affairs administrators creating change for LGBTQ students in the South. *Journal of Diversity in Higher Education, 11*(4), 385–401. https://doi.org/10.1037/dhe0000036

Brookfield, S. D. (2005). *The power of critical theory: Liberating adult learning and teaching.* Jossey-Bass.

Brooks, J., Arnold, N., & Brooks, M. (2013). Educational leadership and racism: A narrative inquiry into second-generation segregation. *Teachers College Record, 115*(11), 1–27. https://doi.org/10.1177/016146811311501101

Brown, L., & Strega, S. (Eds.). (2005). *Research as resistance: Critical, Indigenous, and anti-oppressive approaches.* Canadian Scholars Press.

Brown, R. (Ed.). (2011). *Higher education and the market.* Routledge.

Brown, R. N., Carducci, R., & Kuby, C. R. (2014). *Disrupting qualitative inquiry: Possibilities and tensions in education research.* Peter Lang.

Brown, S. (2022, March 29). This university president is focused on performance and productivity. That worries the faculty. *The Chronicle of Higher Education.* https://www.chronicle.com/article/this-university-president-is-focused-on-performance-and-productivity-that-worries-the-faculty

Bryman, A. (2004). Qualitative research on leadership: A critical but appreciative review. *Leadership Quarterly, 15*(6), 729–769. https://doi.org/10.1016/j.leaqua.2004.09.007

Bryman, A. (2007). Effective leadership in higher education: A literature review. *Studies in Higher Education, 32*(6), 693–710. https://doi.org/10.1080/03075070701685114

Bryman, A., Stephens, M., & à Campo, C. (1996). The importance of context: Qualitative research and the study of leadership. *Leadership Quarterly, 7*(3), 353–370. https://doi.org/10.1016/S1048-9843(96)90025-9

Buras, K. (2011). Race, charter schools, and conscious capitalism: On the spatial politics of whiteness as property (and the unconscionable assault on Black New Orleans). *Harvard Educational Review, 81*(2), 296–331. https://doi.org/10.17763/haer.81.2.6l42343qqw360jo3

Burbules, N. C., & Torres, C. A. (Eds.). (2000). *Globalization and education: Critical perspectives.* Routledge.

Burke, L. (2020, September 16). Close to open revolt. *Inside Higher Ed.* https://www.insidehighered.com/news/2020/09/16/unrest-and-strikes-hit-university-michigan

Burkinshaw, P., & White, K. (2017). Fixing the women or fixing the universities: Women in HE leadership. *Administrative Sciences, 7*(30): 1–11. https://doi.org/10.3390/admsci7030030

Burmicky, J. (2021). Leadership implications for aspiring Latinx community college leaders: Firsthand accounts from community college presidents. *Journal of Applied Research in the Community College, 28*(2), 33–47.

Burns, J. M. (1978). *Leadership.* Harper & Row.

Burns, J. S. (2002). Chaos theory and leadership studies: Exploring uncharted seas. *Journal of Leadership & Organizational Studies, 9*(2), 42–56. https://doi.org/10.1177/10717919020090204

Burris, K., Ayman, R., Che, Y., & Min, H. (2013). Asian Americans' and Caucasians' implicit leadership theories: Asian stereotypes, transformational, and authentic leadership. *Asian American Journal of Psychology, 4*(4), 258–266. https://doi.org/10.1037/a0035229

Bushman, M. F., & Dean, J. E. (2005). *Outsourcing of non-mission-critical functions: A solution to the rising cost of college attendance.* https://www.luminafoundation.org/files/publications/collegecosts/bushman_dean.pdf

Byrne, V. L., Higginbotham, B. L., Donlan, A. E., & Stewart, T. J. (2021). An online occupation of the university hashtag: Exploring how student activists use social media to engage in protest. *Journal of College and Character, 22*(1), 13–30. https://doi.org/10.1080/2194587x.2020.1860775

Bystydzienski, J. M., & Schacht, S. P. (2001). *Forging radical alliances across difference: Coalition politics for the new millennium.* Rowman & Littlefield.

Cabrera, N. L. (2019). *White guys on campus: Racism, white immunity, and the myth of post-racial higher education.* Rutgers University Press.

Cabrera, N. L., Matias, C. E., & Montoya, R. (2017). Activism or slacktivism? The potential and pitfalls of social media in contemporary student activism. *Journal of Diversity in Higher Education, 10*(4), 400–415. https://doi.org/10.1037/dhe0000061

Cajete, G. A. (2016). Indigenous education and the development of indigenous community leaders. *Leadership, 12* (3), 364–376. https://doi.org/10.1177/1742715015610412

Cannella, G. S., Pérez, M. S., & Pasque, P. A. (2015). *Critical qualitative inquiry: Foundations and futures.* Left Coast Press.

Cantwell, B. (2015). Laboratory management, academic production, and the building blocks of academic capitalism. *Higher Education, 70*(3), 487–502. https://doi.org/10.1007/s10734-014-9851-9

Cantwell, B. (2016). The new prudent man: Financial-academic capitalism and inequality in higher education. In S. Slaughter & B. Taylor (Eds.), *Higher education, stratification, and workforce development* (pp. 173–192). Springer. https://doi.org/10.1007/978-3-319-21512-9_9

Capper, C. A. (2015). The 20th-year anniversary of critical race theory in education: Implications for leading to eliminate racism. *Educational Administration Quarterly, 51*(5), 791–833. https://doi.org/10.1177/0013161X15607616

Capper, C. A. (2019). *Organizational theory for equity and diversity: Leading integrated, socially just education.* Routledge.

Carducci, R. (2017). Transforming higher education institutions through critical qualitative leadership inquiry. In P. A. Pasque & V. M. Lechuga (Eds.), *Qualitative inquiry in higher education organization and policy research* (pp. 142–158). Routledge.

References

Carli, L. L., & Eagly, A. H. (2016). Women face a labyrinth: An examination of metaphors for women leaders. *Gender in Management: An International Journal, 31*(8), 514–527. https://doi.org/10.1108/GM-02-2015-0007

Carpenter, B. W., & Diem, S. (2013). Talking race: Facilitating critical conversations in educational leadership preparation programs. *Journal of School Leadership, 23*(6), 902–931. https://doi.org/10.1177/105268461302300601

Carr, J., Truesdell, N., Orr, C. M., & Anderson-Levy, L. (2021). Future thinking and freedommaking: Antidiversity as an intervention to the plantation politics of higher education. In B. C. Williams, D. D. Squire, & F. A. Tuitt (Eds.), *Plantation politics and campus rebellions: Power, diversity, and the emancipatory struggle in higher education* (pp. 141–170). State University of New York Press.

Castagno, A. E. (2014). *Educated in whiteness: Good intentions and diversity in schools.* University of Minnesota Press.

Castagno, A. E., & Lee, S. J. (2007). Native mascots and ethnic fraud in higher education: Using tribal critical race theory and the interest convergence principle as an analytic tool. *Equity & Excellence in Education, 40*(1), 3–13. https://doi.org/10.1080/10665680601057288

Catalyst. (2007). *The double-bind dilemma: Damned if you do, damned if you don't.* Retrieved from https://www.catalyst.org/wp-content/uploads/2019/01/The_Double_Bind_Dilemma_for_Women_in_Leadership_Damned_if_You_Do_Doomed_if_You_Dont.pdf

Catalyst. (2016). *Quick take: Women in academia.* https://www.catalyst.org/research/women-in-academia/

Cavaleri, S., & Sterman, J. D. (1997). Towards evaluation of systems-thinking interventions: A case study. *System Dynamics Review, 13*(2), 171–186. https://doi.org/10.1002/(sici)1099-1727(199722)13:2%3C171::aid-sdr123%3E3.0.co;2-9

Caza, A., & Jackson, B. (2011). Authentic leadership. In A. Bryman, D. Collinson, K. Grint, & M. Uhl-Bien (Eds.), *The SAGE handbook of leadership* (pp. 352–364). SAGE.

Chan, C. D., Harrichand, J. J. S., Anandavalli, S., Vaishnav, S., Chang, C. Y., Hyun, J. H., & Band, M. P. (2021). Mapping solidarity, liberation, and activism: A critical autoethnography of Asian American leaders in counseling. *Journal of Mental Health Counseling, 43*(3), 246–265. https://doi.org/10.17744/mehc.43.3.06

Chance, N. L. (2022). Resilient leadership: A phenomenological exploration into how Black women in higher education leadership navigate cultural adversity. *Journal of Humanistic Psychology, 62*(1), 44–78. https://doi.org/10.1177/00221678211003000

Chávez, A. F., & Sanlo, R. (Ed.). (2013). *Identify and leadership: Informing our lives, informing our practice.* NASPA—Student Affairs Administrators in Higher Education.

Chemers, M. M. (1997). *An integrative theory of leadership.* Lawrence Erlbaum Associates.

Chia, R. (2002). Essai: Time, duration and simultaneity: Rethinking process and change in organizational analysis. *Organization Studies*, 23(6), 863–868. https://doi.org/10.1177/0170840602236007

Chin, J. L. (2011). Women and leadership: Transforming visions and current contexts. *Forum on Public Policy Online*, 2011(2), 1–12. https://doi.org/10.1108/lhs.2008.21121aae.001

Chin. J. L., Lott, B., Rice, J., & Sanchez-Hucles, J., (Eds.). (2007). *Women and leadership: Transforming visions and diverse voices*. Wiley-Blackwell.

Clark, B. R. (1972). The organizational saga in higher education. *Administrative Science Quarterly*, 17(2), 178–184. https://doi.org/10.2307/2393952

Clarke, J., & Newman, J. (2004). Governing in the modern world. In D. L. Steinberg & R. Johnson (Eds.), *Blairism and the war of persuasion: Labour's passive revolution* (pp. 53–65). Lawrence and Wishart.

Clarke, K., & Rosenberg, E. (2018, August 6). *Trump administration has Voting Rights Act on life support*. CNN. https://www.cnn.com/2018/08/06/opinions/voting-rights-act-anniversary-long-way-to-go-clarke-rosenberg-opinion/index.html

Clemons, J. (2022). From "Freedom Now!" to "Black Lives Matter": Retrieving King and Randolph to theorize contemporary white antiracism. *Perspectives on Politics*, 1–15. https://doi.org/10.1017/s1537592722001074

Clifton, J. M. (1981). The rice driver: His role in slave management. *South Carolina Historical Magazine*, 82(4), 331–353.

Coates, S. K., Trudgett, M., & Page, S. (2021). Indigenous higher education sector: The evolution of recognized Indigenous leaders within Australian universities. *Australian Journal of Indigenous Education*, 50(2), 215–221. https://doi.org/10.1017/jie.2019.30

Coates, S. K., Trudgett, M., & Page, S. (2022). Islands in the stream: Indigenous academic perceptions of Indigenous senior leadership roles. *Higher Education Research & Development*, 41(5), 1451–1467. https://doi.org/10.1080/07294360.2021.1920894

Cohen, A. M., Brawer, F. B., & Kisker, C. B. (2014). *The American community college* (6th ed.). Jossey-Bass.

Cole, E. R. (2020). *The campus color line: College presidents and the struggle for Black freedom*. Princeton University Press.

Cole, E. R., & Harper, S. R. (2017). Race and rhetoric: An analysis of college presidents' statements on campus racial incidents. *Journal of Diversity in Higher Education*, 10(4), 318–333. https://doi.org/10.1037/dhe0000044

Colfax, R. S., Santos, A. T., & Diego, J. (2009). Virtual leadership: A green possibility in critical times but can it really work? *Journal of International Business Research*, 8(2), 133–139.

Colket, L., Garrett, J. M., & Shaw, M. S. (2021). Transformative storytelling as critical praxis for educational leaders. In K. Pak & S. M. Ravitch (Eds.), *Critical leadership praxis for educational and social change* (pp. 101–115). Teachers College Press.

Collinson, D. (2011). Critical leadership studies. In A. Bryman, D. Collinson, K. Grint, & M. Uhl-Bien (Eds.), *The SAGE handbook of leadership* (pp. 181–194). SAGE.

Combahee River Collective. (1983). The Combahee River Collective statement. In B. Smith (Ed.), *Homegirls: A Black feminist anthology* (pp. 264–274). Kitchen Table, Women of Color Press. (Original work published 1977)

Coon, D. W. (2001). *A study of gay and lesbian leaders* [Unpublished doctoral dissertation]. Seattle University.

Cooper, J. E., & Ideta, L. M. (1994). *Dealing with difference: Maps and metaphors of leadership in higher education* [Paper presentation]. Annual meeting of the Association for the Study of Higher Education, Tucson, AZ.

Cortez, L. J. (2015). Enacting leadership at Hispanic-Serving Institutions. In A.-M. Núñez, S. Hurtado, & E. Calderón Galdeano (Eds.), *Hispanic-Serving Institutions: Advancing research and transformative practice* (pp. 136–152). Routledge.

Cottom, T. M. (2019). *Thick: And other essays.* New Press.

Cox, O. C. (1959). *The foundations of capitalism.* Monthly Review Press.

Crandall, J. R., Espinosa, L. E., & Taylor, M. (2017, April 14). Looking ahead to diversifying the college presidency. *Higher Education Today.* https://www .higheredtoday.org/2017/08/14/looking-ahead-diversifying-college-presidency/

Crawley, A. T. (2016). *Blackpentecostal breath: The aesthetics of possibility.* Fordham University Press.

Crazy Bull, C. (2018). Tribal Colleges and University leaders: Warriors in spirit and action. In R. T. Palmer, D. C. Maramba, A. T. Arroyo, T. O. Allen, T. F. Boykin, & J. M. Lee (Eds.), *Effective leadership at minority-serving institutions: Exploring opportunities and challenges for leadership* (pp. 150–165). Routledge.

Crenshaw, K. (1989). Demarginalizing the intersection of race and sex: A Black feminist critique of antidiscrimination doctrine, feminist theory and antiracist politics. *University of Chicago Legal Forum, 1989,* 139–167.

Crevani, L., Lindgren, M., & Packendorff, J. (2007). Shared leadership: A postheroic perspective on leadership as a collective construction. *International Journal of Leadership Studies, 3*(1), 40–67.

Cronshaw, S. F. (2012). Is organizational leadership structural or processual? *SSRN Electronic Journal.* https://doi.org/10.2139/ssrn.2104127

Croucher, G., & Lacy, W. B. (2020). The emergence of academic capitalism and university neoliberalism: Perspectives of Australian higher education leadership. *Higher Education, 83,* 279–295. https://doi.org/10.1007/s10734-020-00655-7

Culver, K. C., Harper, J., & Kezar, A. (2021). *Design for equity in higher education.* Delphi Project on the Changing Faculty and Student Success. USC Pullias Center for Higher Education. https://pullias.usc.edu/download/design-for-equity-in-higher -education

Cutright, M. (2001). *Chaos theory & higher education: Leadership, planning, & policy* (Higher Education, Vol. 9). Peter Lang Publishing.

Da'as, R., Schechter, C., & Qadach, M. (2018). Switching cognitive gears: School leaders' cognitive complexity. *NASSP Bulletin, 102*(3), 181–203. https://doi.org/10.1177/0192636518794297

Dache, A. (2019). Ferguson's Black radical imagination and the scyborgs of community-student resistance. *Review of Higher Education, 42*(5), 63–84. https://doi.org/10.1353/rhe.2019.0045

Dahlvig, J. E., & Longman, K. A. (2014). Contributions to women's leadership development in Christian higher education: A model and emerging theory. *Journal of Research on Christian Education 23* (1), 1–23. https://doi.org/10.1080/10656219.2014.862196

Dahlvig, J. E., & Longman, K. A. (2021). Women's leadership in higher education. In N. S. Niemi & M. B. Weaver-Hightower (Eds.), *The Wiley Handbook of Gender Equity in Higher Education* (pp. 29–52). Wiley.

Dancy, T. E., Edwards, K. T., & Davis, J. E. (2018). Historically white universities and plantation politics: Anti-Blackness and higher education in the Black Lives Matter era. *Urban Education, 53*(2), 176–195. https://doi.org/10.1177/0042085918754328

Daniels, J. (2021). *Nice white ladies: The truth about white supremacy, our role in it, and how we can help dismantle it.* Seal Press.

Dator, J. A. (Ed.). (2002). *Advancing futures: Future studies in higher education.* Praeger.

Davis, A., Jansen van Rensburg, M., & Venter, P. (2016). The impact of managerialism on the strategy work of university middle managers. *Studies in Higher Education, 41*(8), 1480–1494. https://doi.org/10.1080/03075079.2014.981518

Davis, A. Y. (2010). *Are prisons obsolete?* Seven Stories Press.

Davis, C. H. F., III. (2021). Introduction. In K. R. Roth & Z. S. Ritter (Eds.), *Whiteness, power, and resisting change in US higher education* (pp. 1–7). Palgrave Macmillan. https://doi.org/10.1007/978-3-030-57292-1_1

Davis, D. R., & Maldonado, C. (2015). Shattering the glass ceiling: The leadership development of African American women in higher education. *Advancing Women in Leadership Journal, 35*, 48–64. https://doi.org/10.18738/awl.v35i0.125

Davis, S. (2015). And still we rise: How a Black college survives the economic recession. *Journal of Negro Education, 84*(1), 7–24. https://doi.org/10.7709/jnegroeducation.84.1.0007

Dawson, P. M. (1994). *Organizational change: A processual approach.* Paul Chapman Publishing.

Dawson, P. M. (2019). *Reshaping change: A processual perspective.* Routledge.

Day, D. V., & Antonakis, J. (2012). Leadership: Past, present, and future. In D. V. Day & J. Antonakis (Eds.), *The nature of leadership* (2nd ed., pp. 3–25). SAGE.

Day, D. V., Gronn, P., & Salas, E. (2006). Leadership in team-based organizations: On the threshold of a new era. *Leadership Quarterly, 17*(3), 211–216. https://doi.org/10.1016/j.leaqua.2006.02.001

Dei, G. J. S. (1999). Knowledge and politics of social change: The implication of anti-racism. *British Journal of Sociology of Education, 20*(3), 395–409. https://doi.org/10.1080/01425699995335

Den Hartog, D. N., House, R. J., Hanges, P. J., Ruiz-Quintanilla, S. A., Dorfman, P. W., Abdalla, I. A., . . . Zhou, J. (1999). Culture specific and cross-culturally generalizable implicit leadership theories: Are attributes of charismatic/transformational leadership universally endorsed? *Leadership Quarterly, 10*(2), 219–256. https://doi.org/10.1016/S1048-9843(99)00018-1

DeRue, D. S., & Ashford, S. J. (2010). Who will lead and who will follow? A social process of leadership identity construction in organizations. *Academy of Management Review, 35*(4), 627–647. https://doi.org/10.5465/amr.2010.53503267

DeRue, D. S., Nahrgang, J. D., Wellman, N., & Humphrey, S. E. (2011). Trait and behavioral theories of leadership: An integration and meta-analytic test of their relative validity. *Personnel Psychology, 64*(1), 7–52. https://doi.org/10.1111/j.1744-6570.2010.01201.x

Dickson, M. W., Castaño, N., Magomaeva, A., & Den Hartog, D. N. (2012). Conceptualizing leadership across cultures. *Journal of World Business, 47*(4), 483–492. https://doi.org/10.1016/j.jwb.2012.01.002

Diehl, A. B., & Dzubinski, L. M. (2016). Making the invisible visible: A cross-sector analysis of gender-based leadership barriers. *Human Resource Development Quarterly, 27*(2), 181–206. https://doi.org/10.1002/hrdq.21248

Dimitrov, A. (2018). The digital age leadership: A transhumanistic perspective. *Journal of Leadership Studies, 12*(3), 79–81. https://doi.org/10.1002/jls.21603

Dinh, J. E., & Lord, R. G. (2012). Implications of dispositional and process views of traits for individual difference research in leadership. *Leadership Quarterly, 23*(4), 651–669. https://doi.org/10.1016/j.leaqua.2012.03.003

Dinh, J. E., Lord, R. G., Gardner, W. L., Meuser, J. D., Liden, R. C., & Hu, J. (2014). Leadership theory and research in the new millennium: Current theoretical trends and changing perspectives. *Leadership Quarterly, 25*(1), 36–62. https://doi.org/10.1016/j.leaqua.2013.11.005

D'Innocenzo, L., Mathieu, J. E., & Kukenberger, M. R. (2016). A meta-analysis of different forms of shared leadership–team performance relations. *Journal of Management, 42*(7), 1964–1991. https://doi.org/10.1177/0149206314525205

Do, V. H. T., & Brennan, M. (2015). Complexities of Vietnamese femininities: A resource for rethinking women's university leadership practices. *Gender and Education, 27*(3), 273–287. https://doi.org/10.1080/09540253.2015.1024619

Dodd, S. D., Anderson, A., & Jack, S. (2013). Being in time and the family owned firm. *Scandinavian Journal of Management, 29*(1), 35–47. https://doi.org/10.1016/j.scaman.2012.11.006

Dorfman, P. W., Howell, J. P., Hibino, S., Lee, J. K., Tate, U., & Bautista, A. (1997). Leadership in Western and Asian countries: Commonalities and differences in effective leadership processes across cultures. *Leadership Quarterly, 8*(3), 233–267. https://doi.org/10.1016/S1048-9843(97)90003-5

Dorfman, P. W., Javidan, M., Hanges, P., Dastmalchian, A., & House, R. (2012). GLOBE: A twenty year journey into the intriguing world of culture and leadership. *Journal of World Business, 47*(4), 504–518. https://doi.org/10.1016/j.jwb.2012.01.004

Dougherty, K. J., & Natow, R. S. (2020). Performance-based funding for higher education: How well does neoliberal theory capture neoliberal practice? *Higher Education, 80*, 457–478. https://doi.org/10.1007/s10734-019-00491-4

Dowdy, J. K., & Hamilton, A. (2012). Lessons from a Black woman administrator: "I'm still here." *Negro Educational Review, 62–63*(1–4), 189–212.

Dray, P. (2011). *There is power in a union: The epic story of labor in America.* Anchor Books.

Drescher, G., & Garbers, Y. (2016). Shared leadership and commonality: A policy-capturing study. *Leadership Quarterly, 27*(2), 200–217. https://doi.org/10.1016/j.leaqua.2016.02.002

Drescher, J. (2021, May 30). Nikole Hannah-Jones, a mega-donor, and the future of journalism. *The Assembly.* https://www.theassemblync.com/long-form/nikole-hannah-jones-a-mega-donor-and-the-future-of-journalism/

DuBois, W. E. B. (1935). *Black reconstruction in America: An essay toward a history of the part which Black folk played in the attempt to reconstruct democracy in America, 1860–1880.* Harcourt, Brace.

Dugan, J. P. (2006a). Explorations using the social change model: Leadership development among college men and women. *Journal of College Student Development, 47*(2), 217–225. https://doi.org/10.1353/csd.2006.0015

Dugan, J. P. (2006b). Involvement and leadership: A descriptive analysis of socially responsible leadership. *Journal of College Student Development, 47*(3), 335–343. https://doi.org/10.1353/csd.2006.0028

Dugan, J. P. (2017). *Leadership theory: Cultivating critical perspectives.* John Wiley & Sons.

Dugan, J. P., & Komives, S. R. (2010). Influences on college students' capacities for socially responsible leadership. *Journal of College Student Development, 51*(5), 525–549. https://doi.org/10.1353/csd.2010.0009

Dumas, M. J. (2016). Against the dark: Antiblackness in education policy and discourse. *Theory into Practice, 55*(1), 11–19. https://doi.org/10.1080/00405841.2016.1116852

Dumas, M. J., & ross, k. m. (2016). "Be real Black for me" imagining BlackCrit in education. *Urban Education, 51*(4), 415–442. https://doi.org/10.1177/0042085916628611

Duncan-Andrade, J. M. R., & Morrell, E. (2008). *The art of critical pedagogy: Possibilities for moving from theory to practice in urban schools.* Peter Lang.

Dunphy, D. C., & Stace, D. (1992). *Under new management: Australian organizations in transition.* McGraw-Hill.

Eagly, A. H. (2015). Foreword. In S. R. Madsen, F. W. Ngunjiri, K. A. Longman, & S. Cherrey (Eds.), *Women and leadership around the world* (pp. ix–xiii). Information Age.

Eagly, A. H., & Carli, L. L. (2007). *Through the labyrinth: The truth about how women become leaders.* Harvard Business School Publishing.

Eagly, A. H., & Chin, J. L. (2010). Diversity and leadership in a changing world. *American Psychologist, 65*(3), 216–224. https://doi.org/10.1037/a0018957

Eagly, A. H., & Johannesen-Schmidt, M. M. (2001). The leadership styles of women and men. *Journal of Social Issues, 57*(4), 781–797. https://doi.org/10.1111/0022-4537.00241

Eagly, A. H., & Karau, S. J. (2002). Role congruity theory of prejudice toward female leaders. *Psychological Bulletin, 109*(3), 573–598. https://doi.org/10.1037/0033-295x.109.3.573

Eberly, M. B., Johnson, M. D., Hernandez, M., & Avolio, B. J. (2013). An integrative process model of leadership: Examining loci, mechanisms, and event cycles. *American Psychologist, 68*(6), 427–443. https://doi.org/10.1037/a0032244

Eddy, P. L. (2003). Sensemaking on campus: How community college presidents frame change. *Community College Journal of Research and Practice, 27*(6), 453–471. https://doi.org/10.1080/713838185

Eddy, P. L. (2012). *Community college leadership: A multidimensional model for leading change.* Stylus.

Eddy, P. L. (2018). Expanding the leadership pipeline in community colleges: Fostering racial equity. *Teachers College Record, 129* (14), 1–18. https://doi.org/10.1177/016146811812001404

Eddy, P. L., & Cox, E. M. (2008). Gendered leadership: An organizational perspective. *New Directions for Community Colleges, 2008*(142), 69–79. https://doi.org/10.1002/cc.326

Eddy, P. L., & Khwaja, T. (2019). What happened to re-visioning community college leadership? A 25-year retrospective. *Community College Review, 47*(1), 53–78. https://doi.org/10.1177/0091552118818742

Eddy, P. L., & VanDerLinden, K. E. (2006). Emerging definitions of leadership in higher education: New visions of leadership or same old "hero" leader? *Community College Review, 34*(1), 5–26. https://doi.org/10.1177/0091552106289703

Eddy, P. L., & Ward, K. (2017). Problematizing gender and higher education: Why leaning in isn't enough. In P. L. Eddy, K. Ward, & T. Khwaja (Eds.), *Critical approaches to women and gender in higher education* (pp. 13–39). Palgrave Macmillan.

Eddy, P. L., Ward, K., & Khwaja, T. (Eds.). (2017). *Critical approaches to women and gender in higher education.* Palgrave Macmillan.

Eden, D., & Leviatan, U. (1975). Implicit leadership theory as a determinant of the factor structure underlying supervisory behavior scales. *Journal of Applied Psychology, 60*(6), 736–741. https://doi.org/10.1037/0021-9010.60.6.736

Ellis, C., & Ginsburg, R. (2010). *Cabin, quarter, plantation: Architecture and landscapes of North American slavery.* Yale University Press.

Emery, F., & Thorsrud, E. (1976). *Democracy at work: The report of the Norwegian industrial democracy program.* Springer.

Emira, M., Brewster, S., Duncan, N., & Clifford, A. (2018). What disability? I am a leader! Understanding leadership in HE from a disability perspective. *Educational Management Administration & Leadership, 46*(3), 457–473. https://doi.org/10.1177/1741143216662923

Endres, S., & Weibler, J. (2016). Towards a three-component model of relational social constructionist leadership: A systematic review and critical interpretive synthesis. *International Journal of Management Reviews, 19*(2), 214–236. https://doi.org/10.1111/ijmr.12095

Erdemir, B., Demir, E., Yıldırım Öcal, J., & Kondakci, Y. (2020). Academic mobbing in relation to leadership practices: A new perspective on an old issue. *Educational Forum, 84*(2), 126–139. https://doi.org/10.1080/00131725.2020.1698684

Evatt-Young, D., & Bryson, B. (2021). White higher education leaders on the complexities of whiteness and anti-racist leadership. *JCSCORE, 7*(1), 47–82. https://doi.org/10.15763/issn.2642-2387.2021.7.1.46-82

Ewing, E. L. (2018). *Ghosts in the schoolyard: Racism and school closings on Chicago's South Side.* University of Chicago Press.

Fairhurst, G. T. (2008). Discursive leadership: A communication alternative to leadership psychology. *Management Communication Quarterly, 21*(4), 510–521. https://doi.org/10.1177/0893318907313714

Fairhurst, G. T., & Grant, D. (2010). The social construction of leadership: A sailing guide. *Management Communication Quarterly, 24*(2), 171–210. https://doi.org/10.1177/0893318909359697

Farley, A. N., Leonardi, B., & Donnor, J. K. (2021). Perpetuating inequalities: The role of political distraction in education policy. *Educational Policy, 35*(2), 163–179. https://doi.org/10.1177/0895904820987992

Farmer, B. A., Slater, J. W., & Wright, K. S. (1998). The role of communication in achieving shared vision under new organizational leadership. *Journal of Public Relations Research, 10*(4), 219–235. https://doi.org/10.1207/s1532754xjprr1004_01

Fassinger, R. E., Shullman, S. L., & Stevenson, M. R. (2010). Toward an affirmative lesbian, gay, bisexual, and transgender leadership paradigm. *American Psychologist, 65*(3), 201–215. https://doi.org/10.1037/a0018597

344 *References*

Felix, E. R., Bensimon, E. M., Hanson, D., Gray, J., & Klingsmith, L. (2015). Developing agency for equity-minded change. *New Directions for Community Colleges, 2015*(172), 25–42. https://doi.org/10.1002/cc.20161

Fenwick, T. (2010). Response to Jeffrey McClellan; Complexity theory, leadership, and the traps of utopia. *Complicity: An International Journal of Complexity and Education, 7*(2), 97–100. https://doi.org/10.29173/cmplct8946

Ferguson, T. L., & Davis, C. H. F., III. (2019). Labor, resources, and interest convergence in the organized resistance of Black male student-athletes. In D. L. Morgan & C. H. F. Davis III (Eds.), *Student activism, politics, and campus climate in higher education* (pp. 77–96). Routledge.

Festekjian, A., Tram, S., Murray, C. B., Sy, T., & Huynh, H. P. (2014). I see me the way you see me: The influence of race on interpersonal and intrapersonal leadership perceptions. *Journal of Leadership & Organizational Studies, 21*(1), 102–119. https://doi.org/10.1177/1548051813486522

Feyerherm, A. E. (1994). Leadership in collaboration: A longitudinal study of two interorganizational rule-making groups. *Leadership Quarterly, 5*(3–4), 253–270. https://doi.org/10.1016/1048-9843(94)90016-7

Fiedler, F. (1997). Situational control and a dynamic theory of leadership. In K. Grint (Ed.), *Leadership: Classical, contemporary, and critical approaches* (pp. 126–148). Oxford University Press.

Finkelstein, M., Conley, V., & Schuster, J. (2016). *The faculty factor.* Johns Hopkins Press.

Fisher, J. L., & Koch, J. V. (2004). *The entrepreneurial college president.* Rowman & Littlefield.

Fitzgerald, T. (2006). Walking between two worlds: Indigenous women and educational leadership. *Educational Management Administration & Leadership, 34*(2), 201–213. https://doi.org/10.1177/1741143206062494

Flagg, B. J. (2005). Foreword: Whiteness as metaprivilege. *Washington University Journal of Law & Policy, 18*(1), 1–11.

Flaherty, C. (2020, August 3). Faculty to students: Stay home. *Inside Higher Ed.* https://www.insidehighered.com/news/2020/08/03/unc-chapel-hill-faculty -students-stay-home

Flaherty, C. (2022a, February 9). "The tip of the iceberg." *Inside Higher Ed.* https:// www.insidehighered.com/news/2022/02/09/harvard-accused-ignoring-reports -against-anthropologist

Flaherty, C. (2022b, February 21). "A new low" in attacks on academic freedom. *Inside Higher Ed.* https://www.insidehighered.com/news/2022/02/21/texas-lt-govs -pledge-end-tenure-over-crt-new-low

Forsyth, D. R., & Nye, J. L. (2008). Seeing and being a leader: The perceptual, cognitive, and interpersonal roots of conferred influence. In C. L. Hoyt, G. R.

Goethals, & D. R. Forsyth (Eds.), *Leadership at the crossroads: Vol. 1. Leadership and psychology* (pp. 116–131). Praeger.

Fox, M., & Fine, M. (2015). Leadership in solidarity: Notions of leadership through critical participatory action research with young people and adults. *New Directions for Student Leadership, 2015*(148), 45–58. https://doi.org/10.1002/yd.20152

Francis, H., & Sinclair, J. (2003). A processual analysis of HRM-based change. *Organization; 10*(4), 685–706. https://doi.org/10.1177/13505084030104004

Frankenberg, R. (1993). *The social construction of whiteness: White women, race matters.* Routledge.

Frankenberg, R. (1997). *Displacing whiteness: Essays in social and cultural criticism.* Duke University Press.

Frawley, R. (2014). The impact of leadership on the role and mission of a Christian college. *Journal of Applied Christian Leadership, 8*(2), 34–48.

Freeman, S., Jr., Commodore, F., Gasman, M., & Carter, C. (2016). Leaders wanted! The skills expected and needed for a successful 21st century Historically Black College and University presidency. *Journal of Black Studies, 47*(6), 570–591. https://doi.org/10.1177/0021934716653353

Freeman, S., Jr., & Gasman, M. (2014). The characteristics of Historically Black College and university presidents and their role in grooming the next generation of leaders. *Teachers College Record, 116*(7), 1–34. https://doi.org/10.1177/016146811411600706

Freire, P. (1970). *Pedagogy of the oppressed.* Bloomsbury Academic.

Fries-Britt, S., Kezar, A., Wheaton, M. M., McGuire, D., Kurban, E., & Dizon, J. P. M. (2020). *Leading after a racial crisis: Weaving a campus tapestry of diversity and inclusion.* American Council on Education.

Frye, V., Camacho-Rivera, M., Salas-Ramirez, K., Albritton, T., Deen, D., Sohler, N., Barrick, S., & Nunes, J. (2020). Professionalism: The wrong tool to solve the right problem? *Academic Medicine, 95*(6), 860–863. https://doi.org/10.1097/ACM.0000000000003266

Furedi, F. (2011). Introduction to the marketisation of higher education and the student as consumer. In M. Molesworth, R. Scullion, & E. Nixon (Eds.), *The marketisation of higher education and the student as consumer* (pp. 1–7). Routledge.

Gaffikin, F., & Perry, D. C. (2009). Discourses and strategic visions: The US research university as an institutional manifestation of neoliberalism in a global era. *American Educational Research Journal, 46*(1), 115–144. https://doi.org/10.3102/0002831208322180

Gaggiotti, H., Kostera, M., & Krzyworzeka, P. (2017). More than a method? Organisational ethnography as a way of imagining the social. *Culture and Organization, 23*(5), 325–340. https://doi.org/10.1080/14759551.2016.1203312

Galloway, M. K., & Ishimaru, A. M. (2015). Radical recentering: Equity in educational leadership standards. *Educational Administration Quarterly, 51*(3), 372–408. https://doi.org/10.1177/0013161x15590658

Gans, H. J. (2012). "Whitening" and the changing American racial hierarchy. *Du Bois Review: Social Science Research on Race, 9*(2), 267–279. https://doi.org/10.1017/s1742058x12000288

Garcia, G. A., & Ramirez, J. J. (2018). Institutional agents at a Hispanic Serving Institution: Using social capital to empower students. *Urban Education, 53*(3), 355–381. https://doi.org/10.1177/0042085915623341

Gardiner, R. A. (2015). Telling tales out of school: A relational approach to authentic leadership. *Values and Ethics in Educational Administration, 11*(4), 1–8.

Gardner, W. L., Avolio, B. J., Luthans, F., May, D. R., & Walumbwa, F. (2005). "Can you see the real me?" A self-based model of authentic leader and follower development. *Leadership Quarterly, 16*(3), 343–372. https://doi.org/10.1016/j.leaqua.2005.03.003

Gardner, W. L., Cogliser, C. C., Davis, K. M., & Dickens, M. P. (2011). Authentic leadership: A review of the literature and research agenda. *Leadership Quarterly, 22*(6), 1120–1145. https://doi.org/10.1016/j.leaqua.2011.09.007

Garner, S. (2007). *Whiteness: An introduction.* Routledge.

Gasman, M. (2011). Perceptions of Black college presidents: Sorting through stereotypes and reality to gain a complex picture. *American Educational Research Journal, 48*(4), 836–870. https://doi.org/10.3102/0002831210397176

Gieseke, A. R. (2014). *The relationship between spiritual intelligence, mindfulness, and transformational leadership among public higher education leaders* [Unpublished doctoral dissertation]. Northeastern University.

Gigliotti, R. A. (2019). *Crisis leadership in higher education: Theory and practice.* Rutgers University Press.

Gildersleeve, R. E. (2016). The neoliberal academy of the anthropocene and the retaliation of the lazy academic. *Cultural Studies ↔ Critical Methodologies, 17*(3), 286–293. https://doi.org/10.1177/1532708616669522

Giles, M. S. (2010). Howard Thurman, Black spirituality, and critical race theory in higher education. *Journal of Negro Education, 79*(3), 354–365.

Gill, E., Clark, L., & Logan, A. (2020). Freedom for first downs: Interest convergence and the Missouri Black student boycott. *Journal of Negro Education, 89*(3), 342–359.

Gilmore, R. W. (1993). Public enemies and private intellectuals: Apartheid USA. *Race & Class, 35*(1), 69–78. https://doi.org/10.1177/030639689303500107

Gilmore, R. W. (2022). *Abolition geography: Essays toward liberation.* Verso Books.

Gilmore, S. (Ed.) (2008). *Feminist coalitions: Historical perspectives on second-wave feminism in the United States.* University of Illinois Press.

Gilroy, P. (2000). *Against race: Imagining political culture beyond the color line.* Harvard University Press.

Giroux, H. A. (2002). Neoliberalism, corporate culture, and the promise of higher education: The university as a democratic public sphere. *Harvard Educational Review, 72*(4), 425–464. https://doi.org/10.17763/haer.72.4.0515nr62324n71p1

Giroux, H. A. (2004). Public pedagogy and the politics of neo-liberalism: Making the political more pedagogical. *Policy Futures in Education, 2*(3–4), 494–503. https://doi.org/10.2304/pfie.2004.2.3.5

Giroux, H. A. (2014). *Neoliberalism's war on higher education.* Haymarket Books.

Giroux, H. A. (2015). *University in chains: Confronting the military-industrial-academic complex.* Routledge.

Gleick, J. (1987). *Chaos: Making a new science.* Penguin Books.

Gluckman, N. (2019, July 19). University of South Carolina Trustees vote for governor's pick for president. *The Chronicle of Higher Education.* https://www.chronicle.com/article/university-of-south-carolina-trustees-vote-for-governors-pick-for-president/

Gmelch, W. H., & Wolverton, M. (2002). *College deans: Leading from within.* Rowman & Littlefield.

Gonzales, L. D., Kanhai, D., & Hall, K. (2018). Reimagining organizational theory for the critical study of higher education. In M. B. Paulsen (Ed.), *Higher education: Handbook of theory and research* (Vol. 33, pp. 505–559). Springer.

Gonzales, L. D., Martinez, E., & Ordu, C. (2014). Exploring faculty experiences in a striving university through the lens of academic capitalism. *Studies in Higher Education, 39*(7), 1097–1115. https://doi.org/10.1080/03075079.2013.777401

Gonzales, L. D., & Rincones, R. (2013). Using participatory action research and photo methods to explore higher education administration as an emotional endeavor. *The Qualitative Report, 18*, 1–17. https://doi.org/10.46743/2160-3715/2013.1481

Gooden, M. A. (2012). What does racism have to do with leadership? Countering the idea of color-blind leadership: A reflection on race and the growing pressures of the urban principalship. *Educational Foundations, 26*(1–2), 67–84.

Gooden, M. A., & Dantley, M. (2012). Centering race in a framework for leadership preparation. *Journal of Research on Leadership Education, 7*(2), 237–253. https://doi.org/10.1177/1942775112455266

Gordon, A. F. (1997). *Ghostly matters: Haunting and the sociological imagination.* University of Minnesota Press.

Gordon, R. (2011). Leadership and power. In A. Bryman, D. Collinson, K. Grint, B. Jackson, & M. Uhl-Bien (Eds.), *The SAGE handbook of leadership* (pp. 195–202). SAGE.

Gray, M., Chambers, E., Southern, S., & Walton, M. (2021, March). Toward a framework for abolitionist leadership: Understanding the relationship between abolitionism and educational leadership. Paper presented at the meeting of the California Association of Professors of Educational Administration, Hayward, CA.

348   *References*

Green, E. L. (2019, June 28). DeVos repeals Obama-era rule cracking down on for-profit colleges. *New York Times.* https://www.nytimes.com/2019/06/28/us/politics/betsy-devos-for-profit-colleges.html

Greenleaf, R. K. (1998). *The power of servant-leadership.* Berrett-Koehler Publishers.

Griesbach, D., & Grand, S. (2013). Managing as transcending: An ethnography. *Scandinavian Journal of Management, 29*(1), 63–77. https://doi.org/10.1016/j.scaman.2012.11.004

Griffin, D. R. (1986). Introduction: Time and the fallacy of misplaced concreteness. In D. R. Griffin (Ed.), *Physics and the ultimate significance of time: Bohm, Prigogine, and process philosophy* (pp. 1–48). State University of New York Press.

Griffin, K. A., Hart, J. L., Worthington, R. L., Belay, K., & Yeung, J. G. (2019). Race-related activism: How do higher education diversity professionals respond? *Review of Higher Education, 43*(2), 667–696. https://doi.org/10.1353/rhe.2019.0114

Grint, K. (Ed.). (1997). *Leadership: Classical, contemporary, and critical approaches.* Oxford University Press.

Gronn, P. (2002). Distributed leadership as a unit of analysis. *Leadership Quarterly, 13*(4), 423–451. https://doi.org/10.1016/s1048-9843(02)00120-0

Grummell, B., Devine, D., & Lynch, K. (2009). The care-less manager: Gender, care and new managerialism in higher education. *Gender and Education, 21*(2), 191–208. https://doi.org/10.1080/09540250802392273

Guajardo, M. A., Guajardo, F., Salinas, C., & Cardoza, L. (2019). Re-membering, re-framing, and re-imagining Latino leadership in education: Reflections on community, higher learning, and higher education. *Journal of Hispanic Higher Education, 18*(2), 141–164. https://doi.org/10.1177/1538192718810433

Guba, E. G., & Lincoln, Y. S. (2005). Paradigmatic controversies, contradictions, and emerging confluences. In N. K. Denzin & Y. S. Lincoln (Eds.), *The SAGE handbook of qualitative research* (3rd ed., pp. 191–215). SAGE.

Gündemir, S., Carton, A. M., & Homan, A. C. (2019). The impact of organizational performance on the emergence of Asian American leaders. *Journal of Applied Psychology, 104*(1), 107–122. https://doi.org/10.1037/apl0000347

Gunnlaugson, O. (2011). Advancing a second-person contemplative approach for collective wisdom and leadership development. *Journal of Transformative Education, 9*(1), 3–20. https://doi.org/10.1177/1541344610397034

Guthey, E., & Jackson, B. (2011). Cross-cultural leadership revisited. In A. Bryman, D. Collinson, K. Grint, B. Jackson, & M. Uhl-Bien (Eds.), *The SAGE handbook of leadership* (pp. 165–178). SAGE.

Gutierrez, M., Castañeda, C., & Katsinas, S. G. (2002). Latino leadership in community colleges: Issues and challenges. *Community College Journal of Research and Practice, 26*(4), 297–314. https://doi.org/10.1080/10668920275354 6457

Gyllenhammer, P. (1977). How Volvo adapts to people. *Harvard Business Review,* 102.

Haar, J., Roche, M., & Brougham, D. (2019). Indigenous insights into ethical leadership: A study of Maori leaders. *Journal of Business Ethics, 160*, 621–640. https://doi.org/10.1007/s10551-018-3869-3

Hale, C. R. (2008). *Engaging contradictions: Theory, politics, and methods of activist scholarship.* University of California Press.

Hall, E. (1990). *Understanding cultural differences.* Intercultural Press.

Hambley, L. A., O'Neill, T. A., & Kline, T. J. B. (2007). Virtual team leadership: The effects of leadership style and communication medium on team interaction styles and outcomes. *Organizational Behavior and Human Decision Processes, 103*(1), 1–20. https://doi.org/10.1016/j.obhdp.2006.09.004

Handy, C. (1999). *Understanding organizations.* Penguin Books.

Harper, J. (2020, September 28). *It's Time for Campus Search Committees to Reconsider Their Hiring Practices.* AAC&U. https://www.aacu.org/liberaleducation/articles/its-time-for-campus-search-committees-to-reconsider-their-hiring-practices

Harper, J., & Kezar, A. (2021). *Leadership for liberation: A leadership framework & guide for student affairs professionals.* USC Pullias Center for Higher Education. https://pullias.usc.edu/download/leadership-for-liberation/

Harper, S. R. (2009). Race, interest convergence, and transfer outcomes for black male student athletes. *New Directions for Community Colleges, 2009*(147), 29–37. https://doi.org/10.1002/cc.375

Harper, S. R., Patton, L. D., & Wooden, O. S. (2009). Access and equity for African American students in higher education: A critical race historical analysis of policy efforts. *Journal of Higher Education, 80*(4), 389–414. https://doi.org/10.1080/00221546.2009.11779022

Harris, A. (2021, May 7). The GOP's "critical race theory" obsession. *The Atlantic.* https://www.theatlantic.com/politics/archive/2021/05/gops-critical-race-theory-fixation-explained/618828/

Harris, A. (2009). Distributed leadership: What we know. In A. Harris (Ed.), *Distributed leadership: Different perspectives* (pp. 11–21). Springer.

Harris, C. I. (1993). Whiteness as property. *Harvard Law Review, 106*(8), 1707–1791. https://doi.org/10.2307/1341787

Harris, C. I. (2020). Reflections on whiteness as property. *Harvard Law Review Forum, 134*(1), 1–10.

Harris, J. C. (2019). Whiteness as structuring property: Multiracial women students' social interactions at a historically white institution. *Review of Higher Education, 42*(3),1023–1050. https://doi.org/10.1353/rhe.2019.0028

Harris, M. (2010). Interdisciplinary strategy and collaboration: A case study of American research universities. *Journal of Research Administration, 41*(1), 22–34.

Harrison, L. M. (2011). Transformational leadership, integrity, and power. *New Directions for Student Services, 2011*(135), 45–52. https://doi.org/10.1002/ss.403

350   *References*

Hart, J. (2008). Mobilization among women academics: The interplay between feminism and professionalization. *NWSA Journal, 20*(1), 184–208.

Hartley, D. (2010). Paradigms: How far does research in distributed leadership "stretch"? *Educational Management Administration & Leadership, 38*(3), 271–285. https://doi.org/10.1177/1741143209359716

Hartman, S. V. (2008). *Lose your mother: A journey along the Atlantic Slave Route.* Farrar, Straus and Giroux.

Hartman, S. V., & Wilderson, F. B. (2003). The position of the unthought. *Qui Parle, 13*(2), 183–201. https://doi.org/10.1215/quiparle.13.2.183

Hartocollis, A., & Bidgood, J. (2015, November 11). Racial discrimination protests ignite at colleges across the U.S. *New York Times.* https://www.nytimes.com/2015/11/12/us/racial-discrimination-protests-ignite-at-colleges-across-the-us.html

Harvey, D. (2007). *A brief history of neoliberalism.* Oxford University Press.

Harvey, R. S. (2021). *Abolitionist leadership in schools: Undoing systemic injustice through communally conscious education.* Routledge.

Hass, M. (2020, April 29). Shared governance is a strength during COVID-19 crisis. *Inside Higher Ed.* https://www.insidehighered.com/views/2020/04/29/colleges-healthy-shared-governance-perform-better-crises-those-top-down-decision

Hechanova, G., & Cementina-Olpoc, R. (2013). Transformational leadership, change management, and commitment to change: A comparison of academic and business organizations. *Asia-Pacific Education Researcher, 22*(1), 11–19. https://doi.org/10.1007/s40299-012-0019-z

Heifetz, R. A. (1994). *Leadership without easy answers.* Harvard University Press.

Heifetz, R. A., & Linsky, M. (2002). *Leadership on the line: Staying alive through the dangers of change.* Harvard University Press.

Heilman, M. E. (2012). Gender stereotypes and workplace bias. *Research in Organizational Behavior, 32*, 133–135. https://doi.org/10.1016/j.riob.2012.11.003

Helgesen, S., & Johnson, J. (2010). *The female vision.* Berrett-Koehler.

Hendrickson, R. M., Lane, J. E., Harris, J. T., & Dorman, R. H. (2013). *Academic leadership and governance of higher education: A guide for trustees, leaders, and aspiring leaders of two- and four-year institutions.* Stylus.

Henningsen, L., Eagly, A. H., & Jonas, K. (2022). Where are the women deans? The importance of gender bias and self-selection processes for the deanship ambition of female and male professors. *Journal of Applied Social Psychology, 52*(8), 602–622. https://doi.org/10.1111/jasp.12780

Heron, J., & Reason, P. (1997). A participatory inquiry paradigm. *Qualitative Inquiry, 3*(3), 274–294. https://doi.org/10.1177/107780049700300302

Herrera, R., Duncan, P. A., Green, M. T., & Skaggs, S. L. (2012). The effect of gender on leadership and culture. *Global Business and Organizational Excellence, 31*(2), 37–48. https://doi.org/10.1002/joe.21413

Hesburgh, T. M. (1994). *The challenge and promise of a Catholic university*. University of Notre Dame Press.

Hewlett, S. A. (2014). *Executive presence: The missing link between merit and success*. HarperCollins.

Higher Ed Workforce Trends. (n.d.). CUPA-HR. https://www.cupahr.org/surveys /workforce-data/changes-in-workforce-size/

Hill, P. (1971). *Towards a new philosophy of management*. Gower Press.

Hoch, J. E., Bommer, W. H., Dulebohn, J. H., & Wu, D. (2018). Do ethical, authentic, and servant leadership explain variance above and beyond transformational leadership? A meta-analysis. *Journal of Management, 44*(2), 501–529. https://doi .org/10.1177/0149206316665461

Hofstede, G. (1994). The business of international business is culture. *International Business Review, 3*(1), 1–14. https://doi.org/10.1016/0969-5931(94)90011-6

Hofstede, G., Hofstede, G. J., & Minkov, M. (2010). *Cultures and organizations: Intercultural cooperation and its importance for survival*. McGraw-Hill.

Holcombe, E., Kezar, A. J., Elrod, S. L., & Ramaley, J. A. (Eds.) (2021). *Shared leadership in higher education: A framework and models for responding to a changing world*. Stylus.

Hollander, E. P. (1995). Ethical challenges in the leader-follower relationship. *Business Ethics Quarterly, 5*(1), 55–65. https://doi.org/10.2307/3857272

Holten, A. L., Bøllingtoft, A., Carneiro, I. G., & Borg, V. (2018). A within-country study of leadership perceptions and outcomes across native and immigrant employees: Questioning the universality of transformational leadership. *Journal of Management and Organization, 24*(1), 145–162. https://doi.org/10.1017/jmo.2017.2

hooks, b. (1990). *Talking back: Thinking feminist, thinking black*. South End Press.

hooks, b. (1994). *Teaching to transgress: Education as the practice of freedom*. Routledge.

hooks, b. (2009). *Teaching critical thinking: Practical wisdom*. Routledge.

hooks, b. (2013, October 28). Dig deep: Beyond lean in. *The Feminist Wire*. Retrieved from https://thefeministwire.com/2013/10/17973/

Horila, T., & Siitonen, M. (2020). A time to lead: Changes in relational team leadership processes over time. *Management Communication Quarterly, 34*(4), 558–584. https://doi.org/10.1177/0893318920949700

House, R. J., Hanges, P. J., Javidan, M., Dorfman, P. W., & Gupta, V. (Eds.). (2004). *Culture, leadership, and organizations: The GLOBE study of 62 societies*. SAGE.

Hughes, B. E. (2018). Resilience of grassroots leaders involved in LGBT issues at a Catholic University. *Journal of Student Affairs Research and Practice, 55*(2), 123–136. https://doi.org/10.1080/19496591.2017.1366330

Hurley-Hanson, A. E., & Giannantonio, C. M. (2017). LMX and autism: Effective working relationships. In T. A. Scandura & E. Mouriño (Eds.), *Leading diversity in the 21st century* (pp. 281–302). Information Age Publishing.

References

Hypolite, L. I., & Stewart, A. M. (2019). A critical discourse analysis of institutional responses to the 2016 U.S. presidential election. *Journal of Diversity in Higher Education, 14*(1), 1–11. https://doi.org/10.1037/dhe0000158

Ibarra, H., Ely, R. J., & Kolb, D. M. (2013). Women rising: The unseen barriers. *Harvard Business Review, 91*(9), 60–66.

Intezari, A., Spiller, C., & Yang, S. (2021). *Practical wisdom, leadership and culture: Indigenous, Asian, and Middle-Eastern perspectives.* Routledge.

Irwin, L. N. (2021). Student affairs leadership educators' negotiations of racialized legitimacy. *Journal of Leadership Education, 20*(4), 133–153. https://doi.org/10.12806/v20/i4/r10

Irwin, L. N., & Foste, Z. (2021). Service-learning and racial capitalism: On the commodification of people of color for white advancement. *Review of Higher Education, 44*(4), 419–446. https://doi.org/10.1353/rhe.2021.0008

Ison, R. (1999). Applying systems thinking to higher education. *Systems Research and Behavioral Science, 16*(2), 107–112. https://doi.org/10.1002/(sici)1099-1743(199903/04)16:2%3C107::aid-sres278%3E3.0.co;2-e

Izadi, E. (2015, November 9). The incidents that led to the University of Missouri president's resignation. *Washington Post.* https://www.washingtonpost.com/news/grade-point/wp/2015/11/09/the-incidents-that-led-to-the-university-of-missouri-presidents-resignation/

Jackson, M. C. (1991). The origins and nature of critical systems thinking. *Systems Practice, 4*(2), 131–149. https://doi.org/10.1007/bf01068246

Jackson, M. C. (2016). *Systems thinking: Creative holism for managers.* John Wiley & Sons.

Jackson, M. C. (2019). *Critical systems thinking and the management of complexity.* John Wiley & Sons.

Jacobs, C. E., & Clonan-Roy, K. (2021). Developing education organizations with gender and queer inclusive cultures. In K. Pak & S. Ravitch (Eds.), *Critical leadership praxis for educational and social change* (pp. 137–150). Teachers College Press.

Jakubik, M. (2021). Searching for practical wisdom in higher education with logos, pathos, and ethos. Case: Finnish Universities of Sciences. *Philosophies, 6*(3), Article 63. https://doi.org/10.3390/philosophies6030063

James, E. A., Milenkiewicz, M. T., & Bucknam, A. (2008). *Participatory action research for educational leadership: Using data-driven decision making.* SAGE.

Jameson, J. (2019). Critical leadership thinking for global challenges. In. J. Jameson (Ed.), *International perspectives on leadership in higher education: Critical thinking for global challenges* (pp. 166–172). Taylor & Francis.

Janfada, M., & Beckett, D. G. (2019). Leading the self, cultivating wisdom: A neo-Aristotelian perspective on experiential learning. *International Journal of Leadership in Education, 22*(3), 335–346. https://doi.org/10.1080/13603124.2018.1481531

Jaschik, S. (2012, June 25). Purdue faculty debate selection of governor as president. *Inside Higher Ed.* https://www.insidehighered.com/quicktakes/2012/06/25/purdue-faculty-debate-selection-governor-president

Jerolmack, C., & Khan, S. R. (Eds.). (2017). *Approaches to ethnography: Analysis and representation in participant observation.* Oxford University Press.

Jessop, B. (2017). Varieties of academic capitalism and entrepreneurial universities: On past research and three thought experiments. *Higher Education, 73,* 853–870. https://doi.org/10.1007/s10734-017-0120-6

Johns, G. (2006). The essential impact of context on organizational behavior. *Academy of Management Review, 31*(2), 386–408. https://doi.org/10.5465/amr.2006.20208687

Johnson, H. H. (2008). Mental models and transformative learning: The key to leadership development? *Human Resource Development Quarterly, 19*(1), 85–89. https://doi.org/10.1002/hrdq.1227

Johnson, H. L. (2017). *Pipelines, pathways, and institutional leadership: An update on the status of women in higher education.* Higher Ed Spotlight Infographic Brief. http://www.acenet.edu/news-room/Documents/HES-Pipelines-Pathways-and-Institutional-Leadership-2017.pdf

Johnson, N. N., & Fournillier, J. B. (2022). Increasing diversity in leadership: Perspectives of four Black women educational leaders in the context of the United States. *Journal of Educational Administration and History, 54*(2), 174–192. https://doi.org/10.1080/00220620.2021.1985976

Jones, S. (2014). Distributed leadership: A critical analysis. *Leadership, 10*(2), 129–141. https://doi.org/10.1177/1742715011433525

Jones, S., Harvey, M., Hamilton, J., Bevacqua, J., Egea, K., & McKenzie, J. (2017). Demonstrating the impact of a distributed leadership approach in higher education. *Journal of Higher Education Policy and Management, 39*(2), 197–211. https://doi.org/10.1080/1360080x.2017.1276567

Jones, S. R., Torres, V., & Arminio, J. (2022). *Negotiating the complexities of qualitative research in higher education: Fundamental elements and issues* (3rd ed.). Routledge.

Jongbloed, B., Enders, J., & Salerno, C. (2008). Higher education and its communities: Interconnections, interdependencies and a research agenda. *Higher Education, 56*(3), 303–324. https://doi.org/10.1007/s10734-008-9128-2

Jordan, G., Miglič, G., Todorović, I., & Marič, M. (2017). Psychological empowerment, job satisfaction and organizational commitment among lecturers in higher education: Comparison of six CEE countries. *Organizacija, 50*(1), 17–32. https://doi.org/10.1515/orga-2017-0004

Joseph, M. (2015). Investing in the cruel entrepreneurial university. *South Atlantic Quarterly, 114*(3), 491–511.

Joslyn, E. (2018). Distributed leadership in H.E: A scaffold for cultural cloning and implications for BME academic leaders. *Management in Education, 32*(4), 185–191. https://doi.org/10.1177/0892020618798670

Jourian, T. J., & Simmons, S. L. (2017). Trans* leadership. *New Directions for Student Leadership, 2017*(154), 59–69. https://doi.org/10.1002/yd.20240

Judge, T. A., & Piccolo, R. F. (2004). Transformational and transactional leadership: A meta-analytic test of their relative validity. *Journal of Applied Psychology, 89*(5), 755–768. https://doi.org/10.1037/0021-9010.89.5.755

Julien, M., Wright, B., & Zinni, D. M. (2010). Stories from the circle: Leadership lessons learned from aboriginal leaders. *Leadership Quarterly, 21*(1), 114–126. https://doi.org/10.1016/j.leaqua.2009.10.009

Junker, N. M., & van Dick, R. (2014). Implicit theories in organizational settings: A systematic review and research agenda of implicit leadership and followership theories. *Leadership Quarterly, 25*(6), 1154–1173. https://doi.org/10.1016/j.leaqua.2014.09.002

Jyoti, J., & Bhau, S. (2015). Transformational leadership and job performance: A study of higher education. *Journal of Services Research, 15*(2), 77–110.

Kark, R., & Shamir, B. (2013). The dual effect of transformational leadership: Priming relational and collective selves and further effects on followers. In B. J. Avolio & F. J. Yammarino (Eds.), *Transformational and charismatic leadership: The road ahead* (10th anniversary ed., pp. 77–101). Emerald.

Kauppinen, I. (2015). Towards a theory of transnational academic capitalism. *British Journal of Sociology of Education, 36*(2), 336–353. https://doi.org/10.1080/01425692.2013.823833

Kawahara, D. M., Pal, M. S., & Chin, J. L. (2013). The leadership experiences of Asian Americans. *Asian American Journal of Psychology, 4*(4), 240–248. https://doi.org/10.1037/a0035196

Kekale, J. (2001). *Academic leadership.* Nova Science Publishers.

Kelchen, R., Ritter, D., & Webber, D. A. (2021). *The lingering fiscal effects of the COVID-19 pandemic on higher education.* Federal Reserve Bank of Philadelphia.

Kellerman, B., & Rhode, D. L. (Eds.). (2007). *Women and leadership: The state of play and strategies for change.* Jossey-Bass.

Kellerman, B., & Rhode, D. L. (2014). Women at the top: the pipeline reconsidered. In K. A. Longman & S. R. Madsen (Eds.), *Women and leadership in higher education* (pp. 24–39). Information Age.

Kendi, I. X. (2019). *How to be an antiracist.* Random House.

Kennedy, A., McGowan, K., & El-Hussein, M. (2023). Indigenous elders' wisdom and dominionization in higher education: Barriers and facilitators to decolonisation and reconciliation. *International Journal of Inclusive Education, 27*(1), 89–106. https://doi.org/10.1080/13603116.2020.1829108

Keohane, N. O. (2014). Leadership out front and behind the scenes: Young women's ambitions for leadership today. In K. A. Longman & S. R. Madsen (Eds.), *Women and leadership in higher education* (pp. 41–55). Information Age.

Kernbach, S. (2018). *Storytelling canvas: A visual framework for developing and delivering resonating stories* [Paper presentation]. 22nd International Conference Information Visualisation.

Keung, E. K., & Rockinson-Szapkiw, A. J. (2013). The relationship between transformational leadership and cultural intelligence: A study of international school leaders. *Journal of Educational Administration, 51*(6), 836–854. https://doi.org/10.1108/JEA-04-2012-0049

Kezar, A. (1998). Trying transformations: Implementing team-oriented forms of leadership. *New Directions for Institutional Research, 1998*(100), 57–72. https://doi.org/10.1002/ir.10005

Kezar, A. (2000). Pluralistic leadership: Incorporating diverse voices. *Journal of Higher Education, 71*(6), 722–743. https://doi.org/10.2307/2649160

Kezar, A. (2001). Investigating organizational fit in a participatory leadership environment. *Journal of Higher Education Policy and Management, 23*(1), 85–101. https://doi.org/10.1080/13600800020047261

Kezar, A. (2002). Expanding notions of leadership to capture pluralistic voices: Positionality theory in practice. *Journal of College Student Development, 43*(4), 558–578.

Kezar, A. (2004). *Promoting student success: The importance of shared leadership and collaboration* (Occasional Paper No. 4). National Survey of Student Engagement.

Kezar, A. (2005). Redesigning for collaboration within higher education institutions: An exploration into the developmental process. *Research in Higher Education, 46*(7), 831–860. https://doi.org/10.1007/s11162-004-6227-5

Kezar, A. (2012a). Bottom-up/top-down leadership: Contradiction or hidden phenomenon. *Journal of Higher Education, 83*(5), 725–760. https://doi.org/10.1353/jhe.2012.0030

Kezar, A. (2012b). *Embracing non-tenure track faculty: Changing campuses for the new faculty majority.* Routledge.

Kezar, A. (2014). Women's contributions to higher education leadership and the road ahead. In K. A. Longman & S. R. Madsen (Eds.), *Women and leadership in higher education* (pp. 117–134). Information Age.

Kezar, A. (2018). *How colleges change: Understanding, leading, and enacting change.* Routledge.

Kezar, A., Acuña Avilez, A., Drivalas, Y., & Wheaton, M. M. (2017). Building social change oriented leadership capacity among student organizations: Developing students and campuses simultaneously. *New Directions for Student Leadership, 2017*(155), 45–57. https://doi.org/10.1002/yd.20249

Kezar, A., Carducci, R., & Contreras-McGavin, M. (2006). *Rethinking the "L" word in higher education: The revolution of research on leadership* (ASHE Higher Education Report, Vol. 31, No. 6). Wiley.

Kezar, A., & Dee, J. R. (2011). Conducting multi-paradigm inquiry in the study of higher education organization and governance: Transforming research perspectives on colleges and universities. In J. Smart & M. Paulsen (Eds.), *Higher education: Handbook of theory and research* (Vol. 26, pp. 265–315). Springer.

Kezar, A., DePaola, T., & Scott, D. T. (2019). *The gig academy: Mapping labor in the neoliberal university*. Johns Hopkins University Press.

Kezar, A., & Eckel, P. (2008). Advancing diversity agendas on campus: Examining transactional and transformational presidential leadership styles. *International Journal of Leadership in Education, 11*(4), 379–405. https://doi.org/10.1080 /13603120802317891

Kezar, A., Eckel, P., Contreras-McGavin, M., & Quaye, S. J. (2008). Creating a web of support: An important leadership strategy for advancing campus diversity. *Higher Education, 55*(1), 69–92. https://doi.org/10.1007/s10734-007-9068-2

Kezar, A., & Fries-Britt, S. (2018). *Speaking truth and acting with integrity: Confronting challenges of campus racial climate*. American Council on Education. https://www .acenet.edu/Documents/Speaking-Truth-and-Acting-with-Integrity.pdf

Kezar, A., Gallant, T. B., & Lester, J. (2011). Everyday people making a difference on college campuses: The tempered grassroots leadership strategies of faculty and staff. *Studies in Higher Education, 36*(2), 129–151. https://doi.org/10.1080 /03075070903532304

Kezar, A., Glenn, W. J., Lester, J., & Nakamoto, J. (2008). Examining organizational contextual features that affect implementation of equity initiatives. *Journal of Higher Education, 79*(2), 125–159.

Kezar, A., & Holcombe, E. (2017). *Shared leadership in higher education: Important lessons from research and practice*. American Council on Education.

Kezar, A., Holcombe, E., Vigil, D., & Dizon, J. P. M. (2021). *Shared equity leadership: Making equity everyone's work*. American Council on Education; University of Southern California, Pullias Center for Higher Education.

Kezar, A., & Lester, J. (2009). Supporting faculty grassroots leadership. *Research in Higher Education, 50*(7), 715–740. https://doi.org/10.1007/s11162-009-9139-6

Kezar, A., & Lester, J. (2010). Breaking the barriers of essentialism in leadership research: Positionality as a promising approach. *Feminist Formations, 22*(1), 163–185. https://doi.org/10.1353/nwsa.0.0121

Kezar, A., & Lester, J. (2011). *Enhancing campus capacity for leadership: An examination of grassroots leaders in higher education*. Stanford University Press.

Kezar, A., & Maxey, D. (2014). Faculty matter: So why doesn't everyone think so? *Thought & Action, 2014,* 29–44.

Kezar, A., & Moriarty, D. (2000). Expanding our understanding of student leadership development: A study exploring gender and ethnic identity. *Journal of College Student Development, 41,* 55–68.

Kezar, A., & Posselt, J. (2020). Introduction: A call to just and equitable administrative practice. In A. Kezar & J. Posselt (Eds.), *Higher education administration for social justice and equity: Critical perspectives for leadership* (pp. 1–18). Routledge.

Khwaja, T. (2017). Finding their own voice: Women's leadership rhetoric. In P. L. Eddy, K. Ward, & T. Khwaja (Eds.), *Critical approaches to women and gender in higher education* (pp. 41–59). Palgrave Macmillan.

Killian, J. (2021, June 3). *UNC mega-donor Walter Hussman denies exerting pressure over Hannah-Jones hiring*. NC Policy Watch. https://ncpolicywatch.com/2021/06/03/unc -mega-donor-walter-hussman-denies-exerting-pressure-over-hannah-jones-hiring/

Kincheloe, J. L., & McLaren, P. (2005). Rethinking critical theory and qualitative research. In N. K. Denzin & Y. S. Lincoln (Eds.), *The SAGE handbook of qualitative research* (3rd ed., pp. 303–342). SAGE.

Kincheloe, J. L., McLaren, P., & Steinberg, S. R. (2012). Critical pedagogy and qualitative research: Moving to the bricolage. In S. R. Steinberg & G. S. Cannella (Eds.), *Critical qualitative research reader* (pp. 14–32). Peter Lang.

King, J. E., & Gomez, G. G. (2008). *On the pathway to the presidency: Characteristics of higher education's senior leadership*. American Council on Education. https:// immagic.com/eLibrary/ARCHIVES/GENERAL/ACE_US/A080130K.pdf

King, T. L., Navarro, J., & Smith, A. (2020). Beyond incommensurability: Toward an otherwise stance on Black and Indigenous relationality. In T. L. King, J. Navarro, & A. Smith (Eds.), *Otherwise worlds: Against settler colonialism and anti-Blackness* (pp. 1–23). Duke University Press.

Kingkade, T. (2015, November 10). *The incident you have to see to understand why students wanted Mizzou's president to go*. HuffPost. https://www.huffpost.com /entry/tim-wolfe-homecoming-parade_n_56402cc8e4b0307f2cadea10

Klenke, K., Martin, S., & Wallace, J. R. (2016). *Qualitative research in the study of leadership* (2nd ed.). Emerald.

Koenig, A. M., Eagly, A. H., Mitchell, A. A., & Ristikari, T. (2011). Are leader stereotypes masculine? A meta-analysis of three research paradigms. *Psychological Bulletin, 137*(4), 616–642. https://doi.org/10.1037/a0023557

Koivunen, N. (2007). The processual nature of leadership discourses. *Scandinavian Journal of Management, 23*(3), 285–305. https://doi.org/10.1016/j.scaman.2007.05 .006

Komives, S. R. (1991). Gender differences in the relationship of hall directors' transformational and transactional leadership and achieving styles. *Journal of College Student Development, 32*(2), 155–165.

Komives, S. R., Lucas, N., & McMahon, T. R. (1998). *Exploring leadership: for college students who want to make a difference*. Jossey-Bass.

Koopmans, M., & Stamovlasis, D. (Eds.). (2016). *Complex dynamical systems in education: Concepts, methods and applications*. Springer.

References

Kortegast, C., McCann, K. Branch, K., Latz, A. O., Turner Kelly, B., & Linder, C. (2019). Enhancing ways of knowing: The case for utilizing participant-generated visual methods in higher education research. *Review of Higher Education, 42*(2), 485–510. https://doi.org/10.1353/rhe.2019.0004

Kouzes, J. M., & Posner, B. Z. (2002). *The Leadership Challenge* (3rd ed.). Jossey-Bass.

Kreissl, K., Striedinger, A., Sauer, B., & Hofbauer, J. (2015). Will gender equality ever fit in? Contested discursive spaces of university reform. *Gender and Education, 27*(3), 221–238. https://doi.org/10.1080/09540253.2015.1028903

Krumm, B. L., & Johnson, W. (2011). Tribal Colleges: Cultural support for women campus presidencies. In G. Jean-Marie & B. Lloyd-Jones (Eds.), *Women of color in higher education: Turbulent past, promising future* (pp. 263–289). Emerald.

Krupnick, M. (2015, December 26). As times get tough, colleges turn to nonacademics to lead. *The Hechinger Report.* https://hechingerreport.org/as-times-get-tough-colleges-turn-to-nonacademics-to-lead/

Ladkin, D., & Patrick, C. B. (2022). Whiteness in leadership theorizing: A critical race analysis of race in Bass' transformational leadership theory. *Leadership, 18*(2), 205–223. https://doi.org/10.1177/17427150211066442

Lafferty, G., & Fleming, J. (2000). The restructuring of academic work in Australia: Power, management and gender. *British Journal of Sociology of Education, 21*(2), 257–267. https://doi.org/10.1080/713655344

Lafreniere, S. L., & Longman, K. A. (2008). Gendered realities and women's leadership development: Participant voices from faith-based higher education. *Christian Higher Education, 7*(5), 388–404.

Langley, A. (1999). Strategies for theorizing from process data. *Academy of Management Review, 24*(4), 691–710. https://doi.org/10.2307/259349

Latta, G. F. (2020). Modelling the interaction of leadership, culture and power in higher education. *Journal of Further and Higher Education, 44*(9), 1188–1206. https://doi.org/10.1080/0309877X.2019.1669770

Latta, G. F. (2021). Eliciting the true self: The effects of doctoral education on students' implicit leadership theories and authentic leader identity development. *Journal of Research on Leadership Education, 16*(1), 30–56. https://doi.org/10.1177/1942775119858638

Law, I. (2017). Building the anti-racist university, action and new agendas. *Race Ethnicity and Education, 20*(3), 332–343.

Lee, C. (2020). Courageous leaders: Promoting and supporting diversity in school leadership development. *Management in Education, 34*(1), 5–15. https://doi.org/10.1177/0892020619878828

Lee, C. (2021). Promoting diversity in university leadership: The argument for LGBTQ+ specific leadership programmes in higher education. *Perspectives: Policy and Practice in Higher Education, 25*(3), 91–99. https://doi.org/10.1080/13603108.2021.1877205

Lee, S. (Director). (2016). *2 fists up* [Film]. ESPN Films.

Lee, T. L., & Fiske, S. T. (2008). Social cognitive perspectives on leadership. In C. L. Hoyt, G. R. Goethals, & D. R. Forsyth (Eds.), *Leadership at the crossroads: Leadership and psychology* (Vol. 1, pp. 101–115). Praeger.

Leithwood, K., & Mascall, B. (2008). New perspectives on an old idea: A short history of the old idea. In K. Leithwood, B. Mascall, & T. Strauss (Eds.), *Distributed leadership according to the evidence* (pp. 1–11). Routledge.

Leon, D. (2005). *Lessons in leadership: Executive leadership programs for advancing diversity in higher education.* Emerald.

Leonardo, Z. (2009). *Race, whiteness, and education.* Routledge.

Leong, L. Y. C., & Fischer, R. (2011). Is transformational leadership universal? A meta-analytical investigation of multifactor leadership questionnaire means across cultures. *Journal of Leadership & Organizational Studies, 18*(2), 164–174. https://doi.org/10.1177/1548051810385003

Leong, N. (2013). Racial capitalism. *Harvard Law Review, 126*(8), 2151–2226. https://doi.org/10.2139/ssrn.2009877

Letizia, A. J. (2016). The evolution of control: The convergence of neoliberalism and neoconservatism in performance based funding policies. *Critical Education, 7*(2), 1–18. https://doi.org/10.14288/ce.v7i2.186031

Levin, J. S., & Aliyeva, A. (2015). Embedded neoliberalism within faculty behaviors. *Review of Higher Education, 38*(4), 537–563. https://doi.org/10.1353/rhe.2015.0030

Liera, R. (2020). Moving beyond a culture of niceness in faculty hiring to advance racial equity. *American Educational Research Journal, 57*(5), 1954–1995. https://doi.org/10.3102/0002831219888624

Lincoln, Y. S., & Cannella, G. S. (2004). Dangerous dialogues: Methodological conservatism and governmental regimes of truth. *Qualitative Inquiry, 10*(4), 5–14. https://doi.org/10.1177/1077800403259717

Linder, C., Quaye, S. J., Lange, A. C., Roberts, R. E., Lacy, M. C., & Okello, W. K. (2019). "A student should have the privilege of just being a student": Student activism as labor. *Review of Higher Education, 42*(5), 37–62. https://doi.org/10.1353/rhe.2019.0044

Lipman-Blumen, J. (1996). *The connective edge: Leading in an interdependent world.* Jossey-Bass.

Lipnack, J., & Stamps, J. (2000). *Virtual teams: People working across boundaries with technology.* Wiley.

Literte, P. E. (2011). Competition, conflict, and coalitions: Black-Latino/a relations within institutions of higher education. *Journal of Negro Education, 80*(4), 477–490.

Liu, H. (2019). Redoing and abolishing whiteness in leadership. In B. Carroll, J. Firth, & S. Wilson (Eds.), *After leadership* (pp. 101–114). Routledge.

Liu, H. (2020). *Redeeming leadership: An anti-racist feminist intervention.* Bristol University Press.

References

Liu, H., & Baker, C. (2016). White knights: Leadership as the heroicisation of whiteness. *Leadership, 12*(4), 420–448. https://doi.org/10.1177/1742715014565127

Liu, S., Hu, J., Li, Y., Wang, Z., & Lin, X. (2014). Examining the cross-level relationship between shared leadership and learning in teams: Evidence from China. *Leadership Quarterly, 25*(2), 282–295. https://doi.org/10.1016/j.leaqua.2013.08.006

Lizier, A., Brooks, F., & Bizo, L. (2022). Importance of clarity, hierarchy, and trust in implementing distributed leadership in higher education. *Educational Management Administration & Leadership.* Advanced online publication. https://doi.org/10.1177/17411432221105154

Lo, M. C., Ramayah, T., & De Run, E. C. (2010). Does transformational leadership style foster commitment to change? The case of higher education in Malaysia. *Procedia Social and Behavioral Sciences, 2*(2), 5384–5388. https://doi.org/10.1016/j.sbspro.2010.03.877

Longman, K. A. (2021). Fresh strategies for empowering women's leadership development: Spirituality as an untapped tool. *Journal of College and Character, 22*(2), 87–97. https://doi.org/10.1080/2194587X.2021.1898983

Longman, K. A., & Anderson, P. S. (2016). Women in leadership: The future of Christian higher education. *Christian Higher Education, 15*(1–2), 24–37. https://doi.org/10.1080/15363759.2016.1107339

Longman, K. A., Drennan, A., Beam, J., & Marble, A. F. (2019). The secret sauce: How developmental relationships shape the leadership journeys of women leaders in Christian higher education. *Christian Higher Education, 18*(1–2), 54–77. https://doi.org/10.1080/15363759.2018.1547031

Longman, K. A., & Madsen, S. R. (2014). *Women and leadership in higher education.* Information Age Publishing.

Lord, R. G., & Emrich, C. G. (2001). Thinking outside the box by looking inside the box: Extending the cognitive revolution in leadership research. *Leadership Quarterly, 11*(4), 551–579. https://doi.org/10.1016/S1048-9843(00)00060-6

Lorde, A. (1984). *Sister outsider: Essays and Speeches.* Crossing Press.

Lorenz, E. N. (1963). Deterministic nonperiodic flow. *Journal of Atmospheric Sciences, 20*(2), 130–141. https://doi.org/10.1175/1520-0469(1963)020%3C0130:dnf%3E2.0.co;2

Love, P., & Estanek, S. M. (2004). *Rethinking student affairs practice.* Jossey-Bass.

Lowe, K. B., Kroeck, K. G., & Sivasubramaniam, N. (1996). Effectiveness correlates of transformation and transactional leadership: A meta-analytic review of the MLQ literature. *Leadership Quarterly, 7*(3), 385–425. https://doi.org/10.1016/S1048-9843(96)90027-2

Lugg, C. A., & Tooms, A. K. (2010). A shadow of ourselves: Identity erasure and the politics of queer leadership. *School Leadership & Management, 30*(1), 77–91. https://doi.org/10.1080/13632430903509790

Luke, T. W. (2001). Globalization, popular resistance and postmodernity. *Democracy & Nature, 7*(2), 317–329. https://doi.org/10.1080/10855660120064628

Lumby, J. (2019). Leadership and power in higher education. *Studies in Higher Education, 44*(9), 1619–1629. https://doi.org/10.1080/03075079.2018.1458221

Luria, G., Kalish, Y., & Weinstein, M. (2014). Learning disability and leadership: Becoming an effective leader. *Journal of Organizational Behavior, 35*(6), 747–761. https://doi.org/10.1002/job.1896

Lynch, K., & Grummell, B. (2018). New managerialism as an organisational form of neoliberalism. In F. Sowa, R. Staples, & S. Zapfel (Eds.), *The transformation of work in welfare state organizations: New public management and the institutional diffusion of ideas* (pp. 203–222). Routledge.

MacBeath, J., Oduro, G.K.T. and Waterhouse, J. (2004). *Distributed leadership in action: A study of current practice in schools.* National College for School Leadership, Nottingham.

Madsen, S. R. (2008). *On becoming a woman leader: Learning from the experiences of university presidents.* Jossey-Bass.

Madsen, S. R., Longman, K. A., & Daniels, J. R. (2012). Women's leadership development in higher education: Conclusion and implications for HRD. *Advances in Developing Human Resources, 14*(1), 113–128.

Maduka, N. S., Edwards, H., Greenwood, D., Osborne, A., & Babatunde, S. O. (2018). Analysis of competencies for effective virtual team leadership in building successful organisations. *Benchmarking: An International Journal, 25*(2), 696–712. https://doi.org/10.1108/bij-08-2016-0124

Magolda, P. M. (2016). *The lives of campus custodians: Insights into corporatization and civic disengagement in the academy.* Stylus Publishing.

Majeed, N., Ramayah, T., Mustamil, N., Nazri, M., & Jamshed, S. (2017). Transformational leadership and organizational citizenship behavior: Modeling emotional intelligence as mediator. *Management & Marketing: Challenges for the Knowledge Society, 12*(4), 571–590. https://doi.org/10.1515/mmcks-2017-0034

Malcom-Piqueux, L. E. (2016). Participatory action research. In F. K. Stage & K. Manning (Eds.), *Research in the college context: Approaches and methods* (pp. 82–94). Routledge.

Malcom-Piqueux, L. E., & Bensimon, E. M. (2017). Taking equity-minded action to close equity gaps. *Peer Review, 19*(2), 5–8.

Marginson, S. (1997). Steering from a distance: Power relations in Australian higher education. *Higher Education, 34*(1), 63–80. https://doi.org/10.1023/A:10030 82922199

Marginson, S. (2007). The new higher education landscape: Public and private goods, in global/national/local settings. In S. Marginson (Ed.), *Prospects of Higher Education* (pp. 29–77). Brill Sense. https://doi.org/10.1163/9789087903213_004

Marginson, S., & Considine M. (2000). *The enterprise university: Power, governance and reinvention in Australia*. Cambridge University Press.

Marshall, J., Roache, D., & Moody-Marshall, R. (2020). Crisis leadership: A critical examination of educational leadership in higher education in the midst of the COVID-19 pandemic. *International Studies in Educational Administration, 48*(3), 30–37.

Marshall, S. J. (2018). Internal and external stakeholders in higher education. In S. J. Marshall (Ed.), *Shaping the university of the future: Using technology to catalyse change in university learning and teaching* (pp. 77–102). Springer.

Martin, G. S., Keating, M. A., Resick, C. J., Szabo, E., Kwan, H. K., & Peng, C. (2013). The meaning of leader integrity: A comparative study across Anglo, Asian, and Germanic cultures. *Leadership Quarterly, 24*(3), 445–461. https://doi.org/10.1016/j.leaqua.2013.02.004

Martin, S. R., Innis, B. D., & Ward, R. G. (2017). Social class, leaders and leadership: A critical review and suggestions for development. *Current Opinion in Psychology, 18*, 49–54. https://doi.org/10.1016/j.copsyc.2017.08.001

Martínez-Alemán, A. M. (2015). Critical discourse analysis in higher education policy research. In A. M. Martínez-Alemán, B. Pusser, & E. M. Bensimon (Eds.), *Critical approaches to the study of higher education: A practical introduction* (pp. 7–43). Johns Hopkins University Press.

Mayorga-Gallo, S. (2019). The white-centering logic of diversity ideology. *American Behavioral Scientist, 63*(13), 1789–1809. https://doi.org/10.1177/0002764219842619

Mazutis, D., & Slawinski, N. (2008). Leading organizational learning through authentic dialogue. *Management Learning, 39*(4), 437–456. https://doi.org/10.1177/1350507608093713

McBain, L. (2021). *2020 AGB survey of board professionals report*. Association of Governing Boards. https://agb.org/wp-content/uploads/2021/04/2020_Board_Professionals_AGB_Survey-web.pdf

McBride, K. (2010). Leadership in higher education: Handling faculty resistance to technology through strategic planning. *Academic Leadership: The Online Journal, 8*(4), Article 41. https://scholars.fhsu.edu/alj/vol8/iss4/41

McCall, K. (2020). *Leadership through an Indigenous lens*. Kathryn M. Buder Center for American Indian Studies. https://openscholarship.wustl.edu/cgi/viewcontent.cgi?article=1024&context=buder_research

McCauley, C. D., & Van Velsor, E. (2004). *The Center for Creative Leadership handbook of leadership development* (2nd ed.). Jossey-Bass.

McClure, K. R. (2016). Building the innovative and entrepreneurial university: An institutional case study of administrative academic capitalism. *Journal of Higher Education, 87*(4), 516–543. https://doi.org/10.1080/00221546.2016.11777412

McElderry, J. A., & Rivera, H. (2017). "Your agenda item, our experience": Two administrators' insights on campus unrest at Mizzou. *Journal of Negro Education, 86*(3), 318–337. https://doi.org/10.7709/jnegroeducation.86.3.0318

McKenna, B., Rooney, D., & Boal, K. B. (2009). Wisdom principles as a meta-theoretical basis for evaluating leadership. *Leadership Quarterly, 20*(2), 177–190. https://doi.org/10.1016/j.leaqua.2009.01.013

McKenna, L. (2015, December 3). Fewer college presidents are academics. *The Atlantic.* https://www.theatlantic.com/education/archive/2015/12/college -president-mizzou-tim-wolfe/418599/

McKinsey & LeanIn. (2020). *Women in the Workplace 2020: Corporate America is at a critical crossroads.* https://wiw-report.s3.amazonaws.com/Women_in_the _Workplace_2020.pdf

McMillan, E. (2004). *Complexity, organizations and change.* Routledge.

McNae, R., & Vali, K. (2015). Diverse experiences of women leading in higher education: Locating networks and agency for leadership within a university context in Papua New Guinea. *Gender and Education, 27*(3), 288–303. https://doi .org/10.1080/09540253.2015.1027669

McNair, T. B., Albertine, S., McDonald, N., Major, T., & Cooper, M. A. (2016). *Becoming a student-ready college: A new culture of leadership for student success.* John Wiley & Sons.

McNair, T. B., Bensimon, E. M., & Malcom-Piqueux, L. (2020). *From equity talk to equity walk: Expanding practitioner knowledge for racial justice in higher education.* John Wiley & Sons.

Meadows, D. H. (2008). *Thinking in systems: A primer.* Chelsea Green Publishing.

Menchaca, V. D., Mills, S. J., & Leo, F. (2016). Latina titans: A journey of inspiration. *Administrative Issues Journal: Connecting Education, Practice, and Research, 6*(2), 96–115. doi:10.5929/2016.6.2.6

Menon, M. E. (2005). Students' views regarding their participation in university governance: Implications for distributed leadership in higher education. *Tertiary Education and Management, 11*(2), 167–182. https://doi.org/10.1007/s11233-005-0686-x

Merriam-Webster. (n.d.). Revolutionary. In *Merriam-Webster.com dictionary.* Retrieved April 18, 2021, from https://www.merriam-webster.com/dictionary /revolutionary

Mertens, D. M. (2020). *Research, and evaluation in education and psychology: Integrating diversity with quantitative, qualitative, and mixed methods* (5th ed.). SAGE.

Meyerson, D. E. (2008). *Rocking the boat: How tempered radicals effect change without making trouble.* Harvard Business Review Press.

Miller, R. A., & Vaccaro, A. (2016). Queer student leaders of color: Leadership as authentic, collaborative, culturally competent. *Journal of Student Affairs Research and Practice, 53*(1), 39–50. https://doi.org/10.1080/19496591.2016.1087858

364 References

Mills, C. W. (1997). *The racial contract*. Cornell University Press.

Mills, C. W. (2003). White supremacy as sociopolitical system: A philosophical perspective. In A. W. Doane & E. Bonilla-Silva (Eds.), *White out: The continuing significance of racism* (pp. 35–48). Routledge.

Mills, C. W. (2007). White ignorance. In S. Sullivan & N. Tuana (Eds.), *Race and epistemologies of ignorance* (pp. 11–39). State University of New York Press

Milner, H. R. (2008). Critical race theory and interest convergence as analytic tools in teacher education policies and practices. *Journal of Teacher Education, 59*(4), 332–346. https://doi.org/10.1177/0022487108321884

Minthorn, R., & Chávez, A. F. (2015a). Collected insights on Indigenous leadership. In R. S. Minthorn & A. F. Chávez (Eds.), *Indigenous leadership in higher education* (pp. 8–46). Routledge.

Minthorn, R., & Chávez, A. F. (Eds.). (2015b). *Indigenous leadership in higher education*. Routledge.

Minthorn, R., & Chávez, A. F. (2015c). Toward an Indigenous transformation of higher education. In R. S. Minthorn & A. F. Chávez (Eds.), *Indigenous leadership in higher education* (pp. 245–267). Routledge.

Mir, A., & Toor, S. (2021). Racial capitalism and student debt in the U.S. *Organization*. Advance online publication. https://doi.org/10.1177/1350508421995762

Mir, G. M., & Abbasi, A. S. (2012). Role of emotional intelligence in developing transformational leadership in higher education sector of Pakistan. *Middle-East Journal of Scientific Research, 12*(4), 563–571. https://doi.org/10.5829/idosi.mejsr.2012.12.4.1715

Monbiot, G. (2016, April 15). Neoliberalism—the ideology at the root of all our problems. *The Guardian*. https://www.theguardian.com/books/2016/apr/15/neoliberalism-ideology-problem-george-monbiot

Montas-Hunter, S. S. (2012). Self-efficacy and Latina leaders in higher education. *Journal of Hispanic Higher Education, 11*(4), 315–335. https://doi.org/10.1177/1538192712441709

Moore, W. L., & Bell, J. M. (2017). The right to be racist in college: Racist speech, White institutional space, and the first amendment. *Law & Policy, 39*(2), 99–120. https://doi.org/10.1111/lapo.12076

Morecroft, J. D. W., & Sterman, J. D. (1994). *Modeling for learning organizations*. Productivity Press.

Morgan, D. L., & Davis, C. H., III. (Eds.). (2019). *Student activism, politics, and campus climate in higher education*. Routledge.

Morris, A. D., & Staggenborg, S. (2004). Leadership in social movements. In D. Snow, S. A. Soule, & H. Kriesi (Eds.), *The Blackwell companion to social movements* (pp. 171–196). Blackwell Publishing.

Morrison, T. (1992). *Playing in the dark: Whiteness and the literary imagination*. Vintage Books.

Mullins, P. R., & Jones, L. C. (2005). Race, displacement, and twentieth-century university landscapes: An archaeology of urban renewal and urban universities. In J. A. Barns (Ed.), *The materiality of freedom: Archaeologies of postemancipation life* (pp. 250–262). University of South Carolina Press.

Mullins, S. M., Suarez, M., Ondersma, S. J., & Page, M. C. (2002). The impact of motivational interviewing on substance abuse treatment retention: A randomized control trial of women involved with child welfare. *Journal of Substance Abuse Treatment, 27*(1), 51–58. https://doi.org/10.1016/j.jsat.2004.03.010

Muñoz, M. (2009). In their own words and by the numbers: A mixed-methods study of Latina community college presidents. *Community College Journal of Research and Practice, 34*(1–2), 153–174. https://doi.org/10.1080/10668920903385939

Murphy, G. (2005). Coalitions and the development of the global environmental movement: A double-edged sword. *Mobilization: An International Quarterly, 10*(2), 235–250. https://doi.org/10.17813/maiq.10.2.8u3626408607643t

Museus, S. D. (2022). Relative racialization and Asian American college student activism. *Harvard Educational Review, 92*(2), 182–205. https://doi.org/10.17763/1943-5045-92.2.182

Museus, S. D., & Sifuentez, B. J. (2021). Toward a critical social movements studies: Implications for research on student activism in higher education. In L. W. Perna (Ed.), *Higher education: Handbook of theory and research* (Vol. 36, pp. 275–321). Springer.

Mustaffa, J. B. (2017). Mapping violence, naming life: A history of anti-Black oppression in the higher education system. *International Journal of Qualitative Studies in Education, 30*(8), 711–727. https://doi.org/10.1080/09518398.2017.1350299

Mustaffa, J. B. (2021). Can we write about Black life? Refusing the unquenchable thirst for Black death in education. *Educational Foundations, 34*(1), 68–84.

Mustaffa, J. B., & Dawson, C. (2021). Racial capitalism and the black student loan debt crisis. *Teachers College Record, 123*(6), 1–28. https://doi.org/10.1177/016146812112300601

NAACP Legal Defense and Educational Fund Media. (2021, July 6). *Nikole Hannah-Jones issues statement on decision to decline tenure offer at University of North Carolina-Chapel Hill and to accept Knight Chair appointment at Howard University* [Press release]. https://www.naacpldf.org/press-release/nikole-hannah-jones-issues-statement-on-decision-to-decline-tenure-offer-at-university-of-north-carolina-chapel-hill-and-to-accept-knight-chair-appointment-at-howard-university/

Nayak, A. (2008). On the way to theory: A processual approach. *Organization Studies, 29*(2), 173–190. https://doi.org/10.1177/0170840607082227

Neilson, P., & Suyemoto, K. L. (2009). Using culturally sensitive frameworks to study Asian American leaders in higher education. *New Directions for Institutional Research, 2009*(142), 83–93. https://doi.org/10.1002/ir.298

Nelson, S. J. (2000). *Leaders in the crucible: The moral voice of college presidents.* Greenwood Publishing Group.

Neumann, A. (1995). Context, cognition, and culture: A case analysis of collegiate leadership and cultural change. *American Educational Research Journal, 32*(2), 251–279. https://doi.org/10.3102/00028312032002251

Newenham-Kahindi, A., & Stevens, C. E. (2021). Ecological sustainability and practical wisdom from the Maasai and Hadza people in East Africa. In A. Intezari, C. Spiller, & S. Y. Yang (Eds.), *Practical wisdom, leadership and culture: Indigenous, Asian and Middle-Eastern perspectives* (pp. 13–33). Routledge.

Nichols, J. C. (2004). Unique characteristics, leadership styles, and management of Historically Black Colleges and Universities. *Innovative Higher Education, 28*(3), 219–229.

Nicolazzo, Z. (2017). Introduction: What's transgressive about trans* studies in education now? *International Journal of Qualitative Studies in Education, 30*(3), 211–216. https://doi.org/10.1080/09518398.2016.1274063

Nonaka, I., & Takeuchi, H. (2011). The wise leader. *Harvard Business Review, 89*(5), 58–67.

Northouse, P. G. (2019). *Leadership: Theory and practice* (8th ed.). SAGE.

Nussbaum, M. (2011). *Creating capabilities: The human development approach.* Harvard University Press.

Nyoni, W. P., He, C., & Yusuph, M. L. (2017). Sustainable interventions in enhancing gender parity in senior leadership positions in higher education in Tanzania. *Journal of Education and Practice, 8*(13), 44–54.

Oc, B. (2018). Contextual leadership: A systematic review of how contextual factors shape leadership and its outcomes. *Leadership Quarterly, 29*(1), 218–235. https://doi.org/10.1016/j.leaqua.2017.12.004

Oc, B., Bashshur, M. R., Daniels, M.A., Greguras, G. J., & Diefendorff, J. M. (2015). Leader humility in Singapore. *Leadership Quarterly, 26*(1), 68–80. https://doi.org/10.1016/j.leaqua.2014.11.005

O'Connor, M. (2014). Investment in edification: Reflections on Irish education policy since independence. *Irish Educational Studies, 33*(2), 193–212. https://doi.org/10.1080/03323315.2014.920609

Odhiambo, G. (2011). Women and higher education leadership in Kenya: A critical analysis. *Journal of Higher Education Policy and Management, 33*(6), 667–678. https://doi.org/10.1080/1360080x.2011.621192

Okello, W. K., Duran, A. A., & Pierce, E. (2021). Dreaming from the hold: Suffering, survival, and futurity as contextual knowing. *Journal of Diversity in Higher Education.* Advance online publication. https://doi.org/10.1037/dhe0000321

Okuwobi, O., Faulk, D., & Roscigno, V. J. (2021). Diversity displays and organizational messaging: The case of Historically Black Colleges and Universities. *Sociology of Race and Ethnicity, 7*(3), 384–400. https://doi.org/10.1177/2332649220980480

Olscamp, P. J. (2003). *Moral leadership: Ethics and the college presidency.* Rowman & Littlefield.

Olson, J. (2004). *The abolition of white democracy.* University of Minnesota Press.

Omi, M., & Winant, H. (1994). *Racial formation in the United States: From the 1960s to the 1990s.* Routledge.

Orlikowski, W. J., & Yates, J. (2002). It's about time: Temporal structuring in organizations. *Organization Science, 13*(6), 684–700. https://doi.org/10.1287/orsc.13.6.684.501

Ortegón-Monroy, M. C. (2003). Chaos and complexity theory in management: An exploration from a critical systems thinking perspective. *Systems Research and Behavioral Science, 20*(5), 387–400. https://doi.org/10.1002/sres.566

Osborn, R. N., Hunt, J. G., & Jauch, L. R. (2002). Toward a contextual theory of leadership. *Leadership Quarterly, 13*(6), 797–837. https://doi.org/10.1016/s1048-9843(02)00154-6

Osborn, R. N., Uhl-Bien, M., & Milosevic, I. (2014). The context and leadership. In D. V. Day (Ed.), *The Oxford handbook of leadership and organizations* (pp. 589–612). Oxford University Press.

Osei-Kofi, N., Torres, L. E., & Lui, J. (2013). Practices of whiteness: Racialization in college admissions viewbooks. *Race Ethnicity and Education, 16*(3), 386–405. https://doi.org/10.1080/13613324.2011.645572

Osland, J. S., Bird, A., Delano, J., & Jacob, M. (2000). Beyond sophisticated stereotyping: Cultural sensemaking in context. *Academy of Management Executive, 14*(1), 65–79. https://doi.org/10.5465/ame.2000.2909840

Ospina, S., & Foldy, E. (2009). A critical review of race and ethnicity in the leadership literature: Surfacing context, power and the collective dimensions of leadership. *Leadership Quarterly, 20*(6), 876–896. https://doi.org/10.1016/j.leaqua.2009.09.005

Ott, E., Grebogi, C., & Yorke, J. A. (1990). Controlling chaos. *Physical Review Letters, 64*(11), 1196–1199. https://doi.org/10.1103/PhysRevLett.64.1196

Owusu-Agyeman, Y. (2019). Transformational leadership and innovation in higher education: A participative process approach. *International Journal of Leadership in Education.* Advance online publication. https://doi.org/10.1080/13603124.2019.1623919

Owusu-Bempah, J., Addison, R., & Fairweather, J. (2014). Commonalities and specificities of authentic leadership in Ghana and New Zealand. *Educational Management Administration & Leadership, 42*(4), 536–556. https://doi.org/10.1177/1741143213502198

Pak, K., & Ravitch, S. M. (Eds.). (2021a). *Critical leadership praxis for educational and social change.* Teachers College Press.

Pak, K., & Ravitch, S. M. (2021b). Critical leadership praxis for educational and social change. In K. Pak & S. Ravitch (Eds.), *Critical leadership praxis for educational and social change* (pp. 1–26). Teachers College Press.

Palacio, A. B., Meneses, G. D., & Perez, P. J. P. (2002). The configuration of the university image and its relationship with the satisfaction of students. *Journal of Educational Administration, 40*(5), 486–505.

Palestini, R. H. (1999). Leadership tendencies of continuing education administrators. *PAACE Journal of Lifelong Learning, 8*, 31–39.

Palmer, R. T., & Freeman, S. (2020). Examining the perceptions of unsuccessful leadership practices for presidents at Historically Black Colleges and Universities. *Journal of Diversity in Higher Education, 13*(3), 254–263. https://doi.org/10.1037/dhe0000120

Palmer, R. T., Maramba, D. C., Arroyo, A. T., Allen, T. O., Boykin, T. F., & Lee, J. M., Jr. (2018). *Effective leadership at minority-serving institutions: Exploring opportunities and challenges for leadership.* Routledge.

Papish, R. (1999). Collaborative common ground: A shared vision of student learning. *College Student Affairs Journal, 19*(1), 44–51.

Paris, L. D., Howell, J. P., Dorfman, P. W., & Hanges, P. J. (2009). Preferred leadership prototypes of male and female leaders in 27 countries. *Journal of International Business Studies, 40*, 1396–1425. https://doi.org/10.1057/jibs.2008.114

Parker, L., & Villalpando, O. (2007). A race(cialized) perspective on education leadership: Critical race theory in educational administration. *Educational Administration Quarterly, 43*(5), 519–524. https://doi.org/10.1177/0013161x07307795

Parry, K. W. (1998). Grounded theory and social process: A new direction for leadership research. *Leadership Quarterly, 9*(1), 85–105. https://doi.org/10.1016/s1048-9843(98)90043-1

Parry, K. W. (2013). Leadership and organization theory. In A. Bryman, D. Collinson, K. Grint, B. Jackson, & M. Uhl-Bien (Eds.), *The SAGE handbook of leadership* (pp. 53–70). SAGE.

Pasque, P. A., & Carducci, R. (2015). Critical advocacy perspectives on organization in higher education. In M. B. Paulson (Ed.), *Higher education: Handbook of theory and research* (Vol. 30, pp. 275–333). Springer.

Pasque, P. A., Carducci, R., Gildersleeve, R. E., & Kuntz, A. K. (2012). *Qualitative inquiry for equity in higher education: Methodological innovations, implications, and interventions* (ASHE Higher Education Report, Vol. 37, No. 6). Jossey-Bass.

Patel, L. (2021). *No study without struggle: Confronting settler colonialism in higher education.* Beacon.

Patton, L. D. (2010). On solid ground: An examination of the successful strategies and positive student outcomes of two Black culture centers. In L. D. Patton (Ed.), *Culture centers in higher education: Perspectives on identity, theory, and practice* (pp. 63–82). Stylus Publishing

Patton, L. D., Harper, S. R., & Harris, J. C. (2015). Using critical race theory to (re)interpret widely-studied topics in U.S. higher education. In A. M. Martínez-Alémán, B. Pusser, & E. M. Bensimon (Eds.), *Critical approaches to the study of higher education* (pp. 193–219). Johns Hopkins University Press.

Pearce, C. L. (2014). The future of leadership: Combining vertical and shared leadership to transform knowledge work. *IEEE Engineering Management Review, 42*(4), 95–107. https://doi.org/10.1109/emr.2014.6966949

Pearce, C. L., & Conger, J. A. (2003). *Shared leadership: Reframing the hows and whys of leadership.* SAGE.

Pearce, C. L., & Sims, H. P. (2002). Vertical versus shared leadership as predictors of the effectiveness of change management teams: An examination of aversive, directive, transactional, transformational, and empowering leader behaviors. *Group Dynamics: Theory, Research, and Practice, 6*(2), 172–197. https://doi.org/10.1037/1089-2699.6.2.172

Pechenkina, E., & Liu, H. (2018). Instruments of white supremacy: People of colour resisting white domination in higher education. *Whiteness and Education, 3*(1), 1–14. https://doi.org/10.1080/23793406.2017.1423242

Pedersen, A. R., & Humle, D. M. (Eds.). (2016). *Doing organizational ethnography.* Routledge.

Pettigrew, A. M. (1985). *The awakening giant: Continuity and change in Imperial Chemical Industries.* Oxford: Blackwell.

Pettigrew, A. M. (1997). What is processual analysis? *Scandinavian Journal of Management, 13*(4), 337–348. https://doi.org/10.1016/S0956-5221(97)00020-1

Pettigrew, A. M., Woodman, R. W., & Cameron, K. S. (2001). Studying organizational change and development: Challenges for future research. *Academy of Management Journal, 44*(4), 697–713. https://doi.org/10.5465/3069411

Pollitt, C. (1990). Managerialism and the public services: The Anglo-American experience. *Public Administration, 69*(3), 404–405.

Posselt, J., Reyes, K., Slay, K. E., Kamimura, A., & Porter, K. B. (2017). Equity efforts as boundary work: How symbolic and social boundaries shape access and inclusion in graduate education. *Teachers College Record, 119*(10), 1–38. https://doi.org/10.1177/016146811711901003

Povey, R., Trudgett, M., Page, S., & Coates, S. K. (2021). On the front foot: Indigenous leadership in Aotearoa/New Zealand higher education. *Higher Education Research & Development, 41*(6), 1–16. https://doi.org/10.1080/07294360.2021.1969542

Povey, R., Trudgett, M., Page, S., & Coates, S. K. (2022). Where we're going, not where we've been: Indigenous leadership in Canadian higher education. *Race Ethnicity and Education, 25*(1), 38–54. https://doi.org/10.1080/13613324.2021.1942820

Powell, G. N. (2011). The gender and leadership wars. *Organizational Dynamics, 40*(1), 1–9. https://doi.org/10.1016/j.orgdyn.2010.10.009

Pryor, J. T. (2021). Queer activist leadership: An exploration of queer leadership in higher education. *Journal of Diversity in Higher Education, 14*(3), 303–315. https://doi.org/10.1037/dhe0000160

Prysor, D., & Henley, A. (2017). Boundary spanning in higher education leadership: Identifying boundaries and practices in a British university. *Studies in Higher Education, 43*(12), 2210–2225. https://doi.org/10.1080/03075079.2017.1318364

Purnell, D. (2021). *Becoming abolitionists: Police, protest, and the pursuit of freedom.* Verso Books.

Quezada, R. L., & Martinez, T. (2021). A culturally tailored Latinx leadership program: Diversifying the nation's community college presidency. *Journal of Applied Research in the Community College, 28*(2), 49–67.

Quijano, A. (2000). Coloniality of power and eurocentrism in Latin America. *International Sociology, 15*(2), 215–232. https://doi.org/10.1177/0268580900 015002005

Rall, R. M. (2021). Modeling equity-minded leadership amid crises: The call for higher education governing boards to lead the way. *Journal of Higher Education Management, 36*(1), 25–31.

Rall, R. M., Morgan, D. L., & Commodore, F. (2020). Toward culturally sustaining governance in higher education: Best practices of theory, research, and practice. *Journal of Education Human Resources, 38*(1), 139–164. https://doi.org/10.3138/jehr .2019-0006

Ralston, S. J. (2020). Higher education's microcredentialing craze: A postdigital-Deweyan critique. *Postdigital Science and Education, 3,* 83–101.

Randers, J. (1980). *Elements of the system dynamics method.* MIT Press.

Ray, V. (2019). A theory of racialized organizations. *American Sociological Review, 84*(1), 26–53. https://doi.org/10.1177/0003122418822335

Reed, L., & Evans, A. E. (2008). "What you see is [not always] what you get!" Dispelling race and gender leadership assumptions. *International Journal of Qualitative Studies in Education, 21*(5), 487–499. https://doi.org/10.1080 /09518390802297797

Reinecke, J., & Ansari, S. (2017). Time, temporality, and process studies. In A. Langley (Ed.), *The SAGE handbook of process organization studies* (pp. 402–416). SAGE.

Renn, K. A. (2007). LGBT student leaders and queer activists: Identities of lesbian, gay, bisexual, transgender, and queer identified college student leaders and activists. *Journal of College Student Development, 48*(3), 311–330. https://doi.org/10 .1353/csd.2007.0029

Renn, K. A., & Bilodeau, B. L. (2005). Leadership identity development among lesbian, gay, bisexual, and transgender student leaders. *NASPA Journal, 42*(3), 342–367. https://doi.org/10.2202/1949-6605.1512

Rescher, N. (1996). *Process metaphysics: An introduction to process philosophy.* State University of New York Press.

Reynolds, R., & Mayweather, D. (2017). Recounting racism, resistance, and repression: Examining the experiences and #hashtag activism of college students with critical race theory and counternarratives. *Journal of Negro Education, 86*, 283–304. https://doi.org/10.7709/jnegroeducation.86.3.0283

Rhoades, G., & Slaughter, S. (1997). Academic capitalism, managed professionals, and supply-side higher education. *Social Text, 51*(Vol. 15, No. 2), 9–38. https://doi.org/10.2307/466645

Rhoads, R. A. (1998). *Freedom's web: Student activism in an age of cultural diversity.* Johns Hopkins University Press.

Rhoads, R. A., Saenz, V., & Carducci, R. (2005). Higher education reform as a social movement: The case of affirmative action. *Review of Higher Education, 28*(2), 191–220. https://doi.org/10.1353/rhe.2004.0039

Rhode, D. L. (2003). *The difference "difference" makes: Women and leadership.* Stanford University Press.

Riad, S. (2011). Invoking Cleopatra to examine the shifting ground of leadership. *Leadership Quarterly, 22*(5), 831–850. https://doi.org/10.1016/j.leaqua.2011.07.006

Rios, V. M. (2011). *Punished: Policing the lives of Black and Latino boys.* New York University Press.

Roberson, Q., Quigley, N. R., Vickers, K., & Bruck, I. (2021). Reconceptualizing leadership from a neurodiverse perspective. *Group & Organization Management, 46*(2), 399–423. https://doi.org/10.1177/1059601120987293

Roberts, L. M., Mayo, A. J., & Thomas, D. A. (2019). *Race, work, and leadership: New perspectives on the Black experience.* Harvard Business Review Press.

Robinson, C. J. (1980). *The terms of order.* SUNY Press.

Robinson, C. J. (2000). *Black Marxism: The making of the Black radical tradition.* University of North Carolina Press.

Rodela, K. C., & Rodriguez-Mojica, C. (2020). Equity leadership informed by community cultural wealth: Counterstories of Latinx school administrators. *Educational Administration Quarterly, 56*(2), 289–320. https://doi.org/10.1177/0013161x19847513

Rodríguez, C., Martinez, M. A., & Valle, F. (2016). Latino educational leadership across the pipeline: For Latino communities and Latina/o leaders. *Journal of Hispanic Higher Education, 15*(2), 136–153. https://doi.org/10.1177/1538192715612914

Rodríguez, C., Martinez, M. A., & Valle, F. (Eds.). (2018). *Latino educational leadership: Serving Latino communities and preparing Latinx leaders across the P-20 pipeline.* Information Age Publishing.

Rohe, W. M., & Watson, H. L. (Eds.). (2007). *Chasing the American dream: New perspectives on affordable homeownership.* Cornell University Press.

Ropo, A., Eriksson, P., & Hunt, J. G. (1997). Reflections on conducting processual research on management and organizations. *Scandinavian Journal of Management, 13*(4), 331–335. https://doi.org/10.1016/s0956-5221(97)88766-0

Rosette, A. S., Koval, C. Z., Ma, A., & Livingston, R. (2016). Race matters for women leaders: Intersectional effects on agentic deficiencies and penalties. *Leadership Quarterly, 27*(3), 429–445. https://doi.org/10.1016/j.leaqua.2016.01.008

Rosette, A. S., Leonardelli, G. J., & Phillips, K. W. (2008). The white standard: Racial bias in leader categorization. *Journal of Applied Psychology, 93*(4), 758–777. https://doi.org/10.1037/0021-9010.93.4.758

Rosette, A. S., & Livingston, R. W. (2012). Failure is not an option for Black women: Effects of organizational performance on leaders with single versus dual-subordinate identities. *Journal of Experimental Social Psychology, 48*(5), 1162–1167. https://doi.org/10.1016/j.jesp.2012.05.002

Rosile, G. A., Boje, D. M., & Claw, C. M. (2018). Ensemble leadership theory: Collectivist, relational, and heterarchical roots from indigenous contexts. *Leadership, 14*(3), 307–328. https://doi.org/10.1177/174271501665

Ross, A. (2022a, April 12). A university asked professors to help quash a grad-student strike: Hundreds have refused. *The Chronicle of Higher Education.* https://www.chronicle.com/article/a-university-asked-professors-to-help-quash-a-grad-student-strike-hundreds-have-refused

Ross, A. (2022b, May 10). Grad students suspend their strike at Indiana U. But the fight's not over. *The Chronicle of Higher Education.* https://www.chronicle.com/article/grad-students-suspend-their-strike-at-indiana-u-but-the-fights-not-over

Rosser, V. J. (2009). Support professionals: The key issues survey. In *The NEA 2009 Almanac of Higher Education* (pp. 93–97). National Education Association.

Rost, J. C. (1991). *Leadership for the twenty-first century.* Praeger.

Roth, K. R., & Ritter, Z. S. (Eds.). (2021). *Whiteness, power, and resisting change in US higher education: A peculiar institution.* Springer Nature.

Roueche, J. E., Baker III, G. A., & Rose, R. R. (2014). *Shared vision: Transformational leadership in American community colleges.* Rowman & Littlefield.

Rowe, A. C., & Tuck, E. (2017). Settler colonialism and cultural studies: Ongoing settlement, cultural production, and resistance. *Cultural Studies Critical Methodologies, 17*(1), 3–13. https://doi.org/10.1177/1532708616653693

Roy, S. R. (2012). Digital mastery: The skills needed for effective virtual leadership. *International Journal of E-Collaboration, 8*(3), 56–66. https://doi.org/10.4018/jec.2012070104

Ruben, B. D., & Gigliotti, R. A. (2016). Leadership as social influence: An expanded view of leadership communication theory and practice. *Journal of Leadership & Organizational Studies, 23*(4), 467–479. https://doi.org/10.1177/1548051816641876

Rubin, H. (2002). *Collaborative leadership: Developing effective partnerships and communities in schools.* Corwin Press.

Rubins, I. (2007). Risks and rewards of academic capitalism and the effects of presidential leadership in the entrepreneurial university. *Perspectives in Public Affairs, 4*(4), 3–18. https://www.asu.edu/mpa/Entre%20University.pdf

Sadeghi, A., & Pihie, Z. A. L. (2012). Transformational leadership and its predictive effects on leadership effectiveness. *International Journal of Business and Social Science*, *3*(7), 186–197.

Salisbury, J. D., Sheth, M. J., & Angton, A. (2020). "They didn't even talk about oppression": School leadership protecting the whiteness of leadership through resistance practices to a youth voice initiative. *Journal of Education Human Resources*, *38*(1), 57–81. https://doi.org/10.3138/jehr.2019-0010

Sanchez-Hucles, J. V., & Davis, D. D. (2010). Women and women of color in leadership: Complexity, identity, and intersectionality. *American Psychologist*, *65*(3), 171–181. https://doi.org/10.1037/a0017459

Sandefur, G., & Deloria, P. J. (2018). Indigenous leadership. *Daedalus*, *147*(2), 124–135.

Santamaría, L. J. (2014). Critical change for the greater good: Multicultural perceptions in educational leadership toward social justice and equity. *Educational Administration Quarterly*, *50*(3), 347–391. https://doi.org/10.1177%2F0013161 X13505287

Santamaría, L. J., & Jean-Marie. G. (2014) Cross-cultural dimensions of applied, critical, and transformational leadership: Women principals advancing social justice and educational equity. *Cambridge Journal of Education*, *44*(3), 333–360 . https://doi.org/10.1080/0305764X.2014.904276

Santamaría, L. J., & Santamaría, A. P. (2012). *Applied critical leadership in education: Choosing change*. Routledge.

Santamaría, L. J., & Santamaría, A. P. (2015). Counteracting educational injustice with applied critical leadership: Culturally responsive practices promoting sustainable change. *International Journal of Multicultural Education*, *17*(1), 22–42. https://doi.org/10.18251/ijme.v17i1.1013

Santamaría, L. J., & Santamaría, A. P. (Eds.) (2016a). *Culturally responsive leadership in higher education: Promoting access, equity, and improvement*. Routledge.

Santamaría, L. J., & Santamaría, A. P. (2016b). Introduction: The urgent call for culturally responsive leadership. In L. J. Santamaría & A. P. Santamaría (Eds.), *Culturally responsive leadership in higher education: Promoting access, equity, and improvement* (pp. 1–14). Routledge.

Santamaría, L. J., Santamaría, A. P., & Dam, L. I. (2014). Applied critical leadership through Latino/a lenses: An alternative approach to educational leadership. *Revista Internacional de Educación para la Justicia Social*, *3*(2), 161–180.

Santamaría, L., Santamaría, A., Webber, M., & Pearson, H. (2014). Indigenous urban school leadership: A critical cross-cultural comparative analysis of educational leaders in New Zealand and the United States. *Comparative and International Education*, *43*(1). https://doi.org/10.5206/cie-eci.v43i1.9240

Schein, E. H. (2010). *Organizational culture and leadership* (4th ed.). John Wiley & Sons.

Schulze-Cleven, T., & Olson, J. R. (2017). Worlds of higher education transformed: Toward varieties of academic capitalism. *Higher Education, 73*(1), 813–831. https://doi.org/10.1007/s10734-017-0123-3

Schuster, J., & Finkelstein, M. (2006). *The restructuring of academic work and careers.* Johns Hopkins Press.

Schwandt, T. A. (2001). *Dictionary of qualitative inquiry* (2nd ed.). SAGE.

Schwartz, S. H. (1999). A theory of cultural values and some implications for work. *Applied Psychology: An International Review, 48*(1), 23–47.

Scott, J. C. (1990). *Domination and the arts of resistance: Hidden transcripts.* Yale University Press.

Scott, W. R. (2015). Organizational theory and higher education. *Journal of Organizational Theory in Education, 1*(1), 68–76.

Scott, K. A., & Brown, D. J. (2006). Female first, leader second? Gender bias in the encoding of leadership behavior. *Organizational Behavior and Human Decision Processes, 101*(2), 230–242. https://doi.org/10.1016/j.obhdp.2006.06.002

Seierstad, C. & Healy, G. (2012). Women's equality in the Scandinavian academy: A distant dream? *Work, Employment and Society, 26*(2), 296–313. https://doi.org/10.1177/0950017011432918

Senge, P. M. (1990). *The fifth discipline: The art and practice of the learning organization.* Doubleday.

Sensoy, O., & DiAngelo, R. (2017). "We are all for diversity, but . . .": How faculty hiring committees reproduce whiteness and practical suggestions for how they can change. *Harvard Educational Review, 87*(4), 557–580. https://doi.org/10.17763/1943-5045-87.4.557

Serban, A., & Roberts, A. J. B. (2016). Exploring antecedents and outcomes of shared leadership in a creative context: A mixed-methods approach. *Leadership Quarterly, 27*(2), 181–199. https://doi.org/10.1016/j.leaqua.2016.01.009

Sexton, J. (2008). *Amalgamation schemes: Antiblackness and the critique of multiracialism.* University of Minnesota Press.

Shahjahan, R. A., & Edwards, K. T. (2021). Whiteness as futurity and globalization of higher education. *Higher Education, 83*, 747–764. https://doi.org/10.1007/s10734-021-00702-x

Shaked, H., & Schechter, C. (2020). Systems thinking leadership: New explorations for school improvement. *Management in Education, 34*(3), 107–114. https://doi.org/10.1177/0892020620907327

Shakeshaft, C. (1999). The struggle to create a more gender inclusive profession. In J. Murphy & K. S. Louis (Eds.), *Handbook of research on educational administration* (2nd ed.). Jossey-Bass.

Shamir, B., & Howell, J. M. (1999). Organizational and contextual influences on the emergence and effectiveness of charismatic leadership. *Leadership Quarterly, 10*(2), 257–283. https://doi.org/10.1016/s1048-9843(99)00014-4

Sharpe, C. (2016). *In the wake: On Blackness and being.* Duke University Press.

Shaver, H. (2004). *Organize, communicate, empower! How principals can make time for leadership.* Corwin Press.

Shields, C. M. (2012). Critical advocacy research: An approach whose time has come. In S. R. Steinberg & G. S. Cannella (Eds.), *Critical qualitative research reader* (pp. 2–13). Peter Lang.

Shondrick, S. J., Dinh, J. E., & Lord, R. G. (2010). Developments in implicit leadership theory and cognitive science: Applications to improving measurement and understanding alternatives to hierarchical leadership. *Leadership Quarterly, 21*(6), 959–978. https://doi.org/10.1016/j.leaqua.2010.10.004

Siangchokyoo, N., Klinger, R. L., & Campion, E. D. (2020). Follower transformation as the linchpin of transformational leadership theory: A systematic review and future research agenda. *Leadership Quarterly, 31*(1), 101–341. https://doi.org/10.1016/j.leaqua.2019.101341

Silsbee, D. (2018). *Presence-based leadership: Complexity practices for clarity, resilience, and results that matter.* Yes! Global.

Skinner, R. A. (2010). Turnover: Selecting the next generation's presidents. *Change, 42*(5), 9–15. https://doi.org/10.1080/00091383.2010.503141

Slaughter, S., & Rhoades, G. (2004). *Academic capitalism and the new economy: Markets, state, and higher education.* Johns Hopkins University Press.

Smerek, R. E. (2013). Sensemaking and new college presidents: A conceptual study of the transition process. *Review of Higher Education, 36*(3), 371–403. https://doi.org/10.1353/rhe.2013.0028

Smith, A. (2016). Heteropatriarchy and the three pillars of white supremacy: Rethinking women of color organizing. In INCITE! Women of Color Against Violence (Eds.), *Color of violence: The INCITE! Anthology* (pp. 66–73). Duke University Press.

Smith, D. G. (2020). *Diversity's promise for higher education: Making it work.* Johns Hopkins University Press.

Smythe, J. (2017). *The toxic university: Zombie leadership, academic rock stars, and neoliberal ideology.* Palgrave Macmillan.

Solórzano, D. G., & Yosso, T. J. (2002). Critical race methodology: Counterstorytelling as an analytical framework for education research. *Qualitative Inquiry, 8*(1), 23–44. https://doi.org/10.1177/107780040200800103

Son, C., Hegde, S., Smith, A., Wang, X., & Sasangohar, F. (2020). Effects of COVID-19 on college students' mental health in the United States: Interview survey study. *Journal of Medical Internet Research, 22*(9), e21279. https://doi.org/10.2196/21279

Sorensen, B. E. (2015). Walking the talk: The balancing act of native women Tribal College presidents. *Tribal College Journal of American Indian Higher Education, 26*(4), 24–27.

Spillane, J. P. (2006). *Distributed leadership.* Jossey-Bass.

Spillane, J. P., & Diamond, J. B. (2007). *Distributed leadership in practice*. Teachers College Press.

Spillane, J. P., Halverson, R., & Diamond, J. B. (2004). Towards a theory of leadership practice: A distributed perspective. *Journal of Curriculum Studies, 36*(1), 3–34. https://doi.org/10.1080/0022027032000106726

Spiller, C., Dell, K., & Mudford, M. (2021). The wisdom of inclusion: Māori leadership and management practices that make a world of difference. In A. Intezari, C. Spiller, & S. Yang (Eds.), *Practical wisdom, leadership and culture: Indigenous, Asian, and Middle-Eastern perspectives* (pp. 46–62). Routledge.

Spiller, C., Maunganui Wolfgramm, R., Henry, E., & Pouwhare, R. (2020). Paradigm warriors: Advancing a radical ecosystems view of collective leadership from an indigenous Māori perspective. *Human Relations, 73*(4), 516–543. https://doi.org/10.1177/0018726719891989

Squire, D., Williams, B. C., & Tuitt, F. (2018). Plantation politics and neoliberal racism in higher education: A framework for reconstructing anti-racist institutions. *Teachers College Record, 120*(14), 1–20. https://doi.org/10.1177/016146811812001412

Stacey, R. D., Griffin, D., & Shaw, P. (2000). *Complexity and management: Fad or radical challenge to systems thinking?* Routledge.

Starratt, R. J. (2004). *Ethical leadership*. Jossey-Bass.

Stein, S. (2017). Internationalization for an uncertain future: Tensions, paradoxes, and possibilities. *Review of Higher Education, 41*(1), 3–32. https://doi.org/10.1353/rhe.2017.0031

Sternberg, R. J. (2003). *Wisdom, intelligence, and creativity synthesized*. Cambridge University Press.

Stewart, C. W. (2019). Coexisting values in healthcare and the leadership practices that were found to inspire followership among healthcare practitioners. *Journal of Values-Based Leadership, 12*(2), Article 12. http://dx.doi.org/10.22543/0733.122.1282

Stewart, K. D., & Gachago, D. (2020). Step into the discomfort: (Re)orienting the white gaze and strategies to disrupt whiteness in educational spaces. *Whiteness and Education, 7*(1), 1–14. https://doi.org/10.1080/23793406.2020.1803760

Stewart, L. J. (2010). A contingency theory perspective on management control system design among U.S. ante-bellum slave plantations. *Accounting Historians Journal, 37*(1), 91–120. https://doi.org/10.2308/0148-4184.37.1.91

Stokes, S., & Davis, C. H. (2022). In defense of dignitary safety: A phenomenological study of student resistance to hate speech on campus. *Peabody Journal of Education, 97*(5), 600–615.

Streufert, S., & Nogami, G. Y. (1989). Cognitive style and complexity: Implications for I/O psychology. In C. L. Cooper & I. Robertson (Eds.), *International review of industrial and organizational psychology* (pp. 93–143). Wiley.

Stroh, D. P. (2015). *Systems thinking for social change: A practical guide to solving complex problems, avoiding unintended consequences, and achieving lasting results.* Chelsea Green Publishing.

Stull, G. C., & Gasman, M. (2017). Tribal College and University leadership: Overcoming challenges through service and collective leadership. In R. T. Palmer, D. C. Maramba, A. T. Arroyo, T. O. Allen, T. F., Boykin, & J. M Lee Jr. (Eds.). *Effective leadership at minority-serving institutions* (pp. 139–149). Routledge.

Sudbury, J., & Okazawa-Rey, M. (2009). *Activist scholarship: Antiracism, feminism, and social change.* Routledge.

Sullivan, L. G. (2009). Informal learning among women community college presidents. In D. R. Dean, S. J. Bracken, & J. K. Allen (Eds.), *Women in academic leadership: Professional strategies, personal choices* (pp. 95–127). Stylus.

Sullivan, S., & Tuana, N. (Eds.). (2007). *Race and epistemologies of ignorance.* State University of New York Press.

Sumara, D. (2021). On the power of not passing: A queer narrative hermeneutics of higher education leadership. *Journal of Educational Administration and History,* 53(2), 144–157. https://doi.org/10.1080/00220620.2020.1814224

Sung, M., & Yang, S. U. (2008). Toward the model of university image: The influence of brand personality, external prestige, and reputation. *Journal of Public Relations Research,* 20(4), 357–376. https://doi.org/10.1287/orsc.13.1.18.543

Tadiar, N. X. (2003). In the face of whiteness as value: Fall-outs of metropolitan humanness. *Qui Parle,* 13(2), 143–182. https://doi.org/10.1215/quiparle.13.2.143

Tanner, N. M., & Welton, A. (2021). Using anti-racism to challenge whiteness in educational leadership. In C. A. Mullen (Ed.), *Handbook of social justice interventions in education* (pp. 395–414). Springer.

Tarker, D. (2019). Transformational leadership and the proliferation of community college leadership frameworks: A systematic review of the literature. *Community College Journal of Research and Practice,* 43(10–11), 672–689. https://doi.org/10.1080/10668926.2019.1600610

Tawa, J., Tauriac, J. J., & Suyemoto, K. L. (2016). Fostering inter-minority race-relations: An intervention with Black and Asian students at an urban university. *Making Connections: Interdisciplinary Approaches to Cultural Diversity,* 16(2), 33–64.

Taylor, K.-Y. (2019). *Race for profit: How banks and the real estate industry undermined Black homeownership.* University of North Carolina Press.

Teague, L. W. J., & Bobby, K. (2014). American Council on Education's IDEALS for women leaders. In K. A. Longman & S. R. Madsen (Eds.), *Women and leadership in higher education* (pp. 59–76). Information Age.

Theoharis, G. (2010). Disrupting injustice: Principals narrate the strategies they use to improve their schools and advance social justice. *Teachers College Record,* 112(1), 331–373. https://doi.org/10.1177/016146811011200105

Thomas, G., Martin, R., & Riggio, R. E. (2013). Leading groups: Leadership as a group process. *Group Processes & Intergroup Relations, 16*(1), 3–16. https://doi.org/10.1177/1368430212462497

Tichavakunda, A. A. (2021a). *Black campus life: The worlds Black students make at a historically white institution.* State University of New York Press.

Tichavakunda, A. A. (2021b). A critical race analysis of university acts of racial "redress": The limited potential of racial symbols. *Educational Policy, 35*(2), 304–322. https://doi.org/10.1177/0895904820983031

Tichavakunda, A. A. (2022). University memorials and symbols of white supremacy: Black students' counternarratives. *Journal of Higher Education,* 1–25. https://doi.org/10.1080/00221546.2022.2031707

Tierney, W. G. (1991). Advancing democracy: A critical interpretation of leadership. *Peabody Journal of Education, 66*(3), 157–175. https://doi.org/10.1080/01619568909538654

Tierney, W. G. (1996). Leadership and postmodernism: On voice and the qualitative method. *Leadership Quarterly, 7*(3), 371–383. https://doi.org/10.1016/S1048-9843(96)90026-0

Tilly, C. (2004). Social boundary mechanisms. *Philosophy of the Social Sciences, 34*(2), 211–236. https://doi.org/10.1177/0048393103262551

Toppo, G. (2019, March 22). UTEP faculty and students protest presidential finalist who serves as Trump Air Force appointee. *Inside Higher Ed.* https://www.insidehighered.com/news/2019/03/22/utep-faculty-and-students-protest-presidential-finalist-who-serves-trump-air-force

Torres, V., & Renn, K. A. (2021). Is metric-centered leadership generating new silos? *Change, 53*(2), 49–56. https://doi.org/10.1080/00091383.2021.1883982

Tourish, D. (2014). Leadership, more or less? A processual, communication perspective on the role of agency in leadership theory. *Leadership, 10*(1), 79–98. https://doi.org/10.1177/1742715013509030

Tourish, D. (2018). Is complexity leadership theory complex enough? A critical appraisal, some modifications and suggestions for further research. *Organization Studies, 40*(2), 219–238. https://doi.org/10.1177/0170840618789207

Townsend, C. V. (2021). Identity politics: Why African American women are missing in administrative leadership in public higher education. *Educational Management Administration & Leadership, 49*(4), 584–600. https://doi.org/10.1177/1741143220935455

Trow, M. (1996). Trust, markets and accountability in higher education: A comparative perspective. *Higher Education Policy, 9*(4), 309–324. https://doi.org/10.1016/s0952-8733(96)00029-3

Tuck, E., & Yang, K. W. (2012). Decolonization is not a metaphor. *Decolonization: Indigeneity Education and Society, 1*(1), 1–40.

Tuck, E., & Yang, K. W. (2014). R-words: Refusing research. In J. Paris & M. Winn (Eds.), *Humanizing research: Decolonizing qualitative inquiry with youth and communities* (pp. 223–258). Sage.

Tuitt, F. A. (2021). The contemporary chief diversity officer and the plantation driver: The reincarnation of a diversity management position. In B. C. Williams, D. D. Squire, & F. A. Tuitt (Eds.), *Plantation politics and campus rebellions: Power, diversity, and the emancipatory struggle in higher education* (pp. 171–197). State University of New York Press.

Tupling, C. L., & Outhwaite, D. (2017). Developing an identity as an EdD leader: A reflexive narrative account. *Management in Education, 31*(4), 153–158. https://doi .org/10.1177/0892020617734819

Tuttle, D. B. (1997). A classification system for understanding individual differences in temporal orientation among processual researchers and organizational informants. *Scandinavian Journal of Management, 13*(4), 349–366. https://doi.org /10.1016/s0956-5221(97)00021-3

Uhl-Bien, M., Marion, R., & McKelvey, B. (2007). Complexity leadership theory: Shifting leadership from the industrial age to the knowledge era. *Leadership Quarterly, 18*(4), 298–318. https://doi.org/10.1016/j.leaqua.2007.04.002

V. Rodríguez, J. J. (2019). The neoliberal co-optation of identity politics: Geopolitical situatedness as a decolonial discussion partner. *Horizontes Decoloniales / Decolonial Horizons, 5,* 101–130.

Van de Ven, A. H., & Huber, G. P. (1990). Longitudinal field research methods for studying processes of organizational change. *Organization Science, 1*(3), 213–219. https://doi.org/10.1287/orsc.1.3.213

Vaughn, G. B. (1992). *Dilemmas of leadership: Decision making and ethics in the community college.* Jossey-Bass.

Villarreal, C. D., Liera, R., & Malcom-Piquex, L. (2019). The role of niceness in silencing racially minoritized faculty. In A. E. Castagno (Ed.), *The price of nice: How good intentions maintain educational inequity* (pp. 127–144). University of Minnesota Press.

Vine, B., Holmes, J., Marra, M., Pfeifer, D., & Jackson, B. (2008). Exploring co-leadership talk through interactional sociolinguistics. *Leadership, 4*(3), 339–360. https://doi.org/10.1177/1742715008092389

Voyageur, C., Brearley, L., & Calliou, B. (Eds.). (2015). *Restorying Indigenous leadership: Wise practices in community development.* Banff Centre Press.

Wang, G., Oh, I. S., Courtright, S. H., & Colbert, A. E. (2011). Transformational leadership and performance across criteria and levels: A meta-analytic review of 25 years of research. *Group & Organization Management, 36*(2), 223–270. https:// doi.org/10.1177/1059601111401017

Warner, L. S., & Grint, K. (2006). American Indian ways of leading and knowing. *Leadership, 2*(2), 225–244. https://doi.org/10.1177/1742715006062936

Warren, K. (2004). Why has feedback systems thinking struggled to influence strategy and policy formulation? Suggestive evidence, explanations and solutions. *Systems Research and Behavioral Science, 21*(4), 331–347. https://doi.org /10.1002/sres.651

Wasden, S. T. (2014). *A correlational study on transformational leadership and resilience in higher education leadership.* [Doctoral dissertation, University of Idaho]. ProQuest Dissertations Publishing. https://www.proquest.com/docview /1552969464

Webb, K. S. (2008). Creating satisfied employees in Christian higher education: Research on leadership competencies. *Christian Higher Education, 8*(1), 18–31. https://doi.org/10.1080/15363750802171073

Weber, K., & King, B. (2014). Social movement theory and organization studies. In P. Adler, P. du Gay, G. Morgan, & M. Reed (Eds.), *The Oxford handbook of sociology, social theory, and organization studies: Contemporary currents* (pp. 487–509). Oxford University Press.

Weber, M. (1924). *The theory of social and economic organization.* Free Press.

Weick, K. E. (1976). Educational organizations as loosely coupled systems. *Administrative Science Quarterly, 21*(1), 1–19. https://doi.org/10.2307/2391875

Weiner, M. F. (1997). *Mistresses and slaves: Plantation women in South Carolina, 1830–80.* University of Illinois Press.

Weissman, J. (1990). Institutional image assessment and modification in colleges and universities. *Journal for Higher Education Management, 6*(1), 65–75.

Welton, A., Owens, D., & Zamani-Gallaher, E. (2018). Anti-racist change: A conceptual framework for educational institutions to take systemic action. *Teachers College Record, 120*(14), 1–22. https://doi.org/10.1177/016146811812001402

Wheatley, M. J. (1999). *Leadership and the new science: Discovering order in a chaotic world* (2nd ed.). Berrett-Koehler.

White, K., & Bagilhole, B. (2012). The gendered shaping of university leadership in Australia, South Africa and the United Kingdom. *Higher Education Quarterly, 66*(3), 293–307. https://doi.org/10.1111/j.1468-2273.2012.00523.x

Whitehall, A. P., Bletscher, C. G., & Yost, D. M. (2021). Reflecting the wave, not the title: Increasing self-awareness and transparency of authentic leadership through online graduate student leadership programming. *Journal of Leadership Education, 21*(1), 114–127. https://doi.org/10.12806/V20/I1/R8

Whitehead, A. N. (1929). *Process and reality: An essay in cosmology.* Cambridge University Press.

White-Lewis, D. K. (2020). The facade of fit in faculty search processes. *Journal of Higher Education, 91*(6), 833–857. https://doi.org/10.1080/00221546.2020.1775058

White-Lewis, D. K. (2022). The role of administrative and academic leadership in advancing faculty diversity. *Review of Higher Education, 45*(3), 337–364. https://doi .org/10.1353/rhe.2022.0002

Whitford, E. (2020, December 7). University of Missouri Board Approves New Governance Rules. *Inside Higher Ed.* https://www.insidehighered.com/quicktakes/2020/12/08/university-missouri-board-approves-new-governance-rules

Wilcox, J. R., & Ebbs, S. L. (1992). *The leadership compass: Values and ethics in higher education* (ASHE-ERIC Higher Education Report 1). School of Education and Human Development, George Washington University.

Wilder, C. S. (2014). *Ebony and ivy: Race, slavery, and the troubled history of America's universities.* Bloomsbury.

Wilkerson, I. (2020). *Caste: The origins of our discontents.* Random House.

Williams, B. C., Squire, D., & Tuitt, F. (Eds.). (2021). *Plantation politics and campus rebellions: Power, diversity, and the emancipatory struggle in higher education.* State University of New York Press.

Williams, D. A., & Wade-Golden, K. C. (2013). *The chief diversity officer.* Stylus.

Wilson, J. L. (2013). Emerging trend: The chief diversity officer phenomenon within higher education. *Journal of Negro Education, 82*(4), 433–445. https://doi.org/10.7709/jnegroeducation.82.4.0433

Wofford, J. C., Goodwin, V. L., & Whittington, J. L. (1998). A field study of a cognitive approach to understanding transformational and transactional leadership. *Leadership Quarterly, 9*(1), 55–84. https://doi.org/10.1016/S1048-9843(98)90042-X

Wolfe, B. L., & Dilworth, P. P. (2015). Transitioning normalcy: Organizational culture, African American administrators, and diversity leadership in higher education. *Review of Educational Research, 85*(4), 667–697. https://doi.org/10.3102/003465431456566

Wolverton, M. (2002). A matter of degree: Men and women deans of education. In W. H. Gmelch (Ed.), *Deans' balancing acts: Education leaders and the challenges they face* (pp. 35–57). AACTE Publications.

Wood, D. F. (2009). Barriers to women's leadership in faith-based colleges and universities: Strategies for change. In D. R. Dean, S. J., Bracken, & J. K. Allen (Eds.), *Women in academic leadership: Professional strategies, personal choices* (pp. 74–94). Stylus.

Wood, F. (2014). Kinship, collegiality and witchcraft: South African perceptions of sorcery and the occult aspects of contemporary academia. *Tydskrif Vir Letterkunde, 51*(1), 150–162. https://doi.org/10.4314/tvl.v51i1.14

Wood, M. (2005). The fallacy of misplaced leadership. *Journal of Management Studies, 42*(6), 1101–1121. https://doi.org/10.1111/j.1467-6486.2005.00535.x

Wood, M., & Dibben, M. (2015). Leadership as relational process. *Process Studies, 44*(1), 24–47. https://doi.org/10.5840/process20154412

World Economic Forum. (2017). *The global gender gap report.* https://www3.weforum.org/docs/WEF_GGGR_2017.pdf

Wright-Mair, R., & Museus, S. D. (2021). Playing the game just enough: How racially minoritized faculty who advance equity conceptualize success in the neoliberal academy. *Journal of Diversity in Higher Education*. Advance online publication. https://doi.org/10.1037/dhe0000304

Yancey, G. A. (2003). *Who is white? Latinos, Asians, and the new black/nonblack divide.* Lynne Rienner Publishers.

Yancy, G. (2012). *Look, a white! Philosophical essays on whiteness.* Temple University Press.

Yang, S. (2011). Wisdom displayed through leadership: Exploring leadership-related wisdom. *Leadership Quarterly, 22*(4), 616–632. https://doi.org/10.1016/j.leaqua.2011.05.004

Yang, S. (2014). Wisdom and learning from important and meaningful life experiences. *Journal of Adult Development, 21*, 129–146. https://doi.org/10.1007/s10804-014-9186-x

Yosso, T. J. (2005). Whose culture has capital? A critical race theory discussion of community cultural wealth. *Race Ethnicity and Education, 8*(1), 69–91. https://doi.org/10.1080/1361332052000341006

Young, M. D., & López, G. R. (2011). The nature of inquiry in educational leadership. In F. W. English (Eds.), *The SAGE handbook of educational leadership: Advances in theory, research, and practice* (2nd ed., pp. 233–254). SAGE.

Yukl, G. (1998). *Leadership in organizations* (4th ed.). Prentice Hall.

Yukl, G. (1999). An evaluation of conceptual weaknesses in transformational and charismatic leadership theories. *Leadership Quarterly, 10*(2), 285–305. https://doi.org/10.1016/s1048-9843(99)00013-2

Yukl, G. (2009). Leading organizational learning: Reflections on theory and research. *Leadership Quarterly, 20*(1), 49–53. https://doi.org/10.1016/j.leaqua.2008.11.006

Zaccaro, S. J. (2012). Individual differences and leadership: Contributions to a third tipping point. *Leadership Quarterly, 23*(4), 718–728. https://doi.org/10.1016/j.leaqua.2012.05.001

Zacharatos, A., Barling, J., & Kelloway, E. K. (2000). Development and effects of transformational leadership in adolescents. *Leadership Quarterly, 11*(2), 211–226. https://psycnet.apa.org/doi/10.1016/S1048-9843(00)00041-2

Zacher, H., & Johnson, E. (2015). Leadership and creativity in higher education. *Studies in Higher Education, 40*(7), 1–16. https://doi.org/10.1080/03075079.2014.881340

Zarate, M. E., & Mendoza, Y. (2020). Reflections on race and privilege in an educational leadership course. *Journal of Research on Leadership Education, 15*(1), 56–80. https://doi.org/10.1177/1942775118771666

Zhang, S., & Fjermestad, J. (2006). Bridging the gap between traditional leadership theories and virtual team leadership. *International Journal of Technology, Policy and Management, 6*(3), 274–291. https://doi.org/10.1504/ijtpm.2006.011253

Zhao, J., & Jones, K. (2017). Women and leadership in higher education in Chinese discourse and the discursive construction of identity. *Administrative Sciences, 7*(21), 1–17. https://doi.org/10.3390/admsci7030021

Zhu, J., Liao, Z., Yam, K. C., & Johnson, R. E. (2018). Shared leadership: A state-of-the-art review and future research agenda. *Journal of Organizational Behavior,* *39*(7), 834–852. https://doi.org/10.1002/job.2296

Zigurs, I. (2003). Leadership in virtual teams: Oxymoron or opportunity? *Organizational Dynamics, 31*(4), 339–351. https://doi.org/10.1016/S0090 -2616(02)00132-8

Zuber-Skerritt, O. (2011). *Action leadership: Towards a participatory paradigm.* Springer.

Zuber-Skerritt, O., Wood, L., & Louw, I. (2015). *A participatory paradigm for an engaged scholarship in higher education: Action leadership from a South African perspective.* Sense.

Index

ability status, 174, 209, 221, 223, 288
abolitionist leadership, 193, 196–98, 200, 230, 287
academic capitalism, 12, 49, 51, 54–58, 62–63, 65, 72–73
academic values, 69–70
affirmative action, 87
alliances, 256–57, 258, 291–92
anti-Blackness, 84, 85–86, 110, 307
applied critical leadership, 35–36, 202–3, 204, 209, 231–34, 241, 290–91
apprenticeships, 168
aspirational capital, 138, 140
attribution research and theory, 30
authentic leadership, 170–73, 179, 286, 296
axiology: critical views of, 26, 33; definition of, 24; paradigm implications for, 44; participatory views of, 26, 41; postmodern views of, 26, 38; postpositivist views of, 26, 27–28; social constructivist views of, 26, 30. *See also* values

backcasting, 300
balance principle, 166–67, 274
Black Lives Matter, 3, 39
boundary control, 106–9
Brown, Michael, 3
bullying, 70–71
Butler, Jonathan, 4

Cañada College, 303–9
capitalism: academic, 12, 49, 51, 54–58, 62–63, 65, 72–73; neoliberal, 50, 51 (*see also* neoliberalism); racial, 86, 91
careless institutions, 71
case studies: on Cañada College merger, 303–9; on Chumash State technology, 310–14; on Webster University programs

and leadership process, 315–19; on Westgate Community College student success, 320–25
chaos and complexity leadership perspectives, 181–201; abolitionist leadership in, 193, 196–98, 200, 287; case examples of, 181–82, 185, 307, 313, 318, 323; collaboration in, 182, 183, 186, 188–89, 190, 193–95; continuous organizational learning in, 184, 194, 198, 199, 200; in crisis situations, 190–91, 193–96, 200, 287; critical systems thinking in, 193, 198–99; critiques of, 191–93; definition and emergence of, 182–83; evolution of, 13, 14 (*see also* new evolutions *subentry*); experimentation in, 184, 195, 197–98, 200; feedback loops in, 187; flexibility in, 184–85, 192, 194–95, 197, 200; future research on, 286–87, 295; key findings and insights on, 186–91; major assumptions and contributions to, 183–86; neoliberalism, white supremacy, and, 188–90, 192–98, 200–201, 286–87; new evolutions in, 193–99, 200–201 (*see also* evolution *subentry*); overview of, 18, 182, 199–201; prediction and statistical measurement of, 187; shared vision in, 187–88, 193–96, 200, 313; on student affairs administration, 189–90; systemic perspective in, 185–86, 193, 194, 197–99, 200–201, 287; transformative leadership rooted in, 295; weaver-leader framework in, 193–96
charismatic leadership theories, 119–20, 121
charter schools, 51
chief diversity officers, 90, 96–97
Choi, Mun Y., 103–4
Chumash State, 310–14

386   Index

class status: cognitive leadership perspectives on, 174; critical social theory on, 32–36, 135, 221; cultural leadership perspectives on, 221–22, 223, 288–89; neoliberal classism and, 50; whiteness, white supremacy and, 80, 86, 93

coalitions, 256–57, 258, 291–92

cognitive leadership perspectives, 147–80; action congruence with understanding in, 164–66, 285; authentic leadership in, 170–73, 179, 286, 296; case examples of, 147–48, 308, 313–14, 318, 322–24; critiques of, 162–66; cultural norms and, 150, 152, 154, 162, 168, 206–7, 308; definition and emergence of, 149–51; equity-minded leadership in, 168, 173–77, 179, 283–86, 308; formal leader prominence in, 162–63; future research on, 283–86, 295, 296; implicit leadership theories and, 154–56, 164–66, 178, 206, 284; key insights and findings on, 154–62; leader qualifications influenced by, 147–49; leadership prototypes in, 153, 164–66, 206, 318; leadership schemas in, 152, 173–74, 284–85, 318; major assumptions and contributions to, 151–53; mental models for framing leadership in, 156–60, 163–64, 175, 178–79, 284–85, 308; neoliberalism and, 147–48, 149, 163–64, 165, 283–86; new evolutions in, 166–77, 179; organizational learning and, 160–62, 163, 168, 170–71, 179; overview of, 18, 148–49, 177–79; perceivers or followers in, 149, 150–51, 153, 154–55, 159, 163, 170; transformational leadership and, 152, 161, 170; transformative leadership rooted in, 295; trauma-informed leadership rooted in, 296; whiteness, white supremacy, and, 149, 155, 165, 283–86; wisdom in, 166–69, 179, 286

collaboration: chaos and complexity leadership perspectives on, 182, 183, 186, 188–89, 190, 193–95; cognitive leadership perspectives valuing, 148, 161; collective leadership with (see collective leadership); critical views of, 33; cultural leadership perspectives on, 210, 219–20; global, 11; neoliberalism effects on, 71, 74, 188–89; organizational learning and, 161; in participatory leadership paradigms, 40–43; research on, 11; in shared-equity

leadership, 134–35, 283; transformational leadership use of, 122, 123, 128–30, 134–35, 144, 283; white supremacy effects on, 188–89

collective leadership: abolitionist leadership and, 197; barriers to, 7, 55–56, 67–68, 72, 254–55; cognitive leadership perspectives on, 148; cultural leadership perspectives on, 211, 224, 235–36; distributed leadership as, 249, 253–54; grassroots leadership as, 254–55, 258, 307–8; Indigenous principles on, 13, 235–36; neoliberalism hampering, 55–56, 67–68, 72, 254–55; oppressive systems vs., 5, 21; processual leadership perspectives on, 248–58, 291–92, 307–8; shared-equity leadership and, 135, 249–50 (see also shared-equity leadership); shared leadership as, 249–51; social constructivist, 29; social movements as, 11, 256–57, 258, 291–92; team leadership as, 249, 251–52; transformational leadership and, 130, 135, 144

colonialism, 50, 82, 84–85, 101, 105, 227. See also decolonization

communication. See language and communication

competition, 52–53, 55–56, 64, 69, 74

complexity theory. See chaos and complexity leadership perspectives

complicity: cognitive leadership perspectives critiqued for, 164–65; leadership for liberation avoiding, 141–42; transparency vs., 275; whiteness and, 84, 88–89, 95–96, 105, 110

Concerned Student 1950, 3–5, 39

consensus decision-making, 171, 233, 236

context: chaos and complexity leadership perspectives on, 183–84, 198; cognitive leadership perspectives in, 153, 154, 159, 160, 162, 175–77; for contemporary leadership and research, 5–9; cultural leadership perspectives specific to, 204–5, 206–7, 210–11, 217–18, 239, 289–90; neoliberal, 67–72; participatory paradigm in local, 40–43; positivist views of, 48; postmodernism on, 38–39, 40; postpositivism on, 28; processual leadership perspectives on, 243, 244–48, 250, 266, 291; for research and theory evolution, 9–17, 20, 23–24; social constructivism on, 29–30, 31, 173, 246;

for transformational leadership, 124–26, 143–44, 205, 218, 283
contingent workforce: chaos and complexity leadership perspectives on, 189, 190; cognitive leadership perspectives on, 164; grassroots leadership challenges for, 254–55; neoliberal, 54–58, 61, 65–66, 67–68, 71, 254–55, 323; in plantation leadership, 98, 107; at Westgate Community College, 320–24
contracts, 100–102
corporatization, 51–54, 58, 61–62, 69, 73–74, 280, 306
counterstorytelling, 36, 216, 229, 233, 297
COVID-19 pandemic: chaos and complexity leadership perspectives during, 181–82, 185, 188, 191, 287; neoliberalism and, 61, 279; research on leadership in, 281; virtual team leadership in, 252
critical disability theory, 221
critical Indigenous theory, 33
critical organizational ethnography, 299
critical race theory: applied critical leadership rooted in, 231–33, 241, 290; in critical leadership paradigm, 34, 35; in cultural leadership perspectives, 202–3, 212, 215–16, 226, 229–33, 240–41, 271–72, 290; future research using, 297; interest convergence in, 107; leadership for liberation and, 138; whiteness, white supremacy, and, 107, 216
critical social movements (CSM) studies framework, 264–65, 267, 291, 307
critical social theory: applied critical leadership and, 35–36, 202–3, 204, 209, 231–34, 241, 290–91; breadth and diversity of, 33; cognitive leadership perspectives and, 164; critical race theory as (see critical race theory); criticisms or limitations of, 26, 36, 141; CSM studies framework rooted in, 264–65, 267, 291, 307; cultural leadership perspectives guided by, 202–3, 204, 209, 218, 221, 231–34, 240–41, 271–72, 290–91 (see also critical race theory); as leadership paradigm, 24–26, 32–36, 204; major assumptions of, 25, 32–36; processual leadership perspectives rooted in, 251 (see also CSM studies subentry); research and theory guided by, 6, 12–13, 15–16, 25–26, 32–36, 297–99; transformational leadership emerging from, 118, 128, 135–36,

138, 141; transformative leadership rooted in, 295; values in, 26, 33
critical systems thinking, 193, 198–99
CSM (critical social movements) studies framework, 264–65, 267, 291, 307
cultural leadership perspectives, 202–41; ability status in, 209, 221, 223, 288; applied critical leadership in, 202–3, 204, 209, 231–34, 241, 290–91; case examples of, 202–3, 313, 318, 324; class status in, 221–22, 223, 288–89; cognitive leadership perspectives and, 150, 152, 154, 162, 168, 206–7, 308; context in, 204–5, 206–7, 210–11, 217–18, 239, 289–90; critical views of, 202–3, 204, 209, 218, 221, 231–34, 240–41, 271–72, 290–91 (see also critical race theory); critiques of, 225–29; cross-cultural, 223–25, 227, 289; definitions and emergence of, 204–6; evolution of, 9–11, 14 (see also new evolutions subentry); future of research on, 287–91; gender in, 202–3, 204, 207, 209, 211–15, 222–23, 224, 227, 228–29, 240, 287–89; Indigenous, 204, 209, 216, 234–38, 241, 290–91 (see also Indigenous principles); key insights and findings on, 208–25; leadership actively shaped by, 206; leaders' role in shaping organizational culture, 207, 208–11, 226, 240; local, 206, 239; major assumptions and contributions to, 206–8; national cultures and, 205, 207, 209, 223–25, 227, 289; neoliberalism and, 69, 204, 220, 226, 234–35, 237–38, 287–91; new evolutions in, 229–38, 240–41 (see also evolution subentry); overview of, 18, 203–4, 238–41; postmodernist, 37; on power, 206, 210–11, 215, 224, 225–27, 230, 236, 290; processual perspectives and, 259–62; race and ethnicity in, 202–4, 207, 209, 215–18, 220, 222–23, 226–38, 240, 287–91, 313, 318; sexual orientation in, 204, 207, 209, 219–20, 223, 288–89; shared beliefs and values in, 206, 234–35, 239; social constructivist, 29, 31, 204; social identities in, 202–5, 207–9, 211–23, 227–29, 239–40, 271–72, 287–90; storytelling in (see counterstorytelling; storytelling); transformational leadership and, 124–25, 133, 144, 205, 218; whiteness and white supremacy vs., 203–4, 216, 218, 220, 226, 229–30, 238, 240, 287–91; wisdom in, 168

388 Index

decolonization, 298–99
DEHE (design for equity in higher education) model, 262–64, 266
dehumanization: humanization vs., 276; neoliberalism and, 66–67, 70, 122; people over profit principle to combat, 272–73; transformative storytelling to combat, 260; whiteness and, 85–86, 87, 90–91, 95, 98, 108, 122
DEI. *See* diversity, equity, and inclusion
deprofessionalization, 55, 63, 71
design for equity in higher education (DEHE) model, 262–64, 266
DeVos, Betsy, 53
disability status, 174, 209, 221, 223, 288
distributed leadership, 249, 253–54
diversity, equity, and inclusion: chaos and complexity leadership perspectives on, 181–82, 187–201, 286–87; cognitive leadership perspectives on, 148, 164, 166–69, 173–79, 283–86; critical views of, 34 (*see also* applied critical leadership; critical race theory); cultural leadership perspectives on, 202–41, 287–91 (*see also* cultural leadership perspectives); DEHE model for, 262–64, 266; equity-minded leadership supporting (*see* equity-minded leadership); future practices and research to improve (*see* future of leadership practice and research); neoliberalism as barrier to, 46–47, 50; politics of representation and, 104–5; postpositivism as barrier to, 28; predatory, 106–9; processual leadership perspectives on, 246, 249–67, 291–92; research and theory reflecting, 5, 7–8, 12–17, 20; shared-equity leadership supporting (*see* shared-equity leadership); strategic plans on, 4; transformational leadership supporting, 125, 128–30, 134–38, 143–45, 249–50, 282–83; whiteness and white supremacy undermining, 80, 89–90, 96–97, 99, 104–9; wisdom to pursue, 166–69, 179, 236, 274, 286

economics: chaos and complexity leadership perspectives on crises of, 190–91, 287; contemporary higher education addressing, 5–6; critical social theory on, 15–16; global, 11, 223; neoliberalism and, 46, 49–51, 61–62, 67–68; predatory inclusion and, 106–7; recessions in, 50, 67, 190, 287

empowerment: chaos and complexity leadership perspectives on, 189; cultural leadership perspectives on, 211–12, 215, 218, 231; DEHE model for, 262–64; neoliberalism removal of, 65–66; power relinquished and acknowledged to alter, 275–76; research and theory reflecting, 11–12; transformational leadership supporting, 129, 130–32, 133, 134–35, 144–45, 283, 313, 317–18
entrepreneurialism, 52–53, 55, 58, 63, 69, 73–74
epistemology: authentic leadership on, 171; critical views of, 36; definition of, 24; Indigenous, 235, 236–37, 274; neoliberal views of, 62–63; organizational learning and (*see* organizational learning); paradigm implications for, 44; participatory views of, 41–42, 43; postmodernist views of, 37; postpositivist views of, 27–28; processual leadership perspectives on, 256; research questions on, 281; social constructivist views of, 28–29; wisdom and, 167, 274
equity. *See* diversity, equity, and inclusion
equity-minded leadership: cognitive leadership perspectives on, 168, 173–77, 179, 283–86, 308; future fostering of, 273–74, 276–77, 283–86; transformational leadership as, 145, 218. *See also* shared-equity leadership
Equity Scorecard projects, 176
ethics and morality in leadership: in authentic leadership, 171, 172–73, 286; critical views of, 33; grassroots leadership advocacy for, 254; neoliberal removal of, 64–66, 121–22, 127; in transformational leadership, 119–20, 121–22, 126–27, 128, 133, 134, 144, 282, 313; wisdom for, 167
ethnic issues. *See* racial and ethnic issues
experimentation, 184, 195, 197–98, 200. *See also* innovation

faculty and staff: contingent (*see* contingent workforce); contracts for, 100–102; disproportionate expectations of nonwhite, 85; as house and field slaves, 97–99; leadership schemas among, 152; politics of representation and, 104–5; Webster University new program hiring of, 315–19
familial capital, 138, 142
feedback loops, 187

Index 389

fellowship, 142

feminist poststructuralism, 34

flexibility, 184–85, 192, 194–95, 197, 200

framing leadership: cognitive/mental models for, 156–60, 163–64, 175, 178–79, 284–85, 308; in plantation leadership, 92–93

Frankfurt School, 32

future of leadership practice and research, 271–301; advocacy for new leadership processes in, 277; case studies reflecting (*see* case studies); centering liberation, social justice, and humanization in, 276; chaos and complexity leadership perspectives in, 286–87, 295; cognitive leadership perspectives in, 283–86, 295, 296; cultural leadership perspectives in, 287–91; equity-minded leadership in, 273–74, 276–77, 283–86; goals for, 16–17, 18–19, 271–72; new and multitheory theories in, 292–96; new research methodologies in, 296–300; otherwise possibilities in, 293–94; overview of, 18–19, 271–72, 279–82, 300–301; people over profit principle in, 272–73; personal and organizational work toward equity-mindedness in, 276–77; power relinquished and acknowledged in, 275–76; processual leadership perspectives in, 291–92, 296; reevaluation of white leadership approaches in, 277–79, 280–81; transformational leadership in, 282–83, 296; transformative leadership in, 294–95; transparency in, 275; trauma-informed leadership in, 295–96; wisdom and wise leadership in, 274, 286

future studies, 300, 314

gender issues: Black women's leadership and, 22–23, 77–80, 175; chaos and complexity leadership perspectives on, 189; cognitive leadership perspectives on, 148–49, 155, 165, 173, 174–75, 284; critical social theory on, 15–16, 32–36, 135; cultural leadership perspectives on, 202–3, 204, 207, 209, 211–15, 222–23, 224, 227, 228–29, 240, 287–89; equity-minded leadership on, 174–75; feminist poststructuralism on, 34; gender continuum vs. binary constructions as, 228–29, 288; gender hierarchies, roles, and stereotypes as, 213–14, 228; masculinity-femininity dimension as, 224;

neoliberal sexism and, 48, 50, 57, 59–60, 68–69, 71; plantation leadership and, 95–96, 104–5; positivist views not legitimizing, 47–48; processual leadership perspectives on, 249, 291; sexual harassment and, 57; transformational leadership and, 129–30, 132–33, 135; whiteness, white supremacy, and, 80, 93, 95–96, 104–5, 212. *See also* sexual orientation issues

generalizability, 27–28, 29, 124

Gig Academy, 49, 54–58, 60, 63, 65–66, 107, 130, 323

Global Leadership and Organizational Behavior Effectiveness Project, 124, 223

global leadership perspectives, 11, 124, 223–25, 227, 289

grassroots leadership, 254–55, 258, 264–65, 266, 307–8

Hannah-Jones, Nikole, 77–80, 94, 101–2, 104, 110–11

heteronormative issues. *See* sexual orientation issues

hidden agendas, 102–4

higher education leadership: audience for study of, 19–20; case studies on (*see* case studies); contemporary landscape of, 5–9; future of (*see* future of leadership practice and research); neoliberalism and (*see* neoliberalism); paradigms of (*see* leadership paradigms); perspectives on (*see* perspectives on leadership); research on (*see* research and theory); whiteness and white supremacy in (*see* whiteness and white supremacy)

human-first approach, 197, 200. *See also* people over profit principle

humanization, centering of, 276

human resource cognitive frames, 156–59, 308

Hussman, Walter, 78–79, 111

identity constructions. *See* social identities

identity politics, 218

implicit leadership theories (ILTs), 154–56, 164–66, 178, 206, 284

impression management, 109–11, 312, 317

inclusion. *See* diversity, equity, and inclusion

Index

Indigenous principles: collective leadership rooted in, 13, 235–36; critical Indigenous theory on, 33; cultural leadership perspectives including, 204, 209, 216, 234–38, 241, 290–91; future of leadership adopting, 19, 274; higher education transformation based on, 237–38; positivist views not legitimizing, 47–48; whiteness and white supremacy vs., 82, 108, 238 (*see also* colonialism); wisdom rooted in, 168, 236, 274

individualism, 47, 49, 52–53, 224

innovation, 72, 123, 161, 167. *See also* experimentation

institutionalization, organizational learning, 161

integration, in organizational learning, 161

intellectual property, 100–102

interest convergence, 107–9, 312

interpretation, in organizational learning, 160–61

Interstate School Leaders Licensure Consortium standards, 176

intuition, in organizational learning, 160

Kimpton, Lawrence, 103, 104

knowledge. *See* epistemology

language and communication: authentic leadership on, 171; chaos and complexity leadership perspectives on, 194–95, 200; cognitive leadership perspectives valuing, 148, 161–62, 167, 171, 178; cultural leadership perspectives on, 224–25, 233, 236; impression management with, 109–11, 312, 317; organizational learning and, 161–62; postmodernist views of, 38, 39; processual leadership perspectives on, 252, 259–62; storytelling using (*see* counter-storytelling; storytelling); transformational leadership on, 140, 171; in trauma-informed leadership, 296; wisdom for clear, 167

LDT (liberatory design thinking), 262–64, 266

leadership consolidation, 103

leadership for liberation, 118, 138–43

leadership paradigms, 22–45; assumptions of, 24, 25, 27; critical, 24–26, 32–36, 204; definition of, 24; overview of, 17–18, 23–27, 43–45; participatory, 24–26, 40–43 (*see also* participatory leadership

paradigms); positivist, 27–28, 47–49; postmodern, 24–26, 37–40 (*see also* postmodernism); postpositivist, 24–26, 27–28 (*see also* postpositivism); research informed by, 23–27, 43–44; social constructivist, 24–26, 28–32, 204 (*see also* social constructivism); theories vs., 24, 27

leadership prototypes, 153, 164–66, 206, 318

leadership schemas, 152, 173–74, 284–85, 318

leadership teams, 249, 251–52

LGBTQ+ issues. *See* sexual orientation issues

liberation: centering of, 276; future practices and research to advance (*see* future of leadership practice and research); as individual value, 139–40; leadership for, 138–43

liberatory design thinking (LDT), 262–64, 266

linguistic capital, 138, 140

Loftin, R. Bowen, 3–4, 39

managerialism / new managerialism, 12, 48, 58–62, 66–67, 70, 72

marketization, 51–54, 58, 61–62, 69, 73–74, 280, 306

masculinity-femininity dimension, 224. *See also* gender issues

mental models, 156–60, 163–64, 175, 178–79, 284–85, 308

mental representations, 149, 151, 153–54. *See also* cognitive leadership perspectives

mentoring, 168

methodology: critical views of, 36, 271–72, 297–99; definition of, 24; future directions in, 296–300; paradigm implications for, 44; participatory views of, 41–42, 297–300; postmodernist views of, 39–40; postpositivist views of, 28; processual leadership perspectives critiques on, 258–59; social constructivist views of, 30–31

microcredentialing, 62

Midwestern University, 108

morality. *See* ethics and morality in leadership

Multifactor Leadership Questionnaire (MLQ), 120

national cultures and nationality, 205, 207, 209, 223–25, 227, 289

navigational capital, 138, 141

neoliberalism, 46–76; academic capitalism and, 12, 49, 51, 54–58, 62–63, 65, 72–73; academic values diminished with, 69–70; careless institutions with, 71; case examples of, 46–47, 52–53, 64, 66–67 (*see also* case studies); chaos and complexity leadership perspectives and, 188–90, 192–95, 197, 200–201, 286–87; cognitive leadership perspectives and, 147–48, 149, 163–64, 165, 283–86; collegiality and community destroyed with, 71–72; comparison of alternative leadership practices to, 280; competition in, 52–53, 55–56, 64, 69, 74; context for leadership with, 67–72; cultural leadership perspectives and, 69, 204, 220, 226, 234–35, 237–38, 287–91; definition and description of, 49–53; dehumanization of leadership with, 66–67, 70, 122; discrimination, bullying, and low morale with, 70–71; entrepreneurialism and, 52–53, 55, 58, 63, 69, 73–74; ethics in leadership removal with, 64–66, 121–22, 127; future practices and research to dismantle (*see* future of leadership practice and research); gender issues and, 48, 50, 57, 59–60, 68–69, 71; Gig Academy and, 49, 54–58, 60, 63, 65–66, 107, 130, 323; Indigenous principles vs., 234–35, 237–38; individualism fostered by, 49, 52–53; innovation destroyed with, 72; leader goals and role redesigned with, 62–64; leader qualifications based on, 4–5, 59–60, 279; leadership decisions driven by, 46–47; leadership participant extrication with, 67–68; leadership reshaped by, 59–67, 280; managerialism, new managerialism, and, 12, 48, 58–62, 66–67, 70, 72; marketization or corporatization goals of, 51–54, 58, 61–62, 69, 73–74, 280, 306; overview of, 18, 48–49, 74–75; participatory paradigm to advance, 43; power concentration with, 52, 54, 60–61, 66, 68–69, 279–80; privatization goals of, 50, 51, 53, 56–57, 63; processual leadership perspectives and, 246, 247, 249, 251, 254–55, 258, 260–61, 264, 266, 291–92; public good vs., 47, 49, 50, 55, 62–63, 72–74, 279; reorientation of leadership aims with, 61–62; research and theory rooted in, 6–8, 12–17, 20; resisting and dismantling influence of, 17, 18–19, 271–301

(*see also under specific perspectives*); traditional views of leadership and, 47–49; transformational leadership and, 118, 121–22, 125, 127, 130, 133, 134, 282–83; whiteness and white supremacy intertwined with, 5, 49, 59–60, 68–69, 81, 95, 98–99, 107

networks, 142, 256–57, 258

neurodiversity, 221. *See also* ability status

neutrality: chaos and complexity leadership perspectives on, 191, 196; cognitive leadership perspectives on, 163–64, 285; critical views of, 32, 36, 265; future research and practices on, 265, 278, 285; whiteness and race, 89, 110, 278

niceness, whiteness as, 230, 278

Obama, Barack, administration of, 53

objectivity, 18, 27–28, 31, 36–37, 41, 47, 265

ontology: critical views of, 36; definition of, 24; paradigm implications for, 44; participatory views of, 41; positivist views of, 47; postmodernist views of, 37; postpositivist views of, 27–28; processual leadership perspectives on, 243–44, 256; social constructivist views of, 28, 30

Oracle, 56

organizational learning: authentic leadership for, 170–71; barriers to, 161–62; chaos and complexity leadership perspectives on continuous, 184, 194, 198, 199, 200; cognitive leadership perspectives and, 160–62, 163, 168, 170–71, 179; wisdom and, 168

otherwise possibilities, 293–94

outsourcing, 56–57, 58, 63–64, 65–66, 67–68

paradigms: assumptions of, 24, 25, 27; definition of, 24; leadership (*see* leadership paradigms); research informed by, 23–27, 43–44; theories vs., 24, 27

participatory leadership paradigms, 24–26, 40–43; criticisms or limitations of, 26, 42–43; cultural leadership perspectives guided by, 204; equity-minded leadership reflecting, 175; major assumptions of, 25, 40–43; processual leadership perspectives and, 244; research and theory guided by, 25–26, 40–43, 281, 297–300; values in, 26, 41

392 Index

people over profit principle, 272–73

perspectives on leadership: chaos and complexity (*see* chaos and complexity leadership perspectives); cognitive (*see* cognitive leadership perspectives); cultural (*see* cultural leadership perspectives); global (*see* global leadership perspectives); overview of, 18; processual (*see* processual leadership perspectives); symbolic (*see* symbolic leadership perspectives); traditional, 47–49, 118, 163 (*see also* positivism); transformational (*see* transformational leadership)

photovoice, 298

plantation leadership, 91–111; boundary control in, 106–9; case examples of, 312, 317; drivers in, 96–97, 99; enslavers in, 93–94, 98–99; framing of, 92–93; hidden agendas in, 102–4; house and field slaves in, 97–99; impression management in, 109–11, 312, 317; managers and overseers in, 95–96, 98–99; oppositional work to dismantle, 111; overview of, 81, 91–92, 111; politics of representation and, 104–5; property ownership and, 100–102; protective strategies in, 93, 105–11; roles and responsibilities in, 93–99; tools of oppression in, 92–93, 100–105

political cognitive frames, 156–57, 159, 164

politics of representation, 104–5. *See also* identity politics

positionality theory, 29

positivism, 27–28, 47–49

postmodernism: chaos and complexity leadership perspectives guided by, 183; cognitive leadership perspectives influenced by, 150; criticisms or limitations of, 26; as leadership paradigm, 24–26, 37–40; major assumptions of, 25, 37–40; research and theory guided by, 12, 25–26, 37–40; values in, 26, 38

postpositivism: authentic leadership anchored in, 171; chaos and complexity leadership perspectives vs., 191; cognitive leadership perspectives informed by, 150; criticisms or limitations of, 26, 28; cultural leadership perspectives and, 223; as leadership paradigm, 24–26, 27–28; major assumptions of, 25, 27–28; research

and theory guided by, 6, 12–13, 18, 25–26, 27–28; values in, 26, 27–28

power: chaos and complexity leadership perspectives on, 189, 192–93, 198; cognitive leadership perspectives on, 164, 167–68, 178, 285; critical views of, 32–34, 36, 141; cultural leadership perspectives on, 206, 210–11, 215, 224, 225–27, 230, 236, 290; Indigenous decentralization of, 236; leadership for liberation acknowledging, 141–42, 145; neoliberal concentration of, 52, 54, 60–61, 66, 68–69, 279–80; participatory views of, 43; positivist views of, 47–48; postmodernist views of, 37, 38, 39; processual leadership perspectives on, 254, 256, 258, 262–64; relinquishing and acknowledging of, 275–76; transformational leadership on, 119, 122, 123, 129, 130–32, 133, 134–35, 141–42, 144–45; transformative leadership dismantling systems of, 295; whiteness, white supremacy, and, 78–82, 85–90, 93–111, 133, 230; wisdom to leverage, 167–68. *See also* empowerment

predatory inclusion, 106–9

prisons, 50, 87

privatization, 50, 51, 53, 56–57, 63, 105

processual leadership perspectives, 242–67; case examples of, 242–43, 307–8, 314, 317, 324–25; collective leadership in, 248–58, 291–92, 307–8; context in, 243, 244–48, 250, 266, 291; critiques of, 258–59; CSM studies framework in, 264–65, 267, 291, 307; definition and emergence of, 243–44; DEHE model in, 262–64, 266; distributed leadership in, 249, 253–54; future research on, 291–92, 296; grassroots leadership in, 254–55, 258, 264–65, 266, 307–8; key findings and insights on, 246–58; major assumptions and contributions to, 244–46; methodology critiques with, 258–59; neoliberalism and, 246, 247, 249, 251, 254–55, 258, 260–61, 264, 266, 291–92; new evolutions in, 259–65, 266–67; overview of, 18, 243, 257–58, 265–67; participation in leadership process in, 244; power in, 254, 256, 258, 262–64; shared leadership in, 249–51, 317; social movements in, 256–57, 258, 264–65, 267, 291–92, 307; team leadership in, 249, 251–52; temporal orientation in, 245–46,

261; transformational leadership and, 122; transformative storytelling in, 259–62, 266, 324; trauma-informed leadership rooted in, 296; whiteness, white supremacy, and, 247, 249–50, 254, 260–61, 264, 266, 291–92
professionalism, whiteness as, 230, 278. *See also* deprofessionalization
property: intellectual, 100–102; ownership of, 100–102; racial hierarchies and, 86; whiteness as, 84, 87–88, 104, 216
prototypes, 153, 164–66, 206, 318
public good: chaos and complexity leadership perspectives on, 188, 192, 200; cognitive leadership perspectives on, 166–68, 177, 285; neoliberalism vs., 47, 49, 50, 55, 62–63, 72–74, 279; transformational leadership for, 127, 134, 282; whiteness and white supremacy as threat to, 80; wisdom applied for, 166–68

queer theory, 34

racial and ethnic issues: abolitionist leadership on, 193, 196–98, 200, 230, 287; anti-Blackness as, 84, 85–86, 110, 307; anti-racist leadership and, 229–30, 240; applied critical leadership addressing, 35–36, 202–3, 204, 209, 231–34, 241, 290–91; Black women's leadership and, 22–23, 77–80, 175; case studies on (*see* case studies); chaos and complexity leadership perspectives on, 181–82, 189–90, 192, 193–201, 287; cognitive leadership perspectives on, 148–49, 155, 165, 173, 174–76; complicity in avoiding, 84, 88–89, 95–96, 105, 110, 141–42; critical social theory on, 15–16, 32–36, 135–36 (*see also* critical race theory); cultural leadership perspectives on, 202–4, 207, 209, 215–18, 220, 222–23, 226–38, 240, 287–91, 313, 318 (*see also* cultural leadership perspectives); equity-minded leadership on, 174–76, 218, 273–74; for Indigenous people (*see* Indigenous principles); leadership for liberation addressing, 138–43; neoliberal racism and, 48, 50, 59–60, 68–69 (*see also under* whiteness and white supremacy); positivist views not legitimizing, 47–48; processual leadership perspectives on,

242–43, 246, 247, 249–50, 254, 260–61, 291–92; race consciousness on, 174; racial capitalism as, 86, 91; racial hierarchies as, 84, 86–87, 94; student protests on, 3–5, 16, 39, 79; transformational leadership addressing, 218, 249–50; transformational leadership and, 118, 129–30, 132–33, 134–36, 138–43, 145; trauma-informed leadership in response to, 295–96; weaver-leader framework on, 193–96. *See also* diversity, equity, and inclusion; whiteness and white supremacy
Reagan, Ronald, 49
reality. *See* ontology
refusal, acts of, 281–82
relationship building, 195–96, 235, 252
representation: mental, 149, 151, 153–54 (*see also* cognitive leadership perspectives; mental models); politics of, 104–5 (*see also* identity politics)
research and theory: acts of refusal in, 281–82; as barrier and pathway to systemic change, 5, 13–16, 20; contemporary landscape of, 5–9; evolution and revolution of, 9–17, 20, 23–24; future of (*see* future of leadership practice and research); leadership practices influenced by, 8–9; methodology or design for (*see* methodology); paradigms informing, 23–27, 43–44 (*see also* leadership paradigms); perspectives in (*see* perspectives on leadership); property ownership and, 100–101
resistant capital, 138, 141

scenario planning, 300, 314
schemas, leadership, 152, 173–74, 284–85, 318
scientific management, 55–56, 156, 164
servant leadership, 126, 234, 235
settler colonialism. *See* colonialism
sexual harassment, 57
sexual orientation issues: chaos and complexity leadership perspectives on, 189; cognitive leadership perspectives on, 155, 174; cultural leadership perspectives on, 204, 207, 209, 219–20, 223, 288–89; processual leadership perspectives on, 242–43, 255, 256; queer theory on, 34
shared beliefs and values, 206, 234–35, 239

394   *Index*

shared-equity leadership: case examples of, 308–9, 313, 323; future practices and research on, 273–74, 276, 282–83; processual leadership perspectives on, 249–50; as transformational leadership, 118, 134–38, 143–45, 249–50, 282–83, 308–9. *See also* equity-minded leadership

shared leadership, 249–51, 317

shared vision, 123, 140, 187–88, 193–96, 200, 220, 313

1619 Project, 77

slavery, afterlife of. *See* plantation leadership

social capital, 138, 142

social class. *See* class status

social constructivism: authentic leadership anchored in, 173; chaos and complexity leadership perspectives guided by, 183; cognitive leadership perspectives influenced by, 150, 162; criticisms or limitations of, 26, 32; cultural leadership perspectives guided by, 29, 31, 204; as leadership paradigm, 24–26, 28–32, 204; major assumptions of, 25, 28–32; processual leadership perspectives rooted in, 243, 244, 246, 251; research and theory guided by, 6, 12, 14, 25–26, 28–32; transformational leadership emerging from, 118; values in, 26, 30

social identities: applied critical leadership and, 231–32; authentic leadership and, 173; awareness of personal, 276; cognitive leadership perspectives on, 164, 165, 173, 178, 179; critical views of, 15, 34–35, 36, 231–32, 271–72; cultural leadership perspectives on, 202–5, 207–9, 211–23, 227–29, 239–40, 271–72, 287–90; emerging research on, 220–22; frag-mented, 39–40; identity politics and, 218; intersectional, 22, 34, 202–4, 207–9, 222–23, 240, 289; politics of representa-tion and, 105; postmodernist views of, 38, 39–40; postpositivist views of, 28; social constructivist views of, 29. *See also* ability status; class status; gender issues; racial and ethnic issues; sexual orientation issues

social justice and social change: centering of, 276; cognitive leadership perspectives on, 164, 166–67, 177; critical social theorists' commitment to, 32–36, 128; cultural leadership perspectives on, 204, 231; future practices and research to advance (*see* future of leadership practice and research); leadership for liberation supporting, 138–43; leadership paradigms supporting, 23 (*see also specific paradigms*); neoliberal-ism as barrier to, 48–49; participatory paradigm commitment to, 41, 42–43; postpositivism as barrier to, 28; processual leadership perspectives on, 246, 251–52, 256–57, 258, 259–62, 264–65, 266–67, 291–92; research and theory as barrier and pathway to, 5, 14–16; shared-equity leadership supporting, 134–38, 276 (*see also* equity-minded leadership); social constructivism not actively pursuing, 32; transformational leadership for, 128–30, 131, 134–43, 145, 282; transformative leadership for, 294–95; whiteness and white supremacy undermining, 80, 89

social movements, 11, 130, 133, 256–57, 258, 264–65, 267, 291–92, 307

socioeconomic class. *See* class status

spirituality, 10–11, 289

staff. *See* faculty and staff

storytelling, 140, 167, 233, 236–37, 259–62, 266, 324. *See also* counterstorytelling

structural cognitive frames, 156–59, 164

students: authentic leadership development in graduate, 172; contracts for graduate, 101; as field slaves, 97–99; protests on racial issues by, 3–5, 16, 39, 79; Webster University new program involvement of, 315–19; Westgate Community College efforts for success of, 320–25

subjectivity, 41

support networks, 142

symbolic leadership perspectives: evolution of, 9–10, 14; social constructivist, 30; symbolic cognitive frames in, 156–59, 308; whiteness and, 90, 96, 99, 105

system challenging, 140–41

systemic perspective: chaos and complexity leadership perspectives on, 185–86, 193, 194, 197–99, 200–201, 287; equity-minded leadership taking, 273–74; on power, 290; in transformative leadership, 295

team leadership, 249, 251–52

technology, 56, 58, 252, 310–14

temporal orientation, 224, 235, 245–46, 261, 296

Thatcher, Margaret, 49
toku, 167
traditional views of leadership, 47–49, 118, 163. *See also* positivism
transactional leadership theories, 119–20, 121, 123, 125–26, 152
transformational leadership, 117–46; applied critical leadership rooted in, 231, 234; authentic leadership and, 170–71; behaviors and characteristics of leaders in, 123, 124, 129, 136, 144; case examples of, 117–18, 143–44, 308–9, 313, 317–18, 323; cognitive leadership perspectives and, 152, 161, 170; critiques of, 132–33, 135, 136, 138; cultural and institutional context for, 124–25, 133, 144, 205, 218, 283; definition and emergence of, 118–20; empowerment with, 129, 130–32, 133, 134–35, 144–45, 283, 313, 317–18; ethics and morality in, 119–20, 121–22, 126–27, 128, 133, 134, 144, 282, 313; future research on, 282–83, 296; idealized influence in, 120; individualized consideration in, 120; inspirational motivation in, 120, 122, 123; intellectual stimulation in, 120; key concepts of, 126–32; key findings and insights on, 122–26; leadership for liberation evolved from, 118, 138–43; major assumptions and contributions to, 121–22; mutual interactions in, 118, 120, 121, 130, 131, 134; neoliberalism and, 118, 121–22, 125, 127, 130, 133, 134, 282–83; new evolutions of, 134–43, 145; organizational learning and, 161; outcomes of, 123–25, 129, 136; overview of, 18, 118, 143–45; shared-equity leadership evolved from, 118, 134–38, 143–45, 249–50, 282–83, 308–9; social change with, 128–30, 131, 134–43, 145, 282; trauma-informed leadership rooted in, 296; whiteness and, 118, 121–22, 128, 129–30, 132–33, 134–35, 141, 145, 249–50, 282–83
transformative leadership, 294–95
transformative storytelling, 259–62, 266, 324
transparency, 165, 170–71, 262, 275
trans* theory and research, 228, 288
trauma-informed leadership, 295–96
Trump, Donald, administration of, 53, 68
trust: authentic leadership grounded in, 170; cultural leadership perspectives on, 225;

234; processual leadership perspectives and, 249, 252, 258, 262; transformational leadership supporting, 122, 123, 131, 136

unbundling, 54–55
uncertainty avoidance, 224
unions, 30, 34, 50, 68, 100–101, 292
University of Chicago, 103
University of Missouri (Mizzou), 3–5, 16, 39, 103–4, 194
University of North Carolina, 77–80, 94, 101–2, 104, 110–11
University of Southern California Center for Urban Education, 176

values: academic, 69–70; axiology as examination of (*see* axiology); community, 128, 139, 142–43; critical views of, 26, 33; cultural leadership perspectives on, 204–7, 210, 217, 234–38, 239–40; group, 128, 139, 140–42; Indigenous, 234–38 (*see also* Indigenous principles); individual, 128, 139–40; in leadership for liberation, 138–43; participatory views of, 26, 41; people over profit, 272–73; postmodern views of, 26, 38; postpositivist views of, 26, 27–28; processual leadership perspectives on, 256, 262; shared, 206, 234–35, 239; in shared-equity leadership, 134–38, 276; social constructivist views of, 26, 30; in transformational leadership, 121, 128–29, 133, 134–43, 145, 282; wisdom for integrity of, 167–69
virtual team leadership, 252
voting rights, 87

Walan Mayiny: Indigenous Leadership in Higher Education project, 236–37
weaver-leader framework, 193–96, 314
Webster University, 315–19
Westgate Community College, 320–25
whiteness and white supremacy, 77–113; anti-Blackness and, 84, 85–86, 110, 307; anti-racist leadership vs., 229–30, 240; case examples of, 77–80, 94, 101–2, 104, 110–11 (*see also* case studies); chaos and complexity leadership perspectives and, 188–90, 192–98, 200–201, 286–87; cognitive leadership perspectives and, 149, 155, 165, 283–86; colonialism and, 82, 84–85, 101, 105; complicity with, 84,

396   *Index*

whiteness and white supremacy (*continued*) 88–89, 95–96, 105, 110; cultural leadership perspectives vs., 203–4, 216, 218, 220, 226, 229–30, 238, 240, 287–91; definition and description of, 80–91; future practices and research to dismantle (*see* future of leadership practice and research); neoliberalism intertwined with, 5, 49, 59–60, 68–69, 81, 95, 98–99, 107; overview of, 18, 80–81, 90–91, 111–12; plantation leadership and, 81, 91–111, 312, 317; positivist views reinforcing, 47–48; processual leadership perspectives and, 247, 249–50, 254, 260–61, 264, 266, 291–92; as property, 84, 87–88, 104, 216; racial hierarchies and, 84, 86–87, 94; recommended resources on, 91; reevalua-tion of, 277–79, 280–81; research and theory rooted in, 6–8, 12–17, 20; resisting and dismantling influence of, 17, 18–19, 111, 271–301 (*see also under specific perspectives*); transformational leadership and, 118, 121–22, 128, 129–30, 132–33, 134–36, 141, 145, 249–50, 282–83; UNC tenure denial reflecting, 77–80, 94, 101–2, 104, 110–11; University of Missouri policies reflecting, 5, 103–4; white gaze as lens of, 84, 89–90, 105, 260, 307

wisdom and wise leadership, 166–69, 179, 236, 274, 286

Wolfe, Tim, 3–5, 39

women. *See* gender issues

Workday, 56

worldviews, 23. *See also* paradigms